P9-ECQ-211

DATE DUE

			PRINTED IN U.S.A

SHAKESPEARE

THE
MAGILL
BIBLIOGRAPHIES

Other Magill Bibliographies:

American Drama: 1918–1960—R. Baird Shuman
American Ethnic Literatures—David Peck
Biography—Carl Rollyson
Black American Women Novelists—Craig Werner
Classical Greek and Roman Drama—Robert J. Forman
Contemporary Latin American Fiction—Keith H. Brower
English Romantic Poetry—Bryan Aubrey
The Modern American Novel—Steven G. Kellman
Restoration Drama—Thomas J. Taylor
The Vietnam War in Literature—Philip K. Jason

SHAKESPEARE

An Annotated Bibliography

Joseph Rosenblum
University of North Carolina at Greensboro

SALEM PRESS

Pasadena, California   Englewood Cliffs, New Jersey

Library of Congress Cataloging-in-Publication Data

Rosenblum, Joseph.
    Shakespeare / Joseph Rosenblum
       p. cm.—(Magill bibliographies)
    Includes bibliographical references and index
    ISBN 0-89356-676-4
    1. Shakespeare, William, 1564-1616—Bibliography.
I. Title. II. Series.
Z8811.R68 1992
[PR2894]   92-4863
016.8223'3—dc20   CIP

To Fluff
January 27, 1977—August 6, 1991
Belov'd till Life can charm no more;
And mourn'd, till Pity's self be dead.

EDITORIAL STAFF

CONTENTS

SHAKESPEARE

ACKNOWLEDGMENTS

It is a pleasure to thank the various people who have assisted me in the course of my work on this bibliography:

John Wilson of Salem Press, Inc., who may be styled the only begetter of the book, who proposed the project, patiently bore with my fumbling efforts with the word processor, and offered many helpful suggestions;

Kathryn White, whose research and typing greatly expedited the completion of the project;

Gaylor Callahan and Wendy Jackson of UNCG's Interlibrary Loans, who kindly summoned numerous volumes and articles from around the country;

My friends and colleagues in McIver 136, who listened sympathetically to my tales of woe;

And my wife, Suzanne, who helped with the typing and proofreading and, what is much more, has borne with the ills that assail the scholar's life.

INTRODUCTION

The Jacobean playwright John Webster commended the "right happy and copious industry" of William Shakespeare; this industry has proved far less copious than that of Shakespeare's critics over the centuries. Whereas Shakespeare's works fit into one volume—admittedly large but still single—libraries have been written about them. The history of this criticism reveals not only the changing perceptions about and fortunes of the plays and poems but also the shifting *Zeitgeist*. As Bonamy Dobree observed in his review of E. M. W. Tillyard's *Shakespeare's Last Plays* (1938),

> The history of criticism is the history of general mental movements, even more so than is the history of "creative" literature; and this is especially true of the history of Shakespearean criticism, which reveals with a disturbing fidelity, not so much what people think of Shakespeare, but what they want of life. This is because in Shakespeare you can, with fatal ease, find anything you look for, not only by way of an "attitude towards life," but also by way of material for any literary or psychological theory which at the moment seems important (*Criterion* 17 [1938]: 740-741).

Even the first recorded criticism of Shakespeare, *Greene's Groats-worth of Wit* (1592) by the playwright and pamphleteer Robert Greene, reflects the truth of Dobree's assertion. Disillusioned with the theater, Greene on his deathbed attacked the rising star of the London stage, that transplant from Stratford whom Greene described as

> an upstart crow, beautified with our feathers, that with his *Tiger's heart wrapt in a player's hide,* supposes he is as well able to bombast out a blank verse as the best of you; and being an absolute *Johannes Factotum,* is in his own conceit the only Shake-scene in a country.

The comment anticipates much of what has been said of the dramatist since. It notes Shakespeare's use of others' plots and plays, implies that he lacks learning, reflects on his prosody, and argues, using a line from the playwright himself, that his reputation is undeserved. This hostile tone provoked responses even in the 1590s. Thomas Nashe and Henry Chettle condemned the tone of Greene's remarks, and in 1598 Francis Meres' *Palladis Tamia, Wit's Treasury* praised Shakespeare as extravagantly as Greene had condemned him: "As Plautus and Seneca are accounted the best for comedy and tragedy among the Latins, so Shakespeare among the English is the most excellent in both kinds for the stage."

As Samuel Schoenbaum notes in *Shakespeare's Lives*, the value of Meres' work as criticism or as a measure of Shakespeare's reputation is questionable, since

Palladis Tamia offers a general panegyric to more than a hundred English authors, artists, and musicians, and it devotes more attention to Michael Drayton than to Shakespeare. Yet Shakespeare certainly had his admirers in his own day. Shortly after the playwright's death, William Basse wrote:

> Renowned Spenser, lye a thought more nye
> To learned Chaucer, and rare Beaumont lye
> A little neerer Spenser to make roome
> For Shakespeare in your threefold fourefold Tomb.

In any event, Edmund Spenser, Francis Beaumont, and Geoffrey Chaucer were not to be crowded by Shakespeare in Westminster Abbey's Poet's Corner, which would not house even a monument to Shakespeare until well into the eighteenth century. Ben Jonson, who "loved [Shakespeare] and [did] honor his memory on this side idolatry as much as any," maintained that Shakespeare needed no such recognition: "Thou art a monument without a tomb." Jonson also took issue with Beaumont's observation that Shakespeare's plays reveal "How far sometimes mortal man may go/ By the dim light of Nature." Greene's sneering at Shakespeare's lack of education has been turned by Beaumont—and later critics as well—into at least a modicum of praise, but for Jonson "a good poet's made as well as born." Jonson denied Shakespeare much learning, claiming that the dramatist had "small Latin and less Greek," though scholars have continued to debate this point. Yet Jonson maintained that whatever natural talent the dramatist possessed was supplemented with artistry and hard work:

> Who casts to write a living line must sweat
> (Such as thine are) and strike the second heat
> Upon the Muses' anvil, turn the same
> (And himself with it) that he thinks to frame.

Jonson's praise is probably sincere, as may be Thomas Walkley's in "The Stationer to the Reader" prefacing the 1622 quarto of *Othello*, which maintains that "the Author's name is sufficient to vent his work." Both Jonson and Walkley are, however, attempting to sell books, Jonson's lines serving as preface and puff to the 1623 First Folio. Perhaps a more just indication of where on Parnassus Shakespeare's Jacobean contemporaries placed him is John Webster's preface to *The White Devil* (1612), which ranks him with Thomas Dekker and John Heywood, below George Chapman, Jonson, Beaumont, and John Fletcher. Another measure is the sale of his works. The First Folio sold out within a decade, not a bad performance for an expensive book. Jonson's works, published in 1616, were not reprinted until 1640. Shakespeare's Second Folio (1632) satisfied demand for more than three decades, though, and by the 1640s Shakespeare's company, the King's Men, was producing three plays by Beaumont and Fletcher to one by Shakespeare.

In the latter half of the seventeenth century, Shakespeare continued to rank below

Beaumont and Fletcher. When the theaters reopened in 1660 after eighteen years of the Puritans' official, if not totally successful, prohibition of stage plays, Thomas Killigrew's company assumed the name and much of the repertoire of the King's Men. His patent granted him the rights to twenty of Shakespeare's plays, but the company produced only four. Three were staged in the spring of 1660, along with nine by Beaumont and Fletcher, three by James Shirley, and one each by Chapman, Jonson, Thomas Middleton, Sir William Davenant, and Killigrew. As patentee of the other licensed London theater, Davenant had the right to produce ten (later thirteen) of Shakespeare's plays. In 1660, he chose to stage only *Pericles*, probably because it mirrored in part the recent experiences of Charles II, a young ruler driven from his throne and then restored. Davenant put on eight works by Beaumont and Fletcher that first season. Commenting on the fare of the London theaters at the end of the 1660s, John Dryden observed that Beaumont and Fletcher "are now the most pleasant and frequent entertainments of the Stage; two of theirs being acted through the year for one of Shakespeare's or Jonson's." Samuel Pepys' *Diary* confirms this observation. In the 1660s, Pepys attended the theater some 350 times. He saw fifteen plays by Shakespeare, twenty-seven adaptations, and seventy-six performances of works by Beaumont and Fletcher.

It was Dryden who coined the phrase "the divine Shakespeare," but even for him the divinity was qualified. As Dryden wrote to explain his revision of *Troilus and Cressida*,

> It must be allowed to the present age, that the tongue in general is so much refined since Shakespeare's time, that many of his words, and more of his phrases, are scarce intelligible. And of those which are understood, some are ungrammatical, others coarse; and his whole style is so pestered with figurative expressions, that it is as affected as it is obscure.

With Davenant, Dryden adapted *The Tempest*; their version influenced performances for two centuries. *Antony and Cleopatra* became Dryden's *All for Love* (1678). Davenant's operatic *Macbeth* (1664) held the boards for eighty years. His *The Law Against Lovers* (1667) fused *Measure for Measure* and *Much Ado About Nothing*, and his *The Rivals* is based on *The Two Noble Kinsmen*. Nahum Tate gave *King Lear* a happy ending; he compensated by killing off Volumnia, Martius, Aufidius, and his new introduction, Nigridius, in his version of *Coriolanus*. John Lacy's *Sawny the Scot* (1667), a farcical version of *The Taming of the Shrew*, continued to be performed into the nineteenth century. As Pepys' diary indicates, Restoration audiences were thus more likely to see a Shakespeare adaptation than Shakespeare undefiled, but these new versions kept the plays alive. Folio editions of the works appeared in 1663-1664 and 1685, and individual plays were reprinted with some regularity. Five *Hamlet* quartos were published between 1676 and 1703.

As in the early 1600s, playgoers and readers alike continued to divide in their opinions. The eccentric Duchess of Newcastle praised Shakespeare after reading the Third Folio. Pepys called *1 Henry IV* "a good play" (June 4, 1661) but regarded

A Midsummer Night's Dream as "the most insipid ridiculous play that ever I saw in my life" (September 29, 1662). He saw *Hamlet* five times and enjoyed it, perhaps because of the acting of Thomas Betterton, whose fine performances did much to enhance Shakespeare's reputation among theatergoers. *Romeo and Juliet*, which Pepys saw on March 1, 1662, displeased him, but, again, the performers influenced his opinion; he claimed the piece was "the worst acted that ever I saw these people do." In 1689 Robert Gould remarked, "When e'er I *Hamlet*, or *Othello* read,/ My *Hair* starts up, and my *Nerves* shrink with dread." Thomas Rymer was less impressed, though like Greene his attacks on Shakespeare reflect hostility to the stage in general. In *A Short View of Tragedy* (1693), Rymer declared, "In the *Neighing* of an Horse, or in the *growling* of a Mastiff, there is a meaning, there is as lively expression, and, I may say, more humanity, than many times in the Tragical flights of Shakespear." Rymer singled out *Othello* for particular castigation:

> The moral, sure, of this fable is very instructive. First, this may be a caution to all maidens of quality how, without their parents' consent, they run away with blacka-moors.
>
> Secondly, this may be a warning to all good wives, that they look well to their linen.
>
> Thirdly, this may be a lesson to husbands, that before their jealousy be tragical, the proofs may be mathematical.

Despite the absurdity of these comments, they anticipate two objections that would often be repeated in the next century: Shakespeare's vocabulary and his lack of poetical justice. Less dyspeptically, James Drake in 1699 observed that "Shakespeare . . . fell short of the Art of *Jonson*, and the conversation of *Beaumont* and *Fletcher*." Yet, in the same year that Rymer published his counterblast against Shakespeare, a Mr. Dowdall made the first recorded literary pilgrimage to Stratford.

In the eighteenth century, Shakespeare's fortunes rose. The University of Cambridge library admitted him to its shelves in 1715, acquiring a copy of the Fourth Folio (1685). In 1736-1737, a Shakespeare Ladies Club formed in London to promote revivals of Shakespeare's plays, and it succeeded: in the 1736-1737 season, about a fifth of the London repertory derived from Shakespeare. The Licensing Act of 1737 that imposed censorship on the theaters also helped Shakespeare because it drove much talented competition away from drama. A monument to Shakespeare was installed in Westminster Abbey in 1741, another sign of his growing reputation. David Garrick's great acting career did even more than Betterton's to advance Shakespeare's theatrical popularity. Though Garrick purged *Hamlet* of what he called "the tedious interruptions" and "its absurd digressions," he restored *Macbeth*, *Coriolanus*, *Cymbeline*, *The Tempest*, and *Antony and Cleopatra* to their pre-Restoration condition. Yet he, too, was not averse to adaptation, turning scenes into entertainments such as *Florizel and Perdita* (1756, based on *The Winter's Tale*) and *Catharine and Petruchio* (1756, derived from *The Taming of the Shrew*). Altogether, though, Garrick's influence was beneficial. During his management of Drury Lane

Theatre, one of four tragedies and one of every six comedies staged were by Shakespeare. Even his rain-sodden Shakespeare Jubilee in 1769 further promoted popular interest in the playwright.

At the same time that audiences could see more (and more accurate) Shakespearean plays, texts, too, multiplied. Arthur Sherbo finds in the eighteenth century the birth of Shakespeare studies. In the seventeenth century, four editions of the collected works appeared; between 1709 and 1809 there were sixty-five, including the first American one (1795-1796). Lewis Theobald's *Shakespeare Restored* (1726) exemplifies the attention being devoted to textual matters. Rather than trying to revise the plays, as the Restoration had done, Theobald and his fellow (often rival) editors hoped to free the plays from corruption so that they could claim their place among the classics.

Like a classic, too, Shakespeare was now being collected. Garrick owned a number of early editions, and the botanist Richard Warner formed a Shakespeare library in anticipation of producing a new edition (preempted by George Steevens). An even greater sign of Shakespeare's popularity was the new phenomenon of Shakespeare forgeries. In the seventeenth century, publishers might attribute another author's play or poem to Shakespeare, but now authors hoped to capitalize on the dramatist's vogue by passing off their work as his. John Jordan of Stratford created a Shakespearean ballad about Sir Thomas Lucy, but this inventiveness paled before that of William Henry Ireland, who wrote an entire play, *Vortigern and Rowena*, staged at Drury Lane in 1796. Ireland also manufactured a manuscript of *King Lear* and many other items. The "Profession of Faith" that Ireland fathered on Shakespeare drew from Dr. Samuel Parr the declaration, "Sir, we have many very fine passages in our church service, and our litany abounds with beauties; but here, sir, here is a man who has distanced us all." Portraits of Shakespeare, no two alike, proliferated. The eighteenth century produced the first illustrated edition of Shakespeare (1709). Paintings based on the plays quickly found their way into the Royal Academy after it opened in 1769 and claimed equality with historical canvases (then regarded as the epitome of artistic achievement). In 1789, John Boydell opened his Shakespeare Gallery in Pall Mall; by 1800, it housed 160 pictures by the finest artists of the day, including Sir Joshua Reynolds, Benjamin West, Angelica Kauffmann, and George Romney.

Though appreciation for Shakespeare rose, critical commonplaces echoed those of the previous century. Nicholas Rowe, Shakespeare's first eighteenth century editor, commented that the playwright, ignorant of Aristotle's rules, "liv'd under a kind of mere light of Nature." Alexander Pope, who succeeded Rowe as editor of Shakespeare for Jacob Tonson, similarly observed that Shakespeare's characters "are so much Nature her self, that 'tis a sort of injury to call them by so distant a name as Copies of her." For them, as for John Milton, Shakespeare was still "Fancy's child,/ Warbling his native woodnotes wild."

Pleasing as these notes were, the wildness sometimes demanded refining. In the prologue to *The Invader of His Country*, formerly *Coriolanus*, John Dennis explained the need to bring order to the play, "Where Master-strokes in wild Confusion lye." Pope blamed the actors of Shakespeare's day and later for distorting the text, and he emended accordingly. Theobald sought to restore Shakespeare's text not only from Pope's efforts but also from earlier corruption. The apparent lack of poetic justice also continued to bother critics. Dennis lamented in 1712, "The good and the bad then perishing promiscuously in the best of Shakespearean tragedies, there can be either none or very weak instruction in them." Samuel Johnson echoed this concern, claiming that Shakespeare "sacrifices virtue to convenience, and is so much more careful to please than to instruct, that he seems to write without any moral purpose."

As long as neoclassical doctrines dominated critical thinking, Shakespeare's reputation remained subject to challenge. No English writer would have gone so far as Voltaire, who in 1748 called *Hamlet* "a piece gross and barbarous, that would not be approved by the lowest populace of France or Italy. . . . One would think that this work was the fruit of the imagination of a drunken savage." The English were less attached to rigid neoclassicism than were their counterparts across the Channel; moreover, Shakespeare represented English liberty opposed to French tyranny. During the Seven Years' War, *Henry V* was performed annually in London. Yet even Samuel Johnson, who appealed from rules to nature to defend Shakespeare's violation of the unities, the mingling of genres, and many of the plays' violations of decorum, objected to what he regarded as poorly constructed plots, hasty endings, anachronisms, and puns.

Romanticism removed theoretical impediments to the enjoyment of Shakespeare. August Wilhelm von Schlegel's *Course of Lectures in Dramatic Art and Literature*—delivered in Vienna in 1808, published in German (1809-1811), and then quickly translated into English by John Black (1815)—agreed with Dryden that Shakespeare was a giant before the Flood, a Gothic genius, but by 1800 Gothicism in literature as in architecture held equal status with the classical. To Schlegel, Shakespeare was the peer of Sophocles, indeed, his superior, as art of the Christian era surpassed that of the pagan. Johnson had to defend Shakespeare's mingling of genres; Schlegel celebrated it, claiming that art "delights in indissoluble mixtures."

Johnson pioneered another area of Shakespearean criticism that persisted into the twentieth century but is generally associated with Romanticism: the treatment of Shakespeare's characters as real people. Writing of Falstaff, Johnson proclaimed, "Unimitated, unimitable *Falstaff*, how shall I describe thee? Thou compound of sense and vice; of sense which may be admired but not esteemed, of vice which may be despised, but hardly detested." The popularity of this approach is evident in the very titles of works such as William Richardson's *A Philosophical Analysis and Illustration of Some of Shakespeare's Remarkable Characters* (1774), Maurice Morgann's *An Essay on the Dramatic Character of Sir John Falstaff* (1777), and Thomas Whateley's *Remarks on Some of the Characters of Shakespeare* (1785). A. C. Bradley's *Shakespearean Tragedy* (1904), with its focus on character, belongs to this tradition, which even L. C. Knights's "How Many Children Had Lady

Macbeth?" (1933), an attack on this approach, could not counteract completely. Psychoanalytical studies such as Ernest Jones's *Hamlet and Oedipus* (1947) also derive from this line of investigation.

A number of Romantics went beyond Morgann or Bradley, identifying Shakespeare's characters with themselves. In a letter to Fanny Brawne dated August, 1820, John Keats wrote, "Hamlet's heart was full of such misery as mine is when he said to Ophelia, 'Go to a Nunnery, go, go!' Indeed I should like to give up the matter at once—I should like to die." Samuel Taylor Coleridge, too, likened himself to Hamlet, and William Hazlitt extended the equation to embrace all who fail to act or who seek in the theater diversion from the miseries of life.

In other ways, Romantic writers on Shakespeare refined earlier views. Though still speaking the language of nature, Shakespeare in the nineteenth century came to be regarded as a conscious artist, a view anticipated by Ben Jonson but then dropped in the neoclassical age. For Johann Wolfgang von Goethe, he was so great a poet that the stage was unworthy of him. Charles Lamb and Hazlitt repeated the view that the plays could not be represented accurately in the theater. With the many editions available—162 were published in the 1850s alone—the library replaced the theater as the place where most people encountered Shakespeare, and criticism increasingly focused on text rather than on performance. With a few notable exceptions such as Harley Granville-Barker, this tendency persisted into the late twentieth century and was even then only partially reversed.

Romantics also discovered in Shakespeare an ethical dimension. According to Coleridge, Shakespeare "never rendered that amiable which religion and reason taught us to detest; he never clothed vice in the garb of virtue." Henrietta Maria Bowdler and her brother Thomas produced *The Family Shakespeare* (1807; 2d ed., 1818) with the profanity removed, but they did not alter the plots. They thus found Shakespeare more moral than do many modern feminist critics, who see in the plays a defense of patriarchy and so condemn the author's stance. Others continue to find in the works the ethical outlook they themselves endorse, reading into the plays and poems orthodox or radical views on religion, war, women, politics, love, or commerce.

Less acceptable at the end of the twentieth century was the Romantics' biographical approach to the works. This effort to find the author in his writings enhanced the popularity of the sonnets, which had been excluded from the four folio editions of the seventeenth century and frequently omitted from eighteenth century editions as well: Rowe's and Pope's included them only in a supplementary volume. Not until 1780 did the great Shakespeare scholar Edmond Malone produce a carefully edited text that returned to the 1609 version. Ten years later Malone issued the *Plays and Poems*, which for the first time integrated the sonnets into the canon. Gary Taylor argues that Shakespeare's poems profited from the late eighteenth century vogue for Spenser and John Milton and the consequent resurgence of the sonnet form. Whatever their artistic appeal, though, Shakespeare's sonnets were read as revealing the life of their creator, about whom so little seemed to be known otherwise. Thus, Schlegel in his lectures maintained that "these sonnets paint most unequivocally the actual situation and sentiments of the poet." William Wordsworth in 1815 claimed that in the poems "Shakespeare expresses his own feelings in his own person," and in "Scorn Not the Sonnet" Wordsworth maintained that "with this key/ Shakespeare unlocked his heart."

Such biographical readings affected the perceived chronology of the plays. Because Leigh Hunt regarded *Twelfth Night* as genial, he claimed that it was Shakespeare's last play, the product of contented age. For Keats, *Hamlet* reflected Shakespearean unhappiness in the playwright's middle years. This approach culminated in Edward Dowden's *Shakspere: A Critical Study of His Mind and Art* (1875). Using the plays, Dowden divided Shakespeare's life into four periods: "In the Workshop," "In the World," "Out of the Depths," and "On the Heights." These four periods correspond roughly to the romantic comedies, histories, tragedies, and late romances (a name that Dowden was the first to apply to these comedies). In this tradition, Frank Harris' *The Man Shakespeare and His Tragic Life Story* (1909) identifies Brutus with his creator, showing "his own sad heart and the sweetness which suffering had called forth in him." Gertrude and Cressida were avatars of the Dark Lady of the sonnets (whom Harris identified as Mary Fitton), who had betrayed the playwright. The success of the Ireland forgeries attests to the hunger for information that continues unabated. Oxfordians, Baconians, and all the other kooks and cranks who deny that William Shakespeare of Stratford wrote the plays and poems cannot accept the gaps in biographical knowledge, and even the learned and orthodox Stratfordian A. L. Rowse claims to have unriddled the sonnets.

As one of the first academic critics, Dowden heralded another change in Shakespearean studies. Shakespeare's first editors, John Heminge and Henry Condell, were men of the theater. In the eighteenth century, his editors and admirers were again not sheltered in academic bowers; Arthur Sherbo's *The Birth of Shakespeare Studies* (1986) illustrates how many people from all occupations contributed comments to the various editions that appeared between 1709 and 1821. Malone, the greatest English literary scholar of the eighteenth century, trained as a lawyer and held no academic post. In the Victorian period, Shakespeare moved into the university. Thus, between 1863 and 1866, William George Clark, John Glover, and William Aldis Wright, all from Cambridge, produced *The Works of William Shakespeare*, in nine volumes, published by Cambridge University Press and dedicated to the university's chancellor. Though nonacademics continued to contribute to scholarship—T. S. Eliot and Granville-Barker come at once to mind, and the publisher Robert Giroux's *The Book Known as Q* provides a fascinating analysis of the sonnets—criticism and editing have become largely the province of academics, who also constitute the primary audience for these writings, which have grown increasingly hermetic and esoteric. Like much modern literature, art, and music, late twentieth century criticism isolated itself from the public. Wordsworth's famous definition of the poet as a man speaking to other men might be paraphrased to define the modern critic as a man (used generically) writing to himself and his colleagues.

Yet the multiplicity of Shakespeare festivals—thirty-one in the United States alone in 1983—the popularity of movies based on the plays, and the British Broadcasting System (BBC) and Grenada television series suggest that the plays remain alive to greater audiences than ever.

In *Reinventing Shakespeare: A Cultural History, from the Restoration to the Present*, Gary Taylor argued that Dowden's fourfold division of Shakespeare's life reflects the Victorian belief in progress. The formation of the New Shakspere Society under F. J. Furnivall in 1873 similarly mirrors the age's faith in science. The Reverend Frederick G. Fleay, one of the society's leading members, proclaimed,

> We must adopt every scientific method from other sciences applicable to our ends. From the mineralogist we must learn to recognize a chip of rock from its general appearance; from the chemist, to apply systematic tabulated tests to confirm our conclusions; from the botanist we must learn to classify; finally, from the biologist we must learn to take into account, not only the state of any writer's mind at some one epoch, but to trace its organic growth from beginning to end of his period of work. When these things are done systematically and thoroughly, then, and then only, may we expect to have a criticism that shall be free from shallow notions taken up to please individual eccentricities.

Dowden's anatomy of Shakespeare's life was a product of such thinking—Dowden was a charter member of the New Shakspere Society. Another product was Fleay's metrical tests to determine the chronology and authenticity of the plays. His results were not always happy: according to Fleay, *Henry VIII, Pericles, Timon of Athens, Macbeth, Julius Caesar*, and *The Taming of the Shrew* all showed signs of other authors. Most of his conclusions have been rejected by modern scholarship. Another member of the society, James O. Halliwell-Phillips, charged with writing the biography, stretched out his meager facts to a thousand pages that again portray an unlearned genius: "Residing with illiterate relatives in a bookless neighbourhood; thrown into the midst of occupations adverse to scholastic progress, it is difficult to believe that when he first left Stratford, he was not all but destitute of polished accomplishments." Modern scholarship finds a very different environment, a very different man.

Victorian sentimentality and belief in progress have not worn well in Shakespeare studies or anywhere else. The scientific method has fared somewhat better. The Hinman collator, developed by Charlton Hinman, greatly aided textual studies, and metrical tests, more sophisticated and aided by computers, continue to be applied to determine authorship, though this approach remains controversial. The twentieth century's belief in the social sciences was mirrored in Shakespearean criticism, with its sociological, anthropological, and psychological approaches. C. L. Barber's *Shakespeare's Festive Comedy* (1959), John Holloway's *The Story of the Night* (1961), and Northrop Frye's *A Natural Perspective* (1965) are products of this methodology. The rise of feminism finds its echo in essays such as Kathleen E.

McLuskie's "The Patriarchal Bard" (1985) and Linda Bamber's *Comic Women, Tragic Men* (1982).

The Victorian concern with the past led to historically accurate productions and the creation of historically accurate texts. In 1838 William Macready offered Shakespeare's *The Tempest* rather than the Davenant/Dryden version, and Shakespeare's *King Lear* instead of Tate's. In 1877 Henry Irving abandoned Colley Cibber's *Richard III* for the original. F. R. Benson, William Poel, and Granville-Barker continued this practice, and Peter Hall's uncut versions demonstrate the vitality of the tradition. This nineteenth century new historicism benefitted criticism also. E. E. Stoll argued for seeing Shakespeare as a product of his time. Thus, he maintained that Shylock reveals the mentality of Shakespeare's audiences, their attitude towards Jews, misers, and moneylenders. This approach provides the background necessary to understand the works and offers a necessary corrective to those who fail to remember that Shakespeare was of his age as well as for all time. E. M. W. Tillyard's influential and controversial *The Elizabethan World Picture* (1943) is a product of this same concern for understanding the literary, intellectual, and cultural background of the works, as is new historicism. Yet no age is monolithic. Even if the majority of Shakespeare's audience hated Jews, Shylock need not be a clone of Barabas in Christopher Marlowe's *The Jew of Malta*. Though a majority of Elizabethans may have envisioned the world as Tillyard claims, Shakespeare may not have agreed. Artists in general, and great artists in particular, are antinomian; Shakespeare may have found other truths more appealing than the orthodoxies of his time.

In a revolt against the biographical-historical approach to literature, New Criticism turned to the texts as self-contained artifacts that would interpret themselves under proper investigation. Caroline F. E. Spurgeon tabulated Shakespeare's imagery, finding in *Macbeth*, for example, repeated references to clothes. The title character wears "borrow'd robes," "strange garments," and "a giant's robe/ Upon a dwarfish thief." Her study does not break completely with those of her predecessors: she hoped to use the imagery to understand the life of the creator, and her tables resemble those of Fleay's chemist. Still, she provided the impetus and much of the information that underlies the work of scholars such as Cleanth Brooks and Wolfgang Clemen. Deconstructionists, much as they claim to reject New Criticism, undertake the same close reading of the text. At its best, such interpretation has illuminated the plays, but it has also encouraged reading them as poems rather than as drama. Theater-based criticism has claimed, with some justice, that such approaches distort the works.

How to Use this Bibliography

The proliferation of critical schools calls to mind Guildenstern's observation, "O, there has been much throwing about of brains" (*Hamlet*, II, ii). *The World Shake-*

speare Bibliography for 1986 alone lists 4,069 items. The figure testifies to the enduring achievement of England's greatest dramatist, but it poses a problem for researchers. This bibliography has sought to examine twentieth century criticism, particularly books, to suggest the range of materials and approaches and to discuss those works that students of Shakespeare are most likely to encounter and need. Though it has sought to include all the classic studies since the beginning of the century, the bibliography is weighted towards more recent scholarship. The primary audience is college undergraduates, but many of the items here will be accessible, physically and intellectually, to high school students as well. Graduate students and scholars, too, will find this volume a good place to begin their research.

The annotations indicate the contents of the book or article and generally evaluate it. While most items are included because they are useful, some (such as the Chelsea House collections edited by Harold Bloom) appear because they are likely to be found on library shelves. Where necessary, commentary places the individual work within the critical conversation it is addressing, and often the user will find references to one or more reviews.

The arrangement seeks to facilitate use. For example, the plays are listed alphabetically to avoid problems of chronology and classification. To avoid excessive repetition, entries appear under one heading only. Therefore, someone seeking material on *The Comedy of Errors* should look at the listings under "General Studies" and "Comedies" as well as under the play itself. Samuel Johnson observed that knowledge is of two kinds: either one knows something, or one knows where to find the information. It is hoped that this book contributes to the latter.

Joseph Rosenblum

Works Consulted

Benzie, William. *Dr. F. J. Furnival: A Victorian Scholar Adventurer*. Norman, Okla.: Pilgrim Books, 1983.

Eastman, Arthur M. *A Short History of Shakespearean Criticism*. New York: Random House, 1968.

Franklin, Colin. *Shakespeare Domesticated: The Eighteenth Century Editions*. Aldershot, England: Scolar Press, 1991.

Grebanier, Samuel. *The Great Shakespeare Forgery*. New York: W. W. Norton, 1965.

Halliday, F. E. *The Cult of Shakespeare*. New York: Thomas Yoseloff, 1957.

Marder, Louis. *His Exits and Entrances: The Story of Shakespeare's Reputation*. Philadelphia: J. B. Lippincott, 1963.

Munro, John, ed. *The Shakespeare Allusion-Book: A Collection of Allusions to Shakespeare from 1591 to 1700*. 2 vols. London: Oxford University Press, 1932.

Schoenbaum, Samuel. *Shakespeare's Lives*. 2d ed. New York: Oxford University Press, 1991.

Sherbo, Arthur. *The Birth of Shakespeare Studies: Commentators from Rowe (1709) to Boswell-Malone (1821)*. East Lansing, Mich.: Colleagues Press, 1986.

Taylor, Gary. *Reinventing Shakespeare: A Cultural History, from the Restoration to the Present*. New York: Weidenfeld and Nicholson, 1989.

BIBLIOGRAPHIES

Bergeron, David Moore, and Geraldo U. de Sousa. *Shakespeare: A Study and Research Guide*. 2d and rev. ed. Lawrence: University Press of Kansas, 1987.
A revision of the authors' 1975 work; aimed primarily at the beginning student. Surveys criticism from Shakespeare's time to 1987 and is especially useful for newer approaches to the works, such as poststructuralism and new historicism. The discussion of the items included, almost all of them books, is useful, but the thematic arrangement is awkward for those seeking material on specific plays. Contains a chapter on how to write research papers.

Berman, Ronald. *A Reader's Guide to Shakespeare's Plays*. Rev. ed. Glenview, Ill.: Scott, Foresman, 1973.
Intended for the general reader, this revision of the 1965 edition includes some three thousand entries. For each play, Berman discusses text, editions, sources, criticism, and staging, with an emphasis on literary analysis. Provides evaluations of most items listed. A reliable, helpful guide, especially good for tracing the development of responses to the plays. Each section concludes with an unannotated list for further reading.

Bevington, David. *Shakespeare*. Arlington Heights, Ill.: AHM Publishing, 1978.
Contains some 4,700 entries arranged topically, treating not only the plays and poems but also such subjects as social, political, and intellectual background. Covers criticism published between 1930 and 1977. Important items are marked with asterisks, which are sparsely allotted, but inclusion indicates that Bevington sees the work as important. The lack of annotations is a serious deficiency for the novice.

Champion, Larry S. *The Essential Shakespeare: An Annotated Bibliography of Major Modern Studies*. Boston: G. K. Hall, 1986.
Offers 1,500 English-language entries for twentieth century criticism through 1984. Clearly organized, this model bibliography is especially good for locating material on specific plays. Aimed at the general reader and the undergraduate, it attempts to present a representative sample of various approaches rather than a comprehensive listing. Annotations give good descriptions but do not evaluate the works.

Ebisch, Walter, and Levin Schucking. *A Shakespeare Bibliography*. Oxford, England: Clarendon Press, 1931.
A selective, unannotated listing of about 3,800 titles. Its chief defect is the baroque arrangement that makes locating items on specific topics difficult. For example, material on Shakespeare's treatment of ghosts and clowns appears under a sub-sub-sub-subheading of "The Art of Shakespeare." A supplement extending

coverage to 1935 was published by Clarendon Press in 1937. Not the first place to look for material on Shakespeare.

Godshalk, William, ed. *Garland Shakespeare Bibliographies*. New York: Garland, 1980-   .
Comprehensive annotated bibliographies for individual plays; covers criticism since 1940, with entries for significant earlier works. Well indexed. The introduction discusses major critical approaches and surveys available scholarship. This front matter is followed by a chronological listing of critical works, discussion of authorship where relevant, textual studies and material treating the dating of the play, sources, adaptations and influences, bibliographies, editions, translations, and stage history. Valuable for its effort to include and annotate virtually everything written during the dates covered.

Harris, Laurie L., et al., eds. *Shakespearean Criticism: Excerpts from the Criticism of William Shakespeare's Plays and Poetry, from the First Published Appraisals to Current Evaluations*. Detroit: Gale Research, 1984-   .
Aimed at the high school student and the undergraduate, this series provides a range of criticism on the works. The first ten volumes examine the texts; volume 11 begins the discussion of plays in performance. After a brief introduction to each play or poem, excerpts from the criticism are presented; each volume includes material from about two hundred books and essays, many of which are prefaced by useful headnotes explaining the importance of the selection. At the end of each unit is an annotated bibliography of additional studies.

Howard-Hill, T. H. *Shakespearian Bibliography and Textual Criticism: A Bibliography*. Oxford, England: Clarendon Press, 1971.
Volume 2 of the *Index to British Literary Bibliography*, this work lists about two thousand items under three broad headings. The first includes general bibliographies and guides: periodicals, indexes, and bibliographies. The second section lists material dealing with Shakespeare's works in general and the quartos, folios, and other editions. This unit also discusses important Shakespeare collections. The final part notes studies on specific plays and poems. Annotations are brief but informative.

McManaway, James G., and Jeanne Addison Roberts. *A Selective Bibliography of Shakespeare: Editions, Textual Studies, Commentary*. Charlottesville: University Press of Virginia, 1975.
Concentrates on works published in English between 1930 and 1970. Includes approximately 4,500 items, most of them dealing with individual plays, including the apocryphal writings. Generally lists editions and textual studies, followed by critical analyses. Lacks annotations, but the selection is rigorous enough to ensure the significance of the material listed.

Quinn, Edward, James Ruoff, and Joseph Grennen, eds. *The Major Shakespearan Tragedies: A Critical Bibliography*. New York: Free Press, 1973.
Aimed at the advanced undergraduate and graduate student, this bibliography surveys writing about *Hamlet*, *Macbeth*, *King Lear*, and *Othello*. Reviews criticism, editions, text, sources, and stage history for each play, with emphasis on criticism, which is discussed chronologically to show trends. Entries are carefully selected and thoroughly annotated.

Smith, Gordon Ross. *A Classified Shakespeare Bibliography, 1936-1958*. University Park: Pennsylvania State University Press, 1963.
Comprehensive, with 20,000 entries; a dinosaur in bulk and organization. Continues the Ebisch-Schucking work (cited above), using its elaborate system of classification, though not necessarily the same headings. Within each class, the listings are generally chronological but occasionally alphabetical, and each entry is designated by a letter followed by a number up to 10,000, at which point the letter changes and the number returns to 1. Thus, A10,000 is followed by B1, though both treat the same topic. Despite this Byzantine arrangement and the lack of annotations, students seeking a complete listing of studies for the years covered should consult this volume.

Wells, Stanley, ed. *The Cambridge Companion to Shakespeare Studies*. Cambridge, England: Cambridge University Press, 1986.
The most recent edition of a work that first appeared in 1934, this volume combines substantive essays with selective bibliographies. The seventeen chapters cover such topics as Shakespeare's life (chapter 1), the theater in Shakespeare's day (chapter 5), Shakespeare's use of history (chapter 9), and critical approaches (chapters 12, 13, and 16). Each unit is written by an authority in the area, and an index connects the chapters.

_____, ed. *Shakespeare: A Bibliographical Guide*. New ed. London: Oxford University Press, 1990.
Contains nineteen chapters, each prepared by an expert in the field. Most discuss books and articles about particular plays, and each chapter concludes with a well-selected bibliography. Additional chapters treat such matters as Shakespeare's text, the plays in performance, and recent critical approaches such as feminism and new historicism. A fine overview, valuable to the novice and scholar alike.

REFERENCE WORKS

Alexander, Marguerite. *A Reader's Guide to Shakespeare and His Contemporaries*. New York: Barnes & Noble Books, 1979.
Thirteen chapters provide plot summaries and brief reviews of criticism for each play. Includes more general discussions of such topics as the English and Roman history plays, comedy, romance, and Shakespeare's life. Also treats selected plays by Shakespeare's contemporaries. Concludes with a three-page bibliography for further reading.

Alexander, Peter. *Introductions to Shakespeare*. London: William Collins Sons, 1964.
Includes an essay by E. A. J. Honigmann on Shakespeare's theater and Alexander's treatment of Shakespeare's life and texts. The book provides introductions to each play and to the poetry, focusing on source, date, text, and interpretation. Peter Hillis Goldsmith called the work "revealing and useful, especially for the novice" (*Shakespeare Quarterly* 18 [1967]:81).

Baker, Arthur Ernest. *A Shakespeare Commentary*. 2 vols. New York: Frederick Ungar, 1938.
The lengthy subtitle details the scope of this work: "Dates of Composition and First Publication; Sources of the Plots and Detailed Outlines of the Plays; together with the Characters, Place-names, Classical, Geographical, Topographical and Curious Historical and Folk Allusions, with glosses; to which are added Appendices, giving Extracts from Holinshed, Plutarch, and the various Romances, Novels, Poems and Histories used by Shakespeare in the formation of the Dramas." Volume 1 covers *Julius Caesar*, *As You Like It*, *Macbeth*, *The Tempest*, *Hamlet*, *King Lear*, *King John*, *The Merchant of Venice*, and *Richard II*. The second volume treats *Henry IV*, *Henry V*, and *Henry VI*. Includes a genealogical table of the family of Edward III and the houses of Lancaster and York.

Boyce, Charles. *Shakespeare A to Z*. New York: Facts on File, 1990.
With some three thousand entries and more than fifty illustrations, this oversize volume includes scene-by-scene summaries of all the plays, biographical sketches of important people concerned with Shakespeare from his own day to the twentieth century, definitions of literary terms, and identifications of real and imaginary places relevant to the man and his works. The attempt at comprehensiveness can lead to silliness, as in the separate listings under "ambassador" for minor characters so designated in three different plays, and the bibliography, though helpful, contains a number of errors.

Browning, D. C. *Everyman's Dictionary of Shakespeare Quotations*. London: J. M. Dent & Sons, 1953.

Browning writes in his introduction that "the present volume is much more than just a collection of pleasant and interesting extracts from and about Shakespeare. It aims at providing within inadequate compass what will be at once an anthology of all that is greatest in Shakespeare's writings, a reference work to the plays and poems and to Shakespeare's allusions, and a companion and guide to Shakespeare's works, enabling the reader to find his way about them and to enjoy their choicest riches without having to quarry for them himself." Arranged by work, with a brief plot summary preceding the selected quotations. A shorter section includes biographical information, tributes, and a page of comments hostile to Shakespeare. The index is based on key words, but one must choose the right term. For example, Lady Macbeth's "A soldier and afeared?" is listed under "afeared," not under "soldier."

Campbell, Oscar James, ed., and Edward G. Quinn, assoc. ed. *The Reader's Encyclopedia of Shakespeare.* New York: Thomas Y. Crowell, 1966.
In one alphabetical listing, this work provides a discussion of Shakespeare's contemporaries, important actors, critics, editors, and the characters in the works. For each play, the editors give not only plot summaries but also sources, date of composition, stage history, and critical commentary, together with helpful references. Concludes with a chronology and selective bibliography. Nicely illustrated.

Clark, Sandra, and T. H. Long. *The New Century Shakespeare Handbook.* Englewood Cliffs, N.J.: Prentice-Hall, 1974.
An alphabetical listing "of all Shakespeare's plays and all the characters in these plays; . . . the principal actors, acting companies, and theatres of the time; other playwrights, writers, and historical figures of Elizabethan times important to Shakespeare's works; contemporary writings that mentioned Shakespeare; and much more." Includes brief plot summaries and a full list of characters for each play. Three introductory chapters deal with Shakespeare's life, theater, and poetry, and a thirty-two-page section depicts scenes from modern productions. Includes a ten-page bibliography for further research.

DeLoach, Charles. *The Quotable Shakespeare: A Topical Dictionary.* Jefferson, N.C.: McFarland, 1988.
More than 6,500 quotations arranged by subject and indexed by character, title of work, and general topics. The subject headings can overlap. "'Tis ever common/ That men are merriest when they are from home" (*Henry V*, I, ii) is listed under "absence" and "merriment" but not under "happiness" or "mirth." Quotations under headings are arranged randomly, not by play—even individual passages may be divided—but one is likely to find one's favorite passages here.

Evans, Gareth Lloyd, and Barbara Evans. *The Shakespeare Companion*. New York:
Charles Scribner's Sons, 1978.
Divided into four sections: Shakespeare and his times, the plays in performance,
the works, and Stratford and Shakespeare. The first section includes a useful
chronology, and the second presents a stage history of the plays, with brief
biographies of important performers. The third unit offers scene-by-scene plot
summaries. Finally, for tourists, the authors, who live in Stratford, provide a ten-
page guide with historical notes. Altogether, a useful compilation.

Fox, Levi, ed. *The Shakespeare Handbook*. Boston: G. K. Hall, 1987.
Begins with essays on the Elizabethan world (by Eric Ives), Shakespeare's life
(by David Daniell), and his theater (by Andy Piasecki). The major portion of the
book offers brief analyses of the plays; these commentaries at times fail to do
justice to the works. The volume concludes with essays on Shakespeare in
performance; Shakespeare's poetry, music, and songs; and films of Shakespeare's
plays. Includes a brief bibliography. Attractively illustrated. Despite its limitations, a good introduction for students in junior high school and high school.

Gooch, Bryan N. S., and David Thatcher. *A Shakespeare Music Catalogue*. 5 vols.
Oxford, England: Clarendon Press, 1990.
Brian Vickers called this "undoubtedly one of the most important Shakespearean
reference works published in our time" (*The Times Literary Supplement*, August
30, 1991, p. 14). Lists and discusses composers who have written music for the
plays or music based on them, from such classics as Felix Mendelssohn's
incidental music to *A Midsummer Night's Dream* to Max Schuurman's 1923
arrangement of "Sigh No More, Ladies" to accompany eurhythmic exercises.
Equally fascinating is information about unfinished projects, such as Wolfgang
Amadeus Mozart's unwritten *Tempest* or Robert Schumann's opera *Hamlet*, the
play that has inspired the most unwritten music. *Twelfth Night*, according to this
catalog, has been the most scored, with 1,762 pieces based on the text. One
learns here that Sir Edward Elgar took the title of his "Pomp and Circumstance"
marches from *Othello*, and that a "Fortinbras Rumba" was composed in 1982.
A fascinating and invaluable work.

Halliday, Frank Ernest. *A Shakespeare Companion, 1564-1964*. Rev. ed. New
York: Schocken Books, 1964.
An updated version of the work first published in 1952. Halliday discusses his
scope in the preface: "This book . . . is a handbook not only to Shakespeare's
life and works, to his friends and acquaintances, to his poems and plays and their
characters, but also to the Elizabethan-Jacobean theatre, the other dramatists who
wrote for it, their most important plays and the companies that performed them,
and to the history up to the present day of Shakespeare's work both on the stage
and in the study, to his printers and publishers, players and producers, editors

and adapters, scholars and critics." Entries tend to be brief, but the work provides excellent thumbnail sketches of the history of the King's Men and the Children of the Chapel, plot summaries of the plays, and descriptions of characters. Includes facsimiles, genealogical tables, maps, and portraits.

Harbage, Alfred. *William Shakespeare: A Reader's Guide*. New York: Noonday Press, 1963.
Divided into five sections. The first discusses Shakespeare's language, the poetry, and "The Script," which includes information about dramatic conventions, characters' names, and structure. The other units treat the plays in chronological order, giving an overview of the works produced during one period (for example, 1587-1596 or 1597-1606) and then offering detailed treatment of the fourteen most popular plays. Harbage not only summarizes every scene in these fourteen works but also analyzes them in some detail.

Howard-Hill, T. H., ed. *Oxford Shakespeare Concordances*. Oxford, England: Clarendon Press, 1969-1973.
A separate volume for each play. Based on the text used for the Oxford Old Spelling Shakespeare. Words are listed alphabetically, with "I" and "J," "U" and "V" treated as one letter rather than as two. Thus, "advised" precedes "adultery." Some common words are counted, but line references are not provided for them, and words with different meanings are not differentiated. Thus, "a" as "he" is grouped with "a" as an article or exclamation.

Lewis, William Dodge. *Shakespeare Said It: Topical Quotations from the Works of Shakespeare, Selected and Annotated*. Syracuse, N.Y.: Syracuse University Press, 1961.
Arranged alphabetically by subject and under each heading by play. Complements Charles DeLoach's *The Quotable Shakespeare* (cited above). Thus, under "England," Lewis includes the gravedigger's comment about Hamlet's being sent to England (not in DeLoach) but omits Rambures' statement in *Henry V* that "England breeds very valiant creatures; their mastiffs are of unmatchable courage" (cited in DeLoach). Provides an index for cross-references.

Martin, Michael Rheta, and Richard C. Harrier. *The Concise Encyclopedic Guide to Shakespeare*. New York: Horizon Press, 1971.
Begins with an alphabetic listing that discusses the plays, characters, and language. In addition to the conventional elements such as plot summary, sources, and brief appraisals, this section presents selected quotations under key words, so it can serve as a Bartlett's *Familiar Quotations* for Shakespeare. Following the main encyclopedic guide is an essay on Shakespeare's life and theater; this unit is succeeded by a dictionary of Shakespearean scholars and theatrical figures, together with a list, by play, of significant twentieth century productions. The

volume concludes with a selected list of Shakespearean music (arranged by composer), a selected list of recordings, a bibliography, and genealogical charts.

Onions, C. T., and Robert D. Eagleson. *A Shakespeare Glossary*. Rev.ed. Oxford, England: Clarendon Press, 1986.
A much expanded edition of a work that first appeared in 1911. Like the original version, this one includes only words or meanings that were current in Shakespeare's time but have since become obsolete, archaic, or provincial. Eagleson has supplied a quotation for each entry but has omitted much of the philological information that Onions provided. The new version is easier to consult; the earlier one is more fun to read.

Partridge, Eric. *Shakespeare's Bawdy: A Scholarly, Fully Documented Examination of Shakespeare's Sexual Allusions*. 2d ed. London: Routledge & Kegan Paul, 1968.
Frequently reprinted since its first appearance in 1948, this may well be the most popular scholarly work on Shakespeare. Partridge presents a lengthy essay, "The Sexual, The Homosexual, and Non-Sexual Bawdy in Shakespeare." The glossary that follows is particularly helpful for noting sexual puns. Partridge has been accused of finding bawdry where none exists, but the work remains useful—and highly entertaining.

Quennell, Peter, and Hamish Johnson. *Who's Who in Shakespeare*. New York: William Morrow, 1973.
An attractively illustrated and nicely printed volume identifying, in alphabetical order, all the characters in the plays (excludes *The Two Noble Kinsmen* and *Sir Thomas More*). Generally avoids interpretation, providing summaries of the characters' actions. Reproductions of prints and photographs show how major characters have been portrayed over the centuries.

Root, Robert Kilburn. *Classical Mythology in Shakespeare*. New York: Henry Holt, 1903.
Provides an alphabetical listing of Shakespeare's mythological characters. Root discusses their use and suggests their source. Another section summarizes the mythology that appears in each play; Root notes the number and types of mythological references. Sees Ovid as Shakespeare's primary source for classical mythology.

Shaheen, Naseeb. *Biblical References in Shakespeare's Tragedies*. Newark: University of Delaware Press, 1987.
An updated version of Richmond Noble's 1935 study (see under "General Studies: Sources"), the work begins with discussions of the English Bible in Shakespeare's age and "Shakespeare and the Anglican Liturgy." The main section

of the study looks at biblical allusions in eleven tragedies. Appendix A lists which plays borrow from which books in the Bible; appendix B does the same for the Book of Common Prayer, and appendix C notes Shakespeare's use of the homilies, which were read weekly in the Anglican churches of Shakespeare's day. Cynthia Lewis observed that "the work furnishes Shakespeareans at all levels with a place to begin exploring . . . possible biblical allusions—and even larger religious concerns" (*Shakespeare Quarterly* 40 [1989]:108).

Spevack, Marvin. *A Complete and Systematic Concordance to the Works of Shakespeare*. 8 vols. Hildesheim, Germany: Georg Olms Verlagsbuchandlung, 1968-1980.
Based on the Riverside edition of Shakespeare, this massive work of more than eleven thousand pages provides a comprehensive, computer-generated listing of every word used by Shakespeare. Includes the bad quartos and even stage directions. Quotes the line in which the word appears and gives act, scene, and line references, making this not only an excellent finding tool but also a complete book of Shakespearean quotations. An indispensable reference tool, this work served as the basis for the one-volume *Harvard Concordance to Shakespeare* (Cambridge, Mass.: Harvard University Press, 1973).

Sugden, Edward H. *A Topographical Dictionary to the Works of Shakespeare and His Fellow Dramatists*. Manchester, England: Manchester University Press, 1925.
Arranged alphabetically by place and containing six plates, five of them showing Shakespeare's London and the sixth reproducing Emerie Mullineux's map of the Indies. Includes the references to the place and provides historical notes. Sugden quotes John Stow, for example, on the absence of any Boar's Head Tavern in Eastcheap in 1410 but adds that a tavern of that name in Southwark "once belonged to Sir John Fastolfe," and another tavern by that name served as the sight of dramatic performances before theaters were built. An entertaining collection of erudition.

Zesmer, David M. *Guide to Shakespeare*. New York: Barnes & Noble Books, 1976.
Begins with discussions of Shakespeare's life and world, text, chronology, and sources. The book then treats the plays and poems in roughly chronological order, providing both plot summary and brief analysis. Each chapter concludes with bibliographical footnotes, and a short bibliography precedes the index. Barry Gaines praised the work in his review for *Shakespeare Quarterly* (28 [1977]:526-528).

EDITIONS

Allen, Michael J. B., and Kenneth Muir, eds. *Shakespeare's Plays in Quarto: A Facsimile of Copies Primarily from the Henry E. Huntington Library.* Berkeley: University of California Press, 1981.
Twenty of Shakespeare's thirty-eight plays first appeared in quarto editions, some fairly accurate ("good"), some differing greatly from the accepted text ("bad"). This work reproduces all twenty-two quartos, including the bad first quartos and the good second quartos of *Romeo and Juliet* and *Hamlet. The Two Noble Kinsmen* (1634), increasingly attributed to Shakespeare, is included. Appendices discuss variant readings, the copies used in the facsimiles, and standard act-scene divisions (lacking in the quartos). Very useful for textual studies, especially since these quartos are extremely rare. *Titus Andronicus* (1594) and *Richard III* (1595) survive in unique copies, and only two copies exist of the bad quarto of *Hamlet*; one of these lacks the first page (British Library), one the last (Huntington).

Barnet, Sylvan, ed. *The Complete Signet Classic Shakespeare.* New York: Harcourt Brace Jovanovich, 1972.
Barnet has written a long introduction on Shakespeare's life, canon, theaters, actors, dramatic background, style, language, intellectual milieu, comedies, histories, tragedies, and poems. Individual editors have provided essays before each play; these treat interpretation, sources, and textual problems. Difficult words are explained at the bottom of each page. Includes a fourteen-page bibliography.

Bevington, David, ed. *The Complete Works of Shakespeare.* 4th ed. New York: HarperCollins, 1992.
A revision of Hardin Craig's acclaimed 1951 edition. Bevington arranges the plays by type: comedies, histories, tragedies, romances, and nondramatic poems. A general introduction treats Shakespeare's England; drama before Shakespeare; London's theaters and acting companies; Shakespeare's life, work, and language; editions; editors; and critical approaches. Appendices cover the canon, sources, and Shakespeare in performance. The volume concludes with a glossary and an extensive bibliography. Short critical essays precede each play. Includes some lovely color photographs and reproductions, and the text provides helpful explanatory notes.

Brockbank, Philip, ed. *The New Cambridge Shakespeare.* Cambridge, England: Cambridge University Press, 1984-   .
A handsome and carefully prepared edition of individual plays. nicely illustrated with photographs of productions. With briefer introductions than *The New Arden Shakespeare* volumes, *The New Cambridge Shakespeare* offers information on composition, sources, staging and stage history—especially strong here—and

critical approaches. Each volume also includes a bibliography for further research. This edition supersedes the earlier Cambridge edition of the plays that
appeared from 1921 to 1966.

Brooke, C. F. Tucker, ed. *The Shakespeare Apocrypha: Being a Collection of
Fourteen Plays Which Have Been Ascribed to Shakespeare.* Oxford, England:
Clarendon Press, 1918.
An important contribution to Shakespeare scholarship, collecting plays attributed
to Shakespeare in whole or in part. Among these are *The Two Noble Kinsmen*,
now often included in standard editions of Shakespeare's works, and *Sir Thomas
More*, believed by many to contain the only extant Shakespeare manuscript of
a play (Hand D). Brooke's introduction remains valuable for its historical
overview of these attributions and for its discussion of the individual works.
Includes a dated but still useful bibliography.

Brooks, Harold F., and Harold Jenkins, eds. *The New Arden Shakespeare.* Cambridge, Mass.: Harvard University Press, 1951-   .
A well-printed, carefully edited series of individual plays especially valuable for
the wealth of introductory material that surveys criticism and interprets the plays
with such lucidity that the views expressed here have become standard readings.
The introductions discuss text, historical questions such as sources and date of
the play, and critical issues. Appendices often reprint relevant sources and treat
other important questions, such as stage history.

Evans, G. Blackmore, ed. *The Riverside Shakespeare.* Boston: Houghton Mifflin,
1974.
An outstanding edition that is handsomely produced. Based on an examination
of every edition since the beginning of the eighteenth century. Contains a general
introduction by Harry Levin on Shakespeare's life, language, style, theater, and
artistic development. The editor has added a discussion of the text and a glossary
explaining bibliographic terms. Helpful introductions precede each play, and
footnotes explain difficult passages. The volume also contains helpful appendices,
such as Charles Shattuck's treatment of the history of the plays on stage from
1660 to 1974. Also provides a selected bibliography. The edition to choose if
buying only one.

Furness, Horace Howard, et al., eds. *A New Variorum Edition of Shakespeare.*
Philadelphia: J. B. Lippincott, 1871-   .
Painstakingly edited, each play is treated in a separate volume (*Hamlet* in two).
The notes include all textual variants, discuss critical controversies, and offer
historical context. Appendices discuss the text, stage history, and critical reception, with excerpts from various commentators. Fascinating for all students and
essential for the scholar. Publication has been taken over by the Modern Language Association of America.

Harbage, Alfred, ed. *William Shakespeare: The Complete Works*. New York: Penguin Books, 1977.
Issued in 1969 as *The Complete Pelican Shakespeare*, this edition has proved popular in undergraduate classes. As in the First Folio, the works are arranged by genre. A general introduction provides discussions of the Elizabethan intellectual and political background, Shakespeare's life and works, his theater, dramatic techniques, texts, and editors. Each of the sections (comedies, histories, tragedies, romances, and nondramatic poetry) and each of the plays is preceded by a brief introduction. Notes to the text appear conveniently at the bottom of the page.

Harrison, G. B. *Shakespeare: The Complete Works*. New York: Brace & World, 1948.
Somewhat dated in its introductory material and text, but much of the apparatus remains useful. The general introduction discusses the universality of Shakespeare, Shakespeare's life, his England, Elizabethan drama and playhouses (especially dated here), the text, the development of Shakespeare's art, and Shakespearean criticism. Appendices comment helpfully on such matters as the Elizabethan worldview, almanacs, funeral customs, and cuckoldry in Shakespeare's day. Each play is preceded by a critical introduction, and the annotations are good.

Hinman, Charlton, ed. *The First Folio of Shakespeare: The Norton Facsimile*. New York: W. W. Norton, 1968.
A number of facsimiles of the 1623 First Folio have been published; this is a reasonably priced and nicely made reproduction. It is not a copy of any particular folio but rather a reconstructed ideal version. Hinman invented a machine that compares seemingly identical pages to detect differences. Using this device (the Hinman collator), he compared twenty-nine of the eighty folios housed at the Folger Library in Washington, D.C., and chose the most accurate copy for each page, which was then reproduced in its original size and condition. Hinman did add line numbers to the margins, hoping that his designation would supplant the act-scene references for passages (the latter being ahistorical, since Shakespeare did not use them). An introduction discusses the authority of the text of the First Folio, its production, the creation of the Norton facsimile, and the seven pairs of variant pages reproduced at the end of the volume. A nice addition to any library, it gives a sense of what the early seventeenth century reader saw when reading a Shakespearean play.

Ribner, Irving, and George Lyman Kittredge, eds. *The Complete Works of Shakespeare*. Rev. ed. Waltham, Mass.: Ginn, 1971.
Based on the 1936 Kittredge edition and revised by Ribner. The text remains unchanged from the first edition, but Ribner has added a general introduction and

shorter essays for each play. The introduction discusses Shakespeare and the English Renaissance, Shakespeare's life, his England, the drama before Shakespeare, theaters and acting companies, publication history of the plays, criticism, and performance. Also provides a bibliography.

Wells, Stanley, and Gary Taylor. *William Shakespeare: The Complete Works.* London: Oxford University Press, 1986.
The most controversial edition. Some editorial decisions reflect modern scholarly views. Thus, both the 1608 quarto and 1623 folio versions of *King Lear* are presented (rather than a conflated edition) because they are now widely regarded as two different editions, each with its own legitimacy. Other editorial decisions are more questionable, such as renaming *Henry VIII* as *All Is True* and Falstaff as Oldcastle (in *1 Henry IV* but not in *2 Henry IV*). In 1987 Oxford added an old-spelling edition and *A Textual Companion*. The plays are also available in individual volumes. While fascinating in many ways, this edition cannot be recommended to the beginning student, who may emerge with some bizarre ideas about the text.

BIOGRAPHIES

Adams, Joseph Quincy. *A Life of Shakespeare*. Boston: Houghton Mifflin, 1923.
Drawing together all that was then known about Shakespeare, Adams produced
a readable and scholarly account that emphasizes the Elizabethan theatrical world
in which the playwright operated. Adams' interpretations, such as his view of
Shakespeare's marriage as happy, will not satisfy everyone, but his account,
enriched with numerous illustrations, offers a good starting place for the serious
student.

Bentley, Gerald Eades. *Shakespeare: A Biographical Handbook*. New Haven,
Conn.: Yale University Press, 1961.
In the opening chapter, Bentley examines what he calls "legends" about Shakespeare and rival claimants to the authorship of the plays. The rest of the book
weaves together some one hundred documents into a biographical narrative that
sets the playwright "against the background of Elizabethan customs and preju-
dices," according to the preface. Bentley's objectivity and brevity—the text runs
to little more than two hundred pages—make this an excellent choice for the
beginning student. Its bibliography remains useful.

Bradbrook, M. C. *Shakespeare: The Poet in His World*. New York: Columbia
University Press, 1978.
The first section of this study ("The World He Found") highlights the influence
on Shakespeare of the Warwickshire landscape and literary tradition, which
includes William Langland and Sir Thomas Malory, as well as a rich oral
heritage. "The World He Made" shifts to London to examine the Elizabethan
theater, events surrounding the plays, and the importance of rival playwrights,
especially Christopher Marlowe, in the creation of the early works. The final,
elegiac section examines Shakespeare's later writing—Ben Jonson emerges as the
major influence here—and Shakespeare's last years. Both the poet and his world
come to life, and though scholars will find little that is new, all readers will
emerge with a renewed appreciation for England's greatest author.

Burgess, Anthony. *Shakespeare*. New York: Alfred A. Knopf, 1970.
An attractive volume with forty-three color plates and many others in black and
white, Burgess' life seeks "to set down the main facts about the life and society
from which the poems and plays arose." The work contains some imaginative
but enjoyable reconstruction, such as Shakespeare's love of two Annes or the first
performance of *Hamlet*. Almost all these conjectures are labeled as such, and the
sprightly style makes this popular biography a joy to read as well as to look
through.

Burton, S. H. *Shakespeare's Life and Stage*. Edinburgh: W & R Chambers, 1989.
The first and longer part treats Shakespeare's life; the last fifty pages discuss his theater, actors and acting companies of the period, audiences, and Shakespeare's text. Appendices provide a family tree and a chronology. Synthesizing the latest research in a readable, concise manner, this book offers a good introduction for the beginning student or general reader. It generally avoids conjecture and notes where scholars differ (for example, Shakespeare's activities in the mid-1580s).

Chambers, Edmund Kerchever. *William Shakespeare: A Study of Facts and Problems*. 2 vols. Oxford, England: Clarendon Press, 1930.
This massive, scholarly, sane work presents and evaluates the facts and legends surrounding Shakespeare. "It is no use guessing," he says about Shakespeare's "lost years" (1585-1592), and he avoids speculation throughout. Chambers was especially interested in the Elizabethan stage; most of the first volume focuses on the world of the theater and on the texts of the plays, with his dating of the works remaining useful. The second volume reproduces in typescript, and sometimes in facsimile, the records of Shakespeare's life, contemporary allusions, and later accounts, including forgeries. The study is daunting but indispensable and marks the division between older and modern Shakespearean scholarship. The inadequate index is supplemented by Beatrice White's *Index to "The Elizabethan Stage" and "William Shakespeare"* (1934).

Chute, Marchette. *Shakespeare of London*. New York: E. P. Dutton, 1949.
Chute produced a popular biography that largely avoids conjecture. She does not look for hidden meanings in the sonnets (which she discusses only in an appendix), and she confines legendary material, such as the deer-poaching episode of Shakespeare's youth, to the back of the book. The text itself relies on contemporary evidence, none later than 1635. While the absence of footnotes is troubling, the book offers excellent treatment of Shakespeare's world—London, the court, and the stage—and the book's focus is on Shakespeare in the theater as actor, businessman, and, of course, playwright.

Fraser, Russell A. *Young Shakespeare*. New York: Columbia University Press, 1988.
Few hard facts are available about Shakespeare's early life. Fraser fleshes out this material with his discussions of the Warwickshire countryside, Stratford and its surrounding villages, and London and the aristocratic world that supplied young Shakespeare's patrons. The background material about Shakespeare's pre-London world is the less familiar and hence the more welcome. Even though the forty pages of notes suggest careful scholarship, Fraser occasionally speculates beyond his evidence, placing the eleven-year old Shakespeare at Kenilworth for Queen Elizabeth's visit to the Earl of Leicester, for example. Fraser also can be sloppy about dates, a problem exacerbated by his "cross-cutting" presentation

that can confuse chronology. Unexplained allusions can confuse the novice, Fraser's dating of the plays will raise eyebrows, and the index could be better. Not a good first biography, Fraser will fascinate those who already know something about Shakespeare.

Holland, Norman N., Sidney Homan, and Bernard J. Paris, eds. *Shakespeare's Personality*. Berkeley: University of California Press, 1989.
The thirteen essays in this collection draw on Shakespeare's works to reach an understanding of the man. Despite their diversity, they portray an angry man seeking to compensate for his father's loss of status or for sibling rivalry. He is troubled by heterosexual relationships, and his world view is dualistic. Many of the ideas offered here suggest excellent readings of the texts; what they say about the poet is problematic. Includes an eleven-page bibliography for those seeking to pursue the psychological approach to Shakespeare.

Honigmann, E. A. J. *Shakespeare: The Lost Years*. Totowa, N.J.: Barnes & Noble Books, 1985.
Drawing on material in the Lancashire, England, archives, earlier studies, tradition, and Shakespeare's writing, Honigmann argues that the playwright began life as a Catholic, earned his living as a schoolmaster for a time, and served Lord Strange, with whom he learned his dramatic craft. Fraser assigns earlier dates than are customary for Shakespeare's first plays; for example, he places *Titus Andronicus* in 1586, rather than 1591-1592, and *The Two Gentlemen of Verona* in 1587, rather than 1593-1594. The ideas here may possibly be correct, but they remain highly speculative.

Levi, Peter. *The Life and Times of William Shakespeare*. New York: Henry Holt, 1989.
A personal view of Shakespeare, intended for the general reader. Includes brief discussions of the plays. Levi's judgments sometimes outstrip his data and contradict general scholarly opinion. For example, his first appendix reprints as Shakespeare's the verses for a masque generally attributed to Sir William Skipwith. To be read with caution.

Quennell, Peter. *Shakespeare: A Biography*. Cleveland: World Publishing, 1963.
An accomplished biographer, Quennell has produced a well-written and well-illustrated life of Shakespeare that offers excellent background without obscuring the subject. Readers should be wary of Quennell's willingness to ascribe to the author certain sentiments expressed by characters, views contradicted elsewhere in the plays. Similarly, Quennell reads tragic gloom back from the major tragedies to their author. Read skeptically, this remains a good biography for the beginning student or the general reader.

Reese, M. M. *Shakespeare: His World and His Work*. Rev. ed. New York: St. Martin's Press, 1980.
Taking a topical approach, Reese begins with a short chapter on Shakespeare's youth. He next discusses the medieval and Renaissance stage, drawing heavily on the work of E. K. Chambers; this is the largest section of the book. The final units treat the dramatist's life and mind ("Shakespeare's Personality") and his work ("Shakespeare's Art"). Appendices briefly discuss Shakespeare's acting company and reprint Chambers' dating of the plays. Reese does not excite, but he will not mislead.

Rowse, A. L. *William Shakespeare*. New York: Macmillan, 1963.
Rowse offers no new information, but he claims to have dispelled all mysteries surrounding Shakespeare except for the identity of the Dark Lady of the sonnets (whom Rowse subsequently named in *Shakespeare the Man*, 1973). Rowse actually offers a readable and accurate account of Shakespeare's social and political milieu—on which Rowse is an acknowledged expert—in a biography aimed at the general reader. He is opinionated, not definitive, but nevertheless fascinating for his quirkiness.

Schoenbaum, Samuel. *Shakespeare's Lives*. New ed. New York: Oxford University Press, 1991.
Surveys the biographies of Shakespeare from the bust and inscription of the Gheerart Janssen monument erected at Holy Trinity Church, Stratford, shortly after the playwright's death in 1616 to Peter Levi's *The Life and Times of William Shakespeare* (1988) and A.L. Rowse's *Discovering Shakespeare: A Chapter in Literary History* (1989). A helpful guide to works about Shakespeare, it shows how the playwright has been regarded through the centuries, and from this welter of often conflicting portraits an image of the man emerges.

_____. *William Shakespeare: A Documentary Life*. New York: Oxford University Press in association with Scolar Press, 1975.
George Bernard Shaw commented that "everything we know about Shakespeare can be put into a half-hour sketch." As Schoenbaum demonstrates in this sumptuous collection of more than two hundred facsimiles, much material about the playwright survives, from the baptismal register recording his christening on April 26, 1564, to his marriage license bond and his will. The text commenting on and linking these materials provides a clear, judicious biography.

_____. *William Shakespeare: Records and Images*. London: Scolar Press, 1981.
A supplement to Schoenbaum's *William Shakespeare: A Documentary Life*, this equally handsome oversize volume includes 165 facsimiles of items relating to Shakespeare and his age. The six chapters explore the authenticity of various

portraits and signatures and present evidence of Shakespeare's activities in London and Stratford. Like its companion, the narrative and documents offer fascinating glimpses into the man and his world.

THE SHAKESPEAREAN STAGE

Adams, John Cranford. *The Globe Playhouse, Its Design and Equipment*. New York: Barnes & Noble Books, 1961.
Very influential though probably erroneous. Based on the 1616 Claes Visscher engraving showing an eight-sided theater. Adams maintained that the Globe "was a three-story octagonal structure surrounding an unroofed octagonal yard." The book dismisses Wenzel Hollar's view of 1647, now regarded as the most accurate depiction despite its mislabeling of the Globe and the Bear Garden. Adams believed that Shakespeare's theater resembled an inn-yard and that each scene was set in a certain area to specify location. Both assumptions have since been questioned. The image of the Elizabethan theater used for the opening scenes of Laurence Olivier's *Henry V* was Adams'.

Adams, Joseph Quincy. *Shakespearean Playhouses: A History of English Theaters from the Beginnings to the Restoration*. Boston: Houghton Mifflin, 1917.
Opens with a discussion of the inn-yards as precursors to actual theaters and then devotes individual chapters to seventeen regular theaters and five others that were temporary or only projected. Includes many maps and illustrations. Adams did not attempt to resolve all questions about the Elizabethan stage, but he offers sober assessments of the wealth of evidence that he presents. Despite its age, this remains an important work on the subject.

Armstrong, William A. *The Elizabethan Private Theaters: Facts and Problems*. London: Society for Theatre Research, 1958.
A short survey of private (that is, indoor) London theaters from 1575 to 1642, based on a study of 150 plays written for these stages. Finds many similarities between the outdoor and indoor theaters, though the latter had a smaller acting area. Since plays were performed indoors at night, the private theaters also provided artificial lighting. Armstrong notes that the private theaters served as the models for staging after the Restoration.

Baldwin, Thomas Whitfield. *The Organization and Personnel of the Shakespearean Company*. Princeton, N.J.: Princeton University Press, 1927.
Discusses the operation of the Lord Chamberlain's/King's Men. The first chapter treats laws and customs governing the actors; Baldwin argues that acting was a mystery like any other occupation, with seven years' apprenticeship for those seeking to join a company. He turns next to membership of Shakespeare's company from 1588 to 1642, drawing on the list of twenty-six actors named in the First Folio. Baldwin sees the Lord Chamberlain's Company as a continuation of Leicester's Men. The third chapter examines the shareholders and owners of the properties the company used. Hired actors who were not patented members of the company are discussed next. Among the hired help were door-keepers and

book-keepers (who served as prompters and safeguarded the copies of the plays). In "Shakespearean Clan," Baldwin tells how the actors lived, clustering in Shoreditch, Southwark, and Aldermanbury. Finances occupy the sixth chapter. Shakespeare probably never earned more than two hundred fifty pounds a year. Baldwin then turns to the roles actors played and maintains that plays were adapted to particular companies; he even tries to determine who played each Shakespearean role. Though the book is dated, it remains useful for its picture of actors' lives in the Elizabethan age.

Barroll, Leeds. *Politics, Plague, and Shakespeare's Theater: The Stuart Years.* Ithaca, N.Y.: Cornell University Press, 1991.
Barroll argues that despite the recognition from King James, Shakespeare's company "remained the plaything of social circumstances," still at the margin of society. The bubonic plague that led to the closing of the theaters threatened actors' livelihoods; other restrictions, such as the banning of performances during Lent, limited actors' freedom. Barroll maintains that these factors inhibited Shakespeare's productivity. Between 1594 and 1602 Shakespeare wrote twenty-seven plays; from 1603 to 1611, when the theaters were closed for a total of sixty-eight months, he composed only ten. Useful for the observations about the state of the theater in the early Stuart period. The argument about Shakespeare's writing habits is less persuasive.

Beckerman, Bernard. *Shakespeare at the Globe, 1599-1609.* New York: Macmillan, 1962.
Drawing his conclusions from fifteen Shakespearean and fourteen non-Shakespearean plays produced at the Globe between 1599 and 1609, Beckerman examines the repertory, dramaturgy, stage, acting, and staging at the theater during its first decade. Appendices note such matters as properties required and scenes needing more than five characters. Among the book's conclusions are that the stage was essentially bare and exposed to the audience on three sides.

Bentley, Gerald Eades. *The Profession of Player in Shakespeare's Time, 1590-1642.* Princeton, N.J.: Princeton University Press, 1984.
Bentley claims that "my principle of organization has been to consider first the relations between the player and his company; then the three components of all adult companies—sharers, hired men, and apprentices; then three aspects of the players' activities—managing, touring, and casting; and then an attempt to draw some of the material together in a [summary]." An appendix lists casts for a number of plays. A judicious summary of the evidence that incorporates a number of previously unpublished records. In her review of the work, Ann Jennalie Cook wrote that "readers ranging from undergraduates to specialists will find Bentley's book a lucid guide to the performers' professional life" (*Shakespeare Quarterly* 37 [1986]:412). Does little with provincial and children's companies.

_____. *Shakespeare and His Theatre*. Lincoln: University of Nebraska Press, 1964.

Five lectures emphasizing the view that the plays were intended to be performed rather than read. Explores Shakespeare's company and theaters and what happened to audiences and theaters after Shakespeare's retirement. His view that Shakespeare wrote for particular companies ignores the plays' flexibility, and he sees a cleavage between the public theater of the Globe and the private theater of Blackfriars, ignoring the fact that many plays appeared in both. Still, this readable, short (128-page) book draws on intimate familiarity with the subject and provides much useful information.

Berry, Herbert, ed. *The First Public Playhouse: The Theatre in Shoreditch, 1576-1598*. Montreal: McGill-Queen's University Press, 1979.

Includes five essays on Shakespeare's first theater. Glynne Wickham looks at the question of whether the stage had a second story. Oscar Brownstein and Richard Hosley examine architectural antecedents; Herbert Berry calculates James Burbage's profits, and William Ingram suggests that from 1585 to 1596 Burbage owned The Curtain as well as The Theatre. Concludes with a valuable handlist of relevant documents, giving location, call number, and a summary of the contents.

_____. *Shakespeare's Playhouses*. New York: AMS Press, 1987.

Discusses the four theaters that were controlled by the companies associated with Shakespeare: The Theatre at Shoreditch, Blackfriars Theatre, and the first and second Globe. Together, these cover the period from 1576 to 1642. Five of the six essays in the book appeared previously; two of these were revised. All the information derives from contemporary documents. Berry avoids conjecture, and his quarrying among old records has revealed may fascinating facts. For example, Berry shows that at the Blackfriars the boxes abutted the stage and were on a level with it. It was here, too, that sitting on the stage itself was most popular. Berry does not attempt to reconstruct Shakespeare's stage; indeed, he argues that facts are insufficient to do so. To cite one example, the available material about the Blackfriars Theatre says nothing about where actors dressed.

Bradbrook, Muriel C. *Elizabethan Stage Conditions: A Study of Their Place in the Interpretation of Shakespeare's Plays*. Hamden, Conn.: Archon Books, 1962.

Originally the Harness Prize Essay of 1931, this book begins with a survey of Shakespearean criticism from the eighteenth century to the twentieth. Succeeding chapters discuss the stage's influence on Shakespeare's dramatic structure, Shakespeare's topicality, characterization, Shakespeare and the acting profession, the relationship between the theater and the poetry, and, finally, "Shakespeare's stage and textual criticism." Rich in suggestions, learned without being tedious, this slim volume stands up well. Bradbrook is one of those Shakespeareans whose work is always readable and worth reading.

_____. *The Living Monument: Shakespeare and the Theatre of His Time.* Cambridge, England: Cambridge University Press, 1976.
Covers the period from 1576 to 1644 and seeks to understand the "sociology of the theatre." Elizabethan drama emerged "from a matrix of undifferentiated seasonal games, craft shows, and public entertainments, civic celebrations, private festivities, and polemics on social and religious questions." Theater was ritualistic, with audience participation creating a sense of community. Bradbrook examines the theater itself; conditions under which plays were created; the relationship among dramatists, actors, and audiences; and the way plays responded to contemporary issues. Much here on Shakespeare's last plays, the masques of Ben Jonson, and the work of Thomas Middleton.

_____. *The Rise of the Common Player: A Study of Actor and Society in Shakespeare's England.* Cambridge, England: Cambridge University Press, 1979.
As the title suggests, Bradbrook traces the improving fortunes of actors from their low status in the early Renaissance to relative affluence and respect under James I. She uses the careers of four actors to support her thesis. In the course of her book, Bradbrook conveys the sense of being an actor or theatergoer during the period, and she examines the actors within their social environment. Clifford Leech remarked of an earlier edition of this study that "no writer on the life of the period—no writer on the theatre of any age—can afford to neglect this book" (*Studies in English Literature* 3 [1962]:281).

Chambers, Edmund Kerchever. *The Elizabethan Stage.* 4 vols. Oxford, England: Clarendon Press, 1923.
More comprehensive than the title suggests, this monument to scholarship covers all aspects of theatrical production and the acting profession to 1616. The first volume covers the court and control of the stage. Volume 2 treats the companies, actors, and playhouses. In volume 3, Chambers discusses staging, plays, and playwrights. The final volume looks at anonymous works and reproduces documents important for the stage history of the period. Like his biography of Shakespeare, this work by Chambers is exhaustive and essential for the serious scholar. It is supplemented by the even more detailed study by Gerald Eades Bentley, *The Jacobean and Caroline Stage* (Oxford, England: Clarendon Press, 1941-1968), which covers the period 1616-1642.

Cohen, Walter. *Drama of a Nation: Public Theater in Renaissance England and Spain.* Ithaca, N.Y.: Cornell University Press, 1985.
Despite the difference in religion, both England and Spain developed theaters that fused classical and popular traditions. Similar theaters arose, Cohen argues, because of the similarities in the nature of English and Spanish absolutism; the differences he attributes to divergent religions and economic conditions. He sees public theaters as precapitalist and subversive. In the first part of his book, Cohen

links developments in European drama to the movement from feudalism to absolutism and a capitalist economy. The second part of the book discusses genres and specific plays and notes the similar phases in each theater. From roughly 1585 to 1600 in both countries, romantic comedy, dealing with "aristocratic adaptation" to society, was popular. The decline of the aristocracy in both nations after 1600 was reflected in the rise of satiric comedy and tragedy. Aristocratic retreat produced the third and final phase before 1640—domestic tragedy and pastoral romance. A far-ranging, learned study despite overreliance on Marxist ideology to explain the drama of the period.

Cook, Ann Jennalie. *The Privileged Playgoers of Shakespeare's London, 1576-1642.* Princeton, N.J.: Princeton University Press, 1981.
Disagreeing with the long-held view that Shakespeare's audience consisted largely of the working class, Cook maintains that only those with money had the time, interest, and finances that allowed them to attend the theater regularly, and therefore the playwrights sought to please this segment of society. Cook's view of privilege is broad: "impoverished students, younger sons of gentry set to a trade, and minor retainers in noble households all the way up to lords, ambassadors, merchant princes, and royalty itself." She includes much social history about both the privileged and the plebeians. Appendices discuss prices and wages. Though she probably overstates the case, Cook provides fascinating information about the age.

Dessen, Alan C. *Elizabethan Stage Conventions and Modern Interpreters.* Cambridge, England: Cambridge University Press, 1984.
Looks at some four hundred plays from Shakespeare's day to determine what settings, action, and symbols Elizabethan audiences expected. For example, actors dressed and behaved in a certain way when they entered "as from dinner." When they appeared on stage after a hunt there would be appropriate sounds offstage to suggest the action. These conventions also have thematic significance. Elizabethans read troubled sleep as a sign of guilt (as in *Macbeth*); wearing riding boots suggested haste. Dessen also discusses conventions of lighting, locality, and combat. For example, a modern production would leave Kent in the stocks in darkness and therefore invisible as Edgar flees across the heath. Shakespeare's audience would see both actions at once and connect the characters' plights. Claire Saunders wrote that "Dessen's admirable book combines scholarship with humour and sanity with imagination" (*Review of English Studies*, n. s. 37 [1986]: 410).

Foakes, R. A. *Illustrations of the English Stage 1580-1642.* Stanford, Calif.: Stanford University Press, 1985.
Many works on Shakespeare's stage choose one illustration or another—Claes Visscher's engraving or Aernout van Buchel's copy of the Swan Theatre's

interior—as the basis of their analysis of the Elizabethan stage. Foakes has gathered 124 reproductions of theaters, stages, and performances from 1580 to 1642 and offers a one-page or two-page commentary on seventy-nine of them, indicating what the pictorial evidence suggests. Foakes refrains from trying to argue a thesis or reconstruct a stage, though in his interpretations he does offer opinions. A short bibliography accompanies each entry. An extremely useful compilation; David George called it "indispensable" (*Shakespeare Quarterly* 37 [1986]:411).

Gair, Reavley. *The Children of Paul's: The Story of a Theatre Company, 1555-1608*. Cambridge, England: Cambridge University Press, 1982.
The children who attended St. Paul's grammar school and those who sang in the choir were involved in drama as early as 1378. During the reign of Elizabeth, they were particularly active and for some time were Elizabeth's favorite actors. Gair traces the history of this troupe in the Renaissance, looking at the physical setting, audiences, the running of the company, its playwrights and repertoire, the abilities of the actors, and the social, cultural, and political milieu in which the children's companies operated. An important contribution to the theater history of the age.

Greg, Walter Wilson, ed. *Dramatic Documents from the Elizabethan Playhouse*. 2 vols. Oxford, England: Clarendon Press, 1931.
Volume 1 provides the commentary; volume 2 reprints the documents, many of which also are reproduced in facsimile. Looking at "plots" (outlines of plays), actors' lists, actors' parts, and prompt books, Greg illuminates Elizabethan theater practices. For example, prompt books often contain warnings to actors and stage hands to be ready to appear or to bring in a necessary property. A particularly fascinating item is the only surviving actor's part, written for Edward Alleyne in Robert Greene's *Orlando Furioso* (1591). The part was written on strips of paper, about fifty lines to the strip, and offers very brief cues and stage directions.

Gurr, Andrew. *Playgoing in Shakespeare's London*. Cambridge, England: Cambridge University Press, 1987.
Covers the period from 1567 to 1642. Disagrees with Ann Jennalie Cook's analysis that audiences of the age consisted of the privileged. Gurr tries to balance Alfred Harbage's view with Cook's but leans more to the former. Among his conclusions are that plays generally ran about three hours; that audiences wore hats to the theater, enjoyed apples and nuts, and smelled of beer, garlic, and tobacco; and that audiences in the public theaters often were noisy. Gurr observes that privileged playgoers, who numbered some 350,000, were too few to supply audiences for London's theaters. He looks at the physical condition and social and intellectual composition of audiences, as well as the evolution of taste,

during the seventy-five years treated. Appendix 1 identifies 162 known playgoers, and the second appendix reproduces more than two hundred references to playgoing. Twenty-two illustrations accompany the text. An excellent survey of what one would have found at an Elizabethan theater.

_____. *The Shakespearean Stage, 1574-1642*. 3d ed. Cambridge, England: Cambridge University Press, 1992.
In 1574 actors received the first royal patent, and in 1642 Parliament officially closed the theaters. Gurr explores the history of the acting companies, theaters, staging, and audiences between these dates, drawing extensively on the work of E. K. Chambers and Gerald Eades Bentley. An appendix lists major plays and their authors, dates, places of performance, and acting companies. Well documented, with some forty illustrations. An excellent introduction to the subject, distilling much information into a readable account.

Gurr, Andrew, with John Orrell. *Rebuilding Shakespeare's Globe*. London: Weidenfeld & Nicolson, 1989.
Beautifully illustrated with eight color and fifty-nine black-and-white plates, this book defends the choices made by those reconstructing the Globe theater complex in Southwark, London. Relying on Wenzel Hollar's etching of the second Globe, Gurr and Orrell conclude that the theater was a twenty-four-sided polygon with an outside diameter of about a hundred feet and inside diameter of seventy feet that contained an elevated rectangular stage and three levels of galleries. The Blackfriars Theatre and an indoor theater designed by Inigo Jones (perhaps The Cockpit) are also discussed. The book provides information about playgoing in 1600, Shakespeare's company, and performances at the Globe. A careful sifting of evidence that does not overwhelm the reader with technicalities.

Harbage, Alfred. *Shakespeare's Audience*. New York: Columbia University Press, 1941.
Treats the size of audiences and their composition, behavior, and intellectual abilities. Shakespeare's spectators were largely working class. Though his conclusions about the audiences have been challenged by Ann Jennalie Cook and modified by Andrew Gurr, Harbage's book remains an important study that offers many insights into Elizabethan society and economics. In an appendix, Harbage examines Philip Henslowe's receipts from June, 1594, through July, 1596, to estimate audience size.

Hattaway, Michael. *Elizabethan Popular Theatre: Plays in Performance*. London: Routledge & Kegan Paul, 1982.
"This study of the popular drama of the late Elizabethan age begins with an account of the stages, performance conditions, and acting of the period and then turns to the analysis of five well known plays of the 1590s"—Thomas Kyd's *The*

Spanish Tragedy, Mucedorus, Christopher Marlowe's *Edward II* and *Doctor Faustus,* and Shakespeare's *Titus Andronicus.* Discusses the academic, sophisticated elements of popular drama, which was highly developed. Especially good on the visual-emblematic aspects of performances.

Henslowe, Philip. *Henslowe's Diary.* Edited by R. A. Foakes and
R. T. Rickert. Cambridge, England: Cambridge University Press, 1961.
An essential source for theater history between 1590 and 1604, this diary was kept by the manager of the Admiral's Men. Henslowe lists receipts and expenditures; in addition, he records practical matters, such as the hiring of actors, and legal problems. This edition includes a lengthy introduction discussing the history of the diary and noting some problems of interpretation. Neil Carson's *A Companion to Henslowe's Diary* (Cambridge, England: Cambridge University Press, 1988) discusses the diary's implications for understanding the actors, playwrights, and plays of the period. The Scolar Press has published a facsimile of the diary (1977) for those who want to read the original. The Foakes-Rickert edition supersedes W. W. Greg's 1904 publication of the diary.

Hillebrand, Harold Newcomb. *The Child Actors: A Chapter in Elizabethan Stage History.* University of Illinois Studies in Language and Literature 11, nos. 1 and 2. Urbana: University of Illinois Press, 1926.
Hillebrand begins his study with a discussion of child acting in the sixteenth century, particularly the Children of the Chapel Royal (1509-1584) and the Children of St. Paul's (1551-1590). He then turns to the fortunes of the Children of the Chapel Royal from 1600 to 1608, Paul's children from 1599 (or 1600) to 1609, the King's Revels Company, and the second Queen's Revels Company. Focus is on the business rather than the literary aspects of these groups, but Hillebrand notes that, for most of the sixteenth century, child actors pioneered the growth of English drama; the best plays were written for them by their masters. By 1600, the children's companies were imitating adult actors or turning to satire, courses which led to their demise. Hillebrand provides an annotated chronological listing of plays the children performed.

Hodges, Cyril Walter. *The Globe Restored.* 2d ed. New York: W. W. Norton, 1973.
Illustrated with seventy-three plates that provide both contemporary and reconstructed views of Elizabethan stages. Appendices list the theaters of London from 1576 to 1660 and present the 1599 contract for construction of the Fortune Theatre. Offers a view of the Globe consistent with more recent scholarship and presents its arguments clearly and convincingly, based on illustrations and plays of the period. Concludes that Shakespeare's stage derives from medieval pageants, so that performers stood well off the ground and had much space below the acting surface.

_____. *Shakespeare's Second Globe: The Missing Monument*. London: Oxford University Press, 1973.

An attractive volume that presents as good an idea as is available of what the Globe looked like, both inside and out. Notes differences between the first Globe and the second, particularly the lack of pillars to support the "heavens" above the stage in the rebuilt theater and its twin-gabled superstructure. A clearly presented text that is well illustrated.

Hodges, Cyril Walter, and Samuel Schoenbaum, eds. *The Third Globe: Symposium for the Reconstruction of the Globe Playhouse*. Detroit: Wayne State University Press, 1981.

This nicely illustrated, handsomely printed volume presents ten essays from a 1979 symposium organized to promote the reconstruction of a model of the Globe in Detroit. The essays provide an excellent overview of Shakespeare's theater—its size, sets, props, mechanical devices, and mode of construction. The related hypothesis that only such a theater can do justice to Shakespeare is more problematical, at least for modern audiences, who may find a more "authentic" staging distracting.

Hotson, Leslie. *Shakespeare's Wooden O*. London: Rupert Hart-Davies, 1959.

Maintaining that the Elizabethan stage imitated the medieval pageant stages of the mystery plays (the most commonly held view), Hotson argues that actors were surrounded by the audience on all sides, that the dressing area was beneath the stage, and that actors entered from "houses" on either side of the stage. The work discusses much fascinating evidence, but Hotson's conclusions have not stood up well. He was, however, the first to suggest that, whereas modern theaters place audiences in darkness and illuminate the stage, Shakespeare's open-air theaters reversed this situation, though almost everyone in the building would be shaded from direct sunlight.

Joseph, B. L. *Elizabethan Acting*. 2d ed. London: Oxford University Press, 1964.

Discusses action, speech, gestures, and character portrayal, drawing on Renaissance rhetorical guides to determine how actors performed. Joseph believes that audiences were meant to respond to the plays as literature, not as representations of reality. The work provides a good survey of the Elizabethan tradition of oratory and shows that director Konstantin Stanislavsky's ideas would have proved congenial to Shakespeare and his contemporaries.

King, T. J. *Shakespearean Staging, 1599-1642*. Cambridge, Mass.: Harvard University Press, 1971.

Examines 276 plays, especially the sixty prompt copies, to determine how Elizabethan, Jacobean, and Caroline plays were performed. Focuses on stage requirements, such as the number and location of entrances, properties, and playing areas. King maintains that fifty-five plays require an acting area above the stage, 102 need a discovery place, forty-two need a platform stage with space below, and eighty-seven need only a surface with two entrances. He believes that sets usually did not specify particular locations and argues that public and private theaters had similar staging requirements. The book includes an extended study of the production of *Twelfth Night* at the Middle Temple. An appendix reviews major scholarship on the Elizabethan stage from 1940 to 1971.

Knutson, Roslyn Lander. *The Repertory of Shakespeare's Company: 1594-1613*. Fayetteville: University of Arkansas Press, 1991.
Knutson's book contains much on the everyday preoccupations of the Lord Chamberlain's Company. Her account puts Shakespeare and his company in historical context, emphasizing their engagement with the practical demands of staging commercially viable plays.

Linthicum, Marie Channing. *Costume in the Drama of Shakespeare and His Contemporaries*. Oxford, England: Clarendon Press, 1936.
R. C. Bald began his review of this work by observing that "this book is an exceedingly useful one, and is certain to find a place on the reference shelf of all students of Elizabethan literature." (*Review of English Studies* 14 [1938]:91). Linthicum sets out to survey and define the colors, textiles, and garments used and to provide "illustrative quotation(s) from drama and contemporary accounts." She includes photographs of some—not enough—of the items she discusses. Helpful for envisioning the lady's cap that Petruchio dislikes, for understanding what "slops" are, and for imagining how audiences might have responded to characters wearing certain colors.

Lomax, Marion. *Stage Images and Traditions: Shakespeare to Ford*. Cambridge, England: Cambridge University Press, 1987.
Focusing on productions from 1607 to 1614, Lomax treats *Macbeth, Pericles, Cymbeline*, and John Webster's *The Duchess of Malfi* as they were performed at the Globe and Blackfriars, Webster's *The White Devil* at the Red Bull, a court masque, and plays by Thomas Middleton and John Ford. Lomax observes that audiences brought with them certain expectations derived from reading, playgoing, and public spectacles such as royal processions, civic pageants, and masques. She tries to reconstruct the attitudes of the Elizabethans, who might associate the cave in *Cymbeline* with Plato's allegory of the cave in his *Republic*, with the resurrection of Christ, and with Pandora's box. Unhappily, no one can guess the iconographic associations of the diverse spectators who made up the theatergoing public; Lomax acknowledges this problem by being tentative in her conclusions.

McMillin, Scott. *The Elizabethan Theatre and the Book of Sir Thomas More*. Ithaca, N.Y.: Cornell University Press, 1987.

The Book of Sir Thomas More has received much attention because it probably provides the only surviving specimen of Shakespeare's dramatic manuscripts. McMillin focuses on another aspect of the work, using it as a guide to Elizabethan theater practices. For example, he notes that the minimal stage directions indicate that scripts were the bare bones of parts that were fleshed out when individual parts were transcribed. The title role, more than eight hundred lines, is large for the period; therefore, Edward Alleyne or Richard Burbage probably acted the part, and more likely it was the former, since Lord Strange's Men, Alleyne's company, more commonly performed politically risky plays. Revisions indicate that a smaller company later sought to adapt the script for its cast. Gerald D. Johnson observed that "the book is engagingly written, treating a complex subject with logic and lucidity" (*Shakespeare Quarterly* 39 [1988]:521).

Mooney, Michael E. *Shakespeare's Dramatic Transactions*. Durham, N.C.: Duke University Press, 1990.

Drawing on the work of Robert Weimann (*Shakespeare and the Popular Tradition in the Theater*, 1978), Mooney concentrates on the interaction between actor and audience to "explore the nature of Shakespeare's dramaturgy and examine the ways in which he presents his major characters." Position is crucial; in *Othello*, for example, Iago's cynicism appears downstage while Othello and Desdemona maintain their ideals of love upstage, removed from the audience and hence from the everyday world. Mooney also discusses the iconographic significance of scenes such as the arming of Antony in IV, iv, of *Antony and Cleopatra*, a scene that suggests Venus' and Eros' arming of Mars. Sound interpretations of the plays emerge from discussions of how the works should be produced to create the effects Shakespeare sought.

Nagler, Alois M. *Shakespeare's Stage*. Translated by Ralph Manheim. Enlarged ed. New Haven, Conn.: Yale University Press, 1981.

A brief survey of the London theaters, the staging of *Romeo and Juliet*, actors and acting styles, Blackfriars Theatre, and Shakespeare's audiences. Nagler believes that Elizabethans witnessed stylized action and did not rely on illusion. Perhaps the most fascinating section is that which reprints documents relating to the stage: Johan de Witt's letter recording his visit to the Swan Theatre, Philip Henslowe's inventory of his stage properties, Thomas Platter's record of his visits to the Globe and The Curtain, the Philip Henslowe-Edward Alleyne contract for constructing the Fortune, and other such material.

Orrell, John. *The Human Stage: English Theatre Design, 1567-1640*. Cambridge, England: Cambridge University Press, 1988.

Andrew Gurr called this book "brilliantly argued and beautifully designed"

(*Shakespeare Quarterly* 40 [1989]:25). Orrell seeks to set the theater of the English Renaissance within the context of the period's architectural theories. Sees Sebastiano Serlio as particularly influential, with his measurements based on the Vitruvian proportions of the human body. Recent excavations of the public theaters suggest that Orrell may be overemphasizing mathematical theories, though the case for private theaters and Inigo Jones's designs remains plausible.

_____. *The Quest for Shakespeare's Globe*. Cambridge, England: Cambridge University Press, 1983.
Defends the use of Wenzel Hollar's 1647 engraving of the Globe. Orrell focuses on pictorial evidence and the contract for building the Fortune Theatre. He concludes that Shakespeare's theater could hold more than three thousand people and was aligned with the sunrise at midsummer. Excellent reproductions appear conveniently in the text. Some of the calculations grow complicated, but the conclusions are sound. Though Orrell does not go as far as Frances Yates here in arguing for Vitruvian influence, he sees certain echoes of Vitruvius in the proportions of the theater.

Reynolds, George Fulmer. *The Staging of Elizabethan Plays at the Red Bull Theater, 1605-1625*. London: Oxford University Press, 1940.
Looks at forty-six plays, which Reynolds divides into three groups. The A group of thirteen plays were certainly performed at the Red Bull, and the texts derive from productions. Another nineteen (the B group) probably were performed at the Red Bull, but the texts may not reflect actual productions. The third group may have been produced at the theater. By looking at stage directions and other textual references, Reynolds draws conclusions about properties, the stage, the production of stage effects, and other related matters. The documents reveal surprisingly little, but that discovery in itself is useful as a warning against rash conjecture.

Rhodes, Ernest L. *Henslowe's Rose: The Stage and Staging*. Lexington: University Press of Kentucky, 1976.
By looking at the plays associated with the Rose Theatre, Rhodes seeks to determine how the works were staged. He concludes that the stage was closed at the sides because actors needed five doors to enter and leave. Rhodes's reading of the plays is speculative; since it contradicts generally received views about the other public theaters, it is probably incorrect. The discussion of action on the stage, however constructed, is more convincing.

Rutter, Carol Chillington, ed. *Documents of the Rose Playhouse*. Manchester, England: Manchester University Press, 1984.
As Rutter writes in her preface, "This book is a 'documentary life': a collection of manuscripts selected and arranged to chronicle the day-to-day operation of one

Elizabethan playhouse, the Rose, over the fifteen years of its existence." Based on Philip Henslowe's account book but reconstructed and rearranged to provide a clearer picture of the theater's operations. A lengthy introduction discusses Henslowe and the city, court, and privy council that affected the theater, actors, and playwrights. An appendix reprints three statutes that regulated theatrical activity. Helpful, especially for the undergraduate, who may find Henslowe's diary daunting.

Shapiro, Michael. *Children of the Revels: The Boy Companies of Shakespeare's Time and Their Plays.* New York: Columbia University Press, 1977.
Discusses the children's acting companies that flourished in the late 1500s and first decade of the seventeenth century. The first chapter deals with the troupes, the second with the physical setting, the third with audiences, and the fourth with style of performance. Shapiro then looks at the plays these groups performed. Appendices treat the music in the children's plays, record court performances from 1559 to 1613, and list the children's repertoire. Reviewing the study for *The Times Literary Supplement* (February 3, 1978, p. 111), noted Shakespearean Kenneth Muir wrote that "the book . . . provides a well-balanced introduction to the subject; it makes sensible use of the information collected by previous scholars, and by Professor Shapiro himself; and it contains a good account of the audiences—intelligent but snobbish, intellectual but self-regarding, appreciating satire more than poetry."

Smith, Irwin. *Shakespeare's Blackfriar's Playhouse: Its History and Design.* New York: New York University Press, 1964.
Traces in great detail the history of the Blackfriars Theatre from its origins as a great hall for Dominican friars to the closing of the second playhouse in 1642. Emphasis is on the two theaters of that name; the study thereby promotes an understanding of the private theaters of the period. Reprints many relevant documents not otherwise easily accessible. Extrapolations to the second Blackfriars from the Globe ignore important differences between indoor and outdoor theaters.

_____. *Shakespeare's Globe Playhouse: A Modern Reconstruction.* New York: Charles Scribner's Sons, 1956.
Based on John Cranford Adams' reconstruction, which Smith helped build. Follows Adams' ideas about the shape of the theater and includes fifteen scale drawings. The Adams-Smith model is the one on display at the Folger Library in Washington, D.C., but it is inaccurate. Smith regards the inn-yard as the progenitor of the Elizabethan stage and ignores the influence of medieval staging. Also fails to consider the Wenzel Hollar engraving that gives the best picture of the second Globe.

Sturgess, Keith. *Jacobean Private Theatre*. London: Routledge & Kegan Paul, 1987.
Part 1 looks at the audiences, playhouses, companies, playwrights, and repertory
of the private theaters. The second section discusses three productions at the
Blackfriars: *The Tempest*, John Webster's *The Duchess of Malfi*, and John
Ford's *The Broken Heart*. Part 3 examines performances at court, especially Ben
Jonson's *Bartholomew Fair* and Thomas Carew's *Coelum Britannicum*. Observes
that, whereas in the open-air public theaters the actor was the star, in the private
(indoor) theaters the writer was the central figure. A solid, informative volume.

Thomson, Peter W. *Shakespeare's Theatre*. London: Routledge & Kegan Paul,
1983.
Focuses on Shakespeare's company during its first decade at the Globe. "Part
One looks at the planning and personnel, the financing, the repertoire, and the
Globe Theatre itself. Part Two sets three of Shakespeare's greatest plays [*Twelfth
Night, Hamlet,* and *Macbeth*] in the theatrical context . . . explored in Part One."
Includes contemporary illustrations and modern reconstructions. Appendices
provide the 1599 inventory of the Lord Admiral's Men, part of the contract for
the Fortune, which gives information about the Globe on which the Fortune was
modeled, and the petition of the residents of Blackfriars, London, seeking to
prevent the acting of plays at the theater there. A useful compendium with a good
bibliography.

Weimann, Robert. *Shakespeare and the Popular Tradition in the Theater: Studies
in the Social Dimension of Dramatic Form and Function*. Edited by Robert
Schwartz. Baltimore: The Johns Hopkins University Press, 1978.
Published in Germany in 1967 and translated and revised by Robert Schwartz,
this work maintains that Shakespeare's theater not only responded to but also
helped shape Elizabethan society. Weimann devotes most of the book to medieval
popular drama, which he sees as presenting an inverted world order. He sees two
elements in medieval and Renaissance theater. One is traditional: the actor fuses
with his role and ignores the audience. This aspect is associated with the locus,
a particular place on the stage. The other element is subversive: the actor ignores
the role and addresses the audience from the platea. This latter function belongs
to the Vice, clowns, and fools. Hamlet first appears on stage divided from the
locus of the court; he stands downstage where the unorthodox perform, and his
irreverently punning language suggests disruptive characters. Weimann's post-
Marxist reading of history and literature distorts his picture by creating polarities
and by siding with figures that playwrights and audiences rejected. For example,
Weimann sympathizes with the Vice and fools, but the Shakespearean descendants of the former, such as Iago and Richard III, are not admirable.

Wickham, Glynne. *Early English Stages, 1300-1600*. 3 vols. London: Routledge
& Kegan Paul, 1959-1981.

Begins with a study of theatrical performances of the Middle Ages. Of greatest interest to Shakespeareans are the two parts of the second volume that discuss the Elizabethan and Jacobean theaters. Wickham believes that staging did not differ between public and private theaters. Speculates that Peter Quince in *A Midsummer Night's Dream* alludes to James Burbage, and suggests that James I's patronage of the theater weakened drama. Good for understanding the development of the English stage and theatrical tradition that Shakespeare inherited.

Wiles, David. *Shakespeare's Clown: Actor and Text in the Elizabethan Playhouse.* Cambridge, England: Cambridge University Press, 1987.
A study of Will Kemp, the comic star of the Lord Chamberlain's Company, from 1594 to 1599. Explores the roles designed specifically for him and thus notes that the playwright interpreted the actor quite as much as the actor interpreted the author. During Kemp's tenure with the Lord Chamberlain's Men, clown characters had low social status, spoke colloquially in prose, and had opportunities to improvise, something Kemp loved to do. Wiles believes that Falstaff was a part designed for Kemp, though this point is unclear; Richard Burbage may have taken the role because he always had the largest part in Shakespeare's plays. Wiles also looks at the role of the clown in general and discusses Richard Tarlton, the great predecessor of Kemp, and Robert Armin, Kemp's successor, who played the Fool in Shakespeare's later works.

Yates, Frances A. *Theatre of the World.* Chicago: University of Chicago Press, 1969.
The classical theories of Vitruvius, as translated by the Elizabethan John Dee, explain the construction of Shakespeare's theaters. Yates also believes that an engraving for Robert Fludd's *Ars Memoriae* (1623) depicts the Globe. Yates sees the Elizabethan theaters as deriving from Roman models rather than inn-yards, English great halls, and medieval pageants. While acknowledging variations from the Vitruvian model, she attributes these to necessity or to misreadings. Sees the theater as a microcosm of the world.

SHAKESPEARE IN PERFORMANCE

Agate, James E. *Brief Chronicles: A Survey of Plays by Shakespeare and the Elizabethans in Actual Performance, 1923-1942.* London: Jonathan Cape, 1943. Agate collected here the reviews that he had written for the *Sunday Times* over two decades, providing a portrait of Shakespeare and his contemporaries on the London stage between the World Wars. Among the performances covered are Laurence Olivier's 1937 *Hamlet*; John Gielgud's *King Lear* (1931); *Romeo and Juliet* (1935) with Gielgud as Romeo, Olivier as Mercutio, Peggy Ashcroft as Juliet; and Tyrone Guthrie's *Macbeth* at the Old Vic (1939). In his discussions, Agate offers observations about the plays themselves and how he believes they should be staged. Lady Macbeth's soliloquy beginning "The raven himself is hoarse" should "be croaked in the lowest tone known to the female register." Agate also states that "Juliet has earthly values as well as spiritual; the containing vessel is the lovely clay in whose perishable beauty is all the ache of the sonnets."

Ball, Robert Hamilton. *Shakespeare on Silent Film: A Strange Eventful History.* London: Allen & Unwin, 1968.
The first part discusses Shakespeare on film, from the 1899 Herbert Beerbohm Tree *King John* to a 1928 German version of *A Midsummer Night's Dream*. Part 2 offers more specific details about the productions. While noting that Shakespeare without words is an oxymoron, Ball observes that silent film brought Shakespeare to new audiences and prepared the way for more sophisticated filmic representations by stressing action and visual appeal. An excellent survey of the subject. Includes works only tangentially Shakespearean, such as *Flying Romeo* and *When Macbeth Came to Snakeville*.

Beauman, Sally. *The Royal Shakespeare Company: A History of Ten Decades.* Oxford, England: Clarendon Press, 1982.
In 1879, under the supervision of Charles Flower, the Royal Shakespeare Company began performing in Stratford-upon-Avon. Flower wanted a permanent group of actors dedicated to exploring and performing Shakespeare, but this vision was realized slowly. Beauman traces the development of Flower's dream; not until 1919 did the Mermaid Theatre have a resident company, for example. This is an account not just of one company but also of a century of stage history. As Beauman writes, "All the major changes that have affected the macrocosm of British theatre over the past hundred years can be seen in microcosm in the development of Stratford and its companies."

Berry, Ralph, ed. *On Directing Shakespeare: Interviews with Contemporary Directors.* New York: Barnes & Noble Books, 1977.
Berry interviewed seven leading Shakespearean directors to understand their

approaches to the plays: Jonathan Miller, Konrad Swinarski, Trevor Nunn, Michael Kahn, Robin Phillips, Giorgio Strehler, and Peter Brook. These seven offer valuable insights into the staging and meaning of the plays. Swinarski, for example, explores the significance of the fifth act of *A Midsummer Night's Dream*; Nunn argues for a dictatorial Julius Caesar and a Brutus who is less than noble. An index by play allows the reader to compare responses to particular works.

Brown, John Russell. *Shakespeare's Plays in Performance.*London: Edward Arnold, 1966.
In the first section, Brown discusses the way actors should respond to the text. The second and third parts examine action and audience response. In the fourth section, Brown reviews various English productions of the 1960s. The work highlights the importance of regarding the plays as theater and offers much information about the history of Shakespearean staging. Illustrations of performances add to the book's value and interest. Provides an important reminder that the critic must be aware of the relationship between text and performance.

Bulman, J. C., and H. R. Coursen, eds. *Shakespeare on Television: An Anthology of Essays and Reviews.* Hanover, N.H.: University Press of New England, 1988.
The first section treats general subjects and examines the possibility of presenting Shakespeare on television. The second part looks at specific productions or groups of performances, and the third reprints a wide selection of reviews. Useful for bringing together so much material. Offers a wide range of responses to television's handling of Shakespeare.

Byrne, M. St. Clare. "Fifty Years of Shakespearean Production: 1898-1948." *Shakespeare Survey* 2 (1949):1-20.
Reviews productions, beginning with the lavish spectacles of Henry Irving and the historicism of F. R. Benson around 1900, through Herbert Beerbohm Tree and Harley Granville-Barker—with the latter's simplified sets and uncut texts—and ending with Shakespeare in modern dress and Tyrone Guthrie's interpretations. Includes some lovely illustrations. Byrne concludes that by the 1940s directors had at last concluded that Shakespeare "knew his business" and that a partnership between academic critics and the theater was possible.

David, Richard. *Shakespeare in the Theatre.* Cambridge, England: Cambridge University Press, 1978.
From 1949 to 1956, David provided the annual review of British productions of Shakespeare for *Shakespeare Survey*, and from 1971 to 1976, he reported on the productions of the Royal Shakespeare Company at Stratford-upon-Avon. The first four chapters examine demands of the theater, text, audience, and historical precedent. The next eight look at specific productions from the 1970s. A conclud-

ing chapter offers suggestions for the successful staging of Shakespeare. David allows for innovation and variation but warns against losing sight of the text and its meaning.

Davies, Anthony. *Filming Shakespeare's Plays: The Adaptations of Laurence Olivier, Orson Welles, Peter Brook, and Akira Kurosawa*. Cambridge, England: Cambridge University Press, 1988.
A study of eight Shakespearean films: Olivier's *Henry V, Hamlet,* and *Richard III*; Welles's *Macbeth, Othello,* and *Chimes at Midnight*; Brook's *King Lear*; and Kurosawa's *Throne of Blood*. While recognizing the difference between film and live theater or text, Davies notes that in these productions such distinctions are reconciled. Contains much on the cinematic qualities of the works discussed and includes a lengthy bibliography.

Dawson, Anthony. *Watching Shakespeare: A Playgoer's Guide*. New York: St. Martin's Press, 1988.
Discusses eighteen of Shakespeare's most popular plays by looking at the diverse ways they can be staged. For example, the forest outside Athens in *A Midsummer Night's Dream* can be decorative or threatening, the rude mechanicals presented with old gags (such as Thisbe's stabbing herself with Pyramus' scabbard; the joke goes back at least to 1607) or as absurd but dignified characters. By citing specific performances, Dawson allows the reader to understand something of Shakespeare's infinite variety. Also provides a brief chronicle of Shakespeare on stage.

Donaldson, Peter Samuel. *Shakespearean Films/Shakespearean Directors*. Boston: Unwin Hyman, 1990.
Each of the seven chapters discusses a particular production. Some, such as Laurence Olivier's *Henry V* and *Hamlet*, are well known; others, such as Jean-Luc Godard's *King Lear* may be less familiar. Even the familiar works are presented in new ways. Olivier's *Hamlet* is read in light not of the title character's Oedipal complex but the director's. Franco Zeffirelli's *Romeo and Juliet* emerges as "an antipatriarchal, homoerotic reading" of the work. The close study of the films provides many good observations. The accompanying illustrations are often too small or too dark.

Eckert, Charles W., ed. *Focus on Shakespearean Films*. Englewood Cliffs, N.J.: Prentice-Hall, 1972.
The first three essays discuss theoretical issues involved in the filming of Shakespeare. The rest of the book provides brief criticism of noted productions, such as the 1944 Laurence Olivier *Henry V* or Grigori Kozintsev's 1964 *Hamlet*. Presents the credits for each of the films and often includes more than one response. The book concludes with a filmography arranged alphabetically by play

title, as well as a short bibliography. Useful for those seeking contemporary responses to the movies, some of which have not worn well (such as Olivier's *Hamlet*).

Foulkes, Richard, ed. *Shakespeare and the Victorian Stage*. Cambridge, England: Cambridge University Press, 1986.
Begins with Foulkes's survey of Victorian attitudes towards and treatment of Shakespeare. The essays that follow explore diverse topics. Some examine a particular production, such as Charles Kean's *Richard II* or William Macready's *Cymbeline*. Others take a broader view and discuss such topics as Shakespeare on the continent, his reception in the English provinces, and costuming. Together the articles provide a picture of how Shakespeare fared during the latter part of the nineteenth century, as well as how his reputation reflected cultural biases of the period.

Jorgens, Jack J. *Shakespeare on Film*. Bloomington: Indiana University Press, 1977.
The first chapter looks at the problems involved in translating the plays to film. The rest of the book examines eighteen important examples, analyzing the work of such directors as Franco Zeffirelli, Peter Hall, Orson Welles, Roman Polanski, and Grigori Kozintsev. Though not a history of Shakespeare in the movies, the book is, as Andrew M. McLean writes in *Shakespeare Quarterly* 29 (1978):315, "well informed, authoritative, and readable."

Leiter, Samuel L., ed. *Shakespeare Around the Globe: A Guide to Notable Postwar Revivals*. New York: Greenwood Press, 1986.
Arranged alphabetically by play. Presents a compilation of about a hundred short essays by seventy scholars, critics, and artists writing about Shakespearean productions since World War II. In addition to the discussions of individual performances, the book offers a short introduction to each play, tracing production trends for the period covered. Focus is on English-language performances.

Manvell, Roger. *Shakespeare and the Film*. Rev. ed. San Diego: A. S. Barnes, 1979.
Treats the important sound movies, examining modifications necessary to translate a Shakespearean play to film. Originally published in 1971, which is the cutoff date for movies included. Individual chapters look at specific directors like Laurence Olivier or Orson Welles and at topics such as Russian movies, film versions of *Julius Caesar*, Italian treatments of Shakespeare, and the filming of stage productions. Altogether, the book covers twenty-five films.

Odell, George C. D. *Shakespeare from Betterton to Irving*. 2 vols. New York: Charles Scribner's Sons, 1920.
Looks at 250 years of Shakespearean performances, from 1660 to the beginning

of the twentieth century, stressing major productions. Studies the shifts in dramatic techniques and changes in the texts used. Each of the eight units discusses the theaters, the texts, staging, scenery, and costuming. In the Age of Thomas Betterton, Shakespeare's plays were freely adapted and lavishly staged. Odell observes that "authors and actors had the knife (or scissors) in the hand that poured out the libation, or offered the sacrifice. They kissed him ere they killed him." Even in the nineteenth century, actors and directors added, cut, and rearranged. Odell's comments on the Age of Henry Irving are especially informative because he wrote from observation. Odell praises Irving's work but finds Forbes Robertson the best Shakespearean actor of the day. Joseph Quincy Adams conceded that Odell may provide more detail than the general reader seeks and less erudition than the scholar might desire. Nevertheless, the study "presents a splendid spectacle of King Shakespeare reigning in crowned sovereignty over the English stage" (*Yale Review* 11 [1921]:646). Montrose J. Moses also praised Odell in his comments in *The Nation* (111 [1920]:660-664).

Rothwell, Kenneth S., and Annabelle Henkin Melzer. *Shakespeare on Screen: An International Filmography and Videography*. New York: Neal-Schuman, 1990. Describes more than 750 films and videos produced from 1899 to 1990. Includes adaptations such as *Kiss Me Kate*, ballets, and opera versions. Records country of origin, year of release, history and evaluation (with references to reviews), color, length, type of film, language, credits, distributor, availability, and price. A well indexed, valuable guide.

Salgado, Gamini. *Eyewitnesses to Shakespeare: Firsthand Accounts of Performances 1590-1890*. New York: Barnes & Noble Books, 1975. Part 1 presents "everything that can be reasonably called a record, a memory or even an allusion to a Shakespearean performance" to 1700. Included are such well-known items as Simon Forman's account of his three visits to the Globe and also more obscure references from the period. After 1700, the entries are more selective. All these references are available elsewhere—Salgado has uncovered no new material—but the compilation is handy and is enriched with apt illustrations. Arrangement by play makes the book easy to use.

Shattuck, Charles H. *Shakespeare on the American Stage*. 2 vols. Washington, D.C.: Folger Shakespeare Library, 1979-1987. Surveys performances of Shakespeare in the United States from the 1752 visit of Lewis Hallam's London Company until the end of World War I. Among Shattuck's observations is that Edwin Forrest in the early 1800s was the first important Shakespearean actor in the United States. Shattuck sees three phases in the growth of Shakespearean performance. The 1700s were dominated by English imports. In the early nineteenth century, realism became important, but by mid-century the genteel tradition had supplanted earlier modes. Both volumes are clearly written and well indexed; the second is sumptuously illustrated.

Speaight, Robert. *Shakespeare on the Stage: An Illustrated History of Shakespearean Performance*. Boston: Little, Brown, 1973.
A survey of Shakespearean performances from the Elizabethans to the Royal Shakespeare Company's production of Peter Brook's *A Midsummer Night's Dream*. Focus is on the United States, Canada, England, and Europe. Intended for the general reader rather than the scholar, the book condenses much information into short, well-illustrated chapters that are more descriptive than analytical. Speaight offers his own views as well. He maintains, for example, that Brook's *Titus Andronicus* is arguably the greatest modern Shakespearean production. Includes many fascinating anecdotes: Junius Brutus Booth would not eat ham before going on stage to play Shylock, for example.

Sprague, Arthur Colby. *Shakespeare and the Actors: The Stage Business in His Plays, 1660-1905*. Cambridge, Mass.: Harvard University Press, 1944.
Covers much the same territory as George C. D. Odell's *Shakespeare from Betterton to Irving* (1920) but is arranged by plays—comedies, histories, *Hamlet*, *Othello*, *Macbeth*, and other tragedies. Discusses the stage business that actors have introduced to interpret and enliven the productions. For example, Sprague notes that in his interview with Ophelia in Act III "Hamlet began to notice Polonius, or Polonius and the King only . . . in the eighteen-twenties." Draws on promptbooks, reviews, and other printed sources. Reflects the wide variation possible in interpreting character and shows how stage business affects audience understanding. A brief supplement appeared in 1954: *The Stage Business in Shakespeare's Plays: A Postscript* (London: Society for Theatre Research, 1954).

_____. *Shakespearean Players and Performances*. Cambridge, Mass.: Harvard University Press, 1953.
The ten chapters examine eight great actors from Thomas Betterton to Edwin Booth by focusing on a particular performance of each: Betterton as Hamlet on September 20, 1709; David Garrick as King Lear in 1776; and Edwin Booth's Iago in 1881. Explains what made each outstanding. Two chapters discuss William Poel's efforts to return to Elizabethan conventions, and the last chapter includes a personal glimpse at twentieth century productions.

Sprague, Arthur Colby, and J. C. Trewin. *Shakespeare's Plays Today: Some Customs and Conventions of the Stage*. Columbia: University of South Carolina Press, 1970.
Looks at stage business, cuts in the text, additions to the text, the manner of delivering lines, visual and sound effects, characterization, and stages and staging. Though informal rather than scholarly—the authors refer to the book as an "essay"—the information here reveals much about twentieth century productions, especially of *Hamlet*. Arthur Sprague objects to a fondness for luggage whenever characters leave or arrive: "To have Hamlet furnished with a trunk,

as he is about to leave for England, simply will not do—if only because a playgoer . . . begins wondering who packed it and what it contains." The book notes that Henry Irving added the appearance of Shylock before his house after Jessica elopes. The authors' concluding remarks have a timeless quality: "We are still in an age of experiment, when anything can happen. . . . It would be happier if directors refrained from discovering new significances that Shakspeare never dreamed about, struggling to make their productions unlike any other, and playing over and over the game of 'relevance to modern life' which can be both irrelevant and tedious."

Styan, J. L. *The Shakespeare Revolution: Criticism and Performance in the Twentieth Century*. Cambridge, England: Cambridge University Press, 1977.
Begins in the late Victorian period and charts shifts in presentation, with good discussion of the influence of critics on performance. For example, Styan argues that William Poel's production of the first quarto of *Hamlet* was stimulated in part by the availability of an inexpensive reprint. Harley Granville-Barker provided both fine productions and solid criticism. Notes the movement away from realism to nonillusory presentations and the recognition by critics that the production is crucial to understanding the text. Argues for integrating critic and actor to arrive at meaning.

Trewin, J. C. *Shakespeare on the English Stage*. London: Barrie & Rackliff, 1964.
Surveys twentieth century British productions, noting the wide variations, from elaborate to spare. Concludes that Theseus in *A Midsummer Night's Dream* is in some ways correct when he says of plays, "The best in this kind are but shadows; and the worst are no worse, if imagination amend them" (V). Appendices list all Shakespearean productions at the West End from 1900 to 1964, at the Old Vic from 1914 to 1964, and at Stratford from 1879 to 1964. Presents many photographs of productions and actors.

Wells, Stanley. *Royal Shakespeare: Four Major Productions at Stratford-upon-Avon*. Greenville, S.C.: Furman University, 1976.
The four lectures collected here treat Peter Hall's *Coriolanus* (1959) and *Hamlet* (1965), and John Barton's *Twelfth Night* (1969-1972) and *Richard II* (1973-1974). Wells was a student at the Shakespeare Institute when he saw *Coriolanus*, with Laurence Olivier in the title role and Dame Edith Evans as Volumnia. Wells remarked that after the performance he "walked the streets of Stratford for twenty minutes before feeling I wanted to talk to anyone. That, I think, is what Aristotle meant by catharsis." Hall's Hamlet suffers from the "disease of disillusionment" that breeds "an apathy of the will so deep that commitment to politics, to religion or to life is impossible." Wells finds this an incomplete view of the character. Wells praises Barton for fusing the serious and comic elements of *Twelfth Night*; Barton's *Richard II* delighted Wells less. Throughout, the book offers discussions

of acting and directing decisions that will assist anyone involved in a production, and the observations here will benefit all students of the plays.

_____, ed. *Shakespeare Survey: An Annual Survey of Shakespearean Study and Production.* Vol. 39. Cambridge, England: Cambridge University Press, 1987.
Each annual volume lists British productions, but this one devotes itself entirely to Shakespeare and the media. The opening essay, by Anthony Davies, offers a retrospective of twentieth century film, radio, and television productions. Other entries discusses specific productions such as Orson Welles's *Othello* (1957), various treatments of a particular play (such as E. Pearlman's "Macbeth on Film: Politics"), and problems ("Two Types of Television Shakespeare," by Neil Taylor). Though the treatment is selective, observations are informative and thought-provoking.

Willes, Susan. *The BBC Shakespeare Plays: Making the Television Canon.* Chapel Hill: University of North Carolina Press, 1991.
Between 1978 and 1985, the British Broadcasting System (BBC) filmed the thirty-seven canonical plays of Shakespeare. Willes discusses the producers, directors, technical elements of filming, and critical reception of the plays; she also includes many photographs. For three of the plays, Willes provides her production diaries. Contains much on the nature of televised Shakespeare. An important discussion of a series that will long be watched by students and the public.

Williams, Simon. *Shakespeare on the German Stage.* Vol. 1. Cambridge, England: Cambridge University Press, 1990.
An illustrated history of Shakespearean productions in Germany, from the first recorded performance by English actors at the court of the Elector of Saxony in the sixteenth century to the eve of World War I. Focuses on the period from 1750 to 1810, when Shakespeare profoundly influenced German literature and when discussions of Shakespeare's works engaged numerous German writers and directors. The appendix, which lists performances, shows a pronounced rise during this period, when many of the works were staged in Germany and Austria for the first time. Williams notes that even Max Reinhart's highly acclaimed cycle of ten Shakespearean plays, staged at the Deutsches Theater, Berlin, in 1913-1914, drew heavily on the romantic legacy. Among the insights here is that the Schlegel/Tieck translation made Shakespeare more accessible to Germans than to Anglophones, who still had to struggle with Elizabethan language. This translation remains popular on the stage as well as among readers.

GENERAL STUDIES

Sources

Bullough, Geoffrey, ed. *Narrative and Dramatic Sources of Shakespeare*. 8 vols. New York: Columbia University Press, 1957-1975.

Bullough has provided a generous selection of sources, analogies, and probable and possible sources; many of these, such as Thomas Lodge's *Rosalynde* (1590), the basis of *As You Like It*, are presented in full. As Bullough comments in the preface to his last volume, his aim is "not to discover new sources but to make those already known accessible to Shakespeare lovers." The introductory essays offer insightful discussions of Shakespeare's transformations of his sources, as well as cogent arguments for accepting or rejecting various works as influences on the plays. Frank Kermode called this set "the most useful adjunct to Shakespeare scholarship published since the war" (*Review of English Studies*, n.s. 11 [1960]: 233).

Dessen, Alan C. *Shakespeare and the Late Moral Plays*. Lincoln: University of Nebraska Press, 1986.

Between 1550 and the 1580's, morality plays were the most frequently produced form of drama. Dessen examines *Richard III, 1, 2 Henry IV*, and *All's Well That Ends Well* in relation to these popular plays. By looking at the tradition of the moral play, one can better understand Bertram's unrealistic conversion (*All's Well*), for example. The Vice figure of the moral plays is transformed in Richard III, Falstaff, and Parolles, and the Vice's initial dominance and final taming is repeated in these works.

Donaldson, E. Talbot. *The Swan at the Well: Shakespeare Reading Chaucer*. New Haven, Conn.: Yale University Press, 1985.

Examines the connections between *A Midsummer Night's Dream* and "The Knight's Tale," as well as three other of Chaucer's works; *The Two Noble Kinsmen* and "The Knight's Tale"; Shakespeare's and Chaucer's versions of the story of Troilus and Cressida; the influence of Chaucer's account of these lovers on *Romeo and Juliet*; and the relationship between the Wife of Bath and Falstaff. The connections go beyond plot and character to the nature of art and reality. Explores the same areas as Thompson's *Shakespeare's Chaucer* (q.v.) but from the perspective of a Chaucerian rather than a Shakespearean.

Gesner, Carol. *Shakespeare and the Greek Romance: A Study of Origins*. Lexington: University Press of Kentucky, 1970.

Gesner begins with an introduction to the Greek romance and then examines the way Giovanni Boccaccio, Miguel de Cervantes, and other Continental writers employed the genre from about 1300 to the mid-seventeenth century. The three concluding chapters trace Shakespeare's use of the form, particularly in the late plays, where he adapts them to create "a new version of reality." An appendix offers a bibliographic survey of a number of the romances, which went through many editions and translations that attest to their enduring popularity.

Hankins, John Erskine. *Shakespeare's Derived Imagery*. Lawrence: University of Kansas Press, 1953.
Looks at twenty Shakespearean metaphors, such as the ages of man or the unweeded garden, and suggests that *Zodiacus Vitae* by Marcellus Palingenius provided the source of all of these. The work was popular as a school text in Latin and was also available in English translation. Though Hankins makes a good case for his view, Palingenius' images were Elizabethan commonplaces; emblem books, observations, paintings, and sculpture all could have provided these metaphors. Hence, the book is less significant for locating a source than for pointing out and discussing the images themselves.

Hart, Alfred. *Shakespeare and the Homilies: And Other Pieces of Research into the Elizabethan Drama*. Melbourne, Australia: Melbourne University Press, 1934.
A collection of essays that examine a number of issues. The title refers to *Certain Sermons or Homilies* (1547), which maintains the divine right of kings and urges passive obedience on the part of subjects. Hart believes that Shakespeare's plays endorse this view and warn against rebellion. Other papers argue that a typical Elizabethan staged play contained 2,400 lines; Shakespeare wrote works that he knew would be cut in performance. Hart also looks at Shakespeare's vocabulary, which was richer than that of any of his contemporaries, and at censorship in *2 Henry IV*. *Modern Language Notes* (30 [1935]: 552) remarked that "altogether, there is much food for thought in these essays, and the evidence of a critical and well-informed mind at work in an original manner."

Hosley, Richard, ed. *Shakespeare's Holinshed: An Edition of Holinshed's Chronicles, 1587*. New York: G. P. Putnam's Sons, 1968.
A good source for students seeking the original stories that Shakespeare used for his histories, *King Lear*, *Macbeth*, and *Cymbeline*, all of which the playwright found in the second (1587) edition of Raphael Holinshed's *Chronicles*, which first appeared in 1577. Hosley gives the citations from Holinshed and their location in the plays. Appendices outline English history from 1154 to 1603, provide genealogies, and suggest sources for further study. By focusing on Holinshed's book as history rather than as a Shakespearean rough draft, Hosley allows the reader to see more clearly how Shakespeare altered his sources. For example, Hosley includes Holinshed's account of Cordelia's reign after the death of King Lear; even Geoffrey Bullough's extensive compilation omits this paragraph.

Jones, Emrys. *The Origins of Shakespeare*. Oxford, England: Clarendon Press, 1977.
At least since Ben Jonson's famous eulogy in the First Folio, Shakespeare has been regarded as largely unlearned, especially in the classics. Jones sets out to demolish this view, discussing in the first chapter the playwright's debt to classical sources—Seneca, Quintilian, and Horace, among others. Later, Jones adds Euripides to the list. Medieval mysteries and moralities (chapter 2) also influenced Shakespeare. The taunting of York in *3 Henry VI* suggests the suffering of Jesus as depicted in the New Testament and perhaps the Passion plays. Much of the book treats the history plays; among Jones's conclusions is that *Richard III* was an afterthought, not part of a tetralogy with the three *Henry VI* plays.

Martindale, Charles, and Michelle Martindale. *Shakespeare and the Uses of Antiquity: An Introductory Essay*. London: Routledge, 1990.
Begins with an examination of Shakespeare's learning: he could read Latin fairly well and would have encountered a number of classical texts at Stratford Grammar School. These he sometimes imitated or borrowed from (as in Prospero's "ye elves of hills," derived from Ovid's *Metamorphoses*—Ovid's poetry was his favorite). His ideas of Greek tragedy did not come from the originals but from Seneca. He probably drew on George Chapman for his knowledge of Troy, as Plutarch taught him about Rome. The last chapter argues that Shakespeare also drew on Stoicism, whatever his own views, in the plays. The authors wear their learning lightly and so provide an accessible, illuminating discussion.

Muir, Kenneth. *The Sources of Shakespeare's Plays*. New Haven, Conn.: Yale University Press, 1978.
Analyzes the way Shakespeare uses his sources, noting that he generally combined versions of a story. In *King Lear*, for example, he fuses an old play, at least one history, two poems, and a pastoral romance. Argues that, while Shakespeare looked at translations of classical works, he could also read Latin well enough to use the original. Muir refers to sources but does not include them. The book is therefore a companion to, but not a substitute for, Geoffrey Bullough's *Narrative and Dramatic Sources of Shakespeare* (1957-1975). The two also do not always agree on works that Shakespeare used. For example, Muir regards Thomas Mouffet's *Of Silkewormes, and Their Flies* (1599) as an influence on *A Midsummer Night's Dream*, but Bullough cautiously rejects this view.

Noble, Richmond. *Shakespeare's Biblical Knowledge and Use of the Book of Common Prayer, as Exemplified in the Plays of the First Folio*. New York: Macmillan, 1935.
After a brief survey of English Bibles and prayer books produced in the sixteenth century, Noble explores Shakespeare's biblical knowledge, which often goes

unnoticed when references are allusive rather than direct. Noble also seeks to identify the version of the Bible that Shakespeare used. Most of the book consists of excerpts from the plays that Noble links with the Bible and the Book of Common Prayer. An appendix lists the plays that draw from the various books of the Bible. Expands on Thomas Carter's important pioneering study *Shakespeare and Holy Scripture, with the Version He Used* (New York: E. P. Dutton, 1905), which maintained that the Geneva version was the source of biblical references in the works.

Potts, Abbie Findlay. *Shakespeare and "The Faerie Queene."* Ithaca, N.Y.: Cornell University Press, 1958.
The plays Shakespeare wrote between 1599 and 1604 show many similarities to Edmund Spenser's allegory. The legends of Friendship and Chastity, for example, appear in the relationship of Helena and Bertram (*All's Well That Ends Well*) and Isabella and Angelo (*Measure for Measure*). Cesaro in *Twelfth Night* resembles Spenser's Sir Calidore, Olivia can be seen as Briana, and her steward Malvolio takes at least part of his name and behavior from Briana's seneschal Maleffort. More significantly, Spenser prompted Shakespeare to add an ethical dimension to his works. The parallels are provocative if not totally convincing, and her discussion of Shakespeare's ethics and vision of dramatic form remains relevant whether or not Shakespeare studied Spenser as carefully as Potts.

Satin, Joseph. *Shakespeare and His Sources*. Boston: Houghton Mifflin, 1966.
Reprints a number of Shakespeare's sources in thirteen plays and lists additional works not anthologized here. Satin also discusses briefly the ways Shakespeare used his material. In some cases, he adhered fairly closely to one source (such as to Raphael Holinshed in *Richard III*). Sometimes he selected and compressed (*2 Henry IV* and *Antony and Cleopatra*), and sometimes he changed much (*Othello* and *King Lear*). Often he altered characters to suit dramatic needs. M. A. Shaber called this volume "a poor man's Bullough" (*Studies in English Literature* 7 [1967]: 362). A portable and affordable work for undergraduates.

Spencer, Terence J. B. *Shakespeare's Plutarch*. Harmondsworth, England: Penguin Books, 1964.
Includes Plutarch's accounts (in Thomas North's translation) of the lives of Julius Caesar, Brutus, Marc Antony, and Coriolanus. Shakespeare borrowed not only these stories but also Plutarch's emphasis on individual action. Spencer discusses Shakespeare's use of the histories and also his willingness to deviate from his sources for dramatic purposes (such as adding Virgilia and the young son in the scene of supplication outside Rome in *Coriolanus*).

Thompson, Ann. *Shakespeare's Chaucer: A Study in Literary Origins*. New York: Barnes & Noble Books, 1978.

Though most of the study focuses on Shakespeare's use of Geoffrey Chaucer's works in *Troilus and Cressida* and *The Two Noble Kinsmen*, the book first explores the use of Chaucer by other dramatists in the Elizabethan and Jacobean period. A second chapter then surveys Shakespeare's use of the poet in other plays. Thompson notes the various ways that Shakespeare used and adapted his predecessor. For example, Shakespeare's version of the Troilus story and *The Two Noble Kinsmen* are darker than Chaucer's.

Thomson, J. A. K. *Shakespeare and the Classics.* London: George Allen & Unwin, 1952.
Plutarch's *Lives* and Ovid's *Metamorphoses* are key sources for Shakespeare. Indeed, Plutarch provides Shakespeare his concept of tragedy because the historian had imbibed the views of Euripides, Aeschylus, and Sophocles. Discusses Shakespeare's education and notes classical influences throughout the works. *Macbeth*, for example, though dealing with British history and drawing heavily on Raphael Holinshed's chronicles, reflects the influences of Seneca and Plutarch. Needs an index.

Whitaker, Virgil. *Shakespeare's Use of Learning: An Inquiry into The Growth of His Mind and Art.* San Marino, Calif.: Huntington Library, 1953.
Shakespeare developed as a playwright as he learned more. His early plays follow their sources closely, but as the dramatist grew intellectually he reshaped old stories to highlight philosophical ideas. Especially important are Shakespeare's schooling, the homilies, chronicles, and Richard Hooker's *Ecclesiastical Polity*, which provided a vision of world order and "a theory of tragedy as a violation of the laws of nature through a failure of reason." Looks at the ways Shakespeare altered his sources and concludes from these changes the chief concerns of the playwright. *King John*, for example, differs from *The Troublesome Raigne of King John* (1591) by emphasizing character and themes (such as the divine right of kings) rather than history. According to Whitaker, *Troilus and Cressida* is "the keystone in the arch of Shakespeare's intellectual development," in which he works out the ideas that inform the greater plays to follow. *Julius Caesar* establishes the pattern of the other tragedies, the focus on a moral choice. Whitaker uses his discussion of the sources to provide an understanding of the plays.

The Text

Bartlett, Henrietta C., and Alfred W. Pollard. *A Census of Shakespeare's Plays in Quarto, 1594-1709.* Rev. and extended ed. New Haven, Conn.: Yale University Press, 1939.
Describes and locates more than twelve hundred quartos of eighty-five different

editions and issues of sixteen plays (excludes *Pericles* and *2, 3 Henry VI*) that appeared in quarto before 1623. The terminal date is 1709, when Nicholas Rowe's edition of the plays appeared. Arranged alphabetically, the work is easy to use and provides a treasure house of bibliographic information. Comparison with the earlier (1916) edition (which includes Pollard's valuable introduction omitted here) shows the growth of various collections, especially in the United States, and the dispersal of many private libraries.

Black, Matthew W., and Mathias A. Shaaber. *Shakespeare's Seventeenth-Century Editors, 1632-1685*. New York: Modern Language Association of America, 1937.
A study of the texts of the Second (1632), Third (1664), and Fourth (1685) Folios. While some differences between these and the First Folio resulted from typographical errors, many reveal editorial decisions that improve the text. Of 1,679 intentional changes made in the Second Folio, 623 have been adopted in later editions. The authors conclude that the editor of the Second Folio was a scholar and that those of the Third and Fourth Folios were competent proofreaders who also introduced some improvements even though their texts lack the authority of the First Folio. Black and Shaaber discuss those emendations that have been adopted by later editors, those that return to earlier readings, and those that have been rejected for a variety of reasons.

Burkhart, Robert E. *Shakespeare's Bad Quartos: Deliberate Abridgements Designed for Performance by a Reduced Cast*. The Hague: Mouton, 1975.
As the subtitle indicates, Burkhart dissents from the widely held view that the "bad quartos" of *2, 3 Henry VI, Romeo and Juliet, Henry V, The Merry Wives of Windsor*, and *Hamlet* are defective, pirated versions of the plays. Rather, he regards them as intentionally and carefully shortened editions designed to be performed for provincial audiences by touring companies that had smaller casts. Tables indicate the number of actors needed for each scene in the "good" and "bad" versions; none of the latter requires more than thirteen actors, whereas the former can demand as many as twenty-two. The one exception is *The First Part of the Contention* (the quarto for *2 Henry VI*), performed initially in the provinces when plague closed the theaters, so more London actors would have been touring.

Feuillerat, Albert. *The Composition of Shakespeare's Plays: Authorship, Chronology*. New Haven, Conn.: Yale University Press, 1953.
Looks at the quarto versions of *2, 3 Henry VI, Titus Andronicus, Richard III, Richard II*, and *Romeo and Juliet* to determine Shakespeare's compositional method. Shakespeare revised older plays owned by his company, and the quarto versions demonstrate the way his new material was joined to the old. Feuillerat believes that *The First Part of the Contention* and *The True Tragedie of Richard*

Duke of York are not corrupt versions of Shakespeare's *2, 3 Henry VI*—the conventional view—but rather are plays by others and adapted by Shakespeare. Similarly, he sees the quarto *Titus Andronicus* as a source of Shakespeare's play, not a pirated printing of it, and he regards the quartos of *Richard II* and *Romeo and Juliet* in the same light. Feuillerat's theory that anonymous authors wrote these pieces and that Shakespeare then revised them seriously weakens an argument that otherwise might shed light on Shakespeare's writing methods. Viewed not as separate plays but as early versions that later were revised for the folio, these quartos might yield the kind of information that Feuillerat sought.

Greg, Walter W. *The Editorial Problem in Shakespeare: A Survey of the Foundations of the Text*. 3d ed. Oxford, England: Clarendon Press, 1954.
Begins with a general treatment of the concerns of a Shakespearean editor. Greg presents rules that should guide the editor in preparing a text as similar as possible to the author's intended version. Greg next discusses the folios and quartos generally and then examines the various forms in which the plays appeared: plots (outline) foul papers (author's rough draft), fair copy (the transcribed version of the foul papers), promptbook, actors' parts, the bad quartos, two doubtful quartos (*Richard II* and *King Lear*), good quartos, and the First Folio.

_____. *The Shakespeare First Folio: Its Bibliographical and Textual History*. Oxford, England: Clarendon Press, 1955.
The First Folio is the basis for the Shakespeare canon. Greg discusses its evolution and the editorial problems that John Heminge and Henry Condell faced in preparing the text. Much of the book examines the printing history of each play and the sources used to prepare the folio copy. Draws on great knowledge of sixteenth and seventeenth theater and printing practices. Though some of Greg's ideas have been refined, his book has not been superseded.

Hart, Alfred. *Stolne and Surreptitious Copies: A Comparative Study of Shakespeare's Bad Quartos*. Melbourne, Australia: Melbourne University Press, 1942.
Concludes that the six bad quartos—*The First Part of the Contention, The True Tragedie of Richard Duke of York, Romeo and Juliet* (1597), *Henry V* (1600), *The Merry Wives of Windsor* (1602), and *Hamlet* (1603)—are in fact pirated versions of the plays based on actor reconstructions of abridged versions. Each of the texts reveals "garbling, petty larceny, solecisms, anacolowthia (lack of proper grammatical references), . . . irrelevance, vulgarity, fustian, and nonsense." This view has become the orthodox position, but Hart rejects the possibility that at least some differences between the bad quartos and the good (or folio) resulted from revisions.

Hinman, Charlton. *The Printing and Proof-Reading of the First Folio of Shake-speare*. 2 vols. Oxford, England: Clarendon Press, 1963.
A study of the publication of the First Folio based on a comparison of more than fifty of the eighty first folios at the Folger Library. Hinman believes that about half the plays printed there derive from manuscripts, though not necessarily Shakespeare's. Others were based on quartos or a combination of manuscript and printed versions. Hinman observes that the proofreading was sketchy and care-less, more concerned with appearance than sense. Argues for five typesetters (compositors) and identifies the work of each; "E" was the least careful. Hinman also believes that production lasted two years rather than the three previously accepted. John Shroeder observed in his review that this study would "eventually prove to be one of the most important Shakespearean contributions to appear in our century" (*Shakespeare Quarterly* 15 [1964]: 104). In the area of textual studies, this statement has proved justified.

Pollard, Alfred W. *Shakespeare's Fight with the Pirates and the Problems of the Transmission of His Text*. London: A. Moring, 1917.
A series of four lectures delivered in 1915. The first discusses the sixteenth century book trade; the second the relationship among authors, actors, and pirates in Shakespeare's time; the third lecture addresses the question of Shakespeare's manuscripts; and the fourth discusses problems facing editors of Shakespeare's texts. Among his conclusions are that actors hired by the company to fill minor parts would collude with shady printers to produce printed versions of the plays. To forestall printing, Shakespeare's company would enter the titles in the Statio-ners' Register so that pirating printers could not secure copyright. The company sometimes responded to a corrupt version by providing a better text, and occa-sionally the plays would be sold to a printer. This copy might well be in the playwright's handwriting. Pollard argues that the First Folio is an edited text lacking the authority of the good quartos.

_____. *Shakespeare's Folios and Quartos: A Study in the Bibliography of Shakespeare's Plays, 1594-1685*. London: Methuen, 1909.
Sidney Lee argued that all the early Shakespeare quartos were pirated and corrupt. Pollard disagreed: the bad quartos were stolen and their texts are unreliable, but the good quartos were entered properly in the Stationers' Register and their texts agree closely with the First Folio, which he defends against Lee's aspersions. Pollard also discusses the attempted quarto edition of 1619 and the four seventeenth century folios. Published to accompany Methuen's facsimiles of the folios, Pollard's work includes reproductions of the title pages of twenty-nine early quartos, together with full bibliographic information.

Prosser, Eleanor. *Shakespeare's Anonymous Editor: Scribe and Composition in the Folio Text of "2 Henry IV."* Stanford, Calif.: Stanford University Press, 1981.

Although her study focuses on one play, it has implications for all the texts in the First Folio that derive from good quartos. She rejects eighty-six readings in the folio version of the play, claiming that changes from the quartos do not reflect legitimate emendations but rather are the consequence of the typesetter's efforts to create a neater page and the scribe's willful alterations.

Walker, Alice. *Textual Problems and the First Folio: "Richard III," "King Lear," "Troilus and Cressida," "2 Henry IV," "Hamlet," "Othello."* Cambridge, England: Cambridge University Press, 1953.
The folio texts of the plays in the title were based on corrected quartos. Argues for the primacy of the quarto rather than the folio version because in the latter the collator or copier intervenes between author and reader. Walker also maintains that even when quarto and folio readings agree they may be erroneous; she therefore says that "to emend only what must unavoidably be emended is not enough." In her edition of *Othello* (Cambridge, England, 1957) she adopted fourteen readings from the quarto rather than the folio.

Walton, James Kirkwood. *The Quarto Copy for the First Folio of Shakespeare.* Dublin, Ireland: Dublin University Press, 1971.
Part 1 surveys Shakespearean textual criticism to the twentieth century. Part 2 discusses the eleven plays in the folio that were printed from quartos and tries to decide which quartos were used. Part 3 seeks to determine whether quartos or manuscripts were the bases for the folio copies of other plays. Maintains that, although good quartos existed for *2 Henry IV*, *Hamlet*, and *Othello*, the folio text goes back to a manuscript. Part 4 summarizes and analyzes the findings and concludes that the collators working on the First Folio were not always careful with their text.

Wells, Stanley, and Gary Taylor, with John Jowett and William Montgomery. *William Shakespeare: A Textual Companion.* Oxford, England: Clarendon Press, 1987.
Prepared in conjunction with the *Complete Oxford Shakespeare* (1986). The general introduction discusses the issues involved in editing the work; among other matters treated is the supposed progress of a play from plot (outline) to promptbook (acting version). Other sections treat canon and chronology, the text used for the Oxford edition, the typesetter for each page of the First Folio (a matter of dispute), and editorial procedures. This introductory section concludes with a bibliography. The main section notes alternate readings to those chosen by the editors and explains their choices, sometimes in witty ways. For example, in V, iii, 7 of *The Two Gentlemen of Verona* the Oxford text has changed the folio "Moyses" to "Moses" and has noted that Clifford Leech, in his 1969 Arden edition, retained the original form because "there seems no need to modernize it here." The editors of this book add that "there seems even less need to retain

it in a modern-spelling edition." Although the textual notes are restricted to the 1986 *Complete Oxford Shakespeare*, the introductory material is valuable.

Willoughby, Edwin Elliot. *The Printing of the First Folio*. Oxford, England: Oxford University Press, 1932.
Seeks to answer such questions as how much the First Folio cost, how many copies were printed, how long the printing took, how it was printed, and how it was proofread. Willoughby believes that two or three typesetters were involved and that (except for about 125 pages) one press was used, which produced six sheets a week. Looks at spelling to determine which typesetter was involved in which pages. Concludes that the typesetters and proofreaders did not corrupt the text to any significant degree. More recent scholarship maintains that perhaps as many as eight typesetters were involved—Charlton Hinman thought five.

Language

Baxter, John. *Shakespeare's Poetic Style: Verse into Drama*. London: Routledge & Kegan Paul, 1980.
Shakespeare's plays derive their power from the fusion of form and language. Baxter focuses on *Richard II*, in which he sees four styles at work: golden (Petrarchan), plain, metaphysical, and Shakespearean. The characters use different styles to reveal their natures. Richard and Bolingbroke appear flawed because their language is elaborate, golden. Only John of Gaunt's speeches indicate morality. Baxter's stylistic scheme may be overly elaborate, but he makes good points about different characters' use of language.

Bevington, David. *Action Is Eloquence: Shakespeare's Language of Gesture*. Chicago: University of Chicago Press, 1984.
Argues that gesture, too, is a language. When Coriolanus turns his back on Rome or Macbeth starts at MacDuff's knocking at the gate, audiences receive a powerful message. In addition to gesture, Bevington discusses costumes, props, the use of space on stage, and "The Language of Ceremony." Sometimes the nonverbal message reenforces the language, but often they contradict each other. Jean E. Howard remarked that "*Action Is Eloquence* contributes to our collective understanding of how the visual dimension of Shakespeare's plays function. . . . Bevington shows how Shakespeare modifies visual traditions to make costume changes, gestures, ritual and the staged facade itself newly meaningful" (*Renaissance Quarterly* 38 [1985]: 579).

Burckhardt, Sigurd. *Shakespearean Meanings*. Princeton, N.J.: Princeton University Press, 1968.
Examines sounds, words, phrases, or structure that illuminates the plays—the

word "nothing" in *King Lear*, for example. Similarly, Burckhardt claims that the striking clock in *Julius Caesar*, a famous anachronism, reflects the outdated attitude of Brutus in seeking to restore the Republic by killing Caesar. *King John* lacks form because history itself is chaotic. Characters' attitudes towards language also help clarify issues in the plays. Lear believes that words convey reality; Gloucester distrusts language and believes in things.

Clemen, Wolfgang H. *The Development of Shakespeare's Imagery*. Cambridge, Mass.: Harvard University Press, 1951.
A study of the ways imagery affects plot, character, and speech. Sees the early plays as using imagery decoratively, unrelated to other elements of the work. *Richard II* is the watershed; imagery here reveals character, and by 1600, Shakespeare had learned to use imagery to illuminate themes and character and to create moods.

_____. *Shakespeare's Soliloquies*. Translated by Charity Scott Stokes. London: Methuen, 1987.
Examines some two dozen passages "to convey an idea of Shakespeare's stage-craft, his exceptional theatrical judgement, and his evocative use of poetic language." Though the soliloquy predates Shakespeare, usually it served only to provide exposition and was addressed to the audience. Shakespeare enriched the possibilities of the form, which he recognized as early as *Richard III*; the opening lines of this play are the first ones Clemen discusses. He observes the repetition of "I" in this speech, revealing Richard's delight in self-observation. Only in the final soliloquy of the play, though, does he examine his thoughts. The speech suggests Macbeth's contemplating the murder of Duncan. This brief study is useful not only for what it says about the soliloquies it discusses but also for its ability to guide the reader/listener in studying other examples.

Colman, E. A. M. *The Dramatic Use of Bawdy in Shakespeare*. London: Longman, 1974.
The book opens with an essay on "What Is Indecency?" that defines bawdy as both comic and sensual, intending not only to shock but also to distance the audience. Colman then looks at Shakespeare's use of bawdry. In the early comedies, bawdry usually serves to enhance humor, though Katherine's (*The Taming of the Shrew*) decreasing use of bawdy language reflects her taming and so reveals character. In *Titus Andronicus* and the first Henriad, language mirrors characters' mental status. Hamlet's bawdry comes from within; Othello's is "caught, like jealousy itself, . . . from Iago." The brevity of the book does not allow full examination, but Colman indicates the wide variety of ways in which the bawdy can function: to parody (*Merchant of Venice*), to introduce a sense of realism (as in *King John*), to reveal character, or to define the world of the play (*King Lear*). Bawdry thus becomes another dramatic tool for the playwright, not

merely entertainment for the groundlings. Includes a forty-three-page glossary, mostly of indecent words though also including such entries as "bed" and "big" (that is, pregnant).

Crane, Milton. *Shakespeare's Prose*. Chicago: University of Chicago Press, 1951.
Crane claims that Shakespeare's prose is simple and natural but subtle, capturing the flavor of speech but effectively portraying various characters. Examines why Shakespeare and other playwrights of the English Renaissance use prose for certain characters, situations, or moods. The focus is on plays that combine prose and verse. Crane finds that writers observe the principle of decorum, giving prose—the lower form—to characters of lower social status, mad characters, comic subplots, scenes of low life, and often using it for satire. Crane praises Shakespeare's prose for its ability to mirror real speech yet embrace subtleties.

Donawerth, Jane. *Shakespeare and the Sixteenth Century Study of Language*. Urbana: University of Illinois Press, 1984.
Begins with a study of Elizabethan attitudes towards language and Shakespeare's views, which drew from various theories. Donawerth finds increasing sophistication in Shakespeare's handling of language. She then looks closely at five plays. In *Love's Labor's Lost*, language is not a theme but a means of education. In *King John*, characters use language to conceal truth. For the first time, in *The Merchant of Venice*, different characters use different verse forms, and Shakespeare shows that the lovers rather than the merchants truly understand language. In *All's Well that Ends Well*, Bertram must learn the difference between language and action, but eloquence, keeping one's word, and restraint in speech are shown as virtues. *Hamlet* treats language in complex ways; in Elsinore, communication repeatedly fails. Throughout, Donawerth resists the argument that the plays are self-reflexive studies of language; they use language to depict "human characters and the stories of the faults and triumphs of human judgement and passion." Charles R. Forker writes that "the book . . . makes a significant contribution to the study of . . . the impingement of Renaissance language theory upon the action, characterization, and thematic structure of Tudor and Stuart plays as a body. . . . Anyone who cares to know how Elizabethan playwrights understood the functions of language and made drama out of that understanding will find this book uncommonly rewarding" (*JEGP* 86 [1987]: 100-103).

Evans, Benjamin Ifor. *The Language of Shakespeare's Plays*. London: Methuen, 1952.
Tracing Shakespeare's use of imagery, his vocabulary, and poetry through the plays, Evans finds progress from ornate to a plain but powerfully compressed style that makes the familiar new. Shakespeare is a poet who restrains his love of embellishment to become more effective as a playwright, and in his maturity his imagination finds its proper idiom.

Halliday, Frank Ernest. *The Poetry of Shakespeare's Plays*. London: Gerald Duckworth, 1954.

Shakespeare was a poet before he was a playwright, and his style matures from being ornamental and diffuse to becoming subordinate to action. Halliday sees five stages in the development of Shakespeare's language: 1590 to 1594, the period of the early histories and comedies; 1594 to 1597, the time of the sonnets and lyrical plays; 1597 to 1601, when Shakespeare wrote the historical and romantic comedies; 1601 to 1608, the years of the great tragedies; and 1608 to 1613, the period of the romances. Looks at three elements in the poetry: vocabulary, rhythmical relationships, and imagery. Aimed at the general reader despite its seemingly technical subject and approach.

Hibbard, G. R. *The Making of Shakespeare's Dramatic Poetry*. Toronto: University of Toronto Press, 1981.

Looks at the early plays and argues that Shakespeare created a new kind of language for the stage. *Titus Andronicus* owes much to Christopher Marlowe and Thomas Kyd, but even by the time he was writing *Richard III* Shakespeare had learned to individualize and enliven characters through language. By *Henry IV*, Shakespeare had mastered this ability. As he discusses Shakespeare's poetic development, Hibbard provides intelligent commentary on the works he examines. Well written and well argued.

Hulme, Hilda M. *Explorations in Shakespeare's Language: Some Problems of Lexical Meaning in the Dramatic Text*. London: Longmans, Green, 1962.

Looks at Elizabethan speech to understand some two hundred obscure words and phrases in Shakespeare's plays. Focuses on proverbs and idioms, bawdry, Latinate meanings, orthography, pronunciation, and provincialisms (Shakespeare was, after all, a Warwicksire native). Among Hulme's observations is that, when Othello laments the loss of his occupation, the word has a sexual as well as military implication. She also notes that in *1 Henry IV* Hotspur rewords the standard proverb "we will not lose a Scot" when he says that the king "shall or smalls not have a Scot of them" (the prisoners). By rejecting the conventional proverb, Hotspur shows his contempt for royal as well as linguistic authority. Though some of the connections between proverbs or bawdry and the language of the plays are far-fetched, the book often enlightens and almost always entertains.

Hussey, S. S. *The Literary Language of Shakespeare*. London: Longman Group, 1982.

Begins with a discussion of the English that Shakespeare inherited, a language enriched with foreign imports, new constructions, and revived archaisms. Syntax was growing less rhetorical and freer. Hussey then devotes chapter 5 to Shakespeare's grammar before the study traces what Hussey sees as the evolution in

Shakespeare's handling of language. For example, the early plays too often lack real exchanges; characters talk but do not respond to each other's speeches. Images in these plays lack vigor, and language is embellished for its own sake. As the playwright matures, these faults fade. A similar development characterizes the soliloquy. Although the earliest plays contain them, only in *Julius Caesar* did the playwright begin to exploit the device to explore the inner workings of characters' minds. In the late romances, soliloquy again serves only to inform audiences about events. A good introduction to a complex subject.

Kennedy, Milton Boone. *The Oration in Shakespeare*. Chapel Hill: University of North Carolina Press, 1942.
Sees Shakespeare as an Aristotelian in his use of oration. Kennedy surveys the relationship between persuasion and poetics from Aristotle to Shakespeare and finds that over the centuries distinctions grew confused. Yet Shakespeare, perhaps intuitively, recognized the difference. This study notes that in the course of his career Shakespeare used progressively fewer orations but used them more effectively as "a point of focusing in the progress of dramatic action." Contains a good survey of rhetorical theory and the role of rhetoric in Elizabethan schools and literary criticism.

Mahood, M. M. *Shakespeare's Wordplay*. London: Methuen, 1957.
Examines levels of word use in the sonnets and in *Romeo and Juliet, Richard II, Hamlet, Macbeth*, and *The Winter's Tale*. The author may at times be over-clever at finding multiple meanings: when Friar Lawrence says that Juliet's foot is so light it "will ne'er wear out the everlasting flint," Mahood suggests that the similarity of "ne'er" and "near" allows for contradictory meanings to coexist. Though such a reading of this speech is unconvincing, it makes excellent sense for sonnet 87, where anger coexists with self-effacement. The book also discusses larger issues that illuminate the plays: the various meanings of time in *Macbeth*, Richard II and Bolingbroke's differing attitudes towards language, and the distinction in punning between the two parts of *Henry IV*. Mahood maintains that in the great tragedies "the discovery that words are arbitrary signs and not right names is made by the heroes and the knowledge that the life of words is in their connotations is put to use by the villains." In the late comedies, words recover their value. As Edward Hubler comments, "There is a great deal to be learned from this book that cannot be found elsewhere" (*Shakespeare Quarterly* 9 [1958]: 192).

Mariam, Joseph. *Shakespeare's Use of the Arts of Language*. New York: Columbia University Press, 1947.
At Stratford Grammar School, Shakespeare would have studied grammar, rhetoric, and logic. He later used the devices he had learned. Thus, grammarians warned against the irrelevant answer, and when Juliet asks whether to marry or

not, the nurse complains of a headache. Yet one wonders whether Shakespeare needed Aristotle or Quintilian to create this situation; would life not have sufficed? As a guide to Elizabethan rhetorical theory, though, Sister Joseph's work is valuable, and many of the connections with the plays are suggestive if not definitive. Includes a guide to Renaissance theory of composition and reading.

Shirley, Frances A. *Swearing and Perjury in Shakespeare's Plays*. London: George Allen & Unwin, 1979.
Shakespeare uses oaths to structure a play, to heighten tension, to shock, to attack, and to delineate character. Vows kept or broken determine the action in a number of plays, including the second Henriad, *Hamlet*, and *Othello*. In *Othello*, Iago's effect on characters is apparent in their use of increasingly stronger oaths. Oaths may also have no effect; *A Midsummer Night's Dream* satirizes lovers' vows, and Falstaff swears merely from habit. The 1606 antiblasphemy statute forced Shakespeare to find alternate means to create these effects. Hans-Jürgen Weckermann observed that Shirley "adds an interesting new facet to the study of Shakespeare" (*Shakespeare Quarterly* 34 [1983]: 512).

Sipe, Dorothy L. *Shakespeare's Metrics*. New Haven, Conn.: Yale University Press, 1968.
Shakespeare used iambic pentameter almost exclusively in his poetry, and he used meter effectively to convey meaning. Choice of variants such as "bide/abide" was determined solely by meter. Sipe is responding to critics who maintain that Shakespeare's line is based not on the number of syllables but rather on the number of accents, so that a line with five accents might contain as many as fifteen syllables. She notes that poetic theory favored syllable rather than accentual lines, and while occasional variation was permissible, iambic pentameter was the preferred form. The work is a useful reminder of how one should read Shakespeare's poetry.

Spurgeon, Caroline F. E. *Shakespeare's Imagery and What It Tells Us*. Cambridge, England: Cambridge University Press, 1935.
A landmark study more valuable for its cataloging of Shakespeare's images than for the conclusions it draws about the author. While one may quarrel with her analysis of Shakespeare the man, Spurgeon provided an important service in examining the leading images in the plays. A particularly fascinating feature of the book is a colored chart comparing the imagery of Shakespeare and Christopher Marlowe. The latter drew most heavily from learning, Shakespeare from nature and daily life. The appearance of mathematical accuracy is deceptive, but that fact does not diminish the book's value. This work opened up a new approach to the study of Shakespeare's work through the study of imagery.

Vickers, Brian. *The Artistry of Shakespeare's Prose*. London: Methuen, 1968.

K. M. Lea (in *Review of English Studies*, n.s. 20 [1969]: 216) comments on the study: "It is a full, spirited, and judicious book and . . .'ought to be required reading.' " Kenneth Muir called it "easily the best book on the subject" (*Modern Language Quarterly* 29 [1968]: 471). Vickers looks at images, linguistic structure, and rhetorical devices that Shakespeare uses in the plays, and he finds increasing sophistication in the handling of the prose. Even in *Love's Labour's Lost*, characters are distinguished by their language, but the result "is never harmonious." By 1600 the range of prose had grown considerably, though poetry remained the higher form. Shifts in tone and from verse to prose reflect characters' changes in mood.

Willcock, Gladys D. *Shakespeare as a Critic of Language*. Oxford, England: Oxford University Press, 1934.

Traces the progress of Shakespeare's verbal skills. In the early plays, language often is merely ornamental, but by the end of the 1590s it has become a tool of the characters. Thus, Benedict and Beatrice in *Much Ado About Nothing* use words to learn about each other. Willcock demonstrates that Shakespeare knew Renaissance theories of rhetoric and employed them with increasing mastery.

Wright, George T. *Shakespeare's Metrical Art*. Berkeley: University of California Press, 1988.

While Shakespeare used iambic pentameter as his verse form, he made it flexible, forceful, and natural. The first chapter defines iambic pentameter. Wright then surveys the form from Chaucer to the Renaissance before he turns to a study of Shakespeare's versification in the sonnets and plays. Wright notes ambiguities in the lines, variations that effectively add or delete syllables, and the abandoning of end-stopped lines to allow sense rather than form to control the poetry.

Yoder, Audrey. *Animal Analogy in Shakespeare's Character Portrayal*. New York: King's Crown Press, 1947.

Shakespeare uses more than four thousand comparisons between animals and characters. These analogies illuminate the figures they describe: Richard III is as a "gilded serpent" and Macduff's children are chickens. Shakespeare often draws on Aesop. For the Greek fabulist, the wolf represents greed, and that is the association Shakespeare primarily employs. The ass is patient and stupid, and Yoder shows how Iago and Antony draw on this understanding. Animal imagery delineates villains, satirizes characters, renders figures sympathetic, sets up contrasts (Henry VI as a lamb surrounded by Yorkist wolves), comments on the nature of humanity, and vivifies abstractions. An appendix notes the number of animal analogies for characters in each play.

Thematic and Topical Approaches

Alexander, Peter. *Alexander's Introductions to Shakespeare*. London: Collins, 1964.
Alexander edited Shakespeare's works for the Collins Classics series, providing
an introduction to each play and to the poems. This volume brings together all
these pieces, adding an essay by E. A. J. Honigmann on Shakespeare's theater.
Also provides a biographical sketch of the playwright and short discussions of
the First and Second Folios. The pieces on the plays are brief but survey the
composition, sources, and central concerns. Good for what they are—prefaces
to orient a novice.

Allman, Eileen Jorge. *Player-King and Adversary: Two Faces of Play in Shakespeare*. Baton Rouge: Louisiana State University Press, 1980.
The Player-King seeks to effect social harmony through play, while the Adversary uses play to gain power for himself. The Player-King's vision is inclusive,
the Adversary's exclusive. In the ten plays, Allman analyzes how the Player-King
suffers a psychic shock. Then a mystic vision causes him to see himself "as
potentially everyone and no one." In the end, he usually regains psychic health
and achieves greater understanding of human nature. The pattern is not consistent, though; Richard II suffers the shock and achieves the vision, but he does
not return to his formal role as educator through play. Hamlet and Coriolanus
also fail in their own ways. Falstaff is an Adversary because his playing "is not
a medium for psychic or spiritual growth, but rather one more manifestation of
his self-aggrandizing search for affirmation."

Armstrong, Edward A. *Shakespeare's Imagination: A Study of the Psychology of
Association and Inspiration*. London: Lindsay Drummond, 1946.
Looks at patterns of imagery to determine Shakespeare's compositional methods.
Concentrates on imagery of kites and coverlets, birds and insects, eagle and
weasel, goose, jay, fish, and fowl. Armstrong argues that Shakespeare juxtaposed
disparate images in the manner of metaphysical poets. The study clarifies certain
passages in the plays but, more important, indicates the combining power of
Shakespeare's imagery and thought.

Arthos, John. *The Art of Shakespeare*. London: Bowes & Bowes, 1964.
A study of eight plays—three tragedies (*Othello*, *Macbeth*, and *Antony and
Cleopatra*), three comedies (*Merchant of Venice*, *All's Well That Ends Well*, and
Troilus and Cressida), and two romances (*Pericles* and *The Winter's Tale*). The
general focus of the book is the unity of Shakespeare's works, but Arthos also
discusses Shakespeare's ability in the tragedies to give his characters an inner
life. Indeed, the inability of characters to balance that life with external reality
becomes the tragedy in *Othello*, *Macbeth*, and *Hamlet*. The comedies affirm a

belief in the happy ending despite corruption and confusion. The romances keep audiences at a distance, as do the comedies, but they raise personal and philosophical questions that the comedies do not. The divided plots of *Pericles* and *The Winter's Tale* come together at the end to represent the resolution and renewal of life.

_____. *Shakespeare: The Early Writings*. Totowa, N.J.: Rowman & Littlefield, 1972.
A study of *Venus and Adonis*, *The Rape of Lucrece*, and the first eight plays. Arthos believes that Shakespeare balances religious, humanistic, and native traditions. For example, the early plays introduce Petrarchan ideals, but they are limited by the realistic attitudes of the clowns. The writing always demonstrates a belief in the sanctity of life, but Shakespeare develops as an author as he moves from work to work.

Bamber, Linda. *Comic Women, Tragic Men: A Study of Gender and Genre in Shakespeare*. Stanford, Calif.: Stanford University Press, 1982.
Distinguishes between the Self (masculine) and Other (feminine). The former is self-conscious, shapes its identity, and can change. The Other belongs to the unchanging outside world. Shakespeare writes from the perspective of the Self; Bamber thus denies that the plays portray men and women with equal sympathy, though she does not condemn Shakespeare for his slanted perspective. Tragedy focuses on the Self; the Other appears to be evil (*Othello*) or actually is (*Macbeth*). Even in *Antony and Cleopatra*, the masculine hero possesses an interior life that his female counterpart lacks; Cleopatra never changes. In the comedies, the Other is subversive but dominant; the female characters move from being shrews in the earlier works to true comic heroines. The history plays deemphasize the feminine. Bamber sees *The Tempest* as unique in its transcendence of the masculine-feminine dichotomy. Mary Beth Rose called the book "compelling, thought-provoking, and bold" (*Shakespeare Quarterly* 35 [1984]: 126).

Berger, Harry, Jr. *Imaginary Audition: Shakespeare on Stage and Page*. Berkeley: University of California Press, 1989.
In the first part of this book, Berger attacks stage-centered critics such as Richard Levin and Gary Taylor. The second and longer section illustrates the method of interpretation that constitutes the book's title. This approach, while recognizing the need to imagine a production, is based on reading. It asks for a double audition—listening to a speech not only as it affects its audience but also as it influences the speaker. Berger illustrates his theory by examining passages from *Richard II*. Rather esoteric for undergraduates; graduate students versed in the theory of speech acts will find it accessible.

Bevington, David, and Jay L. Halio, eds. *Shakespeare: Pattern of Excelling Nature.*
Newark: University of Delaware Press, 1978.
A selection of essays from the 1976 World Shakespeare Conference. The pieces
cover a broad range of topics and approaches. Alistair Cooke's "Shakespeare in
America" offers a polished survey of the playwright's reception. The talk in this
chapter is full of fascinating anecdotes: in the West, Macbeth regularly dispatched
Duncan with a six-shooter, and Erma Abbot played Juliet on a trapeze. Janet
Adelman offers a psychological reading of *Coriolanus.* Three papers discuss
staging the plays, and John Dixon Hunt discusses allusions to paintings. The
volume concludes with summaries of various seminars held at the conference.
Though the essays are not of uniform quality, the book suggests the diverse
approaches to Shakespeare and offers both delight and instruction.

Billington, Sandra. *Mock Kings in Medieval Society and Renaissance Drama.*
Oxford, England: Clarendon Press, 1991.
In the first part of this study, Billington looks at mock kings, those who jestingly
(in festive celebrations) or seriously (in rebellion) assumed the royal title. The
second and longer portion of this study looks at Elizabethan and Jacobean drama
that employs the motif of the mock king. In Shakespeare's first tetralogy, one
mock king succeeds another. Even in the second, where misrule is overcome,
Henry V's title is questionable. *Troilus and Cressida, King Lear,* and *Antony and
Cleopatra* draw on the medieval tradition of mock kingship and the disorder
associated with a false ruler. Billington suggests that *Troilus and Cressida* served
as a Twelfth Night entertainment, the disorder of the play creating a desire for
order in the audience. Two-part plays like *Henry IV* and *Tamburlaine* draw on
the tradition of the rise and fall of the summer king. Shakespeare follows this
pattern; Christopher Marlowe subverts it. The presentation of the mock king
could be subversive, but in *Pericles* and *The Queen and the Concubine,* a flawed
ruler improves and so inspires support for the monarch.

Bilton, Peter. *Commentary and Control in Shakespeare's Plays.* New York: Humanities Press, 1974.
Shakespeare's increasing skill as a playwright is evident in his handling of
"commenting characters" who direct the audience's response. In the early plays,
choric figures such as Launce and Speed (*The Two Gentlemen of Verona*) remain
largely outside the action, though even here Shakespeare divides this role instead
of employing the more conventional single controlling character. In the comedies
of the late 1590s Feste (*Twelfth Night*) and Touchstone (*As You Like It*) move
closer to the center of the plot. In the tragedies, the protagonist is also the
principal commentator, especially through soliloquies.

Birney, Alice Lotuin. *Satiric Catharsis in Shakespeare: A Theory of Dramatic
Structure.* Berkeley: University of California Press, 1973.

Birney believes that satire, whose origins lie in primitive magic, can purge hatred; hence, drama can change society. She examines five satiric figures: Margaret of Anjou in the first tetralogy, Falstaff in *1, 2 Henry IV*, Jacques in *As You Like It*, Thersites in *Troilus and Cressida*, and Apemantus in *Timon of Athens*. Each functions differently. Whereas the rejection of Jacques purges Arden and the audience, Thersites infects his world, so that catharsis occurs neither in the play nor in its spectators.

Bowers, Fredson. *Hamlet as Minister and Scourge and Other Studies in Shakespeare and Milton*. Charlottesville: University Press of Virginia, 1989.
The seventy-fifth anniversary issue of *PMLA* cited the title essay as one of nine published in the journal that "really affected the course of scholarship and criticism." The first four pieces in this collection deal with questions of dramatic structure and Shakespeare's ethos, focusing on the tragedies but also touching on the comedies. The next six deal with *Hamlet*; two others treat structure and theme in *King Lear* and *1 Henry IV*, and the volume concludes with a piece connecting Hamlet and John Milton's Samson. Though all the essays in the book have been previously published in the 1960s and 1970s, this is an important gathering of major criticism.

Bradshaw, Graham. *Shakespeare's Scepticism: Nature and Value in Shakespeare's Plays*. Brighton, England: Harvester, 1987.
Bradshaw claims that Shakespeare does not endorse a particular point of view but rather presents divergent ethical outlooks. Like John Keats's view of Shakespeare's "negative capability," Bradshaw's offers a dramatist who delights in variety. Thersites is no more the author's spokesman in *Troilus and Cressida* than Ulysses. Yet Bradshaw also finds certain values prevalent in the plays. A. D. Nuttall said of this study: "People who enjoy thinking hard, who are willing to engage with the real intricacy and power of Shakespeare, will like it very much" (*Essays in Criticism* 38 [1988]: 156). Peter L. Rudnytsky called this "one of the landmarks of Shakespeare criticism in the twentieth century" (*Renaissance Quarterly* 41 [1988]: 757).

Brissenden, Alan. *Shakespeare and the Dance*. Atlantic Highlands, N.J.: Humanities Press, 1981.
The first chapter discusses the Renaissance view of dancing, examining various treatises on the topic. Brissenden then examines this motif in twenty of the plays in which dance is an important metaphor. Dance indicates celebration and order in the comedies, in tragedy dance imagery is ironic, and in the romances it reflects the movement to freedom. Brissenden notes Shakespeare's familiarity with various dances (which the book clearly explains).

Brownlow, Frank Walsh. *Two Shakespearean Sequences: "Henry VI" to "Richard II" and "Pericles" to "Timon of Athens."* Pittsburgh: University of Pittsburgh Press, 1977.
Early plays in each sequence introduce artistic and thematic issues that are reexamined and redefined in later plays. Both sets of plays progress to reveal "man's loneliness" and a "vast encircling absurdity." Despite the title, Brownlow examines each play on its own terms, offering many incisive observations. His treatment of the histories is ambivalent; he sometimes finds, sometimes rejects, the Tudor providence operating in them. His discussions of the romances are occasionally lacking in originality.

Bryant, Joseph A., Jr. *Hippolyta's View: Some Christian Aspects of Shakespeare's Plays.* Lexington: University of Kentucky Press, 1961.
A Christian reading of eleven plays, this volume derives its title from Hippolyta's response to Theseus in *A Midsummer Night's Dream*, where she offers what may be seen as a definition of poetry: "Something of great constancy;/ But, howsoever, strange and admirable." Though Shakespeare is not a religious writer, Bryant believes that the Bible profoundly influenced the plays and that the playwright "does God's work in God's ways." Specific interpretations will unsettle some: Bryant sees Macbeth as dying "cleaner than he began" and argues that Ophelia's bawdy St. Valentine's song symbolizes "selfless love." Yet Edward Hubler wrote (in *Shakespeare Quarterly* 13 [1962]: 85) that "there is not a chapter which does not in some measure illuminate the play with which it deals."

Bush, Geoffrey. *Shakespeare and the Natural Condition.* Cambridge, Mass.: Harvard University Press, 1956.
Shakespeare's characters are caught between the reality of time, chance, and mutability and the vision of an absolute, unchanging world beyond time. In the comedies, the characters and their world move towards a stable order, and in the histories as well this view triumphs. In the problem plays, the resolution is less clear. The title characters in *Timon of Athens, Othello, Macbeth,* and *Coriolanus* fail to achieve identity; they are overwhelmed by evil. *King Lear* and *Hamlet,* though, permit a measure of triumph despite lingering uncertainty. The plays are neither overtly secular nor overtly religious in their view of existence.

Calderwood, James L. *Shakespearean Metadrama: The Argument of the Play in "Titus Andronicus," "Love's Labour's Lost," "Romeo and Juliet," "A Midsummer Night's Dream," and "Richard II."* Minneapolis: University of Minnesota Press, 1971.
The plays are about drama. According to Calderwood, each (not only these five early pieces) contains a playwright who seeks to control the action—Aaron, Oberon, Iago, and Prospero. Language, too, is a subject. In *Richard II,* ceremo-

nial language is deposed. In *Romeo and Juliet*, language unites the lovers but isolates them from society. In *Titus Andronicus*, action overwhelms language; the union of poetry and spectacle produces a rape rather than a marriage. *Love's Labour's Lost* reverses this situation; here language dominates but fails because it cannot fuse poetic and theatrical demands. In *A Midsummer Night's Dream*, the numerous marriages and reconciliations mirror Shakespeare's success in fusing these requirements, and *Richard II* announces a new freedom for the playwright arising from his sense that "words seem hopelessly alienated from a divinely certified world order." The writer therefore must create his own meaning.

Campbell, Oscar James. *Shakespeare's Satire*. Oxford, England: Oxford University Press, 1943.
Shakespeare employs satire throughout his career. In the early plays, ridicule is good natured; even satirists such as Mercutio are amused by those they mock. Plays of the early 1600's grow harsher: *Troilus and Cressida*, *Measure for Measure*, *Coriolanus*, and *Timon of Athens* are true satire in tone and form, thus imitating a popular genre in the decade from 1598 to 1608. In *Hamlet* and *King Lear*, Shakespeare turned the malcontent into figures of deep tragedy.

Chambers, Edmund Kerchever. *Shakespeare: A Survey*. London: Sedgwick & Jackson, 1925.
Reprints the introductions Chambers wrote for the *Red Letter Shakespeare* (1904-1908). Though the book is largely intended for the general reader, Chambers ventures into such matters as the history of farce. He occasionally presents a theory no longer tenable; for example, Chambers believes that *Henry VIII* was composed in the early 1590s. The essays have worn well, however, and R. H. Case's observation remains valid: "This interpretation is always interesting, and generally reveals that intimate knowledge of the age and its spirit that makes for sound and well-balanced judgement" (*Modern Language Review* 21 [1926]: 200).

Clemen, Wolfgang H. *Shakespeare's Dramatic Art: Collected Essays*. London: Methuen, 1972.
A collection of essays, all but the first ("Shakespeare's Art of Preparation") previously published but here usefully gathered. Among the pieces are discussions of the use of the messenger, time, soliloquies, and illusion. One of Clemen's observations is that Shakespeare, while often sharing confidences with his audiences in various ways, forces them to "watch the development of the play, the delusions, hopes, discoveries, the 'false' and the 'right' actions of the characters on the stage with a mixture of pleasure, apprehension, and critical detachment." "Characteristic Features of Shakespearian Drama" notes Shakespeare's originality and ability to create unity from "the most varied and opposed elements." In "How to Read a Shakespeare Play," Clemen combines a theater-based

and a reader-based approach, writing that "only in performance can [a play's] potentialities be fully realized" but that repeated readings are necessary for full understanding. A particularly useful piece for critics is "Shakespeare and the Modern World," with its warning against reading modern concerns and sensibilities back into the plays. Throughout, Clemen demonstrates Shakespeare's infinite variety.

Cook, Ann Jennalie. *Making a Match: Courtship in Shakespeare and His Society.* Princeton, N.J.: Princeton University Press, 1991.
Courtship in Shakespeare's day differed from modern practices. Cook sets out to clarify the nature of courtship in Elizabethan-Jacobean England and in that context to examine Shakespeare's treatment of this matter. Cook notes, for example, that Juliet is quite young to marry just before her fourteenth birthday, that Shakespeare's emphasis on marrying for love does not mirror contemporary practice, but that the plays do recognize the problems rulers faced in choosing partners. Fascinating for its insights into Shakespeare's society and works.

Cook, Judith. *Women in Shakespeare.* London: Harrap, 1980.
After a brief survey of women in Shakespeare's England and in the plays of his contemporaries (citing actresses as well as reviewers and critics), Cook offers brief explications of the characters and notes important theatrical interpretations, such as Dame Peggy Ashcroft's of Rosalind. The book includes photographs of a number of actresses; these pictures show how the same role has been conceived at different times. A good introduction for the general reader, and serious students may find the actresses' comments valuable.

Council, Norman. *When Honour's at the Stake: Ideas of Honour in Shakespeare's Plays.* London: George Allen & Unwin, 1973.
In his first chapter, Council discusses three visions of honor: the traditional attitude linking private virtue with public recognition; the Stoical (and Calvinist) rejection of honor as irrelevant or impious; and a third attitude that saw honor as a personal, not a social, attitude. He then examines six plays—*1 Henry IV, Julius Caesar, Troilus and Cressida, Hamlet, Othello,* and *King Lear*—in terms of their treatment of these views. In *Hamlet,* for example, Laertes and Fortinbras adhere to convention in seeking revenge, but the title character finds that traditional ideas of honor do not obtain in an uncertain world. Council argues that Shakespeare criticizes the notion of honor throughout—Hotspur is "the true and perfect image of honor" but, as such, reveals the fallacy of this ideal. Lear and Iago also accept and seek conventional notions of honor.

Craig, Hardin. *An Interpretation of Shakespeare.* New York: Dryden Press, 1948.
An introductory chapter treats Shakespeare as an Elizabethan, and the last chapter discusses him as a citizen of the world. In between are interpretative essays

dealing with the plays and poems in chronological order of composition. Craig shows how Elizabethan audiences would have understood the works, and he praises Shakespeare's poetic gift. Though his observations may no longer appear new, even a seasoned Shakespearean may find his insights refreshing. Thus, Craig reminds the reader that *King Lear* is a play about authority and kingship, not about disobedience, that *Coriolanus* concerns itself with "absolute virtue" rather than with pride.

Cutts, John P. *The Shattered Glass: A Dramatic Pattern in Shakespeare's Early Plays*. Detroit: Wayne State University Press, 1968.
Shakespeare's characters in the early plays to *Richard II* unwittingly hide behind masks of goodness. Cutts examines the imagery of mirrors, shadows, vision, "fragmentation and synthesis," and the ways Shakespeare compels his characters to "shatter their own brittleness" to create "new and more powerful dramatic life." Often in the early plays, Shakespeare includes supporting characters who represent aspects of that which protagonists fail to see in themselves. The Dromios, for example, are the baser parts of Antipholus that he has yet to accept (*The Comedy of Errors*). In *Rich and Strange: A Study of Shakespeare's Last Plays* (Pullman: Washington State University Press, 1968), Cutts explores this theme of growing self awareness in the romances.

Dash, Irene G. *Wooing, Wedding, and Power: Women in Shakespeare's Plays*. New York: Columbia University Press, 1981.
Looks at courtship in *Love's Labour's Lost* and *The Taming of the Shrew*; female sexuality in *Romeo and Juliet*, *Othello*, and *The Winter's Tale*; and female power in the first Henriad and *Antony and Cleopatra*. Shakespeare's women rebel against conventions of a patriarchal world: Kate wants to choose her own husband, Cleopatra asserts herself by living in adultery with Antony, and Isabella refuses to sacrifice her virginity. Dash objects to editors, critics, directors, and producers who have diminished Shakespeare's women, and she asserts that Shakespeare transcended not only his own age but also his own sex. Though his characters may be misogynists, Shakespeare is not. Includes a number of fascinating illustrations of female characters.

Dawson, Anthony B. *Indirections: Shakespeare and the Art of Illusion*. Toronto: University of Toronto Press, 1978.
Shakespeare uses disguise and illusion not only to develop his plots but also to comment on the relationship between actor and audience. In the romantic comedies, disguise is therapeutic for characters and audience. Hamlet hopes to use the disguise of an antic disposition to cure the diseased world of Denmark, but the murder of Polonius turns the play from comic rehabilitation to tragedy. Helena in *All's Well That Ends Well* resorts to disguise to regain and reform Bertram. Prospero emerges as the arch artificer who employs illusion to regenerate the world of the play and the theater.

Dessen, Alan C. *Elizabethan Drama and Viewer's Eye*. Chapel Hill: University of North Carolina Press, 1977.

Focuses on the visual aspects of the plays through an exploration of three issues: the function of sets, props, and costumes; the role of visual echoes; and the relationship between medieval and Renaissance visual conventions. The sword in *Hamlet*, for example, serves as a significant symbol. Dessen would have the First Player use a sword in his "Pyrrhus" speech and pause in mid-air before Pyrrhus kills and minces Priam. Later, Hamlet will behave similarly during the duel. The exchange of Hamlet's innocent rapier for Laertes' poisoned one mirrors the action of the play. Hamlet "cannot achieve his ends in a corrupt world without partaking of corruption." Dessen maintains that the Elizabethans retained the medieval psychomachia, with different characters representing various aspects of an individual.

Dickey, Franklin M. *Not Wisely But Too Well*. San Marino, Calif.: Huntington Library, 1957.

Antony and Cleopatra serve as examples of rulers who sacrifice their empire for lust. Dickey warns against reading modern assumptions into Elizabethan plays; the book opens with Dickey's view of how Elizabethans understood passion and then proceeds to examine *Venus and Adonis*, *The Rape of Lucrece*, *Troilus and Cressida*, *Romeo and Juliet*, and *Antony and Cleopatra*. While audiences find Romeo and Juliet, Antony and Cleopatra attractive, the plays still warn against loving unwisely. Roy Walker nicely summarized the work's strengths and weaknesses: "Mr. Dickey's book is valuable as a specialized study of a main element in the three plays; it is too partial to win wide acceptance as a comprehensive critique of their protean values" (*Modern Language Review* 53 [1958]: 425).

Dollimore, Jonathan, and Alan Sinfield, eds. *Political Shakespeare: New Essays in Cultural Materialism*. Ithaca, N.Y.: Cornell University Press, 1985.

This anthology of Marxist essays examines political views of Shakespeare and, to an extent, of those who have discussed and reproduced him. Stephen Greenblatt examines the second Henriad in the context of Elizabethan concepts of power and sees the plays as a celebration not only of Henry V but also of Elizabeth. Paul Brown explores the ambiguities of colonialism as expressed in *The Tempest*. Kathleen McCuskie argues that *Measure for Measure* assumes a male perspective that excludes feminist criticism unless that play is radically revised, and *King Lear* contains "an explicitly misogynistic emphasis." Alan Sinfield discusses the possibility of radical productions of Shakespeare, which he suggests can be done only by abandoning the plays. Graham Holderness looks at the same question with televised and film versions, and he concludes that the media provide potential for radicalism that is generally blocked "by the conservatism of the dominant cultural institutions."

Drakakis, John, ed. *Alternative Shakespeares*. London: Methuen, 1985.
Drakakis' introduction briefly surveys the history of Shakespearean interpretation. Nine essays follow, employing more recent approaches such as deconstruction and new historicism. Terence Hawkes, for example, touches on the relationship of *The Tempest* to the ideological concerns of the early seventeenth century and examines the political implications of various modern readings. Christopher Norris examines F. R. Leavis' 1952 essay on *Othello* and defends poststructuralist interpretations, and Jacqueline Rose discusses the antifeminist readings of *Hamlet* and *Measure for Measure*. Implicit in many, though not all, of the selections is the primacy of criticism rather than the original work, so that the volume will prove more useful to students of criticism than to those seeking to understand Shakespeare.

Dreher, Diane Elizabeth. *Domination and Defiance: Fathers and Daughters in Shakespeare*. Lexington: University Press of Kentucky, 1986.
Shakespeare's fathers and daughters demonstrate complex relationships in the twenty-one works where they play important roles. Fathers are hesitant to relinquish control of their daughters; this attitude inhibits daughters' growth or drives them to escape, perhaps through madness (Ophelia), flight (Hermia), or revenge (Goneril and Regan). The comedies resolve tension between fathers and daughters; in the tragedies, the tensions explode. According to Dreher, intelligent, assertive women are favored in the plays, "patriarchal domination of women" condemned.

Driscoll, James P. *Identity in Shakespearean Drama*. Lewisburg, Pa.: Bucknell University Press, 1983.
Jungian study that sees four types of identity in Shakespeare's plays: real, social, conscious, and ideal. Real identity is communicated directly to the audience. Social identity refers to the character's role in the world of the play and the perception of him or her by that world. The character's own sense of self constitutes conscious identity. Ideal identity fuses self-perception and reality. As characters analyze themselves, they gain what Driscoll calls metastance. According to Driscoll, "Shakespeare's genius . . . resides not in his talent for depicting characters that resemble actual persons so much as in his power to grasp imaginatively how actual persons living their real lives resemble actors on a stage." In the history plays, social and conscious identities distort characters' perceptions and so limit their ability to act. Hamlet seeks self-knowledge before he acts, and he achieves this goal in the fifth act. Othello triumphs by overcoming the malignant Turk within himself, that element that Iago had played upon to distort Othello's perceptions earlier. Driscoll uses identity, among other elements, to distinguish between tragedy and comedy, and he also explores Jungian archetypes in the plays. A final chapter examines various critical approaches to character analysis. Closely argued and illuminating.

Dusinbere, Juliet. *Shakespeare and the Nature of Women*. New York: Barnes & Noble Books, 1975.
Sees drama from 1590 to 1625 as "feminist in sympathy," largely because Puritanism prompted a reevaluation of women's roles in society. Also, humanistic education and Elizabeth's rule created an atmosphere sympathetic to women. The book provides a corrective to studies that regard Shakespeare and Puritanism as misogynist, but this study too, is unbalanced in its failure to recognize tensions between the traditional and newer viewpoints voiced in the plays.

Eagleton, Terry. *William Shakespeare*. Oxford, England: Basil Blackwell, 1986.
An unconventional reading of the plays that claims, for example, "that positive value in *Macbeth* lies with the three witches" and that Feste's lament in *Twelfth Night* about the decline of language as a result of the breaking of bonds expresses Shakespeare's yearning for a precapitalist society. At the center of Shakespeare's plays is the conflict between order and the anarchy of creation. Eagleton can be witty, and the book has the virtue of brevity.

Edwards, Philip. *Shakespeare and the Confines of Art*. London: Methuen, 1968.
Edwards claims that Shakespeare is torn between the conflicting claims of chaos and coherence, recognizing that experience refuses to be confined by art, yet trying in his art to encompass experience. Hence, he experiments with various modes. The early comedies question the form's ability to depict reality. *Troilus and Cressida* denies ideals and takes a cynical view of life. *Measure for Measure* and *All's Well That Ends Well* seek unsuccessfully to impose a pattern on life. *The Winter's Tale* succeeds but (through its artifice) acknowledges the unreality of the vision. The fusion of art and life occurs most notably in *The Tempest*; fittingly, it is the opening play in the First Folio.

Egan, Robert. *Drama Within Drama: Shakespeare's Sense of His Art in "King Lear," "The Winter's Tale," and "The Tempest."* New York: Columbia University Press, 1975.
Characters within the plays use art and illusion to repair or at least cope with reality. Edgar deceives Gloucester to save him. Lear and Cordelia present a vision of the pietà that responds to the tragic events they have experienced. Paulina and Camillo in *The Winter's Tale* regenerate a fallen world through their artifice. Prospero accepts and overcomes the forces of chaos. Audiences, too, share the redemption through art. After Paulina asks disbelievers to depart, those who remain in the theater accept the redemptive power of art. Similarly, the epilogue of *The Tempest* links the world of the play with the larger world outside and redeems both.

Ellis-Fermor, Una. *The Frontiers of Drama*. London: Methuen, 1945.
The author examines the ways Shakespeare and other playwrights from Aeschylus

to the twentieth century expanded the definition of theater. She sees three elements that do not readily yield to dramatic treatment: religion, an epic vision, and a coherent sense of life emerging from conflict. Shakespeare's history plays, for example, fuse the dramatic conflict of individuals with the epic vision of an entire society. *Troilus and Cressida* succeeds in depicting the confusion of life by yoking disparate elements together by violence.

—————————. *The Jacobean Drama: An Interpretation*. London: Methuen, 1936. Not limited to Shakespeare, but places his works within the context of the age. Shakespeare's plays reflect the mood of the time of their composition. *Julius Caesar* and the Henriad reveal uncertainty about life. The tragedies and problem plays mirror a sense of horror in the early 1600s, and the romances indicate a return to a less-pessimistic outlook. Despite this oversimplified interpretation, the book offers useful readings of the plays and shows what Shakespeare's contemporaries were writing. C. J. Sisson remarked that "in general the book deserves close study, for it is the fruit of the long and intimate familiarity of a strenuous and critical mind with a great subject" (*Modern Language Review* 31 [1936]: 569).

Erickson, Peter. *Patriarchal Structures in Shakespeare's Drama*. Berkeley: University of California Press, 1985.
In the early plays, Shakespeare endorses the traditional patriarchal view of women. Male-male relationships are more important for the heroes, who resist heterosexual bonding. *Othello* and *King Lear* reveal more skeptical treatment of this outlook, and in *Macbeth* and *Coriolanus* the primary attachment with the title characters is to a woman, though these women are mother figures rather than partners. Only *Antony and Cleopatra* presents the two title characters as equals. Yet, in *The Winter's Tale*, Shakespeare returned to support of patriarchy. While many of the plays replace a stern patriarchy with a more benevolent one, Shakespeare endorses the conventional Renaissance view.

Farnham, Willard. *The Shakespeare Grotesque: Its Genesis and Transformation*. Oxford, England: Clarendon Press, 1971.
Explores the theme of the grotesque in Falstaff, *Hamlet*, Thersites, Iago, and Caliban. The grotesque originated in medieval art, especially in illuminated manuscripts where it combined the monstrous with the humorous. This fusion appears in the evil but funny character Mak of *The Second Shepherd's Play*; he unites high seriousness with low comedy. Falstaff, according to Farnham, physically resembles the medieval grotesque but is not evil. In *Hamlet*, the grotesque is everywhere: Polonius and Osric unite seriousness with folly, death links Yorick and the king, and Hamlet is both prince and court fool. The animal imagery reenforces this union of high and low. Later plays present more malicious grotesques: Thersites and Iago resemble the evil Vice figure. Caliban marks

a falling off from the diabolical evil of Iago, and the monster of *The Tempest* may even be capable of reform.

Ferguson, Margaret W., Maureen Quilligan, and Nancy J. Vickers, eds. *Rewriting the Renaissance: The Discourses of Sexual Difference in Early Modern Europe*. Chicago: University of Chicago Press, 1986.
Not all the essays deal with Shakespeare, but a number illustrate feminist readings of the plays. Peter Stallybrass' "Patriarchal Territories: The Body Inclosed" discusses *Othello*, and the anthology includes Coppélia Kahn's "The Absent Mother in *King Lear*," Stephen Orgel's "Prospero's Wife," and Louis Montrose's reading of *A Midsummer Night's Dream*. Other pieces treat the roles of women in society and thereby provide historical context for Shakespeare's depiction of his female characters.

Fergusson, Francis. *Shakespeare: The Pattern in His Carpet*. New York: Delacorte Press, 1970.
Assembles in one volume the introductions that Fergusson wrote for the Laurel Shakespeare series published by Dell (1958-1968) together with other essays. Fergusson regards Shakespeare as Dante's successor, envisioning "the symbolic world of the Christian monarchy" in which characters repeat the pattern of sin, the Fall, and redemption through grace. Sees Shakespeare's early plays (to 1594) as catering to popular taste. In the next phase (1594-1599), a monarch or mistress provides a way "to Eden"; these two figures correspond to Dante's guides in *The Divine Comedy*, Virgil and Beatrice. The tragedies and problem plays (1595-1608) are "preoccupied with the hell, or loss of faith, or the pronounced end which always threatens the human scene." The last works (1608-1616) deal with the loss and recovery of innocence, as well as the importance of faith. An accessible and valuable introduction to the plays, recommended for undergraduate and graduate students alike.

Fiedler, Leslie. *The Stranger in Shakespeare*. New York: Stein & Day, 1972.
The four divisions of this work look at Shakespeare's treatment of women (especially in *1 Henry IV*), Jews (as exemplified in *The Merchant of Venice*), Moors (as seen in *Othello*), and New World savages (in *The Tempest*). Fiedler argues that only in the last plays did Shakespeare portray women favorably, but these women are themselves motherless. *The Tempest* excludes Venus in favor of a puritanical Eden. Jews, Moors, and Indians are aliens in the world of Shakespeare's plays, as they were in the Elizabethan world. *The Merchant of Venice* "in some sense celebrates, certainly releases actually, the full horror of anti-Semitism." *The Tempest*, according to Fiedler, is racist and foreshadows "the whole history of imperialist America."

Fitch, Robert E. *Shakespeare: The Perspective of Value*. Philadelphia: Westminster Press, 1969.
Aimed at the nonspecialist but useful for the Shakespearean scholar as well, this work examines Shakespeare's presentation of "the moral order." Beginning with the observation that Christianity pervaded Shakespeare's age, Fitch argues that the plays eventually move away from theology and a faith in the supremacy of reason to belief in the power of wisdom, joy, and love to overcome evil in the world. A wide-ranging discussion that offers many insights and reminders.

Foas, Ekbert. *Shakespeare's Poetics*. Cambridge, England: Cambridge University Press, 1981.
Looks at Shakespeare's ideas about drama and language in the context of the period and sees Shakespeare as highly original, though Michel de Montaigne and Francis Bacon shared a number of his ideas. Argues that *The Winter's Tale* is the key to understanding Shakespeare's thoughts about art and language. Foas sees Shakespeare as the poet of nature, who distinguishes between art and life but who also regards artifice as natural. Foas concludes that for the author of *The Winter's Tale* "there is only one nature, the world of flux and cyclical return, of which human artistic endeavor is as much a part as any 'natural' process."

French, Marilyn. *Shakespeare's Division of Experience*. New York: Summit Books, 1981.
Divides experience and literature into masculine and feminine principles. The former seeks power and ownership, requires physical courage, and desires to transcend nature. The feminine, which French subdivides into inlaw and outlaw, accepts nature. Outlaw feminism is associated with darkness and sexuality and would subvert the masculine principle. Inlaw feminism stresses the kindly aspects of nature, especially fertility, and embraces mercy. French examines the balance of these three elements in the plays and concludes that the tragedies are masculine, the histories are largely masculine, and the comedies feminine. She believes that Shakespeare accepted his era's attitudes towards gender, "never abandon[ing] beliefs in male legitimacy or horror at female sexuality." French's division is simplistic, as a number of reviewers have noted (such as Gayle Green in "Feminist Criticism and Marilyn French: With Such Friends, Who Needs Enemies," *Shakespeare Quarterly* 34 [1983]: 479-486), but it attracted much attention when it appeared. (For a favorable review, see Lawrence Lerner in *The Times Literary Supplement*, June 4, 1982, p. 479.)

Frye, Roland Mushat. *Shakespeare and Christian Doctrine*. Princeton, N.J.: Princeton University Press, 1963.
The first part surveys criticism that finds or ignores Christian archetypes in Shakespeare's plays. Part 2 looks at the religious currents of the age, drawing

on Martin Luther, John Calvin, and Richard Hooker, and the third section analyzes Shakespeare's religious references. Frye disagrees with those who read Shakespeare doctrinally. While conceding Shakespeare's knowledge of theology, Frye argues that the plays focus on universal concerns and that Shakespeare's own religious views are not evident in the works. John E. Hawkins called this "a remarkably helpful book" (*Shakespeare Quarterly* 45 [1964]: 233).

Garber, Marjorie. *Coming of Age in Shakespeare*. London: Methuen, 1981.
The first chapter presents the anthropological-psychological basis of Garber's study, and the following six apply these principles to the plays as they portray various stages of loss and reintegration. Thus, "Separation and Individualism" discusses the passage from childhood to adulthood; "Nomination and Election" looks at the loss and acquisition of names as a mark of maturity. Other chapters discuss language, sexuality, the ability to distinguish, and death and survival. Characters who fail to adapt—Don John, Malvolio, Falstaff—are rejected by the plays, while those who undergo rites of passage and change emerge triumphant, such as Benedict and Beatrice in *Much Ado About Nothing* and Prince Hal. Spectators, too, undergo transformations as they witness the plays. Garber concludes that characters in Shakespeare's plays mirror the human condition and so give the works their universal appeal. A stimulating study.

——————. *Dream in Shakespeare: From Metaphor to Metamorphosis*. New Haven, Conn.: Yale University Press, 1974.
Looks at Shakespeare's use of literal and metaphorical dreams, ghosts, and witches in fourteen plays. Begins with a treatment of the Renaissance view of dreams and then considers their use in the plays. As he matured as an artist, Shakespeare used dreams more subtly and effectively, so that by the end of his career dreams cease to be metaphor and become equal to the waking world, a way of understanding and changing reality. Even in the early *A Midsummer Night's Dream*, though, to which Garber rightly devotes an entire chapter, "dreams are . . . consistently truer than the reality they seek to interpret and transform." Jean-Pierre Maquerlot called this "a book both difficult and stimulating, a most valuable source of information and reflection for advanced students of Shakespeare's drama" and "one of the most significant contributions to Shakespearean studies in the past few years" (*JEGP* 74 [1975]: 235-236).

Girard, René. *A Theater of Envy: William Shakespeare*. New York: Oxford University Press, 1991.
Girard's thesis is that theatrical imitation mirrors human behavior, which is based on mimesis. Love and hate both result from mimetic desire, and this truth informs Shakespeare's plays. Proteus in *The Two Gentlemen of Verona* falls in love with Silvia because Valentine, his childhood friend, loves her and wants Proteus to validate his choice. Friends must become rivals. In politics, imitation

can produce order when properly directed, but in the world of *Troilus and Cressida* or Shakespeare's England—where the leader is flawed—emulation produces chaos. Ulysses wisely uses mimetic desire to cure Achilles of self-love, which results from others' admiring him. Girard makes insightful observations about the plays, but his interpretations do not always satisfy. He rides his hobbyhorse too hard, ignoring other possible explanations and sometimes distorting the text. Thus, he maintains that Cressida turns to the "merry Greeks" to regain Troilus' love, which possession has diminished. The paucity of footnotes is troubling in a scholarly work.

Goldman, Michael. *Shakespeare and the Energies of Drama*. Princeton, N.J.: Princeton University Press, 1972.
Examines the ways the plays in performance affect their audiences. *Hamlet*, for example, is filled with uncompleted actions: Pyrrhus pauses as he is about to kill Priam, Claudius tries to but is unable to pray, and Hamlet prepares to strike the kneeling king but does not do so. *King Lear* utilizes repetition: "rejection by one daughter and then another" and repeated words, such as "Howl, howl howl!" and "Never, never, never, never, never!" Goldman also discusses, inter alia, choreography in *Coriolanus*, the power of art in *The Winter's Tale*, and the enchanted atmosphere of *The Tempest*. He is less concerned with dramatic technique than with effect, though—both on the characters as they mature in the play and on the audience witnessing the unfolding drama.

Goldsmith, Robert Hillis. *Wise Fools in Shakespeare*. Liverpool, England: Liverpool University Press, 1955.
Shakespeare's fools derive from both popular and learned tradition. The first three chapters analyze literary and popular antecedents of the Shakespearean fool. In chapter 4, Goldsmith discusses Touchstone (*As You Like It*), Feste (*Twelfth Night*), Lavache (*All's Well That Ends Well*), and Lear's Fool. Touchstone's parody introduces realism into the romantic forest of Arden. Feste is the voice of the established order and, again, of reason. Lavache is not cynical but realistic. Lear's Fool is clear-sighted, loyal, and almost heroic—one of God's fools. "He is the supremely wise fool who expresses in his heartfelt devotion to Cordelia and to his king the Christian virtues of patience, humility, and love." The fifth chapter examines satirists such as Jacques in *As You Like It* or Ben Jonson's Carlo Buffone (*Every Man out of His Humour*). This short book concludes with an examination of the important fools in the plays, where they serve as voices "of humanity and common sense." Provides both humour and reflection.

Granville-Barker, Harley. *Prefaces to Shakespeare*. 4 vols. Princeton, N.J.: Princeton University Press, 1963.
These observations, written over a period of a quarter of a century by actor-playwright-producer Granville-Barker, offer an excellent introduction to the plays.

Granville-Barker brings to the works his vast theatrical experience and a scholarly familiarity with the texts and their backgrounds. Whether he writes about the double time scheme in *Othello* or Hamlet's heroic struggle to penetrate the mystery of being, to act without full knowledge, he is everywhere illuminating and thought-provoking. H. T. Price observed that "no writer has approached Granville-Barker in his profound understanding of the various skills and techniques that go to the making of a play" (*Modern Language Quarterly* 9 [1948]: 358), and M. A. Shaaber called the prefaces "one of the most distinguished discussions of Shakespeare's art of our time" (*Modern Language Notes* 63 [1948]: 196). Required reading for all students of Shakespeare.

Grudin, Robert. *Mighty Opposites: Shakespeare and Renaissance Contrariety.* Berkeley: University of California Press, 1979.
Paracelsus speaks of nature's effecting its own reversal; disease can be treated with itself, not its opposite. Baldassare Castiglione and Giordano Bruno find this same truth—the former in ethics, the latter everywhere. Shakespeare's characters often employ Paracelsus' method. Helena uses Bertram's lust to bring about marriage. To get Achilles to fight, Ulysses encourages the pride that has left the hero sulking in his tent. Angelo in *Measure for Measure* become vicious through virtue; Isabella's chastity in the play appears a vice. Prospero is the "hero of contraries" who can accept both Ariel and Caliban.

Hallett, Charles, and Elaine Hallett. *Analyzing Shakespeare's Action: Scene vs. Sequence.* Cambridge, England: Cambridge University Press, 1991.
Instead of looking at scenes and acts as units of composition, the authors locate beats, sequences, and frames. Each sequence, composed of beats, has its own climax, and sequences combine to create a frame. Understanding these units of action will allow directors to present plays more effectively and students to recognize the lines of action that are being developed. Includes a glossary defining the authors' terms.

Hamilton, A. C. *The Early Shakespeare.* San Marino, Calif.: Huntington Library, 1967.
This is a largely unsatisfactory attempt to find patterns within and among the early plays. Based on T. S. Eliot's observation, quoted at the end of the introduction, that the meaning of a Shakespearean play lies not only in itself but also in relation to all of Shakespeare's other plays—earlier and later. Sees the image of the labyrinth (and related metaphors) as signifying the theme of the comedies, tragedies, and histories. Hamilton also argues that *Richard III* completes the pattern of the first Henriad in describing a failed monarch and also anticipates the second Henriad's portrayal of the ideal monarch. *The Comedy of Errors, The Two Gentlemen of Verona,* and *Love's Labour's Lost* each focuses on an element of drama—plot in the first, character in the second, and language and spectacle

in the third. All these elements come together in *A Midsummer Night's Dream*. So, too, *Romeo and Juliet* complements *Titus Andronicus* because the earlier tragedy provokes fear, the later one pity. Ernest William Talbert praised the work (*Modern Language Quarterly* 29 [1968]: 354-356), and Hamilton does offer insights into individual plays, though his general scheme is overwrought.

Hapgood, Robert. *Shakespeare the Theatre-Poet*. Oxford, England: Clarendon Press, 1988.
Performance-based analysis that sees the plays as involving author, actors, and audience in an ensemble. Audiences, like characters, must encounter the unknown, experience the unbearable, and interpret their theatrical experience. Hapgood sees the plays as offering a range, though not an unlimited number of possible interpretations, with plot as the best guide to the author's intention. In *Macbeth*, for example, the title character finds murder easier and easier to commit, and his victims grow increasingly defenseless—plot thus reveals degeneration. Especially useful for showing how changes in performance can affect interpretation.

Harbage, Alfred. *As They Liked It: A Study on Shakespeare and Morality*. New York: Macmillan, 1947.
Harbage argues that "Shakespeare is moral without being a moralist." His sole aim is to please, but to do so he draws upon "the moral nature of his audience." Among other approaches, Harbage looks at Shakespeare's alteration of his sources to add an ethical dimension. Characters receive moral coloring; Polonius fails to win an audience's sympathy, but Gonzalo in *The Tempest* does, even though both are trusted counsellors given to verbosity. The plays offer an ideal of life that spectators can understand and accept, a vision of life's basic goodness and of the triumph of justice.

_____. *Shakespeare Without Words and Other Essays*. Cambridge, Mass.: Harvard University Press, 1972.
Presents a dozen essays that appeared between 1940 and 1970. The first section criticizes critics and other interpreters of Shakespeare such as directors, who reduce the plays to some formula. Included here is "Cosmic Card Game," a spoof of New Criticism, first published in 1951. The second part treats the development of Elizabethan drama and Shakespeare's role in the process. Harbage's essay on the dating of *Love's Labour's Lost* (which he places before 1589) presents a number of useful reminders about Elizabethan plays in general, such as the observation that "there is no supporting external evidence to prove that any regular play performed by any regular company, juvenile or adult, was originally written for a special occasion during the period 1558-1616." Harbage also suggests that the *Tragical History . . . of Guy of Warwick*, first printed in 1661, probably dates from 1592-1593 and refers to Shakespeare.

Hartwig, Joan. *Shakespeare's Analogical Scene: Parody as Structural Syntax*. Lincoln: University of Nebraska Press, 1983.

Argues for the significance of small moments in the plays, such as the murder of Cinna the Poet in *Julius Caesar* or York's exposing his son's treachery in *Richard II*. In *Measure for Measure*, Angelo's turning over the questioning of Elbow to Escalus serves as a parodic echo of the duke's abdication of his power and demonstrates that neither Angelo's severity nor Escalus' leniency benefits society, which requires a balance. Hartwig thus shows that apparently irrelevant scenes that are often cut in production are integral to the plays. She also draws helpful parallels from other works, such as her observation that the tomb in *Romeo and Juliet* resembles Edmund Spenser's Cave of Despair (*Faerie Queene*, book I). John W. Velz described the book as "an excellent delineation and interpretation of echo structure in ten plays of Shakespeare" (*Modern Language Quarterly* 45 [1984]: 404).

Henn, T. R. *The Living Image: Shakespearean Essays*. London: Methuen, 1972.

The living image of the title refers to animal allusions in the plays, which Henn explicates through his knowledge of falconry, fishing, hunting, horseriding, and war. Hamlet's reference of "rank sweat of an enseamed bed" derives from ornithology: an enseamed hawk has too much grease in its body. Later in the play "this quarry cries on havoc" alludes to the killing of deer en masse to provide for a feast, quarry meaning the carcasses.

Hirsh, James E. *The Structure of Shakespearean Scenes*. New Haven, Conn.: Yale University Press, 1981.

Argues that Shakespeare worked in scenes rather than in a five-act structure; Hirsh defines a scene as the interval from one empty stage to another. The book posits five types of scenes: solo (one character), duets (two characters), unitary group scenes (same group of actors throughout), two-part scenes (some actors change, some do not), and multipartite scenes (many groupings of characters). Hirsch notes, for example, that lovers never have an entire scene (in Hirsch's sense) to themselves; in *Romeo and Juliet*, this arrangement reminds the audience of the world that surrounds the couple. In two-part scenes, one action comments on the other—for example, the appearance of Ophelia in *Hamlet*, II, i, right after Reynaldo links the two to show that Ophelia, too, becomes Polonius' spy. *King Lear*, II, ii-iv, actually is one long scene running from morning to night, and the presence of Kent and Edgar on stage at once, though the latter is not aware of the former, suggests the similarity between the two loyal, banished characters.

Holderness, Graham, ed. *The Shakespeare Myth*. Manchester, England: Manchester University Press, 1988.

Not about Shakespeare as person or writer but as icon. The ten essays offer a Marxist analysis of the role Shakespeare plays in modern culture. Holderness, for example, sees the effort to reconstruct the Globe as "an example of the operation of a cultural imperialism . . . in which culture and a philanthropic international capital combine to engage in an act of urban renewal upon their own hegemonic terms." Ann Thompson surveys feminist criticism, David Margolies explores the ideological uses of Shakespeare by the dominant culture, and David Hornbach discusses knowledge of Shakespeare as a means of social advancement. Interviews with directors are confrontational, seeking to elicit and then demolish what Terry Eagleton calls their "dismally regressive opinions." A fascinating glimpse into how the radical Left seeks to exploit Shakespeare to belabor the establishment for exploiting Shakespeare.

Holderness, Graham, Nick Potter, and John Turner. *Shakespeare: The Play of History.* Iowa City: University of Iowa Press, 1988.
Holderness discusses the second tetralogy, Turner *King Lear* and *Macbeth*, Potter *The Merchant of Venice* and *Othello*. All three maintain that in particularizing the society of each play, Shakespeare turns away from the medieval chronicle and writes as a Renaissance humanist historian. Shakespeare also shows how change results form the struggles for power that are inherent in society, and the plays consider not only what happened but also what might have been, giving play to the imagination (as the book's subtitle implies). In *The Merchant of Venice*, for example, Venice and Belmont represent two social visions—the former of willful, ruthless individualistic capitalism, the latter of love, mutual respect, the feudal order. The play reconciles the two worlds, though reality could not. Informative and useful.

Holland, Norman N. *Psychoanalysis and Shakespeare.* New York: McGraw-Hill, 1966.
Part 1 examines the psychoanalytic approach to literature. Part 2 assembles Sigmund Freud's observations about Shakespeare and his writings, subsequent psychoanalytic statements about the playwright, and a summary, arranged alphabetically by work, of the major psychoanalytic studies. Holland defends the psychoanalytical approach, though he concedes that many of the studies discussed here lack validity. The final section, "Psychoanalysis, Shakespeare, and the Critical Mind," presents Holland's own views, which look at author, character, and audience as parts of a continuum. This section tries to reconcile psychoanalytic approaches and New Criticism, an effort not totally successful: even if sex and death are linked in *Hamlet*, the skulls in the graveyard are not necessarily testicles; and *Othello* may be about love and war, but Iago need not be a homosexual and Desdemona may not suffer from penis envy. Most useful as a bibliography of psychoanalytical criticism.

_____. *The Shakespearean Imagination.* London: Macmillan, 1964.
A good introduction aimed at the general reader. Early chapters discuss Shake-

speare's theater, his reputation since 1616, and major twentieth century critical approaches. Holland then looks at sixteen plays, focusing on structure, images, themes, and character. He finds two overriding principles: a *Macbeth*-principle ("the tragedy of our uncertainty about the way supernatural penetrates nature") and a *Tempest*-principle ("how the dramatist imitates God"). His discussion of the split in Shakespeare's plays between the public and private worlds is sound; his view, echoing the Romantics, that the plays cannot be staged successfully is twaddle.

Homan, Sidney. *When the Theater Turns to Itself: The Aesthetic Metaphor in Shakespeare*. Lewisburg, Pa.: Bucknell University Press, 1981.
An examination of Shakespeare's use of the theater as metaphor in nine plays. *The Taming of the Shrew*, *Love's Labour's Lost*, and *A Midsummer Night's Dream* show how actors and plays blur the boundaries of art and reality. In *Othello*, *As You Like It*, and *Measure for Measure*, a figure—Iago, Rosalind, the Duke—behaves as a playwright-director in controlling the action. *Hamlet*, *Antony and Cleopatra*, and *The Tempest* at once celebrate and question the role of art and its relationship to life. Homan presents sound readings of the plays; his scheme illuminates themes, characters, and action.

Howard, Jean E. *Shakespeare's Art of Orchestration: Stage Technique and Audience Response*. Urbana: University of Illinois Press, 1984.
Arguing for a theatrical rather than a textual approach to Shakespeare, Howard looks at how the playwright controls what the audiences hear and see and hence how they respond to the plays. The study examines speech, juxtaposition, silence, movement, and dramatic structure; this last element receives extended treatment in a chapter devoted to *Twelfth Night*. Offers many suggestions for handling scenes in the plays; for example, when Lear awakes in IV, viii, Howard prefers the quarto's use of music to the folio's silence. Later in the play, she advocates using silences to punctuate Lear's speech over the dead Cordelia.

Howard, Jean E., and Marion F. O'Conner, eds. *Shakespeare Reproduced: The Text in History and Ideology*. London: Methuen, 1987.
A collection of essays, first presented at the April, 1986, Shakespeare Association meetings in Berlin, offering Marxist, feminist, new historicist, and poststructuralist analyses of Shakespeare and his interpreters. Howard reads *Much Ado About Nothing* as a debate over "who will control the theater, and whose theatrical practices will be considered legitimate." Michael Bristol and Thomas Sorge look at *Coriolanus* as a play about legitimate authority. Sorge finds in the work "the failure of orthodoxy." Peter Erickson looks at class and gender in *The Merry Wives of Windsor*, which he claims portrays female control as a threat to patriarchy. For Thomas Cartelli, *The Tempest* embodies "colonial presumptions," especially to Third-World readers. Useful for acquainting readers with modern critical approaches and disagreements.

Jochum, Klaus Peter. *Discrepant Awareness: Studies in English Renaissance Drama*. Frankfurt, Germany: Peter Lang, 1979.
The title refers to the different levels of information characters and audience possess in the plays. In *Richard III*, spectators know not only the protagonist's thoughts but also his ultimate fate. In *Romeo and Juliet*, each character lacks crucial knowledge, and this ignorance produces catastrophe; only the audience has full knowledge. The book also examines this technique in medieval drama and among Shakespeare's contemporaries and successors. Concludes that Shakespeare is one of the few playwrights who rarely seeks to deceive his audience. Though the book's style is labored, it offers solid interpretations.

Jorgensen, Paul A. *Shakespeare's Military World*. Berkeley: University of California Press, 1956.
Looks at Shakespeare's knowledge and use of military conditions, with Jorgensen relating events in the plays to the situation in Elizabethan armies. Thus, the first chapter discusses marches, battles, and maneuvers, especially involving fife and drum music. Chapter 3 examines Shakespeare's treatment of rank (especially in *1, 2 Henry IV* and *Othello*); Chapter 4 deals with the role of the common soldier, the Earl of Essex, and the difficulty of readjusting to civilian life. T. R. Henn called this "a broad and useful book, with much material which is not readily accessible elsewhere" (*Modern Language Review* 53 [1958]: 104).

Kahn, Coppélia. *Man's Estate: Masculine Identity in Shakespeare*. Berkeley: University of California Press, 1981.
In this psychoanalytic study, Kahn argues that the plays concern men's efforts to find their proper places in a patriarchal world. In the history plays, war and politics bring men together. *Romeo and Juliet* and *The Taming of the Shrew* treat marriage as a means to manhood. In *Othello*, men unite against female betrayers. Macbeth and Coriolanus seek manhood through violence.

Kastan, David Scott. *Shakespeare and the Shapes of Time*. Hanover, N.H.: University Press of New England, 1982.
Shakespeare deals with linear and circular concepts of time. Both the histories and the tragedies use linear time, but the histories are open-ended, the tragedies "terrifyingly closed." In the former, then, Shakespeare abandons both medieval drama's sense of a providential ending and the classical tradition of exemplary history, and the tragedies depict a pattern imposed not by divinity but by human limitations. Kastan reads the tragedies as pessimistic. Shakespeare's romances escape tragedy by looking at experience from a perspective outside of time. Though these plays depict losses, redemption offsets deprivation, at least in part. Kastan's scheme distorts the tragedies, which many read as redemptive. Comments on the history plays, however, are perceptive.

Kernan, Alvin B. *The Playwright as Magician: Shakespeare's Image of the Poet in the English Public Theater.* New Haven, Conn.: Yale University Press, 1979. Kernan argues that artistic self-consciousness developed in the Renaissance. In the sonnets and the interpolated plays, Shakespeare indicates his feelings about drama, which he regarded as equal to poetry in ability to reveal truths about human nature and the world. These plays within plays also demonstrate that limitations of stage effects, actors, and audiences could weaken a work, and these restrictions also caused Shakespeare to question the ultimate effect of two hours' traffic on the stage. Kernan concludes that "Shakespeare was . . . suspended between a vision of his art as noble as the highest Renaissance views on the subject, and questions about that art as it had to be practiced in the actual conditions of playing in the public theater."

Kirschbaum, Leo. *Character and Characterization in Shakespeare.* Detroit: Wayne State University Press, 1962.
A study of various characters in Shakespeare. Though he quotes A. C. Bradley repeatedly, Kirschbaum seeks to move beyond independent character analysis to understand how characters function in a play. Most are not realistic but rather behave as theme or plot dictates. Shylock derives from literary stereotypes but becomes the representative of emergent capitalism threatening communal values. Albany's growth is a key to *King Lear*; Banquo and Edgar are not fully realized individuals but "dramatic functions." Other chapters speculate on the relationship of Ophelia and Hamlet, the portrayal of Cleopatra, Romeo's shift from Petrarchan to romantic love, Angelo's dual portrait, and the reality of Beatrice and Benedict in the otherwise unrealistic *Much Ado About Nothing*. The short volume concludes with a brief discussion of the opening scenes of *Richard II* and of *Othello*; Kirschbaum objects to the portrayal of Othello as totally noble.

Knight, G. Wilson. *The Crown of Life: Essays in Interpretation of Shakespeare's Final Plays.* 2d ed. London: Methuen, 1948.
Contains six essays, including Knight's 1929 "Myth and Miracle," his first publication on Shakespeare, that provides the basis for much of the book's criticism. Each of the following five chapters considers one of the final plays (*Pericles, The Winter's Tale, Cymbeline, The Tempest,* and *Henry VIII*). Knight examines the works themselves without regard to literary source or social, cultural, and political developments of the age, though he does argue that the plays exalt British destiny. Sees the works as resolving conflicts through harmony and ritual and revealing Shakespeare's mystic understanding of suffering humanity. Though much of the criticism is impressionistic, Knight emphasizes the excellence of the last plays.

_____. *The Shakespearean Tempest: With a Chart of Shakespeare's Dramatic Universe.* Oxford, England: Oxford University Press, 1932.

Looks at images of storm and music, which Knight sees as the organizing principle of the plays. The former includes imagery of disease, earthquakes, and comets; the latter includes flowers, jewels, gold, and "other pleasant suggestions." Knight rejects readings that focus on character, psychology, or poetics. Finds in the plays a movement from conflict to harmony. The early historical tragedies are dominated by tempests of civil wars, and in the comedies to 1600 "tempests are but the condition through which are attained the dreamland melodies of romance." In the tragedies, tempest dominates, but one hears "the siren music of peace and love." In the romances, again harmony prevails. Knight's exclusive focus on imagery is narrow but can be illuminating.

Knights, L. C. *Some Shakespearean Themes.* Stanford, Calif.: Stanford University Press, 1960.
The opening chapter examines twentieth century critical approaches to Shakespeare and sets forth Knights's effort to find a pattern in the plays. Knights concludes that Shakespeare deals not with abstract philosophy but with ethical questions. *King Lear* is central to Shakespeare's thought; all the earlier plays lead to it, and later works depend upon it. The tragedy of *King Lear* depicts the necessity of love "in spite of everything." Stimulating though subjective, with many provocative observations about the plays and sonnets.

Kott, Jan. *Shakespeare Our Contemporary.* Translated by Boleslaw Taborski. Garden City, N.Y.: Doubleday, 1964.
Argues that twentieth century audiences can more readily appreciate Shakespeare's nihilistic, absurdist world than could those in the nineteenth century. *King Lear*, for example, resembles Samuel Beckett's *Endgame* in its rejection of the absolute and in its vision of an absurdist universe. *Macbeth* offers no redemption, only destruction; *Hamlet* reveals the corrupt nature of politics; and *A Midsummer Night's Dream* is a nightmare. A dark reading of the plays.

Laroque, François. *Shakespeare's Festive World: Elizabethan Seasonal Entertainment and the Professional Stage.* Translated by Janet Lloyd. Cambridge, England: Cambridge University Press, 1991.
In part 1, Laroque looks at popular celebrations in Shakespeare's day, and in part 2 he uses this information to explain Shakespeare's plays. *Love's Labour's Lost*, for example, can be seen as moving from Carnival to Lent; this movement appears again in *Henry IV* and *Antony and Cleopatra*. Benedict's reference in the opening scene of *Much Ado About Nothing* to May 1 and December 31 calls to mind the spring and winter festivals. Hero's association with the latter foreshadows her symbolic journey to the underworld through mock death. *All's Well That Ends Well* uses the rivalries of Hocktide. Laroque devotes a chapter to *Othello*'s use of festival motifs. The study concludes that "in his comedies and his romances Shakespeare makes direct use of the symbolism attached to festivals. In

his histories and tragedies, he reverses the liberating dynamic of festivity, turning it into an instrument of moral perversion, a conveyor of darkness and a herald of chaos." A fruitful fusion of anthropology and literary analysis.

Lenz, Carolyn, Ruth Swift, Gayle Greene, and Carol Thomas Neely, eds. *The Woman's Part: Feminist Criticism of Shakespeare*. Urbana: University of Illinois Press, 1980.
Eighteen essays surveying the body of Shakespeare's work from a feminist perspective. Paula S. Berggren opens the volume with "Female Sexuality as Power," in which she argues that women in the tragedies appear as victims or monsters. Catherine R. Stimpson's "Shakespeare and the Soil of Rape" sees aggression against women as a form of male rivalry. Carol McKewin looks at the plays' treatment of conversations between women; these talks allow for "self-expression, adjustment to social codes, release, relief, rebellion, and transformation." Marianne Novy notes that in the comedies women play a more active role than they do in the tragedies, and in the latter men are suspicious of active women. Madelon Gohlke sees Shakespeare as sympathetic to women in the tragedies, but anxiety still vexes "the feminized male." In "Coming of Age in Verona," Coppélia Kahn argues that Romeo's tragedy arises from the conflict of defining manhood as aggressive or loving. Clara Claiborne Park's delightful 1973 essay about *As You Like It*, "How a Girl Can Be Smart and Still Popular," notes that Shakespeare creates intelligent women, but they all dwindle into wives. She notes that Erich W. Segal's novel *Love Story* (1970) demonstrates the continued viability of this tradition.

Levin, Harry. *Shakespeare and the Revolution of the Times: Perspectives and Commentaries*. New York: Oxford University Press, 1976.
A collection of sixteen essays, addresses, and reviews that offer a balanced, reasonable view of Shakespeare. Levin's discussion of Roy W. Battenhouse's *Shakespearean Tragedy: Its Art and Its Christian Premises* (1969) expands to an analysis of the nature of tragedy in the plays, which he locates in the interaction of "faith and doubt, or hope and despair." "Evangelizing Shakespeare" argues against turning the plays into orthodox Christian dogma. Other essays look at Shakespeare's treatment of the monarchy, *Twelfth Night*, *Othello*, *The Tempest* (which Levin nicely contrasts with Ben Jonson's *The Alchemist* to show the authors' divergent views of human nature), *King Lear*, and the conditions necessary for great drama to emerge. An appendix demolishes the pretensions of those who would make Edward de Vere, seventeenth Earl of Oxford the "real" author of Shakespeare's plays.

Lewis, Percy Wyndham. *The Lion and the Fox: The Role of the Hero in the Plays of Shakespeare*. London: Grant Richards, 1927.
Sees Niccolò Machiavelli as a key influence on Elizabethan thought in general

and Shakespeare's in particular. The first two sections of the book explore the Elizabethan world and Machiavelli's pervasive ideas. Part 3 looks at Shakespearean treatment of kings and heroes. In the fourth section, Lewis presents Shakespeare as responsive rather than active. Lewis then examines Othello, Lear, Antony, Macbeth, Timon, and Coriolanus ("The Colossus of the Third Period"). The text concludes with discussions of Shakespeare and Miguel de Cervantes ("The Two Knights"), of *Troilus and Cressida*, and of George Chapman and Ernest Renan. Sees Shakespeare's heroes as idealists defeated by lesser realists. Shakespeare himself was neither lion nor fox, neither a plain man nor a machiavel, but both at once. Rosamund Gilder called the book "a rare and precious stimulant to those who delight in new approaches and unusual angles of attack" (*Theatre Arts* 11 [1927]: 375).

Long, John H. *Shakespeare's Use of Music: A Study of the Music and Its Performance in the Original Production of Seven Comedies*. Gainesville: University of Florida Press, 1955.
Long examined contemporary plays, music books, and accounts of drama and music to understand how songs are used in *The Two Gentlemen of Verona*, *Love's Labour's Lost*, *A Midsummer Night's Dream*, *The Merchant of Venice*, *Much Ado About Nothing*, *As You Like It*, and *Twelfth Night* to further the plot, suggest action, and indicate the passage of time. The inclusion of scores makes the volume especially helpful for producers, though when Long has to settle for analogues not all the music fits the words equally well. Altogether, a valuable study.

_____. *Shakespeare's Use of Music: The Final Comedies*. Gainesville: University of Florida Press, 1961.
As in his other volumes on music in Shakespeare's plays, Long seeks "to determine the functions of the performed music in the comedies, the manner of performance, the original musical scores used (when possible)," and, when no score exists, contemporary music that will serve for modern productions seeking authenticity. Long notes how music serves as an integral part of the plays, enhancing the force of the opening scene of *The Taming of the Shrew* and highlighting the theme of harmony in *The Tempest*.

_____. *Shakespeare's Use of Music: The Histories and Tragedies*. Gainesville: University of Florida Press, 1971.
Discusses the instruments and songs that might have been used in the plays and how music enhanced the plays theatrically as well as aesthetically. He suggests, for example, that Hamlet sang rather than spoke the snatches from the ballads that he quotes. The imperial trumpet flourish that announces Antony's entrance at the beginning of *Antony and Cleopatra* disappears from all but one of his later appearances, suggesting the decline of Antony from triumvir to lover. Long

indicates which tunes the actors might have used and, more significantly, might adapt for modern performances.

McAlindon, Thomas. *Shakespeare and Decorum*. London: Macmillan, 1973.
A study of *Richard II, Hamlet, Othello, Macbeth,* and *Antony and Cleopatra* that examines them in terms of their representation of "natural order as perceived by the senses or the aesthetic imagination." Language and action comprise this decorum, which is the ideal, and violations of naturalness lead to disaster. As McAlindon observes in his discussion of *Macbeth,* "All choices which are to bear fruit . . . must be in perfect harmony with time and place." In its own way, the book restores E. M. W. Tillyard's Elizabethan world picture.

Marienstras, Richard. *New Perspectives on the Shakespearean World*. Translated by Janet Lloyd. Cambridge, England: Cambridge University Press, 1985.
Draws on the ideology of Shakespeare's day to understand a number of polarities operating in the plays—sacrifice and sacrilege, near and far, subject and foreigner. Includes sensitive readings of *Titus Andronicus, Julius Caesar, Macbeth, Othello,* and *The Tempest,* noting that the plays reflect the ambiguities of reality. For example, Brutus' killing of Caesar could be sacrifice or bloodshed; only the decision of the populace makes it the latter. As Marienstras writes of *Macbeth,* "Good and evil are not opposed in any simple way." Marienstras also looks at *Mucedorus* and John Ford's *'Tis Pity She's a Whore.* Includes an extensive bibliography.

Masefield, John. *William Shakespeare*. New York: Barnes & Noble Books, 1954.
An introduction to the life and works, with a bibliographical essay and discussion of the sonnets, the major poems, and each of the plays. A revision of a 1922 study, this volume aimed at the general reader offers brief plot summaries and observations that are both impressionistic and valuable, coming as they do from England's poet-laureate. Masefield is, however, no scholar and should not be trusted on matters of chronology.

Murry, John Middleton. *Shakespeare*. London: Jonathan Cape, 1936.
Begins with a biographical essay, followed by a discussion of the works. A sensitive reading of Shakespeare, though the autobiographical interpretation of the sonnets is pure speculation and Murry's rhapsodizing can cloy. Includes many useful observations. For example, Murry sees the Bastard in *King John* as dividing into the witty Falstaff and the heroic Hotspur, and he regards Prospero's island as a world of nature transformed through art. His comments about language in *Othello,* time in *Macbeth,* sadness in *Twelfth Night,* and the role the Duke of York in *Richard II* are enlightening.

Naylor, Edward W. *Shakespeare and Music.* 2d ed. London: J. M. Dent & Sons, 1931.

Almost all of Shakespeare's plays deal in some way with music. Naylor begins his discussion by looking at the important role of music in the social life of sixteenth and seventeenth century England. He then examines passages in Shakespeare's work that deal with "Technical Terms and Instruments," "Musical Education," "Songs and Singing," "Serenades and Other Domestic Music," "Dances and Dancing," and "Miscellaneous." The book is enriched with illustrations of contemporary instruments and examples of Elizabethan and Jacobean music. Useful as a gloss on terms such as "canary"(a lively dance).

Neely, Carol Thomas. *Broken Nuptials in Shakespeare's Plays.* New Haven, Conn.: Yale University Press, 1985.

Begins with a survey of attitudes towards marriage in Renaissance England, where Protestant theologians approved of sexual pleasure within the context of marriage but equated sex with sin and advocated both equality of husband and wife and also female subordination. In the comedies, "broken nuptials, even when initiated by men, give women the power to resist, control, or alter the movement of courtship," but in the end men reassert control. The tragedies depict male fears of female sexuality; Cleopatra can express her eroticism only because she will be rendered nonthreatening through death. The romances also use real or imagined death to render female sexuality harmless. Without trying to determine Shakespeare's attitudes towards women, Neely shows how the plays offer full portraits, "absorbing and recreating in another dimension all of the contradictions that surround women's status." The important feminist critic Coppélia Kahn observed that "no Shakespearean, feminist or not, should fail to read this book, the boldest, most tough-minded and meticulous feminist interpretation of the plays that has been written thus far" (*Shakespeare Quarterly* 38 [1987]: 371).

Nicoll, Allardyce. *Shakespeare: An Introduction.* New York: Oxford University Press, 1952.

Intended for the general reader, this work begins with a discussion of Shakespeare's world. It then looks at approaches to Shakespeare and offers a chronological treatment of the plays to trace the playwright's artistic development. Though Nicoll offers no profound insights, his observations are sound. Thus, he says that "Hamlet is Shakespeare's Everyman; his tragedy is Shakespeare's *Humana Commedia.*" He notes that Othello and Desdemona are blinded by idealism, Iago by cynicism, and reminds the reader that among the issues the late romances confront are primitivism and culture, spirit and sense.

Noble, Richmond. *Shakespeare's Use of Song: With the Text of the Principal Songs.* Oxford, England: Oxford University Press, 1923.

Shakespeare was the first dramatist to integrate his songs into the action of his plays. "Who Is Sylvia" in *The Two Gentlemen of Verona* links the two plots. In *The Merchant of Venice*, the casket song directs Bassanio's choice. The songs of *Twelfth Night* echo the diverse moods of the piece. Finds increasing skill in making the songs an integral part of the play. Includes the words of all these songs in the plays with a discussion of their significance.

Novy, Marianne. *Love's Argument: Gender Relations in Shakespeare*. Chapel Hill: University of North Carolina Press, 1984.
Like Carol Thomas Neely, Novy sees a tension in Shakespeare's England between theories of patriarchy and sexual equality, and this ambivalence affects the plays. The comedies portray men and women as mutually dependent; if women submit, so do men. *The Taming of the Shrew*, for example, presents not masculine victory but compromise. In the tragedies, except for *Antony and Cleopatra*, women are weak. In these plays, Shakespeare examines the unfortunate consequences of patriarchy and male domination, especially in *King Lear*. The romances offer an alternative vision of men as passive and as sharing female interests in such matters as pregnancy and children. Novy concludes that "the tragedies focus much more on ideals of manhood; the romances use cross-gender imagery more often to show men transcending a narrow masculinity, while the comedies use such imagery more often to show women transcending conventional limitations."

Parker, M. D. H. *The Slave of Life: A Study of Shakespeare and the Idea of Justice*. London: Chatto & Windus, 1955.
Argues that Shakespeare writes within a Christian framework, so that theology looms large in the works. The study begins with a discussion of Shakespeare's religious milieu, with its conflicts about the rules of reason and grace. In his early plays, Shakespeare presents justice operating in this world, mercy in the next. Later plays allow for mercy in this world as well. Claudius and Macbeth reject repentance; though their consciences prick them on, their wills prick them off. Antony and Cleopatra are saved through love. *Measure for Measure, All's Well That Ends Well*, and *King Lear* provide for redemption. In the tragedies, redemption generally occurs through the heroes' achievement of self-knowledge. An appendix explores the question of whether Shakespeare was Catholic or Anglican.

Parker, Patricia, and Geoffrey Hartman, eds. *Shakespeare and the Question of Theory*. London: Methuen, 1985.
Examines decontructionist, feminist, and historical-political approaches to Shakespeare. Stephen Greenblatt's "Shakespeare and the Exorcists" rejects deconstructionist readings that deny ideology, and he seeks to place the dramatist in the context of the Elizabethan and Jacobean "struggle . . . to redefine the central values of society." Hartman, in "Shakespeare's Poetical Character in

Twelfth Night," sees too much ambiguity to impute to Shakespeare any one ideological vision. Jonathan Goldberg's "Shakespearean Inscriptions: The Voice of Power" suggests that the plays reject a patriarchal vision. The volume concludes with a series of essays on *Hamlet* that link these various theoretical approaches. Thomas Docherty called the work "an indispensable collection for any serious critical student of Shakespeare" (*Review of English Studies* 38 [1987]: 554).

Pitt, Angela. *Shakespeare's Women.* Totowa, N.J.: Barnes & Noble Books, 1981. Intended for the general reader, this nicely illustrated volume begins with a discussion of women in Shakespeare's plays. The next three chapters survey the women in the tragedies, comedies (and romances), and histories, offering essentially plot summaries of their roles. The most fascinating section deals with the actresses who have played the heroines. Chapter five presents a historical overview, and an epilogue interviews various actresses, including Judith Dench, Glenda Jackson, and Janet Suzman.

Rabkin, Norman. *Shakespeare and the Common Understanding.* New York: Free Press, 1967.
The volume takes its title and central idea from Robert Oppenheimer's *Science and the Common Understanding* (1966). According to Rabkin, Shakespeare's plays may be explained by the concept in physics called "complementarity," which recognizes that paradoxes and irresovable contradictions coexist in life as in art. Choices are not clear in Shakespeare's plays, which Rabkin sees as based on dialectic—reason and passion in *Hamlet,* worldly values and the transcendent in *Antony and Cleopatra,* mercy and justice in *The Merchant of Venice* and *King Lear.* By one set of standards—political success—Bolingbroke is the hero of *Richard II,* but in terms of humanity Richard is more admirable. Franklin M. Dickey praised the book for appreciating individual plays' complexity and providing a framework for the entire "oeuvre" (*Renaissance Quarterly* 25 [1972]: 508-510).

_____. *Shakespeare and the Problem of Meaning.* Chicago: University of Chicago Press, 1981.
Attacks both those who deny the possibility of finding any meaning in the plays and those who insist on a reductive, universal reading of Shakespeare. Restoration adaptations of Shakespeare, Rabkin notes, prove unsatisfactory because they ignore the originals' complexity. In the course of his argument, Rabkin sheds light on many passages and individual works that he discusses, and his comment on Shakespearean tragedy as both demanding a choice and "making that choice impossible" is perceptive. Rabkin sometimes forgets his own warning and advocates a single reading. Thus, he admits multiple allegiances in *The Merchant of Venice* but not in *Henry V.* Also, his insistence on dualities rather than multiple choices seems reductive.

Raleigh, Walter. *Shakespeare*. London: Macmillan, 1907.
Raleigh looks at the ways Shakespeare used his world and his reading to produce
the plays. Though scholarship has added much in the decades since Raleigh
wrote, his impressions often remain valuable, and, unlike too many more modern
books, his is a pleasure to read. He does, however, retain the traces of his
time—the view of Shakespeare as Nature's child and the belief that Shakespeare's
"best things are not very effective on the stage."

Righter, Anne. *Shakespeare and the Idea of the Play*. London: Chatto & Windus,
1962.
Claims that medieval drama links audience and performance without pretense of
illusion; the mystery cycles joined player and spectator in biblical truth, and
audiences participated as they would at a mass. The influence of classical drama
caused a separation between the two in the Renaissance and prompted the
metaphor of stage as world. After discussing the evolution of stage illusion in
part 2, Righter turns to a chronological survey of Shakespeare's plays. She sees
three phases to Shakespeare's use of this metaphor. In the early works, the
metaphor is detached from the action. In the middle works, the Player-King
assumes a central role. The last plays again fuse life and art to redeem and
remove the notion of stage as world, but after *Hamlet* Shakespeare's language
indicates a belief that the play cheapens life and is corrupt. Kathleen M. Lea
observed that "this is a most pleasant book; apart from the easy movement of
its prose it is full of ideas which stir the mind long after the actual reading"
(*Modern Language Review* 59 [1964]: 265).

Rose, Mark. *Shakespearean Design*. Cambridge, Mass.: Harvard University Press,
1972.
Each scene is independent, but each depends on its context for complete understanding and enrichment. Rose argues that Renaissance drama accepts the notion
of *ut pictura poesis*—a poem is like a picture. Thus, *A Midsummer Night's Dream*
is a triptych, with the nighttime forest panel framed by the bright scenes in
Athens, and the central panel in moonlight depicts the nature of love. *The
Winter's Tale* is a diptych, the first part tragedy, the second comedy, divided by
the chorus. A scene, which Rose defines as the interval between two empty
stages, also is built as triptych or diptych and is emblematic. "The Murder of
Gonzago" scene in *Hamlet*, where the court watches a play revealing reality in
Elsinore, mirrors the experience of the Globe, where the audience watching
Hamlet is seeing the truth about its life. Ralph Berry called the study "a useful
contribution to our understanding of Shakespearean methods, lucidly written and
well-judged in its line of advance" (*Modern Language Review* 70 [1975]: 143).

Sanders, Wilbur. *The Dramatist and the Received Idea: Studies in the Plays of
Marlowe and Shakespeare*. Cambridge, England: Cambridge University Press,
1968.

Examines how a playwright translates society's norms to the stage. Whereas Christopher Marlowe did not challenge the views of his age, Shakespeare did, though *Richard III* is weakened by the imposition of Tudor propaganda in the treatment of Providence as a directing force. *Richard II* is a better play, for it rejects received ideas and so gives comfort neither to those who believe in the divine right of kings nor to those who favor deposing an incompetent ruler. In *Macbeth*, Shakespeare "is a Manichean, and an Augustinean, and a Pelagian," expressing various approaches to evil but not accepting the conventional Christian attitudes. Sanders concludes that Shakespeare found grace in a natural order, not in divinity. Sanders is better on Shakespeare—whom he admires—than on Marlowe—for whom he shows little sympathy.

Schanzer, Ernest. *The Problem Plays of Shakespeare: A Study of "Julius Caesar," "Measure for Measure," and "Antony and Cleopatra."* London: Routledge & Kegan Paul, 1963.
Defines a problem play as one "in which we find a concern with a moral problem which is central to it, presented in such a manner that we are unsure of our moral bearings, so that uncertain and divided responses to it in the minds of the audiences are possible or even probable." In *Julius Caesar*, the problem lies in the justice of killing Caesar. The audience first sympathizes with Brutus, then recognizes the horrible consequences. In *Measure for Measure*, Isabel's ardent chastity may be excessive. Also, does Antony make the correct choice in preferring love to empire? Schanzer offers a good analysis of these works, but his distinction between these and *Hamlet* or *Henry V* seems arbitrary, since those, too, allow for more than one "correct" response to the issues.

Sen Gupta, S. C. *The Whirligig of Time: The Problem of Duration in Shakespeare's Plays*. Bombay, India: Orient Longman's, 1961.
Sen Gupta distinguishes between Time and Duration. The former, which predominates in the early histories, is chronological and can be measured by clocks and calendars. Duration is used in plays that focus on "development in character and action, . . . ideas and imagery." *Othello*, for example, relies on Duration, not Time. *Measure for Measure* "immobilizes Time so that life may be viewed as a whole." A novel though not totally satisfactory approach to the problem of time in the plays.

Seng, Peter J. *The Vocal Songs in the Plays of Shakespeare: A Critical History*. Cambridge, Mass.: Harvard University Press, 1967.
Looks at the texts of seventy songs in twenty-one plays and presents thematic and textual commentary, information about musical setting, sources and analogues, and the songs' role in the plays. Seng's glosses on the songs suggest new readings. For example, Ophelia's "He Is Dead and Gone Lady" refers to Hamlet, not Polonius, according to Seng. A comprehensive study that will be most useful

for anyone seeking information on the subject. Cyrus Hoy called this "a meticu-
lously executed work of scholarship, and one for which students of Shakespeare
can be distinctly grateful" (*Studies in English Literature* 8 [1968]: 381). Includes
an excellent bibliography.

Siegel, Paul N. *Shakespeare in His Time and Ours.* South Bend, Ind.: University
of Notre Dame Press, 1968.
Reprints earlier pieces and adds new essays on *King Lear* and *Much Ado About
Nothing*, as well as overviews of Shakespearean tragedy and comedy. Siegel sees
the tragedies as Christian, providential, and drawing on biblical archetypes. The
comedies reflect the political and social conditions of the age: the shifts from
romantic to satiric comedy, and from satire to tragicomedy, respond to the
dissolution of the Elizabethan Compromise that balanced aristocracy and the
middle class. Christian humanism informs these plays, too; the last comedies,
with their miraculous conclusions, suggest hope for England's future. Siegel's
interpretations sometimes surprise: he sees Shylock as a Puritan, for example.

Skulsky, Harold. *Spirits Finely Touched: The Testing of Value and Integrity in Four
Shakespearean Plays.* Athens: University of Georgia Press, 1976.
A moral reading of the plays that condemns Hamlet for "intellectual vanity" and
"self-indulgence," the duke in *Measure for Measure* as a "legalist" and "machiavellian confessor" who lacks "sympathetic imagination," and Othello for "abject
lovelessness." These bizarre readings are balanced by an excellent discussion of
King Lear, where Skulsky argues persuasively for the play's affirmation of love
and justice despite its bleakness.

Smith, Marion Bodwell. *Dualities in Shakespeare.* Toronto: University of Toronto
Press, 1966.
A study of the sonnets, *Romeo and Juliet, Twelfth Night, Measure for Measure,
Macbeth, Antony and Cleopatra,* and *The Tempest.* Smith defines duality as "a
lively awareness of contradictions accompanied by a particularly keen sensitivity
to interdependent relationships." The opening chapter discusses duality in Renaissance thought. In her next chapter, Smith looks at thematic treatment of duality
in Shakespeare. She finds the early plays more conventional, the middle plays
full of doubt, and the final works a synthesis of opposing viewpoints. The rest
of the book looks at individual works; the discussion includes, but does not limit
itself to, duality.

Soellner, Rolf. *Shakespeare's Patterns of Self-Knowledge.* Columbus: Ohio State
University Press, 1972.
Opens with a discussion of the meaning of self-knowledge for such Renaissance
figures as Desiderius Erasmus, John Calvin, Michel de Montaigne, and Francis
Bacon. Soellner then looks at these ideas as they are developed in twelve plays

throughout Shakespeare's career and finds "three major periods." At first, Shakespeare accepts humanistic ideals, then he questions them, and finally he returns to a belief in reason and self-control. *The Comedy of Errors* is about the loss and recovery of identity. Richard II does not know himself, but by the end of the play he has achieved limited awareness. Henry V, whom Soellner sees as a true hero, possesses self-knowledge. Brutus, on the other hand, lacks this quality (though Plutarch admired Brutus, Shakespeare does not), and Hamlet's quest for self-knowledge ends in failure. In *Measure for Measure*, Angelo, Isabella, and the Duke discover things about themselves. This play anticipates Lear's attainment of self-knowledge and Prospero's triumph over his passions.

Spencer, Theodore. *Shakespeare and the Nature of Man.* New York: Macmillan, 1942.
The essential element in Shakespeare's intellectual and emotional background is the Renaissance's distinction between humanity's ideal and real nature. Spencer explores the working out of this dichotomy in the tragedies and later plays. He notes three stages in Shakespeare's career: "a period of experiment and adaptation, a period of tragic vision, and a period of affirmation." He also treats this development as the cycle of life—birth (comedies), struggle (tragedies), death (*Timon of Athens*), and renewal (romances).

Sternfeld, Frederick W. *Music in Shakespearean Tragedy.* London: Routledge & Kegan Paul, 1963.
Presents the texts and musical setting for songs in Shakespeare's tragedies and in some of the comedies, simplifying some arrangements that would be too challenging for an average production. The first chapter ("Tradition of Vocal and Instrumental Music in Tragedy") traces the rise in use of music from early Renaissance tragedies to Shakespeare. Chapter 2 treats Desdemona's "Willow Song," chapter 3 Ophelia's singing. Following chapters treat "Magic Songs" that influence mood, "Adult Songs" that offer insight into character, music in *King Lear*, and instrumental music. The book concludes with a survey of scholarship on music in Shakespeare's works. Roy Lamson praised the book as a "rare accomplishment" in "combining . . . scholarship in . . . music, dramatic literature, and theater history" (*Shakespeare Quarterly* 16 [1965]: 117). Sternfeld observes that tragic songs in these plays complement speeches, while comic songs relate to the events of the entire play. Sternfeld maintains that "only Mozart can approach or equal Shakespeare's talent for integrating passages of dramatic action with lyrical utterances." Another of his observations is that "in Elizabethan and Jacobean drama song had two major functions: to characterize and to influence the disposition of men."

Stirling, Brents. *The Populace in Shakespeare.* New York: Columbia University Press, 1949.

Shakespeare, like his fellow Elizabethans, distrusted the mob, as is evident in the Jack Cade scenes of *Henry VI* and the treatment of mobs in *Julius Caesar* and *Coriolanus*. This attitude echoes Anglican propaganda against Puritanism: nonconformity in religion would lead to riot and anarchy. Stirling sees these religious warnings, not actual fear of civil unrest, as the source of Shakespeare's treatment of the populace. Includes a good survey of critical response to the mob scenes in the three plays he treats.

Summers, Joseph H. *Dreams of Love and Power: On Shakespeare's Plays*. Oxford, England: Clarendon Press, 1984.
Looks at *A Midsummer Night's Dream, The Winter's Tale, Hamlet, Measure for Measure, King Lear, Antony and Cleopatra*, and *The Tempest*. Dreams and imaginings reveal the characters' inner hopes and fears and often reflect on the theme of the play—sometimes confronting, at other times transcending, reality. Summers regards the plays as rooted in Christian humanism; good characters possess true love and do not seek to control the beloved, instead loving selflessly. An accessible and insightful interpretation of the plays that offers sound observations about the ways they work to influence audience response.

Sundelson, David. *Shakespeare's Restorations of the Father*. New Brunswick, N.J.: Rutgers University Press, 1983.
A study of the second Henriad (*Richard II* through *Henry V*), *Measure for Measure*, and *The Tempest*, each of which deals with the loss and return of a father figure. The discussion touches on many other plays as well, as Sundelson examines the role of patriarchy in the plays and finds a fear of female dominance and female sexuality. In *Twelfth Night*, for example, powerful women are tolerated, but *Measure for Measure* restores patriarchal power and Prospero rules *The Tempest*.

Talbert, Ernest Williams. *Elizabethan Drama and Shakespeare's Early Plays: An Essay in Historical Criticism*. Chapel Hill: University of North Carolina Press, 1963.
In the thirteen plays written before 1596, Shakespeare manipulates response by playing on audiences' familiarity with dramatic practices such as multiple plots and by appealing to biases such as love of England or hatred of France and Catholicism. Argues that the plays both use and subvert audience expectations and that they present the ambivalent attitudes of their audiences towards questions such as the deposition of Richard II or the nature of love. Talbert observes that, even early in his career, Shakespeare surpassed his contemporaries in controlling audience reaction.

Taylor, Mark. *Shakespeare's Darker Purpose: A Question of Incest*. New York: AMS Press, 1982.

In twenty-one plays, a father or the memory of a father poses an obstacle to marriage, and these fathers feel a "degree of sublimated desire" that prompts them to cruel and arbitrary actions. *The Tempest* marks the culmination of the theme of incest. Alonso forces his daughter into a biracial marriage, and Prospero must overcome his possessive feelings for Miranda to permit her marriage to Ferdinand.

Tennenhouse, Leonard. *Power on Display: The Politics of Shakespeare's Genres.* London: Methuen, 1986.
In this new historicist interpretation, Tennenhouse treats the plays as political documents. The comedies, which portray the pursuit of an unavailable woman, mirror the court of Elizabeth. Like the histories, these plays support both hierarchy and patriarchy. In the Jacobean tragedies, "the punishment of unchaste aristocratic women . . . displays the truth of the subject's relation to the state." Shakespeare's shift from comedy and chronicle history to tragedy and romance responds to the change in rule from a Virgin Queen to a man, a change demanding new representations of power: "The desiring aristocratic woman of romantic comedy suddenly found herself out of place on the stage. She could no longer rectify the disorder there, for she had become one of its causes."

Thaler, Alwin. *Shakespeare and Our World.* Knoxville: University of Tennessee Press, 1966.
Part 1 of this collection of essays discusses the similarities between Shakespeare's world and the twentieth century. Thaler addresses the question of Shakespeare's identity and offers an optimistic, religious reading of the tragedies. Part 2 discusses Shakespeare's plotting and use of absent or invisible characters. John Milton's debts to Shakespeare are also traced. Peter G. Phialus remarked of Thaler's book that "here one finds not only devotion to the poet but reasonableness and common sense, clarity of style, and not infrequently eloquence" (*South Atlantic Quarterly* 66 [1967]: 482).

_____. *Shakespeare's Silences.* Cambridge, Mass.: Harvard University Press, 1929.
Shakespeare uses silences in various ways. Characters may say nothing when one expects them to—Isabella says nothing to Vincentio's proposal in *Measure for Measure*. Characters may vanish silently, such as Rosaline in *Romeo and Juliet* or the Fool in *King Lear*. There also may be details that are not developed, such as the question of Macbeth's children. Another of the five essays in this volume examines "The Unhappy Happy Ending" of the comedies. Readers may find the conclusions contrived because of the seriousness of the situations that the plays treat, but on stage these happy endings work, and that is the test of their appropriateness. The other pieces look at Shakespeare's influence on Thomas Browne and John Milton.

Turner, Frederick. *Shakespeare and the Nature of Time: Moral and Philosophical Themes in Some Plays and Poems of William Shakespeare.* Oxford, England: Clarendon Press, 1971.
Time in the sonnets destroys. In *Hamlet*, the ghost introduces the eternal world into the temporal. Shakespeare used time to show how characters develop. In the opening chapter, Turner defines nine varieties of time: historical, personal, as destroyer or creator, as "opposed to the eternal," as cyclical or natural, as "the medium of cause and effect," as "occasion," and as "revealer and unfolder." He then examines the uses of time in the sonnets and eight of the plays. In the sonnets, love opposes "the destructive and corrupting forces of time." Hamlet confronts two conflicting realms, "the world of time in which the crime was committed and within which he must work his revenge; and the timeless world where he has been shown the crime and commanded to revenge it." Despite the limited focus of the study, it offers a helpful way to view the works it treats. An appendix offers various readings on time from Heraclites to the Renaissance.

Turner, Robert Y. *Shakespeare's Apprenticeship.* Chicago: University of Chicago Press, 1974.
Examines Shakespeare's use of rhetoric, dialogue, scene division and focus, irony, staging, and the mingling of the tragic and comic. Turner thereby traces the playwright's increasing artistic maturity mirrored in his plays' increasing ambiguity, their movement from rhetoric to mimesis. Observes that the early plays (to *A Midsummer Night's Dream*) repeat the course of sixteenth century drama "from the generalized didactic morality play to the relatively literal drama as a distinctive art form." David Riggs called the book "thoughtful, learned, and often sensitive to nuances in the text" (*Shakespeare Quarterly* 28 [1977]: 110).

Van den Berg, Kent T. *Playhouse and Cosmos: Shakespearean Theater as Meta-phor.* Newark: University of Delaware Press, 1985.
Van den Berg explores "the ways in which relationships of play and reality inside the . . . theater and within [Shakespeare's work] define the relationship of the theatrical event as a whole to the world outside." The Elizabethan theaters were little worlds in which actors behave as authors and authors as God, all directing life within their realm. The playgoers withdraw into the world of the theater but also recognize the other world outside to which they will soon return. This movement of withdrawal, recognition, and return operates in all of Shakespeare's plays. Van den Berg uses his model to analyze representative works and audience reaction to them—*As You Like It* for the comedies, *Henry V* for history, and *Macbeth* for tragedy.

Van Doren, Mark. *Shakespeare.* New York: Henry Holt, 1939.
An introduction to the plays and poems. Treats style, structure, imagery, and character, focusing on particular elements in the discussion of each play. An

essay about *Richard III* concentrates on character, one about *Titus Andronicus* on plot. Impressionistic but frequently illuminating interpretations presented clearly. Especially good for the high school student or college undergraduate.

Van Laan, Thomas F. *Role-Playing in Shakespeare.* Toronto: University of Toronto Press, 1978.
Characters assume four types of roles in the plays. The first is "a role in the literal sense, a part in a play, pageant, or other entertainment." A second type involves temporarily adapting a role vis-à-vis the world of the play; this type "is an alien identity that [the character] appropriates." The third type is a traditional type—Falstaff as braggart soldier, for example—and the fourth is the character's function in the play—such as "lover, friend, servant." In the tragedies, characters lose their roles and therefore their identities. This loss, not death, is the essence of the pathos. In the comedies, when characters lose one role they find another. John W. Velz called this "a challenging and perceptive book" (*JEGP* 79 [1980]: 117).

Wain, John. *The Living World of Shakespeare: A Playgoer's Guide.* New York: St. Martin's Press, 1964.
A charming, often insightful introduction aimed at the novice. Treats the plays on their own terms but also seeks to relate them to the concerns of modern audiences. Interpretations are presented without qualifications and will not please all. For example, Wain regards *The Winter's Tale* as the playwright's best work and sees Henry V as a Machiavellian manipulator. Though not aimed at the scholar, the book may provide some insights even for the seasoned Shakespearean.

Watson, Robert N. *Shakespeare and the Hazards of Ambition.* Cambridge, Mass.: Harvard University Press, 1984.
Characters seek to forge new identities, which is for Watson the essence of ambition. In his Freudian reading of the plays, Watson sees Hal pursuing "normal psychological development" as he subjects the id to the superego and controls his Oedipal impulses. Lady Macbeth drives her husband as Volumnia controls her son Coriolanus. In *The Winter's Tale*, Leontes suffers from an "overly ambitious superego." Though primarily a psychological study, the work links ambition with the doctrine of Original Sin and notes that Leontes may be viewed as one who falls because he does not accept the Fall.

Weiss, Theodore. *The Breath of Clowns and Kings: Shakespeare's Early Comedies and Histories.* New York: Atheneum, 1971.
A study of "the growth and change of the plays' language, the matter of words and deeds or poetry and drama" in the works to 1600. In the comedies, love educates the young men; the women are teachers as well as objects of love. The

histories explore the relationship between language and action. Richard III uses language only to express himself; he is a man of action, whereas Richard II substitutes words for deeds. In *1, 2 Henry IV* language and action fuse. R. W. Dent describes the study as "lively, challenging, engaging" (*Renaissance Quarterly* 25 [1972]: 507). Especially but not exclusively useful to the undergraduate.

West, Robert H. *Shakespeare and the Outer Mystery*. Lexington: University of Kentucky Press, 1968.
Looks at the four major tragedies and *The Tempest*, in which West finds ambiguous treatment of external reality. The world of the plays is overtly neither providential nor absurdist. West thus takes issue with both the "Christianizers" and "contemporizers" who try to impose their own views on the plays, which they read as univocal rather than as complex. The ghost in *Hamlet*, for example, may be a spirit of health or a goblin damned. This lack of certainty allows the audience to appreciate Hamlet's plight, for characters must act despite the mystery that surrounds them. The plays do not resolve the nature of this world or the next. Mark Eccles called this "a wise and thoughtful book" of sound scholarship (*Studies in English Literature* 9 [1969]: 366). Reginald Saner similarly praised the study: "All in all, West's is a wise book, beautifully balanced in method and tone, clearly the result of long thought, but short enough to be useful" (*English Language Notes* 7 [1970]: 299).

Women's Studies 9, nos. 1-2 (1981-1982).
Both issues, which were edited by Gayle Greene and Carolyn Ruth Smith, deal with feminist criticism of Shakespeare. Carol Neely opens the first number with a discussion of feminist criticism generally. Marianne Novy notes the difficulty of applying this approach to Shakespeare, who has been viewed either as an uncritical supporter of Tudor orthodoxy or as a universal genius transcending issues of gender. Greene suggests fusing feminist and Marxist criticism because both believe that society determines literature and both critique patriarchal values. Subsequent essays look at Shakespeare's treatment of women in the plays. Shirley Nelson Garner looks at *A Midsummer Night's Dream*, which "affirms patriarchal order and hierarchy, insisting that the power of women must be circumscribed, and recognizes the tenuousness of heterosexuality." Not all the essays go in for Bard-bashing. Martha Andersen-Thom, for example, sees *The Taming of the Shrew* as "a celebratory dance of life" and a parody of patriarchy.

Wright, George T. *Shakespeare's Metrical Art*. Berkeley: University of California Press, 1988.
A useful analysis of the technical aspects of Shakespeare's poetry and also of the theatrical effects the poetry achieves. Wright provides guidance in dealing with contractions and elisions. As he explores the nature of Shakespeare's iambic verse, Wright notes that blank verse suggests that the speaker knows more than

he or she is saying. He points out the contrast between the poetry of Claudius and Gertrude and Ophelia's prose in the mad scene of *Hamlet*. In *King Lear*, when they appear before Regan, Oswald recites half a line of iambic verse for Kent to finish, but Kent rejects Oswald with a two-syllable response. A useful study that shows the connection between the technicalities of verse and the meanings of the text, though Wright sometimes protests too much that Shakespeare's poetic line is strictly iambic.

Zeeveld, W. Gordon. *The Temper of Shakespeare's Thought*. New Haven, Conn.: Yale University Press, 1974.
Sees Shakespeare's plays as dealing with contemporary issues. The Roman plays, for example, explore the then current question of monarchy versus commonwealth. The English encounters with brave new worlds prompt exploration of civility and barbarism in the romances. Zeeveld looks closely at four topics. The first—ceremony—proves significant for Shakespeare. Like Richard Hooker, Shakespeare upholds "customary observances of tradition." The second issue deals with commonwealth, the third with equity (which Zeeveld relates to Elizabethan reforms in the legal system), and the fourth concern is civility. By looking at the works as Shakespeare's audiences might have understood them, Zeeveld enhances the plays' meanings without trying to reduce the works to a single message.

Zukofsky, Louis. *Bottom: On Shakespeare, with Music to "Pericles" by Celia Zukofsky*. 2 vols. Austin: University of Texas Press, 1963.
Not a scholarly exegesis but a prolonged poetic meditation in prose on the writings of Shakespeare, all of which Zukofsky regards as one long work. Part 1 focuses largely on *A Midsummer Night's Dream*, part 2 on *Pericles*. The third and longest section is an exploration of diverse Shakespearean topics alphabetically arranged from the surprising "A-Bomb and H" and the more conventional "After All Eyes and the Birthplace" to "Young" and "Z (signature)." Much of this section, indeed much of this book, is filled with quotations from, about, or related to the plays. Zukofsky draws fascinating parallels between, for example, Spinoza's concept of love and Shakespeare's (part 1) or Aristotelian philosophy and dialogues between Speed and Launce in *The Two Gentlemen of Verona*. Full of thought-provoking suggestions, startling insights, and delightful passages. A companion volume presents Celia Zukofsky's musical scoring of *Pericles*, counterpoint to her husband's essay on the play.

Comedies

Anderson, Linda. *A Kind of Wild Justice: Revenge in Shakespeare's Comedies*. Newark: University of Delaware Press, 1987.

Revenge works in two ways in Shakespeare's comedies. Serious forms of retribution must be thwarted, while comic revenge is visited on hypocrites or those behaving improperly. This latter type relies on reason, not emotion, and is undertaken to restore social harmony as well as to punish and reform the object of revenge. Revenge in the comedies thus serves a positive function. In the course of her discussion, Anderson speaks of the Elizabethan concept of vengeance and thus helps the reader understand more serious treatment of this concept in the tragedies as well.

Barber, C. L. *Shakespeare's Festive Comedy: A Study of Dramatic Form and Its Relation to Social Custom*. Princeton, N.J.: Princeton University Press, 1959.
The first three chapters discuss Elizabethan modes of celebration, especially holiday shows. Later chapters examine *Love's Labour's Lost, A Midsummer Night's Dream, The Merchant of Venice, Henry IV, As You Like It*, and *Twelfth Night*. This highly original and extremely influential study looks at the comedies as artistic renditions of the spirit of folk and court festivals. Thus, *A Midsummer Night's Dream* recreates a May day celebration; Sir Toby Belch in *Twelfth Night* is a lord of misrule. The plays do not reject either idyll or reality. Instead, each element comments on the other, but the plays do offer a temporary release from the everyday world. Highly praised by reviewers.

Bergeron, David M. *Shakespeare's Romances and the Royal Family*. Lawrence: University Press of Kansas, 1985.
Studies *Pericles, Cymbeline, The Winter's Tale, The Tempest*, and *Henry VIII* from the perspective of family and politics, especially the family of James I. The plays reflect the political world of the early seventeenth century. Unlike many of his contemporaries, Shakespeare portrays the Stuarts favorably. This study tells much about the Stuarts' domestic life, but the connections between the plays and the historical events Bergeron sees reflected in them are tenuous. For example, Bergeron suggests that the death of Mamilius in *The Winter's Tale* represents the demise of Prince Henry, but the prince attended the play's first production at court (November 5, 1611).

Berry, Edward. *Shakespeare's Comic Rites*. Cambridge, England: Cambridge University Press, 1984.
A study of eight comedies from *The Comedy of Errors* to *Twelfth Night*; looks at the plays in the light of rites of passage. In these plays, the major characters suffer separation from familiar surroundings and undergo turmoil, reflected in disguises and clowning, before they are reunited with society. The rites of passages portrayed on stage mirror life in Shakespeare's England, but the plays transform reality through art. The author finds this model preferable to those of C. L. Barber (festive comedy) or Northrop Frye (green world).

Berry, Ralph. *Shakespeare's Comedies: Explorations in Form.* Princeton, N.J.:
Princeton University Press, 1972.
Treats the ten comedies that culminate with *Twelfth Night.* While each play is
different, all mock the upper class and all treat the issue of illusion versus reality.
Looks at each play in terms of its "governing idea." For example, *Love's
Labour's Lost* is concerned with language, *The Taming of the Shrew*, with wooing
and *Much Ado About Nothing* with knowing. Sees the comedies as leading
Shakespeare to the major tragedies. Takes issue with C. L. Barber's notion of
festive comedy because Berry sees the plays more closely tied to reality than to
escape. A well-written, informative study.

Brown, John Russell. *Shakespeare and His Comedies.* 2d ed. London: Methuen,
1962.
Sees a serious purpose in the comedies: "In them Shakespeare sought to affirm
a generous, true, and ordered mode of existence." He achieved this end subtly,
not through satire or explicit moralizing. Brown helps illustrate certain motifs
in the plays, all of which he sees as analyzing the nature of love. Brown's
emphasis on Shakespeare's serious intentions ignores the charm and theatricality
of the works.

Bryant, J. A., Jr. *Shakespeare and the Uses of Comedy.* Lexington: University Press
of Kentucky, 1986.
A study of sixteen plays. Bryant finds in the comedies the same sense of mortality and limits of existence that pervade the tragedies. A fascinating but dark
reading of the plays that sees Shakespeare as anticipating many of the findings
of modern psychology. Though much of what Bryant says in this regard has been
said before, he makes his points well and occasionally offers fresh readings.

Carroll, William C. *The Metamorphoses of Shakespearean Comedy.* Princeton, N.J.:
Princeton University Press, 1985.
Marriage in Shakespeare is a metamorphosis, one of many in the plays, and is
typified by the numerous changes in *A Midsummer Night's Dream.* Shakespeare
depicts both internal and external alterations—of love, language, and identity.
The broad definition of metamorphosis, from puns to resurrection, weakens the
argument, and Carroll makes little effort to distinguish between the way Shakespeare used this motif and its employment by his contemporaries. He also does
not examine varying uses of the idea in different plays. Carroll does note that
metamorphosis adds a dark tone to the comedies and so enriches them.

Champion, Larry S. *The Evolution of Shakespeare's Comedy: A Study in Dramatic
Perspective.* Cambridge, Mass.: Harvard University Press, 1972.
Creates four categories: comedies of action, comedies of identity, problem
comedies, and comedies of transformation. The earliest comedies focus on action,

and the next plays stress character. In the third group, plays deal with sin and catharsis, while the final comedies concern themselves with shifts in values. Champion's primary concern throughout is the changing way that Shakespeare treats his characters, and he sees increasing artistry in the works because the characters after 1600 develop in the course of the action. The book includes forty-five pages of notes that evaluate criticism. Highly recommended.

Charlton, H. B. *Shakespearian Comedy*. London: Methuen, 1938.
Eight lectures given annually at the John Rylands Library. Traces Shakespeare's development as a writer of comedies. Prefers the "romantic" comedies such as *A Midsummer Night's Dream*, Shakespeare's first masterpiece, to the "classical" comedies such as *The Comedy of Errors* and *The Taming of the Shrew*, plays that Charlton sees as a "recoil from romanticism." His belief in the playwright's progress led to his rearranging the chronology of the works to fit his theory, for he sees *As You Like It*, *Twelfth Night*, and *Much Ado About Nothing* as the culmination of the comedies. Charlton also maintains that Falstaff is a comic failure, and he denies the darkness of *Troilus and Cressida*, *All's Well That Ends Well*, and *Measure for Measure*. Despite its sometimes perverse readings, this book is a landmark because it was the first attempt to define the characteristics of Shakespearean comedy. More valuable today for the history of Shakespearean criticism than for its insights into the plays themselves.

Charney, Maurice, ed. *Shakespearean Comedy*. New York: New York Literary Forum, 1980.
The opening two sections discuss Shakespeare's debt to classical models—Plautus, Terence, Donatus, and Ovid. The third section looks at the darker side of pastoral, and the next section examines Falstaff and Malvolio. The work concludes with a section on theories of comedy, another that provides a translation and analysis of Evanthius and Donatus, and, finally, Malcolm Kiniry's reviews of twentieth century work on Shakespeare.

Elam, Keir. *Shakespeare's Universe of Discourse: Language-Games in the Comedies*. Cambridge, England: Cambridge University Press, 1984.
Drawing on Ludwig Wittgenstein's concept of language, Elam discusses Shakespeare's use of linguistic games in twelve of the comedies. Given Elam's interest in language, *Love's Labour's Lost* not surprisingly becomes the central text for interpreting Shakespeare. The book offers many insights into the plays and suggests a wide familiarity with theories of language, but it is not for the novice or the fainthearted because it is very difficult to read.

Evans, Bertrand. *Shakespeare's Comedies*. Oxford, England: Clarendon Press, 1960.
Evans offers a look at the seventeen comedies from the perspective of "aware-

ness"—differences in knowledge among characters and between characters and audience. Shakespeare's dramatic craftsmanship is evident in his handling of the latter. His treatment of the former suggests in the early comedies that the world is manageable by witty heroines. Later comedies present a more confused picture that requires outside intervention by Jupiter or Prospero or some such character. Throughout the comedies, the audience knows more than the characters and so enjoys the misadventures it observes. For example, in *Measure for Measure* the audience is not troubled by Angelo's plotting because it knows that the Duke will intervene to ensure a satisfactory conclusion. Evans' approach is somewhat narrow, but T. S. Dorsch wrote (in *Review of English Studies*, n.s. 12 [1961]:424) that Evans "argues his points clearly and persuasively, and there can be no doubt that he has made an important contribution to the study of Shakespearean comedy, and indeed of comedy in general."

Felperin, Howard. *Shakespearean Romance.* Princeton, N.J.: Princeton University Press, 1972.
Shakespeare draws on classical romance, medieval romance, and, most importantly, religious drama of the Middle Ages, not only in the last comedies but also in the tragedies. Felperin's book opens with a definition of romance. The second part treats Shakespeare's use of romance and distinguishes between the romances on the one hand, comedy and tragedy on the other. The third and final section offers close readings of *Pericles, Cymbeline, Henry VIII, The Winter's Tale,* and *The Tempest.* An appendix explores the popular and critical response to these plays from the seventeenth century onward. Mark Eccles called this "an exciting book, brilliantly written and a pleasure to read" (*Studies in English Literature* 13 [1973]:382).

Foakes, R. A. *Shakespeare: The Dark Comedies to the Last Plays, from Satire to Celebration.* Charlottesville: University Press of Virginia, 1971.
Focuses on the dramatic structure of the works. Sees Shakespeare as responding to the early Jacobean vogue for satiric comedy and so presenting inconsistent, inexplicable characters who fail to win the audience's sympathy. Instead, these figures become objects of analysis and satire. Foakes argues that the plays show a world ruled by chance or inscrutable Providence.

Frye, Northrop. *The Myth of Deliverance: Reflections on Shakespeare's Problem Comedies.* Toronto: University of Toronto Press, 1983.
Studies *Measure for Measure, All's Well That Ends Well,* and *Troilus and Cressida.* Argues that the first two are not "problem plays" at all but typical comedies with happy endings that inaugurate a new social order. *Troilus and Cressida* looks ahead to the last plays in its search for reality behind illusion.

_____. *A Natural Perspective: The Development of Shakespearean Comedy and Romance*. New York: Columbia University Press, 1965.

Whereas Ben Jonson seeks to create a semblance of reality on the stage, Shakespeare is concerned with telling a story that has multiple meanings. Myth, especially that of Orpheus, is central to the comedies in general and the romances in particular. Even *The Comedy of Errors* introduces the element of resurrection, as the twins' parents are reunited. The four lectures that compose the book touch on a wide variety of thought-provoking topics. Frye's approach has proved influential; many of his ideas have become commonplaces in Shakespearean criticism: the contrast between the "green world" and everyday experience; the loss and recovery of identity; patterns of loss and recovery, death and resurrection; and the rejection of blocking figures such as Shylock or Malvolio at the end of the play to allow the new society to emerge.

Hart, John A. *Dramatic Structure in Shakespeare's Romantic Comedies*. Pittsburgh: Carnegie-Mellon University Press, 1980.

Deals mainly with *A Midsummer Night's Dream*, *The Merchant of Venice*, *Much Ado About Nothing*, *As You Like It*, and *Twelfth Night*, with less attention given to *The Two Gentlemen of Verona* and *Love's Labour's Lost*. While the plotting of these plays appears disorganized, other devices operate to hold them together. In *A Midsummer Night's Dream*, *The Merchant of Venice*, and *As You Like It*, there is the contrast between the court or city and what Northrop Frye calls the green world—the woods outside Athens, Belmont, and the forest of Arden. Characters also balance each other—Jessica and Lorenzo play against Portia and Bassanio, for example. The rulers and their laws also determine the action of the comedies. Taken together, place, characters, and rules make up the world, or, more precisely, worlds, of the play. Much of the comedy derives from the pastoral world's seeing itself as the whole universe, and the multiple viewpoints allow for the nonjudgmental portraits that characterize Shakespearean comedy.

Hartwig, Joan. *Shakespeare's Tragicomic Vision*. Baton Rouge: Louisiana State University Press, 1972.

A reader-response approach that examines audience reaction to the plays' use of illusion. Shakespeare presents a world ruled by Providence, and characters must recognize their interdependence as well as their need for divine intervention. Despite the similar message in each work, Shakespeare explores different methods to convey this theme: ritual in *Pericles*, wonder in *The Winter's Tale*, and magic in *The Tempest*.

Hassel, R. Chris, Jr. *Faith and Folly in Shakespeare's Romantic Comedies*. Athens: University of Georgia Press, 1980.

A study of six early comedies: *Love's Labour's Lost*, *A Midsummer Night's Dream*, *Much Ado About Nothing*, *As You Like It*, *Twelfth Night*, and *The*

Merchant of Venice. Finds in the plays an expression of Christian doctrines concerning faith and folly, love and charity. Hassel does not argue that Shakespeare held particular religious beliefs, only that the plays draw on ideas and quotations emphasizing the need for humility and recognition of one's limited knowledge. Recognition of one's folly leads to fulfillment.

Hunt, Maurice. *Shakespeare's Romance of the Word.* Lewisburg, Pa.: Bucknell University Press, 1990.
This study of the language of *Pericles, Cymbeline, The Winter's Tale,* and *The Tempest* argues that these plays depict redemption through their linguistic devices. Faulty communication leads to problems that are resolved through improved speech that overcomes limitations. Admitting that the plays are not merely about language, Hunt illuminates the various manipulations of words in these works, tying the plays to the traditions of pastoral and romance and to Renaissance theories of rhetoric.

Hunter, Robert G. *Shakespeare and the Comedy of Forgiveness.* New York: Columbia University Press, 1965.
Concentrates on *Much Ado About Nothing, All's Well That Ends Well, Measure for Measure, The Winter's Tale, Cymbeline,* and *The Tempest.* Two chapters discuss medieval and Renaissance models for a drama of forgiveness that is largely but not rigidly Christian. Shakespeare focuses on salvation in this world through contrition and pardon, two ingredients necessary for comic resolution in the plays. Though he focuses only on this aspect of the plays, Hunter demonstrates that it is an important element. The readings offered here, however, may seem skewed at times. To suit his theories, he must make Alonso the central figure of *The Tempest* and concentrate on Claudio rather than Benedict in *Much Ado About Nothing.*

Huston, J. Dennis. *Shakespeare's Comedies of Play.* New York: Columbia University Press, 1981.
Finds in *The Comedy of Errors, Love's Labour's Lost, The Taming of the Shrew, A Midsummer Night's Dream,* and *Much Ado About Nothing* a focus on play on many levels. Shakespeare plays with audience expectations, there are plays within plays, and characters play with words, often in play worlds drawn from fairy tales. Argues that the last of these works is less festive than the others because it recognizes that illusion can deceive and destroy as well as create. This sober realization suggests Shakespeare's increased artistic maturity.

Jensen, Ejner. *Shakespeare and the Ends of Comedy.* Bloomington: Indiana University Press, 1991.
Despite their differences, both Northrop Frye and C. L. Barber have focused attention on the endings of comedy. Jensen dissents in favor of a moment-by-

moment appreciation that highlights the lighter elements of these plays. Thus, Jensen writes that "the joyousness of *The Merchant of Venice* is not . . . something that emerges only at its close. It is there throughout the play, and it is communicated chiefly through the device of onstage performers acting out their roles before an onstage audience." Also looks at *Much Ado About Nothing, As You Like It, Twelfth Night,* and *Measure for Measure,* all of which Jensen finds less problematic than many other modern critics.

Kay, Carol McGinnis, and Henry E. Jacobs, eds. *Shakespeare's Romances Reconsidered.* Lincoln: University of Nebraska Press, 1978.
Eleven essays on *Pericles, Cymbeline, The Winter's Tale,* and *The Tempest*; one essay surveys criticism of these works. Includes a bibliography of some six hundred titles dealing with the late comedies. Offers a range of approaches and views. Thus, Northrop Frye treats the romances as fusions of Greek Old Comedy and Roman New Comedy into a mythic pattern. Howard Felperin responds, arguing that Frye's scheme oversimplifies. Some essays are more conventional than others, but all are helpful. F. David Hoeniger opened his review (in *Shakespeare Quarterly* 31 [1980]:101) by declaring, "I recommend this book strongly" despite its inclusion of some weak pieces.

Krieger, Elliot. *A Marxist Study of Shakespeare's Comedies.* London: Macmillan, 1979.
Krieger looks at *The Merchant of Venice, A Midsummer Night's Dream, As You Like It, Twelfth Night,* and *1 Henry IV* and finds class struggle implicit in the movement from the world of the court to another, second world such as Belmont or Eastcheap. Shakespeare undercuts the aristocratic attempt to equate universal values with the rulers' values. The book is provocative but limited because of its insistence on its ideology.

Lawrence, William Witherle. *Shakespeare's Problem Comedies.* Rev. ed. Harmondsworth, England: Penguin Books, 1969.
A reprint of the 1931 edition with an updated bibliography. Good on the tradition behind Shakespeare's late comedies *All's Well That Ends Well, Measure for Measure, Troilus and Cressida,* and *Cymbeline.* These literary antecedents condition audience response. Bertram's change of heart in *All's Well That Ends Well,* for example, would be accepted by Elizabethan audiences as part of the convention; hence there are no dark shadows lurking in the ending of the play. Lawrence argues against applying realistic standards in judging these plays; they were meant to entertain. They do, however, treat serious matters and could easily become tragedies. Reviewing the 1931 edition, Peter Alexander remarked that "Professor Lawrence's judgment is equal to his learning, which is extensive and accurate, and he has written a very helpful book" (*Review of English Studies* 8 [1932]:336).

Leech, Clifford. *"Twelfth Night" and Shakespearean Comedy*. Halifax, Nova Scotia: Dalhousie University Press, 1965.
Traces the evolution of Shakespearean comedy. In "The Beginnings," Leech focuses on *The Two Gentlemen of Verona* and sees the early comedies as burlesques rather than romance interspersed with comic elements. Valentine's offering of Silvia to Proteus should not be taken seriously but rather seen as a satire on the cult of friendship. The second chapter addresses *Twelfth Night* as following Sir Philip Sidney's preference for "delight" over "laughter," yet the play also maintains a disquieting undertone. The book concludes with a study of the late comedies—especially *Troilus and Cressida* and *The Winter's Tale*—in which Shakespeare successfully fuses "the sense of triumph with the sense of defeat, a rejoicing in the nature of things with an insistence on human limitations." M. M. Mahood remarked that the three lectures that constitute the book are "eloquent without either modishness or pedantry" (*Modern Language Review* 65 [1970]:378).

Leggatt, Alexander. *Shakespeare's Comedy of Love*. London: Methuen, 1973.
Looks at nine comedies to *Twelfth Night*. With sensitivity to the plays as theater, Leggatt notes the ways that reality confronts illusion. Though the plays all treat this same issue, each comedy develops in its own manner. Leggatt sees the endings as generally contrived because they banish the darker possibilities inherent in life. Much good discussion of the characters.

Lerner, Laurence, ed. *Shakespeare's Comedies: An Anthology of Modern Criticism*. Harmondsworth, England: Penguin Books, 1967.
Assembles important essays dealing with the comedies of the 1590s. Most of the anthology presents pieces on particular plays, from *The Comedy of Errors* to *The Merry Wives of Windsor*, reprinting such seminal discussions as C. L. Barber on *As You Like It* and W. H. Auden on *Twelfth Night*. A concluding section looks at Shakespearean comedy more generally. Among the authors represented here are George Meredith, Northrop Frye, and H. B. Charlton. An excellent introduction for the student beginning research on a topic or for the general reader, who will find here sound explications of the works.

Levin, Richard A. *Love and Society in Shakespearean Comedy: A Study of Dramatic Form and Content*. Newark: University of Delaware Press, 1985.
Treats *The Merchant of Venice*, *Much Ado About Nothing*, and *Twelfth Night*, with references to *As You Like It*. These plays are not romantic comedies for Levin but rather studies in how one improves one's social status through marriage. He does not deny that love appears in the plays, but love is only one factor in bringing men and women together. Outsiders are not less good than those who succeed, only less well connected. Levin offers a darker reading of these comedies than standard interpretations suggest and fails to distinguish between the moral qualities of the successful and unsuccessful characters.

MacCary, W. Thomas. *Friends and Lovers: The Phenomenology of Desire in Shakespearean Comedy*. New York: Columbia University Press, 1985.

Studies ten comedies and concludes that Shakespeare's male lovers pass through four stages—from self-love, to love of reflected self in twin or friend, to love of a young woman like themselves, to true love of a woman seen as an individual. A helpful summary reviews the book's major arguments. Sees the plays' central concern as not marriage but the evolving nature of love.

Macdonald, Ronald R. *William Shakespeare: The Comedies*. New York: Twayne, 1992.

Introductory essays to ten plays, from *The Comedy of Errors* through *Twelfth Night*. Macdonald offers some useful reminders in his discussions; for example, he notes that in *As You Like It* the Forest of Arden does not offer absolute freedom, and that play's resolution balances self and society. The book concludes that while the ten comedies differ, all explore "the dialectic of self and other, individual and collective, the one and the many," and the question of maturation. For Macdonald, the comedies are as intellectually provocative as the tragedies. Good for undergraduates; advanced students will find nothing new here.

McFarland, Thomas. *Shakespeare's Pastoral Comedy*. Chapel Hill: University of North Carolina Press, 1972.

Looks at *Love's Labour's Lost*, *A Midsummer Night's Dream*, *As You Like It*, *The Winter's Tale*, and *The Tempest* to find a common thread running through them: a critique of real life through the use of pastoral. The plays hold out the possibility of a new golden age. McFarland discusses Shakespeare's unconventional handling of pastoral—the use of winter landscapes, for example. An appendix discusses Falstaff as an outcast from the world of pastoral. Norman Rabkin called the study "a fresh and valuable addition to the small library of first-rate books on Shakespeare" (*Modern Language Quarterly* 35 [1974]:195).

Mowat, Barbara A. *The Dramaturgy of Shakespeare's Romances*. Athens: University of Georgia Press, 1976.

Looks at *Cymbeline*, *The Winter's Tale*, and *The Tempest* from the viewpoint of certain dramatic issues. The first chapter treats the blending of comedy and tragedy; the second deals with presentation versus representation; the third examines the use of plot and narrative; the fourth contrasts open and closed forms; and the fifth considers the plays' meaning. Isolating individual scenes, Mowat sometimes distorts the impact of the action. Leontes' jealousy may be comic in itself, but in the context of the play it is not. She does point out connections with earlier plays (Leontes has much in common with Othello) and suggest that the earlier comedies resolve problems and create a new order in the final scenes, whereas the last plays attempt to return to the status quo of the opening—an effort that only partially succeeds.

Muir, Kenneth, ed. *Shakespeare: The Comedies*. Englewood Cliffs, N.J.: Prentice-Hall, 1965.
Twelve essays on the comedies, from John Middleton Murry's 1936 chapter on *The Merchant of Venice* to Harold Brooks's 1961 piece on *The Comedy of Errors*. Among the other important contributors are Clifford Leech, R. W. Chambers, M. C. Bradbrook, and G. Wilson Knight. Muir's introduction surveys criticism from H. B. Charlton's 1938 study (*Shakespearean Comedy*) to the mid-1960s and places the anthologized essays in their critical context. Includes a chronology and a selected bibliography. A useful compilation.

_____. *Shakespeare's Comic Sequence*. Liverpool, England: Liverpool University Press, 1979.
Denies that one can speak of Shakespearean comedy because each play differs so much from the others. Discusses Shakespeare's debt to Roman comedy, interludes, and medieval moralities; sees the plays as didactic. Maurice Charney recommended the volume to undergraduates because of its "easy learning, judiciousness, and a gracefully humanistic style and range of references" (*Modern Language Review* 77 [1982]:407).

Muir, Kenneth, and Stanley Wells, eds. *Aspects of Shakespeare's Problem Plays: "All's Well That Ends Well," "Measure for Measure," "Troilus and Cressida."* Cambridge, England: Cambridge University Press, 1982.
Reprints articles from *Shakespeare Survey*, including reviews of productions. Among the pieces included is R. L. Smallwood's examination of the changes that Shakespeare made from his sources in *All's Well That Ends Well*; Smallwood concludes that the play ends with hope for the future. Roger Warren looks at that play from the perspective of the sonnets and finds the triumph of love. Elizabeth Marie Pope illuminates the Christian view underlying *Measure for Measure*; Harriett Hawkins challenges that reading. Muir and R. A. Yoder offer sympathetic readings of the enigmatic *Troilus and Cressida*, and Michael Jamieson surveys critical approaches to the play from 1920 to 1970.

Nevo, Ruth. *Comic Transformations in Shakespeare*. London: Methuen, 1980.
Studies ten early comedies and sees progress in their art as the heroes and (especially) the heroines become more perceptive and as the plays incline less to polarities. Nevo explores Shakespeare's debt to Roman New Comedy and analyzes how Shakespeare's complications enrich his plays. Nevo also discusses the therapeutic nature of comedy. An appendix argues for Lewis Theobald's act and scene division of *Love's Labour's Lost*, rather than the First Folio arrangement.

Newman, Karen. *Shakespeare's Rhetoric of Comic Character: Dramatic Convention in Classical and Renaissance Comedy*. London: Methuen, 1985.

Looks at monologues and soliloquies to see how they reveal characters' complexities. Newman explores Shakespeare's debt to classical rhetoric and contemporary practice. She does not explain how Shakespeare differs from his contemporaries, nor does she resolve the long-noted dichotomy between realistic characters and contrived plots in the works. Good on the rhetorical traditions and dramatic conventions upon which Shakespeare draws.

Ornstein, Robert. *Shakespeare's Comedies: From Roman Farce to Romantic Mystery*. Newark: University of Delaware Press, 1986.
Examines thirteen comedies, largely by means of character analysis. Like a number of other mid-1980s studies of the comedies, Ornstein's finds many dark elements but regards the plays as finally triumphant and sympathetic to human failure. His account is readable and offers many new insights through its close examination of the plays. Many maligned figures are rehabilitated; Helena in *A Midsummer Night's Dream*, for example, emerges as stronger than she is usually understood. Other figures fare less well. Ornstein dislikes Petruchio and Cymbeline, perhaps because he is seeking realism in the characters. Andrew Leggatt concluded that this book "is full of sharp illumination, and of finely balanced, thoughtful readings. . . . It is, all told, a welcome contribution to the study of Shakespearean comedy" (*English Language Notes* 25 [1987]:87).

Palmer, David, and Malcolm Bradbury, eds. *Shakespearean Comedy*. Stratford-upon-Avon Studies 14. New York: Crane, Russak, 1972.
Includes ten essays and a brief survey of criticism. John Russell Brown, Stanley Wells, and Anne Barton look at the structure of the comedies. R. A. Foakes, Gareth Lloyd Evans, and Tony Nuttall focus on character types. Inga-Stina Ewbank interprets *The Two Gentlemen of Verona*, John Dixon Hunt writes on the courtly values of *Love's Labour's Lost*, Palmer treats *The Merchant of Venice*, and Jocelyn Powell examines the theatrical effects of *Measure for Measure*.

_____, eds. *Shakespeare's Later Comedies: An Anthology of Modern Criticism*. Harmondsworth, England: Penguin Books, 1971.
A companion to Laurence Lerner's *Shakespeare's Comedies* (1967), this volume deals with the comedies of the 1600s. Reprints a wide range of criticism, most of it from the 1950s and 1960s but including Samuel Taylor Coleridge's comments on *The Tempest*. Though any selection will omit some important material, this anthology will serve students well as an introduction to the criticism of these rich, elusive works.

Palmer, John Leslie. *Comic Characters of Shakespeare*. London: Macmillan, 1946.
Left incomplete at the author's death, this book treats the principal comic characters in *Love's Labour's Lost*, *As You Like It*, *The Merchant of Venice*, *A Midsum-*

mer Night's Dream, and *Much Ado About Nothing.* Sees the essence of Shakespearean comedy as joy and harmony, most clearly represented through the marriages that conclude the works. Much of the book presents Palmer's favorite passages and his interpretations. Some of these, like the reading of Dogberry, are enlightening. Elsewhere, Palmer is less convincing. If Shylock is the main character of *The Merchant of Venice,* then the play is a strange sort of comedy. Is Hero the focus of *Much Ado About Nothing,* or are Beatrice and Benedict, who in any case "run away with the play"?

Peterson, Douglas L. *Time, Tide, and Tempest: A Study of Shakespeare's Romances.* San Marino, Calif.: Huntington Library, 1973.
Draws on Renaissance ideas of time and on the emblem tradition to interpret *Pericles, Cymbeline, The Winter's Tale,* and *The Tempest.* These plays are not realistic but emblematic, intended to demonstrate moral truths and the underlying nature of the observed world. Characters' reaction to time as providential or mechanical marks one distinction between the good and the bad, and tempest represent divine intervention. These plays reject Jacobean skepticism by explicitly accepting a providential universe: "Whatever the follies of men, their depravity and inconstancy, and despite the seeming indifference of nature, the gods protect and finally crown the virtuous with happiness." A well-researched exploration that offers much information on how Shakespeare's contemporaries viewed these plays.

Pettet, E. C. *Shakespeare and the Romance Tradition.* London: Staples Press, 1949.
Examines Shakespeare's use of prose and poetic romances; Pettet sees these as more influential than classical or medieval drama in shaping the comedies. Interprets the later comedies as a critique of the way romances treat love, though Pettet notes that even the early plays offer realistic assessments that comment on the ideals of the lovers. Thus *Romeo and Juliet* (included here) presents the Nurse and Mercutio as well as the star-crossed hero and heroine. Best on the romantic comedies, less successful with the later works discussed because Pettet is less appreciative of them.

Phialas, Peter G. *Shakespeare's Romantic Comedies: The Development of Their Form and Meaning.* Chapel Hill: University of North Carolina Press, 1966.
Studies the relationship among structure, theme, and character in the comedies to *Twelfth Night.* Shakespeare uses the structure of New Comedy but adds internal, psychological barriers to a happy ending. The comedies end not only with the union of hero and heroine but also with integration of the individual. Love gives meaning to life, and Rosalind (*As You Like It*) is the perfect heroine because she can balance the ideals of love with its reality. Argues that Shakespeare's ability to present his views and to develop characters matures as his career progresses. A wordy but still enlightening analysis.

Richman, David. *Laughter, Pain, and Wonder: Shakespeare's Comedies and the Audience in the Theater.* Newark: University of Delaware Press, 1990.
Arguing from the perspective of a producer and theatergoer, Richman sees the three elements in his title as essential to Shakespearean comedy, with the evocation of a sense of wonder being unique to these plays. Richman draws on these ideas to interpret the plays, especially from the perspective of how they should be presented to audiences to achieve full effect. For example, he argues that Malvolio's confinement—often presented in grim detail on stage—should not be seen because presenting Malvolio's suffering weakens the humor of the episode. Richman advocates a strict reading of the stage directions here in the First Folio: "Malvolio within," which Richman applies to the entire scene.

Riemer, A. P. *Antic Fables: Patterns of Evasion in Shakespeare's Comedies.* New York: St. Martin's Press, 1980.
Claims that Shakespeare toys with convention to create plays that at once surprise and delight. Thus, *Love's Labour's Lost* ends without the expected marriage of the couples. *Measure for Measure* ends happily but contains many dark elements. The plays thereby celebrate artifice and call attention to the ambiguities of existence.

Salinger, Leo G. *Shakespeare and the Traditions of Comedy.* Cambridge, England: Cambridge University Press, 1974.
Looks at Shakespeare's sources. Medieval romance provided the trials that lovers endure and the family divisions and reunions. Roman comedy contributed disguises and mistaken identity. Plays from the Italian Renaissance suggested the double plot, and the Italian novella offered legal complications and threatened marriages. Some plays, such as *The Comedy of Errors*, depend heavily on classical tradition as modified by Renaissance practice. Others, such as *Much Ado About Nothing*, derive from the Italian novella, while those set in the "green world" draw mostly from romances. A valuable exploration of these sources, though Salinger sometimes fails to recognize the plays' rejection of earlier conventions. The forest of Arden, for example, may derive from Ovid's description of the Golden Age, but Shakespeare undercuts the pastoral ideal. Still, a learned and comprehensive study.

Sen Gupta, S. C. *Shakespearean Comedy.* London: Oxford University Press, 1950.
Opens with a discussion of theories of comedy (chapter 1) and the practice of English comedy (chapter 2). The next six chapters trace Shakespeare's art from the early comedies to the last plays, and the last chapter discusses Falstaff. Focuses on character, which Sen Gupta sees as the central concern of these plays: "The *real excellence* of a Shakespearean comedy lies . . . in the unity and diversity, logic and inconsistency, vividness and incomprehensibility, which mark his study of *human personality.*"

Smidt, Kristian. *Unconformities in Shakespeare's Early Comedies*. New York: St. Martin's Press, 1986.
A sequel to Smidt's study of the histories. The introduction discusses ideas about and types of comedy current in Shakespeare's day. Subsequent chapters examine the comedies to *The Merchant of Venice*. As in the earlier book, Smidt looks at inconsistencies in the plays to determine Shakespeare's methods of composition and to note difficulties not always overcome. Sometimes overemphasizes seeming contradictions.

Smith, Hallett. *Shakespeare's Romances: A Study of Some Ways of the Imagination*. San Marino, Calif.: Huntington Library, 1972.
Begins with a discussion of romance and the connections between Shakespeare's comedies and tragedies on the one hand and his last works on the other. The main portion of the book compares Thomas Lodge's *Rosalynde* and *As You Like It*, *Pandosto* and *The Winter's Tale*, *A Midsummer Night's Dream* and *The Tempest*. Smith concludes with chapters on landscape, scenery, and style. Appendices examine mythological criticism (much of which Smith condemns) and the relationship of the romances to contemporary events. Despite some reservations, Robert Ornstein observed that "Shakespeareans will enjoy the many insights into the last plays which this book affords. Students will profit from its store of useful information about romance tradition and Shakespeare's use of source materials" (*Modern Philology* 71 [1973]:426).

Swinden, Patrick. *An Introduction to Shakespeare's Comedies*. London: Macmillan, 1973.
A brief introduction intended for the beginning student. The first chapter discusses the nature of Shakespearean comedy, focusing on the sense of play and games. Short chapters then treat thirteen plays and Falstaff. The work concludes with a brief bibliography. Adopts C. L. Barber's view of these works as festive. Swinden's judgments, generally sound, sometimes oversimplify. He dismisses some of the early comedies as pure farce, and he sees *The Merchant of Venice* and *Much Ado About Nothing* as muddled.

Thomas, Vivian. *The Moral Universe of Shakespeare's Problem Plays*. Totowa, N.J.: Barnes & Noble Books, 1987.
After surveying criticism of Shakespeare's problem plays—*Troilus and Cressida*, *All's Well That Ends Well*, and *Measure for Measure*—Thomas offers his own understanding of their nature. Among his observations are that they defy genre, puzzle the audience, question authority, and explore the underlying darker reality beneath an attractive surface. The plays create distance between audience and actors, introduce detractors rather than clowns, examine ideas of honor and sex, and produce disillusion. The societies portrayed are flawed. The plays raise questions but fail to resolve them. Thomas denies that Shakespeare is working

within a religious context and sees *Troilus and Cressida* as Shakespeare's crowning achievement.

Tillyard, E. M. W. *Shakespeare's Early Comedies*. London: Chatto & Windus, 1965.
Treats *The Comedy of Errors*, *The Taming of the Shrew*, *The Two Gentlemen of Verona*, *Love's Labour's Lost*, and *The Merchant of Venice*. Begins by looking at Shakespeare's sources in romance, drama, and folk festival. Sees the comedies linked chiefly by their common concern with social interaction. Shakespearean comedy delights in the marvelous and in the fulfillment of daydreams. Tillyard died before he finished revising this book, so it contradicts itself in places and fails to develop some of its ideas. Nevertheless, the interpretations offer many new insights, and Tillyard's pronouncements are always worth reading.

_____. *Shakespeare's Last Plays*. London: Chatto & Windus, 1938.
Short but important study of *Cymbeline*, *The Winter's Tale*, and *The Tempest* that offered new ways of looking at these works, not as romantic comedies but as romances. Rejected the then fashionable views that saw them as imitations of Francis Beaumont and John Fletcher, reflections of Shakespeare's boredom, not entirely successful attempts to break away from the tragedies that preceded them, efforts to capitalize on the popularity of masques in the private theaters, or failures compared to the earlier works. Tillyard noted that the plays follow the movement of tragedy—prosperity followed by reversal and regeneration—but add "planes of reality tending to the religious" to become redemptive and comment on human nature. The criticism is impressionistic rather than detailed.

_____. *Shakespeare's Problem Plays*. Toronto: University of Toronto Press, 1949.
Treats *All's Well That Ends Well*, *Measure for Measure*, *Troilus and Cressida*, and *Hamlet*. Sees the plays as dealing with doctrinal issues of justice and mercy. The plays are serious but not gloomy; they are aware of evil, but evil does not triumph over goodness. In these plays, young men mature and old values confront new, each of these flawed in some way. *All's Well That Ends Well* and *Measure for Measure* anticipate the final plays, which more successfully deal with forgiveness.

Toole, William B. *Shakespeare's Problem Plays: Studies in Form and Meaning*. The Hague: Mouton, 1966.
Objecting to the phrase assigned to *Hamlet*, *All's Well That Ends Well*, *Measure for Measure*, and *Troilus and Cressida*, Toole nevertheless sees connections among the plays. All four rely on a "pattern of temptation, sin, remorse, repentance, penance, and pardon." This scheme derives from medieval morality and mystery plays. Toole offers good interpretations of the medieval works and

Dante, whose view of comedy he sees as Shakespeare's: a reflection of salvation through grace. Bertram saves Helena, the Duke and Mariana save Angelo, and Hamlet saves himself. Toole may overemphasize his model. Contains a good survey of criticism in the opening chapter.

Traversi, Derek. *Shakespeare: The Last Phase*. Stanford, Calif.: Stanford University Press, 1955.
A study of *Pericles, Cymbeline, The Winter's Tale*, and *The Tempest*. Sees the plays as concerned with the loss and recovery of a child, a pattern that first appears in *King Lear*. The plays are symbolic, not realistic; failure to recognize this fact has led to misunderstanding and dissatisfaction. For Traversi, these works are Shakespeare's greatest achievement.

Uphaus, Robert W. *Beyond Tragedy: Structure and Experience in Shakespeare's Romances*. Lexington: University Press of Kentucky, 1981.
Argues that Shakespeare's romances emphasize life's continuation even in the face of individual death. By focusing on resurrection and renewal, these plays offer a second chance; time is reversible. Providence rules, probability is defied, and so the plays challenge commonly held views of reality and art.

Weil, Herbert, Jr., ed. *Discussions of Shakespeare's Romantic Comedy*. Boston: D. C. Heath, 1966.
An anthology offering a wide range of essays, from Samuel Johnson's observations on *As You Like It* and *Twelfth Night* to Charles Lamb's discussion of Malvolio in *Twelfth Night* to more modern interpretations. C. L. Barber and Northrop Frye are, of course, represented, as are critics who are less familiar. Weil includes several essays on *Much Ado About Nothing, As You Like It*, and *Twelfth Night*, allowing the reader a multiplicity of views. The compensating loss is the absence of any discussion of the late comedies as well as *The Two Gentlemen of Verona, The Taming of the Shrew, The Merchant of Venice*, and *A Midsummer Night's Dream*. Good for the plays covered.

Westlund, Joseph. *Shakespearean Reparative Comedy: A Psychological View of the Middle Plays*. Chicago: University of Chicago Press, 1984.
A study of *The Merchant of Venice, Much Ado About Nothing, As You Like It, Twelfth Night, All's Well That Ends Well*, and *Measure for Measure*. Intended for the general reader, this book examines the way these comedies overcome conflict and thereby help audiences deal with their own hostilities. When the lovers find their ideal mates, audiences enjoy the wish fulfillment of the characters and themselves. Plays that question this ideal are also restorative because they put spectators in contact with reality.

White, R. S. *"Let Wonder Seem Familiar"*: *Endings in Shakespeare's Romance Vision*. Atlantic Heights, N.J.: Humanities Press, 1985.
Argues that the open-ended mode of romance lets Shakespeare present multiple views of truth, all of them at once correct and suspect. The extreme artifice constitutes an accurate picture of elusive reality. A brief appendix traces the origins of Elizabethan prose romance and its translation to the stage. White's argument is illuminating but turns virtually every Shakespearean play into a romance.

Williamson, Marilyn L. *The Patriarchy of Shakespeare's Comedies*. Detroit: Wayne State University Press, 1986.
Draws on feminist and historical analysis to explain the changes in Shakespeare's comedies over the years. In the 1590s, Shakespeare presented powerful women and profitable marriages because these fantasies fulfilled audience needs. With the accession of James I, the plays turn to powerful men and forced marriages as the Parliament considers stricter control over private behavior. *Measure for Measure*, to cite one example, reflects efforts to regulate sexual activity and responds to the concern that such restrictions might affect gentlemen as well as the poor. The last comedies support Jacobean ideals by equating king and father as natural rulers of their respective domains: state and family.

Wilson, John Dover. *Shakespeare's Happy Comedies*. Evanston, Ill.: Northwestern University Press, 1962.
The happy comedies are *The Comedy of Errors*, *The Two Gentlemen of Verona*, *Love's Labour's Lost*, *The Merchant of Venice*, *As You Like It*, *Twelfth Night*, *A Midsummer Night's Dream*, *The Merry Wives of Windsor*, and *Much Ado About Nothing*. All but *The Merry Wives of Windsor* have a Continental or Mediterranean setting, much clowning, and noble friends and lovers. Despite their common elements, each play is different; Shakespeare was too great an artist to tie himself to any formula. Though the observations here are not profound, and though Wilson ignores most of the criticism about the plays, the book is readable and informative. Especially useful as an introduction to the early comedies.

Young, David P. *The Heart's Forest: A Study of Shakespeare's Pastoral Plays*. New Haven, Conn.: Yale University Press, 1972.
An examination of *As You Like It*, *King Lear*, *The Winter's Tale*, and *The Tempest*. Argues that all four draw on pastoral conventions, such as the opposition of urban and rural, court and country. Central characters are exiled into nature and then return. Yet, Shakespeare questions the pastoral assumptions of humanity's harmonious relationship with nature and comments on the values and limitations of art. Young's study concludes with a discussion of the staging of pastorals.

Histories

Armstrong, William A., ed. *Shakespeare's Histories: An Anthology of Modern Criticism*. Harmondsworth, England: Penguin Books, 1972.
Armstrong's introduction surveys the critical and theatrical history of these works. Following an annotated bibliography, the volume presents twelve essays. Irving Ribner and S. C. Sen Gupta discuss the nature of the history plays. J. P. Brockbank looks at the way *Henry VI* creates and questions community. A. P. Rossiter examines the structure of *Richard III*. For William H. Matchett, the central issue in *King John* is who should rule and by what right. Peter Ure and Sir John Gielgud discuss *Richard II*; Harold Jenkins sees *2 Henry IV* as repeating some of the material found in the first part. A. R. Humphreys focuses on Falstaff, M. M. Reese on *Henry V*, and Frank Kermode on *Henry VIII*. Arthur Colby Sprague concludes the volume with a brief stage history amplifying Armstrong's prefatory remarks.

Berry, Edward. *Patterns of Decay: Shakespeare's Early Histories*. Charlottesville: University Press of Virginia. 1975.
Sees a unity in the first tetralogy. *1 Henry VI* offers a vision of heroic chivalry exemplified by Talbot. As the *Henry VI* plays continue, society degenerates into civil war and tyranny because old bonds of allegiance are broken and replaced by progressively tenuous ones. Berry argues that the works are further unified by episodes in one play that are mirrored in another. A concluding chapter discusses the later histories, which Berry sees as focusing more on character, less on events. Cogently and concisely argued.

Bloom, Harold, ed. *William Shakespeare: Histories and Poems*. New York: Chelsea House, 1986.
A collection of previously published material. Includes a brief bibliography and an engaging introduction by Bloom on Falstaff, in which he uses the character to demonstrate the inadequacy of Marxist and deconstructionist interpretations of Shakespeare. Among the classical works excerpted here are E. M. W. Tillyard's *Shakespeare's History Plays* (1944) on *Richard II*, C. L. Barber's *Shakespeare's Festive Comedy* (1959) for *Henry IV*, and A. P. Rossiter's *Angel with Horns* (1961) about *Richard III*.

Blanpied, John W. *Time and the Artist in Shakespeare's English Histories*. Newark: University of Delaware Press, 1983.
Shakespeare progresses from an objective recorder of facts to a commentator on the relationship between past and present. The kings shift from "antic" revelers in freedom to Machiavellian controllers of the plays' action and audience response. Yet the antic does not vanish, as Falstaff most clearly demonstrates in *Henry IV*. When Blanpied attempts to extrapolate from the plays to their creator, his arguments are unconvincing.

Calderwood, James L. *Metadrama in Shakespeare's Henriad*. Berkeley: University of California Press, 1979.
A study of Shakespeare's language in the second tetralogy. Richard II believes that words are reality. His successor, Bolingbroke, uses language for convenience. Falstaff, like Richard II (and Shakespeare), uses words to create a world. Henry V, whom Calderwood admires, uses language to move others to action. The early death of Henry V suggests to Shakespeare the insubstantial nature of the dramatic enterprise. A complex argument clearly presented.

Campbell, Lily Bess. *Shakespeare's "Histories": Mirrors of Elizabethan Policy*. San Marino, Calif.: Huntington Library, 1947.
Looks at *King John, Richard II, Henry IV, Henry V*, and *Richard III*. Begins with a study of Renaissance historiography and relates the plays to contemporary political concerns, such as the obligations of kingship and the dangers of rebellion. Sees the plays as supporting Tudor orthodoxy. Campbell sometimes pushes too hard on analogies between England's past and Shakespeare's present; she is excellent when discussing the age's view of history.

Champion, Larry S. *"The Noise of Threatening Drum": Dramatic Strategy and Political Ideology in Shakespeare and the English Chronicle Plays*. Newark: University of Delaware Press, 1990.
Looks at thirteen plays, eight of them by Shakespeare (*1, 2, 3 Henry VI, King John, Richard II, 1, 2 Henry IV*, and *Henry V*). Finds in all of them an ambiguity and complexity that would appeal to a variety of viewpoints held by a diverse audience. Censorship prevented overt subversion of authority, but the plays do not uncritically endorse orthodoxy. The ambivalence of the plays mirrors Renaissance historiography in recognizing the complexity of interpreting events.

_____. *Perspectives in Shakespeare's English Histories*. Athens: University of Georgia Press, 1980.
Analyzes the histories in separate chapters. Champion sees a balance between historical panorama and focus on character. Some plays, such as *Richard II*, tilt more to the latter; others, such as *Henry V*, to the former. Unlike the tragedies, however, all include a concern with historical events that is demonstrated by diverse settings, multiple plots, and essentially static characters.

Coursen, Herbert R. *The Leasing Out of England: Shakespeare's Second Henriad*. Washington, D.C.: University Press of America, 1982.
Sees a decline from the Edenic world lost by Richard II. Henry IV's world is still more corrupt, and Henry V only temporarily stays the decay that will lead to the Wars of the Roses. Argues that Providence plays no role in the works; Shakespeare shows the survival of the fittest. The book is physically unattractive but offers sound, well-supported arguments.

Holderness, Graham. *Shakespeare's History*. New York: St. Martin's Press, 1985.
A Marxist reading that sees Shakespeare's plays as demonstrating sophisticated historical understanding, especially of feudal society. The book criticizes other commentators and productions of the plays as nationalistic. Often enlightening, occasionally abstruse.

Hodgdon, Barbara. *The End Crowns All: Closure and Contradiction in Shakespeare's History*. Princeton, N.J.: Princeton University Press, 1991.
The analysis of endings in the ten English history plays provides a means of understanding the works' legitimization of royalty and absolute power. At the same time, the endings subtly challenge received views about monarchy. Hodgdon looks not only at the text but also at various productions to note how they ignore or exploit the contradictions inherent in the works. For example, Richard II can be seen as Elizabeth, Bolingbroke as Essex, but Essex also resembles Richard II, returning from an unsuccessful Irish campaign to be imprisoned and executed.

Jones, Robert C. *These Valiant Dead: Renewing the Past in Shakespeare's Histories*. Iowa City: University of Iowa Press, 1991.
In this study of the two tetralogies and *King John*, Jones looks at how Shakespeare uses the image of the fallen leader. The plays, especially in the second tetralogy, recognize the fictional nature of history and its glorification of dead heroes, but these works also indicate a belief in the value of such evocations. The book offers a reading of each of the nine plays in terms of its attitude towards history. *1 Henry IV*, for example, largely ignores the past; *I Henry VI* repeatedly invokes the heroism of Henry V and Talbot as models that could inspire English success. Richard III seeks to bury the past, but it returns to overwhelm him in his dreams before the battle of Bosworth Field.

Kelly, Henry A. *Divine Providence in the England of Shakespeare's Histories*. Cambridge, Mass.: Harvard University Press, 1970.
Begins with a good survey of fifteenth and sixteenth century histories and then examines *A Mirror for Magistrates* and Samuel Daniel's *The Civile Warres* (1595-1609) before turning to Shakespeare's two tetralogies. Denies a providential view in the plays or in the chronicles that served as sources, which reveals not only a Tudor myth but also a Yorkist myth and a Lancaster myth. Argues that Shakespeare allows his characters to take sides in this controversy, but the dramatist remains silent.

Ornstein, Robert. *A Kingdom for a Stage: The Achievement of Shakespeare's History Plays*. Cambridge, Mass.: Harvard University Press, 1972.
Denies that the plays posit a providential universe or a Tudor ideology. Regards the plays as treating the same themes that pervade the comedies and tragedies:

the danger of violating human bonds and the need for loyalty not only to one's king but also to one's family and friends if society is to survive. Shakespeare portrays history as personal: "The height of treachery in *Henry IV Part I* is not Worcester's conspiracy against the king but his betrayal of his nephew Hotspur at Shrewsbury." "A fresh and stimulating reappraisal of Shakespeare's achievement in the English Histories," according to Andrew S. Cairncross (*Renaissance Quarterly* 26 [1973]: 234). Derek A. Traversi called the study "a first-rate piece of criticism" (*Modern Language Quarterly* 34 [1973]: 318).

Pierce, Robert B. *Shakespeare's History Plays: The Family and the State*. Columbus: Ohio State University Press, 1971.
Focuses on the ways Shakespeare uses family in the plays. In *Henry IV*, for example, disorder in the family mirrors civil strife. In *Richard II*, the fate of families highlights the tragic events in the play. In *3 Henry VI*, a father's discovery that he has killed his son and a son's discovery that he has killed his father represent the chaos and tragedy of civil war. The family thus serves as "a microcosm of the state and an echo of its values."

Porter, Joseph A. *The Drama of Speech Acts: Shakespeare's Lancasterian Tetralogy*. Berkeley: University of California Press, 1979.
Like James L. Calderwood's 1979 study *Metadrama in Shakespeare's Henriad* (which Porter's often duplicates), this book examines the uses of language in the *Richard II-Henry V* tetralogy and reaches similar conclusions. Richard II is a poet with an absolute faith in words; Hotspur, too, though no poet, takes words seriously. Hal, on the other hand, recognizes the various types and uses of language and so can rule. Porter sees the plays as being ultimately about drama, but drama as language rather than as performance.

Rackin, Phyllis. *Stages of History: Shakespeare's English Chronicles*. Ithaca, N.Y.: Cornell University Press, 1990.
"This book represents an attempt . . . to situate [Shakespeare's] English history plays in the context of Tudor historiography, in his theater, and in his world." Discusses the polarities operating in the plays: providential order versus Machiavellian secularism; past versus present; male versus female; and fact versus fiction. Highlights the complexities of the plays and surveys much of the criticism. A demanding book that repays the reader's efforts.

Reed, Robert Rentoul, Jr. *Crime and God's Judgment in Shakespeare*. Lexington: University Press of Kentucky, 1984.
Returns to the view that the history plays, *Hamlet*, and *Macbeth* demonstrate God's punishment of homicide. Bolingbroke avenges Richard II's murder of Gloucester, for example, but this murder of Richard II leads to the downfall of Henry VI. Shakespeare's plays thus embody the orthodox Tudor view that guilt

is inherited, and God uses humanity to avenge wrongdoing. Reed's interpretation of the Elizabethan worldview is simplistic and assumes that the second tetralogy is completed by the first. It also assumes that the eight history plays he discusses were conceived of as a unit, though they were never produced that way and not composed that way, either.

Reese, M. M. *The Cease of Majesty: A Study of Shakespeare's History Plays.* New York: St. Martin's Press, 1961.
Discusses Tudor historians Polydore Vergil, Sir Thomas More, Robert Fabyan, Edward Hall, and Raphael Holinshed as well as Samuel Daniel, Michael Drayton, and *A Mirror for Magistrates*. Reese finds a providential universe in Shakespeare's histories and believes that this element derives from medieval miracle and morality plays. The history plays explore universal questions of the relationship between morality and power. At the same time, they reflect on contemporary issues. Thus, Richard II is a prototype of Elizabeth I, a ruler who through inefficiency has brought the kingdom to the edge of ruin. Shakespeare is a spokesman for order achieved through mutual obligation, respect, and love. William A. Armstrong called the book "a solid and thought-provoking contribution to a complicated subject" (*Review of English Studies*, n.s. 13 [1962]: 410). Accessible to undergraduates.

Ribner, Irving. *The English History Play in the Age of Shakespeare.* Rev. ed. New York: Barnes & Noble Books, 1965.
An improved edition of the 1957 (first) edition. Ribner notes the popularity of history during the English Renaissance and traces the development of historical drama from its literary antecedents in medieval morality plays, Senecan tragedy, and plays about conquerors. Ribner defines a history play by its purpose rather than through any formal elements. Shakespeare uses his histories to teach his audience about the dangers of civil war (*Henry VI*) and tyranny (*Richard III*). The second tetralogy presents the ideal prince in Hal/Henry V. These plays glorify England and Tudor values. An appendix lists English history plays and their sources from 1519 to 1653, and the book concludes with sources for further study.

Saccio, Peter. *Shakespeare's English Kings: History, Chronicle, and Drama.* London: Oxford University Press, 1977.
Summarizes the material that Shakespeare used to create his plays about English history. Includes genealogical and chronological tables and discusses the way Shakespeare colored later generations' perceptions of the period and characters he portrayed. Very helpful for those who need a refresher course in the history being treated or for those who are innocent of any knowledge of the period.

Sen Gupta, S. C. *Shakespeare's Historical Plays*. London: Oxford University Press, 1964.
A study of the ten English history plays. Rejects the idea that Shakespeare was trying to promote a particular ideology. Sees the second tetralogy especially as focusing on individuals rather than on political philosophy. The plays sometimes present conflicting political messages. The observations about characters are good, but the book suggests a false division in arguing, for example, that Hotspur (*1 Henry IV*) cannot embody chivalric ideals because he appears as an individual.

Siegel, Paul N. *Shakespeare's English and Roman History Plays: A Marxist Approach*. Rutherford, N.J.: Fairleigh Dickinson University Press, 1986.
Begins with a summary of Marxist criticism and then argues that Shakespeare's plays show the evolving relationship among king, nobles, and the middle class. These works reflect the class struggle that will culminate in the execution of Charles I in 1649. Shakespeare analyzes the Tudor myth of cosmic order to show its dark underside of absolutism. Contains a good (though dated) survey of criticism about the histories and offers many useful insights that might be more fully developed.

Smidt, Kristian. *Unconformities in Shakespeare's History Plays*. Atlantic Highlands, N.J.: Humanities Press, 1982.
The English history plays show evidence of revision and of difficulties not fully overcome. Smidt believes, for example, that Shakespeare did not initially plan three plays for Henry VI. At the beginning of *Richard II*, the king is accused of complicity in Gloucester's murder, but this question disappears later in the play. Richard II's heir, Mortimer, figures prominently in the opening scenes of *1 Henry IV* but fades from the action by the second act. The study's title derives from the geological term for fault lines. Smidt's speculations are fascinating, but the argument would be more convincing if it focused on differences among quarto versions of the plays and between quarto and folio readings.

Thayer, C. G. *Shakespearean Politics: Government and Misgovernment in the Great Histories*. Athens: Ohio University Press, 1983.
Looks at the second tetralogy and finds movement from injustice in *Richard II* to justice in *Henry V*. Richard II believes in the divine right of kings to govern wrong; Bolingbroke forces him to recognize the error of that view. Henry IV represents a human-centered monarchy, as does Henry V, who restores England. Shakespeare thus rejects the notion of a divinely ordained monarchy.

Tillyard, E. M. W. *Shakespeare's History Plays*. London: Macmillan, 1944.
A classic work on the topic that has largely framed the debate over the plays since the book's appearance. Contains much information on the Elizabethan worldview and the age's treatment of history. Tillyard sees Shakespeare as

orthodox in believing that Providence rules and justice triumphs. For Tillyard, England is the hero of the plays, which derive from the chronicles and medieval morality plays. Tillyard also sees Shakespeare as an apologist for the Tudor regime. Essential reading.

Traversi, Derek. *Shakespeare from "Richard II" to "Henry V."* Stanford, Calif.: Stanford University Press, 1957.
Sees this second tetralogy as dealing with the education of the prince. Falstaff is a corrupting influence that Hal must reject. The tetralogy ends on a somber but not tragic note. The plays illustrate the ideal personal qualities of the good king, as well as his political character. Shakespeare recognizes that the old notion that the king rules by divine authority is dead, but without that belief Henry IV has trouble ruling. Henry V succeeds because he is a good person, is politically astute, and has the advantage of royal birth, which confers legitimacy.

Waith, Eugene M., ed. *Shakespeare, the Histories: A Collection of Critical Essays.* Englewood Cliffs, N.J.: Prentice-Hall, 1965.
Contains eleven essays, a chronology, and a brief bibliography of works dealing with the English history plays. Waith's introduction surveys the criticism to the mid-1960s. A useful collection of important works that is especially helpful for the beginning student.

Watson, Donald G. *Shakespeare's Early History Plays: Politics at Play on the Elizabethan Stage.* Athens: University of Georgia Press, 1990.
Examines the first tetralogy and *King John*. Focusing on the theatrical spectacle, Watson finds in these works a critique of Elizabethan political ceremony. The stage is inherently subversive; when an actor plays a king, he implies that the king is a player. The arbitrariness of the theater and its ambiguities are like those of politics; there are no absolutes. Yet a portion of Shakespeare's audience could find in the histories an endorsement of orthodoxy. Thus, King John's rejection of papal authority can be seen as support for Elizabeth's Protestantism or as a questioning of John's—and hence Elizabeth's—right to reign. This reading of the plays is consistent with a trend towards reading the plays in multiple ways at once.

Wilders, John. *The Lost Garden: A View of Shakespeare's English and Roman Plays.* New York: Macmillan, 1978.
The histories demonstrate the failure of people to attain an ideal of permanence or perfection. Argues that people are naturally savage and resist the forces of law necessary to protect them from one another. Henry V is not an ideal ruler, nor does his play end triumphantly. Shakespeare's view of history is tragic, as exemplified by the concluding chorus of *Henry V* projecting not a new Eden but civil war. Anne Barton called the book "a most persuasive and thoughtful

introduction to Shakespeare's histories" (*Review of English Studies*, n.s. 31 [1980]: 343).

Winny, James. *The Player King: A Theme of Shakespeare's Histories*. New York: Barnes & Noble Books, 1968.
Shakespeare's kings in the second tetralogy always face the danger of being deposed. Each ruler tries to assert himself and control events. Winny regards the works as artistic artifacts, not as political statements.

Tragedies

Battenhouse, Roy W. *Shakespearean Tragedy: Its Art and Its Christian Premises*. Bloomington: Indiana University Press, 1969.
Offers a Christian reading of *The Rape of Lucrece*, *Hamlet*, *King Lear*, *Coriolanus*, *Romeo and Juliet*, and *Antony and Cleopatra*. According to Battenhouse, Othello rejects grace in his treatment of Desdemona; *Romeo and Juliet* concludes with a reversal of the Easter story. Tragedy results from mistaking the source of true happiness but concludes with the recognition that there is a divinity that shapes human destiny. Battenhouse sees all the tragic heroes except Lear damned for eternity at the end of the plays. Battenhouse also finds analogies between the works and the Bible, sometimes pushing the parallels too far.

Bayley, John. *Shakespeare and Tragedy*. London: Routledge & Kegan Paul, 1981.
Sees Shakespeare's greatness residing in his ability to avoid the conventions of tragedy. In Shakespeare's tragedies, Bayley finds "the incompatibility of the protagonist with the situation, . . . treatment unsuited to the form." For example, *Othello* presents tragedy in the guise of romance, Cordelia refuses to play a role in *King Lear*, and Hamlet is unsuited to revenge. Robert M. Adams praised this study as "the subtlest and most steadily enlightening piece of literary discussion that I've encountered in a long time. It is a work of the highest imaginative quality, unpretentious in its methods, and rich in literary sensibility" (*New York Review of Books*, October 22, 1981, p. 32).

Bloom, Harold, ed. *William Shakespeare: The Tragedies*. New York: Chelsea House, 1985.
Better than a number of books in the Chelsea House "Modern Critical Views" series. Bloom provides a thoughtful essay on *Hamlet* to introduce the volume, which includes Northrop Frye's discussion of the nature of tragedy (drawn from his 1967 work *Fools of Time: Studies in Shakespearean Tragedy*) and an important study on each of nine tragedies from *Romeo and Juliet* to *Coriolanus*. Among the critics represented are G. Wilson Knight on *King Lear* (from the 1930 *The Wheel of Fire*), David Daiches on *Antony and Cleopatra*, and Howard

Felperin on *Macbeth* (from his 1977 *Shakespearean Representation*). The work concludes with a helpful bibliography.

Booth, Stephen. *"King Lear," "Macbeth," Indefinition, and Tragedy*. New Haven, Conn.: Yale University Press, 1983.
Booth uses two tragedies and *Love's Labour's Lost* to develop a concept of tragedy. For the author, tragedy is the failure of character and audience to achieve completeness or resolution. Thus, the ambiguity of the witches' sex in the opening scene of *Macbeth* and the uncertainty of their relationship with the title character serve as an emblem for that play—indeed, for tragedy in general—which leaves only questions. Whereas comedy accepts underlying norms, "Tragedy operates from . . . the proposition that there is a way things are and that fools assume it is knowable and known." An appendix explores Shakespeare's use of doubling—having the same actor play more than one role—and suggests that the dramatist exploited this technique to comment on the indefinition of reality.

Bradbrook, Muriel C. *Themes and Conventions of Elizabethan Tragedy*. London: Cambridge University Press, 1935.
The first part of this important study presents the conventions of presentation, action, and speech in Elizabethan tragedy, and the second part examines how Christopher Marlowe, Cyril Tourneur, John Webster, Thomas Middleton, and a number of other playwrights applied these. Bradbrook provides a good background for understanding the expectations of Shakespeare's audiences and the dramatic milieu in which Shakespeare functioned. For example, she notes that Elizabethan drama was didactic and that narrative and characterization were less important than language to theatergoers.

Bradley, Andrew C. *Shakespearean Tragedy*. London: Macmillan, 1904.
A detailed analysis of *Hamlet, Othello, King Lear*, and *Macbeth* and of the nature of Shakespearean tragedy. For Bradley, Shakespearean tragedy emerges from characters whose very greatness becomes fatal. He sees the tragedies as elevating, not depressing, for they show humanity's potential and present "a world travailing for perfection." For Bradley, these plays show that "extreme evil cannot long endure." Though this study is best known for its character analyses, Bradley also speaks lucidly about imagery and structure. His reputation has risen and fallen over the years, but his work has been immensely influential, and critics have found more in him to like than to reject.

Brooke, Nicholas. *Shakespeare's Early Tragedies*. London: Methuen, 1968.
A study of *Titus Andronicus, Richard III, Romeo and Juliet, Richard II, Julius Caesar*, and *Hamlet* that presents no unifying thesis but examines the central concern of each play. Thus, *Romeo and Juliet* equates love and death, and *Titus*

Andronicus shows how passion can dehumanize. Seeks to rehabilitate the reputation of the early tragedies, which have been regarded as immature apprentice pieces leading to the great works of the 1600s. Provides detailed analysis of the works discussed.

Brower, Reuben Arthur. *Hero and Saint: Shakespeare and the Greco-Roman Heroic Tradition*. New York: Oxford University Press, 1971.
The first half of the book, dealing with classical authors and their Elizabethan translators, presents the text of Brower's Martin Lectures at Oberlin College. The discussion provides the basis for understanding Shakespearean tragedy, which is treated in the second part of the volume. Brower maintains that Shakespeare's ideas of the heroic derive from the classical tradition but are modified by a Christian outlook. Hence, Shakespeare presents a critique of Greco-Roman heroism in plays such as *Troilus and Cressida* and *Coriolanus*. *King Lear* is the greatest of the tragedies because in the title character it offers a life-seeking, life-affirming version of a hero. Brower also notes that Renaissance translations of the classics, such as George Chapman's rendition of Homer, tend "to replace physical [with] moral heroism, to make the great battle the inner one of the soul or of reason against passion." This habit Shakespeare shares with his contemporaries. Especially useful for undergraduates.

Bulman, James C. *The Heroic Idiom of Shakespearean Tragedy*. Newark: University of Delaware Press, 1985.
Shakespeare drew on audience expectations of heroism as depicted in Homer, Virgil, Plutarch, Seneca, medieval romances, and early Renaissance English drama. Shakespeare did not reject these models, but he presents them in such a way as to elicit a complex response, one that simultaneously exalts and questions the heroic ideal. His early plays accept the heroic models; in the plays of the late 1590s, the heroic conventions are treated ironically. With *Troilus and Cressida*, *Othello*, *Timon of Athens*, and *King Lear* Shakespeare offers characters who again believe in the absolutes of heroism and maintain their ideals in the face of a flawed world. Despite some reservations, Robert Y. Turner observed that "it would be a rare student of Shakespeare who could not learn from [this] account of the heroic tradition and the ways Shakespeare used it" (*Shakespeare Quarterly* 38 [1987]:257).

Campbell, Lily B. *Shakespeare's Tragic Heroes: Slaves of Passion*. Cambridge, England: Cambridge University Press, 1930.
Each of the four major tragedies examines a particular passion. *Hamlet* is a study of the effects of grief, *Othello* of jealousy, *King Lear* of anger, and *Macbeth* of fear. Includes much about Renaissance psychology and philosophy. Responds to A. C. Bradley's view that tragedy lies in action, arguing instead that tragedy lies in passion. Campbell divides her book into three sections: the first examines the

purposes and methods of tragedy as the Renaissance saw them, the second explores "Moral Philosophy in Shakespeare's Day," and the third and longest section devotes a chapter to each of the tragedies she studies.

Cantor, Paul A. *Shakespeare's Rome: Republic and Empire.* Ithaca, N.Y.: Cornell University Press, 1976.
Maintains that *Coriolanus* and *Antony and Cleopatra* are meant to contrast the Roman Republic and the Roman Empire. The former encouraged civic virtue and restrained eros, while the latter discouraged public-spiritedness and promoted the erotic. Thus, Coriolanus chastely loves his wife, whereas Antony marries and then abandons Octavia. *Coriolanus* and *Julius Caesar* are rhetorical (republican Rome is not musical), *Antony and Cleopatra* is lyrical. The argument would be stronger if it provided some analysis of Elizabethan perceptions of Rome or discussion of Shakespeare's sources.

Champion, Larry S. *Shakespeare's Tragic Perspective.* Athens: University of Georgia Press, 1976.
Sees greater complexity in the later tragedies, but all present a hero who must act in the face of ambiguity. The character ultimately gains knowledge, and at the end of the play order is restored. Champion offers no novel interpretations and tends to oversimplify character and plot, but he makes some good observations about Shakespeare's use of surprise, irony, and the double vision the audience receives from the protagonists' soliloquies and other characters' comments.

Charlton, H. B. *Shakespearean Tragedy.* Cambridge, England: Cambridge University Press, 1948.
Charlton, a disciple of A. C. Bradley, sees tragedy as "the picture of mankind's struggle towards a goodness." In tragedy, death is balanced by "a growing sense of the immeasurable spiritual potentiality within man." Especially concerned with Shakespeare's four major tragedies, though earlier ones receive some discussion (and are regarded as less successful). Includes discussions of Shakespeare's sources. M. E. Prior commented that Charlton's "analyses are always discerning, and the approach to crucial and traditional questions is characterized by a reassuring combination of learning and common sense" (*Modern Language Notes* 65 [1950]:562).

Charney, Maurice, ed. *Discussions of Shakespeare's Roman Plays.* Indianapolis: D. C. Heath, 1964.
Contains fourteen essays on *Julius Caesar, Antony and Cleopatra,* and *Coriolanus.* In the opening essay, T. J. B. Spencer demonstrates the significance of Roman history in the works and maintains that they give a good picture of Roman life. The selections treating *Julius Caesar* address its complexity; both Caesar

and Brutus are at once admirable and flawed, so that audience sympathy is divided. The treatment of *Antony and Cleopatra* begins with Samuel Taylor Coleridge's high praise of the work for its great style. Derek Traversi maintains that the poetry redeems the play, but L. C. Knights focuses on the play's realism. Samuel Johnson leads off the essays on *Coriolanus*, finding the play entertaining. Willard Farnham calls it a "magnificent failure" because the hero is so flawed. Paul A. Jorgensen recognizes Coriolanus' faults but also his nobility. D. J. Enright sees the play as debate rather than as tragedy.

_____. *Shakespeare's Roman Plays: The Function of Imagery in the Drama.* Cambridge, Mass.: Harvard University Press, 1961.
Julius Caesar offers little imagery; what it has is associated usually with storms and omens. *Antony and Cleopatra* abounds with imagery; Egypt and Rome serve as symbolic contrasts. In *Coriolanus*, food, disease, and animal imagery reinforces the conflict between plebeians and patricians. Notes that nonverbal imagery (for example, the eunuchs' fanning of Cleopatra when she first appears) is as important as the language and can grow out of verbal allusions. The asp that stings Cleopatra is the culmination of the various references to serpents in the play. An appendix makes the case for treating the Roman plays as a distinct grouping. Norman Sanders observed that "Mr. Charney has produced a book which is of permanent value, and obligatory reading for any future critic of the Roman plays" (*Review of English Studies*, n.s. 14 [1963]:197).

Coursen, Herbert R., Jr. *Christian Ritual and the World of Shakespeare's Tragedies.* Lewisburg, Pa.: Bucknell University Press, 1976.
Examines *Richard II, Othello, King Lear, Macbeth*, and *The Tempest*. Sees all but the last of these plays as presenting a symbolic rejection of the Eucharist and of grace. *Richard II* perverts ritual, *Hamlet* concludes with an anti-Mass that uses poisoned wine, and Othello fails to understand true marriage. *King Lear* is more ambiguous and may conclude with a true "marriage" of Lear and Cordelia. Coursen does not insist that Shakespeare held any particular religious beliefs, only that the playwright uses conventional religious views in his works.

Creeth, Edmund. *Mankynde in Shakespeare.* Athens: University of Georgia Press, 1976.
Compares the medieval moralities dealing with the character Mankynde and the tragedies *Macbeth, Othello*, and *King Lear*. Specifically, Creeth points out the similarities between *The Castell of Perseverance* and *Macbeth*, between *A Morality of Wisdom Who Is Christ* and *Othello*, and between *The Pride of Life* and *King Lear*. The insistence on specific parallels weakens Creeth's arguments: there is no evidence that Shakespeare saw or read these particular moralities, there are important differences between the medieval and Shakespearean works, and other, less esoteric sources (such as the Bible) could have influenced the

tragedies. Creeth's position that Shakespeare used medieval moralities only in these three plays seems extreme, as does his view that Shakespeare alone among his contemporaries drew on them.

Danson, Lawrence. *Tragic Alphabet: Shakespeare's Drama of Language.* New Haven, Conn.: Yale University Press, 1974.
Shakespeare's plays are about language. "The variety of expressive modes, the need to speak and to be understood; the great importance of the self-expressive task and its tragic precariousness: these are among the radical facts of Shakespeare's tragedies." Characters struggle to express themselves and frequently recognize that they are playing a role; *Hamlet*, for example, is a play within a play. As Danson writes, "Hamlet's quest . . . is a quest for the shape of his own play." Iago as artist tries to shape his world, but Shakespeare as divinity demonstrates the unreality of Iago's evil creation.

Evans, Bertrand. *Shakespeare's Tragic Practice.* Oxford, England: Clarendon Press, 1979.
As in his discussion of the comedies, Evans explores the gaps in awareness between various characters and between characters and audience. The approach is theoretically sound but falters in practice. The readings here surprised Evans and will astonish others as well. Antony does not love Cleopatra; "The Mousetrap" in *Hamlet* is aimed at Horatio, not Claudius; and Hamlet is not mad because he says he will "put an antic disposition on."

Everett, Barbara. *Young Hamlet: Essays on Shakespeare's Tragedies.* Oxford, England: Clarendon Press, 1989.
A collection of ten essays. The first four comprise the Lord Northcliffe Lectures, presented in 1988 at University College, London, and treat the four major tragedies under the general heading of "Purchasing Experience." The other six discuss aspects of *Romeo and Juliet*, *Hamlet*, *Troilus and Cressida*, *Othello*, and *Twelfth Night*. Everett notes that the tragedies retain their appeal because of their "truth to ordinary experience." Hamlet, for example, tells of a young man's maturation, though the subject has added resonance in the context of the Elizabethan view of youth as a period of "freedom and impotence." Lear's kingship is important, but so are his feelings as father and man. Everett's comments everywhere illuminate the plays.

Farnham, Willard. *Shakespeare's Tragic Frontier: The World of His Final Tragedies.* Berkeley: University of California Press, 1950.
A study of *Timon of Athens*, *Macbeth*, *Antony and Cleopatra*, and *Coriolanus*. Farnham explores the characters' sources of nobility. The heroes of all four plays are paradoxically noble yet deeply flawed, and their greatness emerges from their "ignobleness." Macbeth has an active but flawed conscience that allows remorse

but not repentance. Coriolanus' pride is the cause of both his grandeur and his fall. Along the way, Farnham discusses Shakespeare's sources and notes his deviations from them.

Felperin, Howard. *Shakespearean Representation: Mimesis and Modernity in Elizabethan Tragedy.* Princeton, N.J.: Princeton University Press, 1977.
Shakespeare uses older forms at the same time that he subverts them. *Hamlet* draws on morality and revenge plays but goes beyond those models. *Macbeth* draws on the mystery cycles but subverts its source to suggest the inadequacy of the medieval plays to depict reality. Felperin also explores the ways Jacobean dramatists used Shakespeare's plays as models. Thomas Middleton, for example, responded to *Othello* with *The Changeling.* Although one may question Felperin's overriding scheme or specific details, his observations about the plays are frequently enlightening.

Foreman, Walter C., Jr. *The Music of the Close: The Final Scenes of Shakespeare's Tragedies.* Lexington: University Press of Kentucky, 1978.
Examines the conclusions of *Hamlet, King Lear, Othello,* and *Antony and Cleopatra.* Shakespeare's tragedies move from an old order to a new, passing through disorder in between. The new order is diminished, though, because of the absence of the tragic hero. The endings of these plays are dictated by those heroes, who have failed to shape their worlds but can at least shape their own deaths. Larry S. Champion commended the book as "a helpful and carefully reasoned contribution to our understanding of Shakespeare's tragic technique" (*JEGP* 79 [1980]:119).

Frye, Northrop. *Fools of Time: Studies in Shakespearean Tragedy.* Toronto: University of Toronto Press, 1967.
Sees three main types of Elizabethan tragedy: the tragedy of order, dealing with the death of rulers; the tragedy of passion, concerned with the separation of lovers or the conflict between duty and love; and the tragedy of isolation, in which the hero must discover who he is. *Julius Caesar, Macbeth,* and *Hamlet* belong to the first group; *Romeo and Juliet, Antony and Cleopatra, Troilus and Cressida* and *Coriolanus* to the second; and *King Lear, Othello,* and *Timon of Athens* to the third. Typical of Frye, the book discusses archetypes, such as analogues to Cain and Absalom. A short, illuminating study.

Goldman, Michael. *Acting and Action in Shakespearean Tragedy.* Princeton, N.J.: Princeton University Press, 1985.
Sees three types of action: what characters do, how audiences respond, and what actors do. Looking at how these actions interrelate, Goldman analyzes *Hamlet, Othello, King Lear, Macbeth, Antony and Cleopatra,* and *Coriolanus,* especially the title roles. He is concerned with how actors and audiences interpret roles and

how Shakespeare wrote to guide these interpretations. Though writing from the viewpoint of performance, Goldman frequently clarifies the text.

Harbage, Alfred, ed. *Shakespeare: The Tragedies, a Collection of Critical Essays*. Englewood Cliffs, N.J.: Prentice-Hall, 1964.
Following a short editorial introduction are two essays on the nature of tragedy. Harbage then presents a judicious selection of essays and extracts about the individual plays. Among the pieces reprinted here are Maynard Mack's excellent article on "The World of *Hamlet*" and L. C. Knights's careful analysis of *Macbeth*. Despite its age, this book remains a useful anthology for students seeking sound interpretations of the plays.

Harrison, George Bagshawe. *Shakespeare's Tragedies*. London: Routledge & Kegan Paul, 1951.
Harrison discusses eleven Shakespearean tragedies but is not a partisan of all of them. He regards only *Othello* and *King Lear* as "deep tragedy," Harrison's term for the most profound works. *Macbeth* is not deep tragedy; Harrison admires parts of the play but regards it as hastily written and sees in it the hand of a collaborator. Harrison draws parallels between the plays and contemporary events. Thus, *King Lear*'s pessimism echoes that of England in 1605; the food riots in *Coriolanus* reflect social unrest in the Midlands of 1607.

Heilman, Robert B., ed. *Shakespeare: The Tragedies, New Perspectives*. Englewood Cliffs, N.J.: Prentice-Hall, 1984.
Sixteen articles drawn from journals and books that supplement the pieces collected in *Shakespeare: The Tragedies, a Collection of Critical Essays* (1964), edited by Alfred Harbage. Nine of the selections deal with the four major tragedies, two each with *Hamlet*, *Macbeth*, and *Othello* and three with *King Lear*; the other tragedies are discussed in one essay each. Among the authors represented are James L. Calderwood ("*Romeo and Juliet*: A Formal Dwelling," from his 1971 *Shakespearean Metadrama*), Kenneth Muir on *Hamlet* (from the 1979 *Shakespeare's Tragic Sequence*), and the editor on *Timon of Athens*. A good survey of criticism from the late 1960s to the early 1980s, though the pieces lack the status of those in the Harbage volume.

Holloway, John. *The Story of the Night: Studies in Shakespeare's Major Tragedies*. London: Routledge & Kegan Paul, 1961.
Looks at *Hamlet*, *Othello*, *King Lear*, *Macbeth*, *Antony and Cleopatra*, *Coriolanus*, and *Timon of Athens*. The word tragedy derives from *tragos*, the Greek word for goat; Holloway sees the tragic hero as beginning in the center of the world of the play but becoming the scapegoat, the outcast, because tragedy in general is the ritualization of myth. Holloway offers a useful warning against overmoralizing the plays, but his formula does not fit the works equally well in

all cases. Hamlet, for example, is isolated at the beginning of his play, perhaps more so than at the end. The book shows a debt to Northrop Frye and the Jungian use of archetypes.

Honigmann, E. A. J. *Shakespeare: Seven Tragedies, the Dramatist's Manipulation of Response.* London: Macmillan, 1976.
Describes the ways that Shakespeare controls his audiences. Among Shakespeare's devices are blurred impressions, requiring the suspension of judgment; repetition that reinforces or reinterprets previous impressions; the use of conventional elements in unconventional ways; and soliloquies. Honigmann posits an ideal audience that reads and sees the plays as he does, but even if one dissents from his interpretation one profits from his implied injunction to examine both one's responses to the works and the ways that the playwright has produced those reactions.

Hunter, Robert G. *Shakespeare and the Mystery of God's Judgments.* Athens: University of Georgia Press, 1976.
Looks at the effects of the Protestant Reformation on *Dr. Faustus, Richard III, Hamlet, Othello, Macbeth,* and *King Lear.* Hunter maintains that Shakespeare wrote his plays in such a way that different believers could interpret the plays differently—hence the works' ambiguity. Hunter assumes that playgoers made clear doctrinal distinctions between, for example, Saint Augustine and John Calvin. He concludes that Shakespeare remained a skeptic, though one intensely interested in theology.

Jorgensen, Paul A. *William Shakespeare: The Tragedies.* Boston: Twayne, 1985.
Sees suffering, not death, as the essence of Shakespearean tragedy; suffering humanizes and ennobles the hero. Jorgensen surveys all the tragedies and provides a useful introduction to them. He does not stray beyond the conventional views and so will have little to offer advanced students or scholars. The book includes a useful annotated bibliography.

Kirsch, Arthur. *The Passions of Shakespeare's Tragic Heroes.* Charlottesville: University Press of Virginia, 1990.
A study of the four major tragedies. "The premise of this book is that Shakespeare's plays represent enduring truths of our emotional and spiritual lives, that these truths help account for Shakespeare's enormous vitality in the classroom as well as the theater, and that they deserve our direct attention," Kirsch writes. *Hamlet* depicts the sorrows and gains of confronting grief. *Othello* offers "a full and moving tragic anatomy of love." Self-imposed isolation dominates *Macbeth,* and *King Lear* recognizes the loss through death, the inadequacy of Christian consolation to assuage the pain. A humane and humanistic reading of the plays.

Knight, G. Wilson. *The Imperial Theme*. 3d ed. London: Methuen, 1951.
A study of *Julius Caesar, Hamlet, Macbeth, Coriolanus*, and *Antony and Cleopatra*. In the plays, positive values conflict—love and honor in *Julius Caesar*, for example—and love triumphs, as it does in *Coriolanus* and *Antony and Cleopatra*. The plays rely on specific image patterns to convey their meanings. Many of these images derive from nature, others from music and feasting. Knight regards *Antony and Cleopatra* as Shakespeare's masterpiece because it unites opposites to create a coherent whole.

_____. *The Wheel of Fire*. Rev. ed. London: Methuen, 1949.
A collection of fifteen essays, most of them about the tragedies. Looking at the plays' language and actions, Knight examines the works' central concerns. Thus, *Macbeth* is a study of evil. In *Othello*, Iago's efforts at uncreation combat Othello's artistry, and the latter triumphs even in the death of the main character. Knight's high estimate of *Timon of Athens* is misplaced, but the close readings that he offers provide many stimulating suggestions.

Lawlor, John. *The Tragic Sense in Shakespeare*. New York: Harcourt, Brace, 1960.
Examines the plays as the interaction of opposites: the real and the apparent in the second Henriad, conflicting visions of the hero in *Hamlet* (as "agent" or "patient"), accident and design in *Othello*, natural and supernatural in *Macbeth*, human and inhuman (among other dichotomies) in *King Lear*, and fate and free will throughout. Lawlor sometimes digresses from his main point, and the style can be infelicitous occasionally. Though Lawlor may be reductive in his insistence on polarities, he makes a solid contribution to an understanding of the plays.

Leech, Clifford, ed. *Shakespeare: The Tragedies, a Collection of Critical Essays*. Chicago: University of Chicago Press, 1965.
Eighteen essays, from John Dryden in the late seventeenth century to the mid-twentieth, with an introduction by Leech discussing the criticism of Shakespeare's tragedies. Among the important works represented are A. C. Bradley's "The Substance of Shakespearean Tragedy," G. Wilson Knight on *Macbeth* and *Antony and Cleopatra*, and Robert Ornstein's treatment of *Othello* and *Macbeth*. Leech seeks to present diverging views. For Knight, Shakespearean tragedy ends in triumph; other selections deny redemption in *Coriolanus* and *Othello*. A useful anthology that can lead the reader to fuller discussions.

Lerner, Laurence, ed. *Shakespeare's Tragedies: A Selection of Modern Criticism*. Harmondsworth, England: Penguin Books, 1963.
A collection of thirty-five pieces on the tragedies revealing a wide range of critical approaches. Among the essays included are Ernest Jones's Oedipal reading of *Hamlet*, Harley Granville-Barker on *Antony and Cleopatra*, and

Wayne Booth on *Macbeth*. Not all the selections are "critical"; Lerner includes John Keats's sonnet on *King Lear* and Delmore Schwartz's verses on *Hamlet*. Lerner concludes the volume with a section on tragedy in general and Shakespearean tragedy in particular, presenting an excerpt from Friedrich Nietzsche's *The Birth of Tragedy*, Clifford Leech's opening chapter of *Shakespeare's Tragedies*, an essay on "The Elizabethan View of Tragedy," and T. S. Eliot's "Shakespeare and the Stoicism of Seneca." Still a useful anthology.

Long, Michael. *The Unnatural Scene: A Study in Shakespearean Tragedy*. London: Methuen, 1976.
Drawing on Arthur Schopenhauer's and Friedrich Nietzsche's theories, Long explores the role of the social order in the downfall of the tragic hero. The tragic hero is both a part of society and its victim; he is torn between social and natural demands. *Coriolanus*, for example, depicts a Roman society divorced from nature, and the result is catastrophic. Similarly, Othello has adopted the Venetian Petrarchan outlook and is overwhelmed by Iago's naturalism. Whereas traditionally tragedy is seen as the consequence of passion's triumph over reason, Long argues that the genre depicts the failure of reason to accept emotion. The essays in the book addressing the comedies are less effective because Long shows more sympathy with the tragic outlook.

McAlindon, Thomas. *Shakespeare's Tragic Cosmos*. Cambridge, England: Cambridge University Press, 1991.
Shakespeare inherited two visions of the world: one as a Great Chain of Being, ordered and hierarchical; the other, dynamic, interactive. This latter concept, that the "natural order [is] a precarious balance of contrary forces," informs the tragedies. The book looks first at Geoffrey Chaucer's *The Knight's Tale* and *A Midsummer Night's Dream*, both of which articulate the same worldview as the tragedies, which McAlindon then examines.

MacCallum, Mungo W. *Shakespeare's Roman Plays and Their Background*. London: Macmillan, 1910.
Discusses other Roman plays of the period, Shakespeare's use of history, and his sources. Includes detailed analysis of the characters. Calls attention to the treatment of Roman history by the French imitators of Seneca and Shakespeare's use of their works. Also discusses the use of Plutarch, Shakespeare's chief source for his Roman drama. Despite the book's age and occasional lapses in judgment, this remains an important study and underlies subsequent examinations of the Roman plays.

McElroy, Bernard. *Shakespeare's Mature Tragedies*. Princeton, N.J.: Princeton University Press, 1973.
Focuses on the tragic hero in *Hamlet*, *Othello*, *Macbeth*, and *King Lear*, particu-

larly his conflict with the world of the play. This central tension unites the four great tragedies and makes them more similar than different. Hamlet seeks absolute values in a relativist universe. Othello wishes to believe in love's power to transcend differences but cannot overcome his own doubts. Macbeth commits himself to a certain view of life but never can deny other possibilities. Lear believes in medieval hierarchies, but his world practices self-aggrandizement. The tragic hero must try to reach a better understanding of his world. McElroy sees a darkening vision as the tragedies progress. Hamlet succeeds in reaching a new understanding of the world of the play, but for Lear death is the only release.

Marsh, Derick R. C. *Passion Lends Them Power: A Study of Shakespeare's Love Tragedies.* Manchester, England: Manchester University Press, 1976.
A detailed study of *Romeo and Juliet*, *Othello*, and *Antony and Cleopatra*, with some discussion of *Troilus and Cressida* and the romances (in which the tragic pattern is reversed). Love is crucial to life, but committing oneself to love leaves one vulnerable to tragedy. In the comedies, time and chance aid the lovers; in the tragedies, these forces destroy them, so that the love tragedies "are the extreme statement of the tragedy of time, and as such, they seem to (be) absolute statements of the universal tragedy of human existence." Yet the lovers triumph despite their deaths, especially in *Antony and Cleopatra*.

Mason, Harold A. *Shakespeare's Tragedies of Love: An Examination of the Possibility of Common Readings of "Romeo and Juliet," "Othello," "King Lear," and "Antony and Cleopatra."* London: Chatto & Windus, 1970.
Sees Shakespeare's greatest creations—Othello, Desdemona, Lear, Antony, and Cleopatra—as flawed because they are not, like Macbeth, fully explained. When Shakespeare writes about love, he gets into trouble. Mason apparently objects to theatrical artifice and ambiguity in general; he seems to want realistic, rational characters without passion and divorced from dramatic conventions. Mason's standards are strange indeed when they cannot appreciate the supreme achievements of the world's preeminent dramatist.

Mehl, Dieter. *Shakespeare's Tragedies: An Introduction.* Cambridge, England: Cambridge University Press, 1987.
A survey of the early tragedies *Titus Andronicus* and *Romeo and Juliet*; the "great tragedies" of *Hamlet*, *Othello*, *King Lear*, and *Macbeth*; and the Greek and Roman tragedies, including *Troilus and Cressida*, even though Mehl agrees that it is hardly a "conventional tragedy." Aimed at the undergraduate, the essays discuss sources and indicate important critical approaches. The book offers no new insights or provocative observations but provides a sound, sane starting point for those seeking to understand what they are seeing or reading.

Milward, Peter. *Biblical Influences in Shakespeare's Great Tragedies*. Bloomington: Indiana University Press, 1987.
Lamenting the relative lack of emphasis on Shakespeare's use of the Bible in the
four great tragedies, not only for language but also for meaning, Milward has
focused on the theological implications of these works. From his reading,
Milward determines that certain parts of the Bible particularly appealed to
Shakespeare, since he used them repeatedly. Also, Milward suggests that action
and language would convey particular messages to Elizabethan audiences steeped
in the Bible. For example, Shakespeare's audiences would recognize Lear as
reenacting the parable of the prodigal son.

Miola, Robert S. *Shakespeare's Rome*. Cambridge, England: Cambridge University
Press, 1983.
Shakespeare remained fascinated with Rome from his early *The Rape of Lucrece*
to *Cymbeline*. His first two Roman works, *The Rape of Lucrece* and *Titus
Andronicus*, are conventional apprentice pieces. With *Julius Caesar* and *Antony
and Cleopatra*, he created masterpieces. Coriolanus is closer to Titus than to
Brutus or Antony, and *Cymbeline* marks the triumph of British pastoral over
Roman tragedy. Shakespeare drew on a number of sources, which Miola outlines
in his first chapter; Virgil is particularly important. The playwright focused on
the Roman ideals of "constancy, honor, and *pietas* (the loving respect owed to
family, country, and gods)." Stanley Wells called the book "a coherent, deeply
pondered study" (*The Times Literary Supplement*, November 30, 1984, p. 1390).

Muir, Kenneth. *Shakespeare's Tragic Sequence*. London: Hutchinson University
Library, 1972.
Good for beginning students. Discusses each of the tragedies. Muir sees no
overarching theme in the tragedies but does find a growing maturity. Looks at
the plays as theater as well as text. Having no thesis to argue (other than the view
that each play is unique), Muir confronts each play on its own terms. Discussion
focuses on characters, plot, and the way the works shape audience response.
Muir ably summarizes various critical approaches.

Nevo, Ruth. *Tragic Form in Shakespeare*. Princeton, N.J.: Princeton University
Press, 1972.
Provides a five-part outline of Shakespeare's tragedies: "Predicament," Psychomachia," "Peripeteia" (reversal), renunciation of previously held views, and
catastrophe. Sees in each play a central action, an error that effects reversal.
After presenting her outline of tragedy, Nevo devotes a chapter to each of nine
plays from *Romeo and Juliet* to *Coriolanus*. She focuses on the characters'
humanity and their conflicts with ideals that dehumanize. Philip Edwards praised
the book (in the *Review of English Studies*, n.s. 25 [1974]:333-334) by arguing
that "Professor Nevo sustains her study of Shakespeare's tragedy with a concen-

tration, an intelligence, and an originality which are not often found together in modern Shakespearean criticism." He finds her best on *Julius Caesar*, *Macbeth*, *Hamlet*, and *Richard II*, but he adds that "there is not a single essay in the book without many shrewd insights and many original notes struck." A valuable study.

Proser, Matthew N. *The Heroic Image in Five Shakespearean Tragedies.* Princeton, N.J.: Princeton University Press, 1965.
The five tragedies are *Julius Caesar*, *Macbeth*, *Othello*, *Coriolanus*, and *Antony and Cleopatra*. Proser includes much on critical views of the plays. He sees the heroes as reacting to their own self-images as much as to external factors, and all the tragic heroes are self-deluded. Brutus acts to fulfill his self-image as Roman Republican patriot and in the process becomes a tyrant. Macbeth seeks to demonstrate his manliness and becomes bestial. The theme of self-delusion pervades literature, but Proser uses this motif to discuss the plays intelligently. As Franklin M. Dickey remarked, "This is a sensible and imaginative study which fulfills the aim of criticism: to give the reader the benefit of the meditations of a good mind upon literature" (*Modern Language Quarterly* 28 [1967]:494).

Rackin, Phyllis. *Shakespeare's Tragedies.* New York: Frederick Ungar, 1978.
Opens with a Shakespeare chronology, followed by a brief introduction. Short essays treat ten tragedies from *Titus Andronicus* to *Timon of Athens*, and the book concludes with a discussion of the staging of these works. Includes a bibliography for further study. Not intended as a comprehensive survey but helpful for beginning students trying to cope with the works. For each play, Rackin suggests one or two strategies useful in gaining an understanding of the piece. Thus, she discusses language in *Romeo and Juliet* and *Macbeth*, plot in *Hamlet*, and character in *Othello*.

Ribner, Irving. *Patterns in Shakespearean Tragedy.* New York: Barnes & Noble Books, 1960.
Traces the growth of Shakespeare's artistry from play to play, but even in the earliest tragedies the hero achieves greatness through discovery of the nature of evil. The focus is not on the characters Shakespeare creates but on the concept the plays illustrate, often the triumph of justice and regeneration despite the existence of powerful evil forces. Ribner examines the allegorical function of the characters and sees Shakespearean tragedy as a sophisticated form of the medieval morality play; he sees both as endorsing a Christian outlook. The book finds three types of tragedy: the good man's fall through deception (*Titus Andronicus*), the rise and fall of the evil man (*Richard III*), and "the ordinary man's rise and fall" (*Romeo and Juliet*). John Lawlor wrote (in *Review of English Studies*, n.s. 13 [1962]:185-186) that "Dr. Ribner . . . is everywhere clear and often has strikingly perceptive things to say. . . . All his readers will find profit . . . in his carefully detailed examination of a wide range of plays."

Rosen, William. *Shakespeare and the Craft of Tragedy*. Cambridge, Mass.: Harvard University Press, 1960.

Examines Shakespeare's technique of controlling audience response to the heroes in four tragedies. In *King Lear* and *Macbeth*, the audience sympathizes with the title characters, whereas in *Antony and Cleopatra* and *Coriolanus* that rapport is lacking. The first two plays present action from the perspective of the protagonist, whereas the latter two allow for distance and analysis. Those characters that earn audience sympathy do so because they move out of their private worlds to assume "universal significance." Rosen concludes that "*King Lear* is Shakespeare's greatest tragedy because it is most universal"; Lear's transformation becomes the spectators', his death their "loss of . . . potential perfection."

Siegel, Paul N. *Shakespearean Tragedy and the Elizabethan Compromise*. New York: New York University Press, 1957.

Sees a balance in Shakespeare's four great tragedies mirroring that in the political sphere under Elizabeth. The works express Christian humanism and the outlook of the new aristocracy that balanced queen and commons. By the time Shakespeare wrote his tragedies, the Elizabethan compromise had broken down, but the works extol the ideals that had existed before 1588. The plays also draw on biblical analogues. In *Othello*, for example, Iago is the devil, Desdemona the redeemer who sacrifices herself. Cordelia serves this latter role in *King Lear*. Macbeth partakes of Lucifer and Judas, Lady Macbeth of Eve and Pontius Pilate.

Siemon, James R. *Shakespeare's Iconoclasm*. Berkeley: University of California Press, 1985.

Treats *The Rape of Lucrece*, *Henry V*, *Julius Caesar*, *Hamlet*, *King Lear*, and, more briefly, *The Winter's Tale*. Discusses iconoclasm in Protestant England and Shakespeare's destruction of images in the plays. Siemon thus rejects the more conventional view of critics such as Dieter Mehl and Maurice Charney who maintain that the plays draw on "speaking pictures" or emblems. Siemon agrees that the emblems appear on stage, but only to be undercut. Henry V, for example, is portrayed as an ideal king, but the speeches of Pistol and the Archbishop question such an image. The book's protest against oversimplification is salutary, but it goes too far in the other direction in denying the significance of stage imagery. Protestants as well as Catholics produced and enjoyed emblem books in this period and read the world emblematically.

Simmons, J. L. *Shakespeare's Pagan World: The Roman Tragedies*. Charlottesville: University Press of Virginia, 1973.

Because the plays are set in the pagan world, characters are limited, without hope of salvation or glory. The heroes seek ideals in a fallen world devoid of the possibility of transcendence and are therefore doomed to fail. *Coriolanus* is the tragedy of "a public hero without a public"; Brutus is blind to his failings and to his world's because he does not recognize the Christian doctrine of the Fall. Antony partially succeeds in his quest for the ideal, but his non-Christian world prevents triumph. Simmons' reading isolates the three Roman plays (he dismisses *Titus Andronicus* as "uncertain" in its plotting and characterization) from Shakespeare's other works of the same period and so creates certain distortions.

Smidt, Kristian. *Unconformities in Shakespeare's Tragedies*. New York: St. Martin's Press, 1990.
The third in a series of Smidt's studies, this volume again examines those inconsistencies or gaps in the text that provide insights into the workings of Shakespeare's mind. Early in *King Lear*, for example, Shakespeare apparently planned for a rift between Albany and Cornwall, an idea subsequently abandoned. The fool vanishes inexplicably in act III. Antony in *Julius Caesar* and Hamlet change in the course of their plays. These observations are fascinating but not necessarily enlightening. Some of the "unconformities" are invisible on stage; others may be hints that Shakespeare thought required no further discussion.

Snyder, Susan. *The Comic Matrix of Shakespeare's Tragedies: "Romeo and Juliet," "Hamlet," "Othello," and "King Lear."* Princeton, N.J.: Princeton University Press, 1979.
Considers the ways that comedy influences the tragedies in the title. *Romeo and Juliet* begins in comedy and becomes tragic only through error. *Othello* begins with marriage, where comedy ends, and the forces usually defeated by comedy triumph here. *Hamlet* turns the multiple views of comedy into a nightmare quest for reality, and *King Lear* juxtaposes comic order and comic chaos to produce its "special, devastating tragic effect." Sees the tragedies as a response to and questioning of the comic worldview. Gary Taylor ranked this book "among the finest Shakespearean criticism of recent years" (*Review of English Studies*, n.s. 33 [1982]:76).

Speaight, Robert. *Nature in Shakespearean Tragedy*. London: Hollis & Carter, 1955.
Shakespeare looks carefully at nature, is concerned with ethical problems, and from nature arrives at the divine. Speaight offers a religious reading of the plays: *King Lear* presents "the teaching of the Cross"; the ending of *Antony and Cleopatra* emphasizes resurrection; and the point of *The Tempest* is incarnation. The viewpoint here is limited, and the Shakespeare that is presented is simplistic.

Spivack, Bernard. *Shakespeare and the Allegory of Evil: The History of a Metaphor in Relation to His Major Villains*. New York: Columbia University Press, 1958.
Shakespeare transformed the Vice of medieval morality plays to create Iago, Richard III, Aaron the Moor, and Don John. Iago, for example, embodies much of the medieval Vice figure's hatred of characters simply because they are good.

As Shakespeare matured, his treatment of the Vice figure grew more subtle, but the villain continued to reveal his true nature to the audience. Spivack is most informative about the medieval conventions that Shakespeare drew upon in creating his evil characters.

Spurgeon, Caroline F. E. *Leading Motives in the Imagery of Shakespeare's Tragedies*. London: H. Milford, Oxford University Press, for the Shakespeare Association, 1930.
Finds a particular image or cluster of images that predominates in each of the tragedies. In *Romeo and Juliet*, the key metaphor is light, expressed in "the sun, moon, stars, fire, lightning, the flash of gunpowder, and the reflected light of beauty and of love," and this image contrasts with "night, darkness, clouds, rain, mist, and smoke." *Hamlet* contains many allusions to disease and corruption, *Troilus and Cressida* to taste. *Othello* is filled with animal and sea imagery; *King Lear* repeatedly depicts "a human body in anguished movement" and draws heavily on animal references. *Coriolanus* relies on the motifs of sickness and the body, *Antony and Cleopatra* repeatedly refers to food and to the cosmos. *Macbeth*, despite its brevity, contains a number of key images (clothes, echoes, light and darkness, disease). *Julius Caesar*, though, is rather barren of imagery. These various references "play a part in raising, developing, sustaining, and repeating emotion in the tragedies, which is somewhat analogous to the action of a recurrent theme or motif in a musical fugue or sonata, or in one of Wagner's operas." An important study that subsequent critics drew upon heavily.

Stampfer, Judah. *The Tragic Engagement: A Study of Shakespeare's Classical Tragedies*. New York: Funk & Wagnalls, 1968.
The classical tragedies are *Titus Andronicus*, *Julius Caesar*, *Troilus and Cressida*, *Timon of Athens*, *Antony and Cleopatra*, and *Coriolanus*. Unlike the "Christian tragedies," these plays "are . . . not really about pain, but about loss of role." Except for *Antony and Cleopatra*, they are plays without a true hero. Stampfer posits three versions of the tragic hero, the ethical, the willful, and the political. Frank Kermode was not impressed with Stampfer's scholarship or writing (*New York Review of Books*, November 5, 1970, p. 35).

Stirling, Brents. *Unity in Shakespearean Tragedy: The Interplay of Theme and Character*. New York: Columbia University Press, 1956.
Each of the major tragedies focuses on a particular theme that unifies the play. Haste dominates *Romeo and Juliet*; reputation controls *Othello*. These themes emerge through images and characterization, structure, and action. Stirling sees the characters as subordinate to the theme of the play, so that Macbeth or Brutus is symbolic, not realistic. Stirling's interpretations do not fully explain the plays, but his points are sound and informative.

Traversi, Derek. *Shakespeare: The Roman Plays*. Stanford, Calif.: Stanford University Press, 1963.
A detailed analysis of the three Roman plays, which Traversi sees as fusing the political concerns of the histories with the focus on the hero that characterizes the tragedies. The book proceeds methodically through each play, analyzing every episode. The discussions clarify the works, but they are best taken in small doses, since the study amounts to a gloss on the texts, almost a variorum commentary.

Whitaker, Virgil K. *The Mirror Up to Nature: The Technique of Shakespeare's Tragedies*. San Marino, Calif.: Huntington Library, 1965.
Another Christian reading of the tragedies that sees the Aristotelian tragic flaw in Shakespeare's plays as "moral error." The tragic hero who commits it serves as a "moral *exemplum*," which is how Whitaker understands Hamlet's famous definition of drama as holding a mirror up to nature. Whitaker believes that Shakespeare "saw drama as moral philosophy," and in *Macbeth*, *Othello*, and *King Lear* the dramatist gave realistic portrayals to the issues central to morality plays. Because *Antony and Cleopatra* and *Coriolanus* do not exemplify Christian morality, Whitaker sees them as falling off from their great predecessors, especially *King Lear*, which for Whitaker is the greatest of the tragedies because it is the most Christian.

White, R. S. *Innocent Victims: Poetic Injustice in Shakespearean Tragedy*. 2d ed. London: Athlone Press, 1986.
By showing the deaths of innocent women and children, Shakespeare demonstrates the weakness of "male and political dominance." Richard III, King John, and Macbeth forfeit audience sympathy by killing children. Ophelia's death serves as an "emblem of the victimization and official secrecy of a whole political world headed by a corrupt monarch." White thus demonstrates that seemingly peripheral events play a significant part in the plays.

Wilson, Harold S. *On the Design of Shakespearean Tragedy*. Toronto: University of Toronto Press, 1957.
Christian premises underlie *Romeo and Juliet*, *Hamlet*, *Othello*, and *Macbeth* (plays belonging to the "order of faith") but not *Julius Caesar*, *Coriolanus*, *Troilus and Cressida*, *Timon of Athens*, *Antony and Cleopatra*, or *King Lear* ("order of nature"). Wilson also groups pairs of plays into thesis and antithesis. Thus, *Julius Caesar* and *Coriolanus* study great men; *Troilus and Cressida* and *Timon of Athens* present their opposites. *Antony and Cleopatra* and *King Lear* are the synthesis, stressing the value of love over justice and so fusing human and Christian values. Kenneth Muir said of this study that "the interpretations of individual plays are always intelligent and sensitive, though they are not always convincing" (*Review of English Studies*, n.s. 10 [1959]:87).

Wilson, John Dover. *Six Tragedies of Shakespeare: An Introduction for the Plain Man*. London: Longmans, Green, 1929.
Discusses *Romeo and Juliet, Hamlet, Macbeth, King Lear, Othello,* and *Antony and Cleopatra* in brief, impressionistic essays that offer many riches in little room. For example, Wilson notes the comedic and triumphant elements of *Romeo and Juliet,* the mundane aspects of *Macbeth* for all its surrealistic trappings, and the treatment of old age in *King Lear*. The observations are intelligent and reflect much thought and reading by one who loves the works he treats.

Young, David. *The Action to the Word: Structure and Style in Shakespearean Tragedy*. New Haven, Conn.: Yale University Press, 1990.
Treats the four major tragedies and concludes that "by acknowledging and exploiting conflicts between the action of a play and its characteristic uses of language, Shakespeare . . . was able to confront problems the solution of which contributed significantly to the distinctiveness and richness of his tragedies." For example, *Hamlet* offers much talk but little action; *King Lear*'s style is intimate, its action grand, sweeping.

INDIVIDUAL PLAYS

All's Well That Ends Well

Bergeron, David. "The Mythical Structure of *All's Well That Ends Well.*" *Texas Studies in Literature and Language* 14 (1972):559-568.

Helena, who resembles Venus as symbol of life and love, triumphs over Bertram as Mars, the god of death and war. The play recreates a fertility ritual depicting regeneration. A play that begins with death ends in health and pregnancy. Bergeron traces the play's allusions to the Mars-Venus myth and notes the story's popularity among writers and artists of the period.

Bradbrook, Muriel C. "Virtue Is the True Nobility: A Study of the Structure of *All's Well That Ends Well.*" *Review of English Studies* 1 (1950):289-301.

The play explores the question of the nature of honor. Bertram believes that birth conveys nobility; Helena represents the view that deeds determine this quality. Helena and Parolles may be regarded respectively as Bertram's good and bad angels, and Bertram is redeemed by Helena's real virtue. Sees the play as unsuccessful because of Shakespeare's attempt "to write a moral play."

Cole, Howard C. *The "All's Well" Story from Boccaccio to Shakespeare.* Urbana: University of Illinois Press, 1981.

Surveys Shakespeare's sources from Giovanni Boccaccio to William Painter's *The Palace of Pleasure.* Observes that this troublesome play's sources themselves contain ambiguities. Cole also looks at the nonliterary contexts, such as the enforced marriage of wards, medicine, and politics around 1600. The source study concludes with an interpretation of the play as a spectator around 1600 would have regarded it. Cole sees the work as an ironic commentary on providence and reveals that for Helena religion may be used to cloak earthly motives.

Dennis, Carl. "*All's Well That Ends Well* and the Meaning of *Agape.*" *Philological Quarterly* 50 (1971):75-84.

Addresses the problem ending that bothers most critics: Bertram is unworthy of happiness at the end of the play, and Helena's devotion to him appears excessive, "casting the pearl of her love before a swine." Dennis argues that Shakespeare wants to make Bertram unsympathetic to highlight the nature of Helena's love, which is *agape*—unmerited and unreciprocated. Such unconditional love redeems Bertram, encouraging him to improve. In another example of *agape*, Parolles is pardoned despite his unworthiness and comes to accept a divine order. The play presents "the divine illogic that lies at the heart of the idea of grace."

Donaldson, Ian. "*All's Well That Ends Well*: Shakespeare's Play of Endings." *Essays in Criticism* 27 (1977):34-54.

Notes how throughout the play Shakespeare toys with the idea of endings. The first scene introduces death and dying, which are at once ends and beginnings—the death of Bertram's father frees the youth to go to Paris. That departure is like death for Helena but prompts her to follow her beloved and revivify both herself and the king of France. Though the end of the play has its faults, it also is not the end; Diana's situation remains unresolved, and even after the last line is spoken, an epilogue follows that anticipates repeated performances for a play that may never end.

Lawrence, William Witherle. "The Meaning of *All's Well That Ends Well*." *PMLA* 37 (1922):418-469.
Explores how Elizabethan audiences would have regarded the play. For them, Helena is virtuous, and Bertram's conversion follows literary convention; therefore, however incredible spectators or readers find his transformation in reality, it is meant to be accepted as real. Lawrence discusses in detail Helena's literary antecedents. An important study that has served as the starting point for much subsequent criticism.

Leggatt, Alexander. "*All's Well That Ends Well*: The Testing of Romance." *Modern Language Quarterly* 32 (1971):21-41.
The play juxtaposes the worlds of romance and realism. Bertram and Parolles belong to the latter, Helena to the former. Her winning of Bertram seems to mark the victory of romance, but Bertram's ambiguous acceptance leaves the question unresolved. The play disturbs audiences because it tests conventions of romance and idealism that underlie comedy; Leggatt concludes that Shakespeare showed courage in creating such a problematic work.

Parker, R. B. "War and Sex in *All's Well That Ends Well*." *Shakespeare Survey* 37 (1984):95-113.
Aggression is a masculine trait, love a feminine trait. In *All's Well That Ends Well*, Bertram must accept love, while Helena learns to become aggressive. The ending appears to reconcile the two, but ambiguity lingers, as is reflected in the "if"s of the concluding couplet and epilogue.

Price, Joseph G. *The Unfortunate Comedy: A Study of "All's Well That Ends Well."* Toronto: University of Toronto Press, 1968.
Recounts the theatrical history of the play, which, according to Price, has been rarely and poorly produced. After this book was written, the Royal Shakespearean Company twice staged this play successfully (1967 and 1981), and the BBC production in 1980 also did justice to the performance. Also surveys the criticism from the seventeenth century onward. Helena was popular among the Romantics; early twentieth century writers disliked the work, but appreciation for the play began to grow about 1950. Price concludes with a forty-page, scene-by-scene analysis of the work.

Smallwood, R. L. "The Design of *All's Well That Ends Well.*" *Shakespeare Survey* 25 (1972):45-61.
The problems that critics have with the play derive from the source. Shakespeare has improved his original by adding new characters (older people and comic figures). These make Helena more sympathetic and Bertram appear less base because of the contrast with Parolles. Helena becomes less experienced in Shakespeare's play, and her reduced rank makes Bertram's rejection of her again more understandable. The altered and expanded ending allows Bertram to expose his true nature and to begin his redemption. Argues that, while the story remains flawed, a good production can make the play effective on stage.

Styan, J. L. *"All's Well That Ends Well."* Manchester, England: Manchester University Press, 1984.
A volume in the "Shakespeare in Performance" series. The first part of this slim volume addresses "Issues of Performance," and part 2 looks at each scene. The work concludes with a bibliography and a list of major productions. Styan notes that the play was for many years presented as a romance, but more recent productions have tended towards realism, particularly the David Myerscough-Jones 1981 television version. Although the focus is on performance, Styan includes a goodly amount of critical and historical background.

Antony and Cleopatra

Adelman, Janet. *The Common Liar: An Essay on "Antony and Cleopatra."* New Haven, Conn.: Yale University Press, 1973.
Antony and Cleopatra offers numerous points of view as it mixes comedy, tragedy, and romance. Focusing on audience response, Adelman maintains that the play's very ambiguity demands support for the lovers' vision. The book offers useful information on the literary tradition that Shakespeare used, noting that Antony and Cleopatra were often praised, and discusses the treatment of their analogues—Dido and Aeneas, Venus and Mars. Even Roman writers admired as they condemned Antony and Cleopatra. Adelman also offers careful analysis of the play's rich language, which often contradicts the action but retains its own vitality and validity. Repeatedly, the language exaggerates, but its hyperbole offers a fertile alternative to the sterility of measure.

Barroll, J. Leeds. *Shakespearean Tragedy: Genre, Tradition, and Change in "Antony and Cleopatra."* Washington, D.C.: Folger Shakespeare Library, 1984.
Uses *Antony and Cleopatra* to understand the nature of Shakespearean tragedy. Sees the two protagonists as tragic heroes, which for Barroll means that they are flawed. Both are self-deluded—Antony wedded to an image of himself as soldier, Cleopatra to her perception of herself not only as queen but also as beautiful

woman. Their insistence on maintaining these images becomes self-destructive. Yet, despite their lack of self-perception and their insistence on playing roles that are inappropriate, both enlist audience sympathy, and in their deaths they are grand though isolated.

Bono, Barbara J. *Literary Transvaluation: From Vergilian Epic to Shakespearean Tragicomedy.* Berkeley: University of California Press, 1984.
Looks at the treatment of Dido and Aeneas from Virgil's account through Saint Augustine, Dante, Edmund Spenser, and Renaissance drama, culminating in *Antony and Cleopatra.* Bono argues that Shakespeare sees Cleopatra, as he does all women in the tragedies, as part of that world "which cannot be perfectly controlled." She believes that Lucretius' vision of Venus as creator influenced Shakespeare's vision of Cleopatra and that the play incorporates the resurrection myth of Isis and Osiris in Cleopatra's apotheosis. In Shakespeare's play, excess becomes a virtue, thus inverting the values of the *Aeneid.*

Fawkner, H. W. *Shakespeare's Hyperontology: "Antony and Cleopatra."* Rutherford, N.J.: Fairleigh Dickinson University Press, 1990.
A deconstructionist reading of the play scene by scene. Beneath the opaque jargon, Fawkner examines the motif of leaving and following as it relates to the two worlds of Rome (restraint) and Egypt (excess). A good discussion of the play's imagery and irony. For example, by towing Antony to the top of the monument, Cleopatra also follows him because he has preceded her in death.

Lamb, Margaret. *"Antony and Cleopatra" on the English Stage.* Rutherford, N.J.: Fairleigh Dickinson University Press, 1980.
Discusses forty-two British productions from the Globe theatre performance with Richard Burbage to the 1978 Royal Shakespeare Company version directed by Peter Brook. Lamb notes the wide variety of theatrical interpretations of the characters; for example, are Antony and Cleopatra weak or strong? She also comments on problems the play presents for a modern stage, with the demand for scenery and the presence of the proscenium arch. Nicely illustrated stage history that reveals the play's varying fortunes.

Markels, Julian. *The Pillar of the World: "Antony and Cleopatra" in Shakespeare's Development.* Columbus: Ohio State University Press, 1968.
Sees in Shakespeare a growing disillusion with the public vision of the Elizabethan world picture and the division of public and private life. This development culminates in Antony's refusal to choose between public Rome and private Egypt; instead he endorses both values. Cleopatra, too, finally chooses Antony's path. Another element in Shakespeare's development is his treatment of death, which here conveys immortality; thus *Antony and Cleopatra* moves beyond *King Lear.* Markels examines the play's language to support his argument of Antony's transcendence.

Riemer, A. P. *A Reading of Shakespeare's "Antony and Cleopatra."* Sydney, Australia: Sydney University Press, 1968.
An introduction aimed at readers confronting the play for the first time. Opens with a discussion of the play's sources and concludes with a review of the criticism. In between, Riemer offers his own reading, which likens the play to George Bernard Shaw's *Caesar and Cleopatra*; Riemer sees the work as icono-clastic in its attack on received ideas. Because Riemer believes that the play lacks a religious or metaphysical background, he argues that it only appears to be a tragedy but actually is not. Antony is not the great hero that Cleopatra imagines; Cleopatra is irresistible because of her "vulgarity and vivacity." The play remains open-ended and unbiased, just like Plutarch's account that serves as the basis of Shakespeare's play.

Rose, Mark, ed. *Twentieth Century Interpretations of "Antony and Cleopatra."* Englewood Cliffs, N.J.: Prentice-Hall, 1977.
Rose introduces this collection with a discussion of the peculiarities of the play. Its Rome evokes epic yet is not heroic. Egypt suggests contempt of worldly success but in other ways inverts the medieval morality's theme of *contemptus mundi*. Unlike the great tragedies that precede this play, here no final truth emerges. The play distances its audiences, and it moves towards the romances, especially *The Winter's Tale*. Following Rose's essay are eleven selections commenting on various aspects of the play. Maurice Charney speaks of the play's use of hyperbole; Julian Markels discusses the treatment of public and private worlds; Reuben Brower looks at other Renaissance treatments of Cleopatra and concludes that Antony is a traditional tragic hero, Cleopatra an Ovidian heroine. Maynard Mack's piece, which concludes the volume, notes how changeable the world of the play is.

Scott, Michael. *"Antony and Cleopatra": Text and Performance.* London: Macmillan, 1983.
In part 1, Scott discusses various issues that have concerned the play's critics, such as the question of whether the play is a tragedy. This section ends with a detailed analysis of the conclusion. The second section examines various produc-tions from Shakespeare's day to 1982, focusing on five late twentieth century versions. Each has its virtues, but none completely captures the totality of the work.

Steppat, Michael. *The Critical Reception of Shakespeare's "Antony and Cleopatra" from 1607-1905.* Amsterdam: Grüner, 1980.
Looks at responses to the play from its first appearance around 1607 to A. C. Bradley's discussion of the work. Early writers frowned on the play's unconven-tional structure, the conflict between art and nature, the question of poetic justice, and the language. Nineteenth century readers often took a more romantic view

of the work. John Abraham Heraud in 1865 writes, for example, that the lovers "live in an ideal region far above the reach of a moral code," and Algernon Charles Swinburne called it "the greatest love-poem of all time." Bradley, of course, looked at the characters. Steppat includes a survey of German and French criticism after the Romantics and some post-Bradley criticism to 1919. Includes helpful tables noting, for example, which critics prefer Antony and which prefer Octavius. The volume concludes with a lengthy bibliography of criticism to 1977.

Traci, Philip J. *The Love Play of Antony and Cleopatra: A Critical Study of Shakespeare's Play*. The Hague: Mouton, 1970.
Traci begins by surveying the criticism of the play. Subsequent chapters examine characterization, language, the theme of love, and structure. He concludes that Antony and Cleopatra are better than Octavius, Charman, Octavia, and the others. The play examines love from many aspects and sees love as magical. The play moves to a sexual union of Antony and Cleopatra in death, and from this union comes the rebirth of Antony as emperor.

As You Like It

Barber, C. L. "The Use of Comedy in *As You Like It*." *Philological Quarterly* 21 (1942):353-367.
Argues that Shakespeare's comedies make serious statements. The play posits romantic, pastoral ideals, which Touchstone and Jacques undercut by introducing reality. One cannot have the comforts and sophistication of the court and rustic simplicity. Barber decides that the mockery does not satirize real life because reality is not ideal; rather, it genially reveals that all attempts to achieve perfection must reconcile themselves to actuality. Concludes that most of Shakespeare's so-called comedies are actually romances, and the use of humor here does not differ from its function in the tragedies. Both comedies and tragedies, moreover, "express the difference between what life might be and what it is."

Bracher, Mark. "Contrary Notions of Identity in *As You Like It*." *Studies in English Literature* 24 (1984):225-240.
Comedy can be satiric, rejecting difference, or it can emphasize reconciliation; both types of comedy appear in *As You Like It*. Oliver and Duke Ferdinand represent the former mode, Celia and Rosalind the latter. Shakespeare sides with the latter, romantic vision. *As You Like It* leads the audience to accept multiple perspectives.

Cirillo, Albert R. "*As You Like It*: Pastoralism Gone Awry." *ELH* 38 (1971):19-39.
According to Cirillo, the forest of Arden provides an alternative to the court, but Shakespeare recognizes the unreality of the pastoral world. Rosalind teaches the

need to fuse ideal and actual. The return to the court is not a rejection of pastoral because the characters bring back with them the vision of an orderly world better than the court they left. Argues that their new vision allows for an improved world at the end of the play. Rosalind's epilogue summons audiences to share the transforming experience by allowing the play to become their forest of Arden.

Halio, Jay L., ed. *Twentieth Century Interpretations of "As You Like It": A Collection of Critical Essays*. Englewood Cliffs, N.J.: Prentice Hall, 1968.
In his introduction, Halio discusses the contrasts that characterize the play—for example, nature and nurture, court and the forest of Arden, and Petrarchan and sexual love. Among the essays included are the influential and excellent pieces by Harold Jenkins and Helen Gardner. Gardner discusses the variety of the play, which has something for everyone: romance, debate about court and country, pastoral, music, spectacle, and masque. Jenkins observes that the play juxtaposes idealism and cynicism; though it tempers illusion with reality, it never rejects romance. Halio's essay, " 'No Clock in the Forest': Time in *As You Like It*," arrives at a similar interpretation by looking at the motif of time-consciousness that dominates the court and the timelessness of traditional pastoral. The volume concludes with brief excerpts treating Shakespearean comedy in general and a chronology of important dates in the life of Shakespeare and his age.

Jamieson, Michael. *Shakespeare: "As You Like It."* London: Edward Arnold, 1965.
An introduction intended for high school and college students. Surveys the play's history and context. Jamieson goes through the play scene by scene, offering a conventional interpretation of the work. He concludes that *As You Like It* ranks high among the romantic comedies but is less impressive than some of the romances that follow it. Includes a short bibliography.

Morris, Harry. "*As You Like It*: Et in Arcadia Ego." *Shakespeare Quarterly* 26 (1975):269-275.
Touchstone's announcement in II, iv, "Ay, now am I in Arden" echoes death's statement, most famously portrayed by painter Nicolas Poussin, "Et in Arcadia ego." The forest of Arden is a fallen Arcadia, where unrequited love (William's for Audrey, Phoebe's for Ganymede), passing time (the word appears forty-three times in a pastoral where time supposedly stands still), and reminders of death (such as Jacques' speech on the seven ages of man) constantly intrude. The allusion to Marlowe as dead shepherd reemphasizes this theme of death in Arcadia. Although specific pictographic evidence of the "Et in Arcadia ego" theme postdates the play by two decades, and the play does not fully elaborate the idea of Arcadian death, it certainly incorporates reminders of mortality that were popular in the sixteenth century. One possibility that Morris does not consider is that *As You Like It* may have contributed to later painterly versions of a fallen pastoral world.

Palmer, D. J. "*As You Like It* and the Idea of Play." *Critical Quarterly* 13
  (1971):234-245.
  As You Like It introduces many games. At court, play turns serious as the
  wrestling match becomes an attempt to kill Orlando. In the forest of Arden, the
  banished Duke plays various roles—philosopher, hunter, Robin Hood—but even
  here play partakes of cruelty in the killing of deer. The chief pastime is courtship, which has its escapist but also its melancholy side. Play thus mirrors the
  confusion of reality. The ambiguity of existence persists to the conclusion, with
  its vows that include "if."

Shaw, John. "Fortune and Nature in *As You Like It*." *Shakespeare Quarterly* 6
  (1955):45-50.
  The Renaissance saw Nature and Fortune as rivals. This conflict influences
  characterization and action in the play. Indeed, the central conflict can be seen
  as pitting Duke Frederick and Oliver (Fortune's minions at the play's beginning)
  against Duke Senior, Rosalind, and Oliver (who are wise and virtuous by nature).
  The virtuous characters flout Fortune, and at the end of the play their virtue—and
  hence Nature—triumphs.

Taylor, Michael. "*As You Like It*: The Penalty of Adam." *Critical Quarterly* 15
  (1973):76-80.
  Traces the religious allegory in the play. Arden, like the court, partakes of the
  Fall of Adam, and goodness is persecuted by evil precisely because it is good.
  Grace in the form of love redeems the world of the play, but the epilogue returns
  the audience to reality.

Tolman, Albert H. "Shakespeare's Manipulation of His Sources in *As You Like It*."
  Modern Language Notes 37 (1922):65-76.
  Compares the play to its chief source, Thomas Lodge's *Rosalynde* (1590), to
  consider Shakespeare's alterations and their effects. Though Tolman praises most
  of the changes, in some places he finds the original more pleasing. Lodge does
  not "lose" Adam, for example, and the usurping duke's conversion is less
  plausible than his death in battle. Tolman also considers other debts—to John
  Marston's *The Malcontent* and Desiderius Erasmus' *The Praise of Folly* for
  Jacques, to plays and ballads about Robin Hood for the choice of a pastoral play.

The Comedy of Errors

Arthos, John. "Shakespeare's Transformation of Plautus." *Comparative Drama* 1
  (1967):239-253.

Argues that, although Shakespeare took his story for *The Comedy of Errors* from Plautus, Shakespeare's world differs from that of his source. Plautus posits conflict as the norm, not only in society but also in nature, whereas for Shakespeare harmony is the norm. Shakespeare adopted Plautus' flouting of verisimilitude and also the sense of harmonious structure in the design of the drama.

Baldwin, Thomas Whitfield. *On the Compositional Genetics of "The Comedy of Errors. "* Urbana: University of Illinois Press, 1965.
Ephesus to the Dromios is like London to Shakespeare; Ephesus' relationship with Syracuse is like England's with Spain. The play is actually set in Hollywell Priory, where two priests were executed; the Theater stood in that vicinity. Shakespeare thus mingles his own experiences with the Plautine plot, which he doubles, and fits it into a conventional five-act structure. Baldwin dates the composition to late 1589 and traces themes and images from this play to Shakespeare's later works.

_____. *William Shakespeare Adapts a Hanging.* Princeton, N.J.: Princeton University Press, 1931.
The hanging of William Hartley, a priest, on October 5, 1588, influenced the creation of *The Comedy of Errors*. Like Baldwin's later book (cited above), this one argues for the setting as Hollywell Priory, the site of Egeon's execution (resembling that of Hartley's). Baldwin discusses the background of Hartley's case and concludes his study by drawing parallels between the play and the historical event. Valuable for its treatment of Elizabeth's attitude towards Catholics in the period of the Spanish Armada.

Barber, C. L. "Shakespearean Comedy in *The Comedy of Errors*." *College English* 25 (1964):493-497.
Barber claims that Shakespeare adapts Roman comedy to Elizabethan manners, depicting daily life more fully here than in any other play except *The Merry Wives of Windsor*. Shakespeare also humanizes the characters because his creations are not partial but full people, and his play offers serious commentary on marriage. Even in this early play, one sees the pattern of Shakespearean comedy, in which death threatens but is overcome by the forces of renewal and rebirth.

Brooks, Harold F. "Themes and Structure in *The Comedy of Errors*." In *Early Shakespeare*, edited by John Russell Brown and Bernard Harris. Stratford-upon-Avon Studies 3. London: Edward Arnold, 1961, 57-71.
Even in this early work, Shakespeare shows more skill in structure than any of his contemporaries except Thomas Kyd. Brooks examines the play's second scene to demonstrate the comedy's architectural artistry, which looks ahead and behind without losing the audience's interest in the present. Shakespeare, in common

Renaissance fashion, embellishes his original with other borrowings from Latin comedy, medieval drama, romances, and even the Bible. The play introduces a number of themes that pervade Shakespeare's work: the importance of relationships, cosmic order, and the dangers of illusion.

Elliott, G. R. "Weirdness in *The Comedy of Errors.*" *University of Toronto Quarterly* 9 (1939):95-106.
Praising the structure of the comedy, Elliott points out various ways that the work gains integrity. For example, Antipholus of Syracuse is mistaken for his brother by Adriana at the end of act III, and Dromio of Syracuse is mistaken for his twin by the cook in the next act. Elliott recognizes the pathos inherent in the play and believes that this element is not sufficiently controlled at the beginning. By the end, the play's comic effects have offset potential tragedy.

Grennan, Eamon. "Arm and Sleeve: Nature and Custom in *The Comedy of Errors.*" *Philological Quarterly* 59 (1980):150-164.
Argues that the conflict between nature and custom is central to the play. Characters assume that things are as they appear, whereas in fact appearance is deceptive. Similarly, they assume that what is customary is natural; Luciana tells her sister that it is natural for wives to obey their husbands. Adriana recognizes, however, that she naturally resents her husband's behavior, so that custom does not necessarily reflect nature. Language here, too, observes convention and pattern, but punning reveals its artificiality as the "physical and metaphysical meanings of a word . . . are divorced." Antipholus of Syracuse speaks conventionally about Luciana, using Petrarchan conceits; Dromio undercuts this tradition by speaking to Nell realistically. In the Abbess, nature and custom are reconciled, and the last act significantly avoids punning. The conflict between the natural and the conventional will continue to concern Shakespeare throughout his career.

Parker, Patricia. "Elder and Younger: The Opening Scene of *The Comedy of Errors.*" *Shakespeare Quarterly* 34 (1983):325-327.
Critics have been puzzled by the apparent contradiction in the first scene. Initially Egeon says that he was responsible for the older twin, but later in that scene he says that he had the "youngest" when the mast split. Parker argues that Egeon's description is consistent: the wife, caring for the younger twin, bound him closer to Egeon. Having introduced the idea of crossing, Parker explores how the comedy begins with ideas of the Old Law and concludes in reconciliation, thus echoing the second chapter of Paul's Epistles to the Ephesians, which refers to the cross of Christ as reconciling former strangers. Elsewhere in these epistles, Paul speaks of ending the enmity between Jacob and Esau. Parker's argument about the play's biblical echoes is more convincing than her discussion of the family tied to the mast.

Sanderson, James L. "Patience in *The Comedy of Errors.*" *Texas Studies in Literature and Language* 16 (1974-1975):603-618.
Dissents from those critics who regard the play as lacking serious import. Sanderson argues that the need for patience is an important theme here, as it is throughout Shakespeare's work. Lack of patience leads to the many errors of the comedy, and patience leads to the comic resolution. The word itself appears twelve times in the play, and Shakespeare's audiences would have been alert to this virtue, as it was fundamental to Christian and Renaissance philosophy.

Williams, Gwyn. "*The Comedy of Errors* Rescued from Tragedy." *Review of English Literature* 5 (1964):63-71.
Although often regarded as a farce, *The Comedy of Errors* barely escapes being a tragedy. If Shakespeare had not doubled Dromio, then the play would not have been comic; loss of identity could have turned the play into a *King Lear*. Williams examines the play scene by scene to show how the Dromios, especially Dromio of Syracuse, prevents disaster. Williams exaggerates the play's seriousness, since the Plautine original proves comic with only one Dromio, but she does show how the second Dromio provides more than farcical humor.

Coriolanus

Adelman, Janet. " 'Anger's My Meat': Feeding, Dependency, and Aggression in *Coriolanus.*" In *Shakespeare: Pattern of Excelling Nature*, edited by David Bevington and Jay L. Halio. Newark: University of Delaware Press, 1978, 108-124.
A feminist, psychoanalytical interpretation focusing on imagery dealing with eating. Coriolanus lacked female nurturing. Volumnia has taught him that feeding is equivalent to vulnerability, and "his masculine identity depends on his transformation of his vulnerability into an instrument of attack." He wishes to be self-sufficient; hence, even praise proves offensive, and he cannot ask for popular favor because he sees such pleading as emasculating. He seeks to destroy Rome to assert his mastery over his mother, but he cannot. Coriolanus' effort to stand alone isolates him from the audience and diminishes grief at his death. Also argues that the play denies any resolution to the dilemma it creates—the desire to be omnipotent and independent and the need for dependence.

Barton, Anne. "Livy, Machiavelli, and Shakespeare's *Coriolanus.*" *Shakespeare Survey* 38 (1985):115-129.
Shakespeare drew heavily on Plutarch's life of Coriolanus, but he also consulted Livy's history of Rome, not only for details of his story but also for his outlook. Coriolanus is an anachronism: he is a warrior in a Rome that wants peace and a rigid aristocrat who fails to recognize the importance of the plebeians. Barton

links this view of Livy with Niccolò Machiavelli's in his *Discorsi*, available in manuscript; Machiavelli takes a dim view of Coriolanus' antiplebeian stance. At the end of the play, Coriolanus tries to link commoners and patricians, but Aufidius easily turns him back to his old self and so causes the populace to destroy him.

Berry, Ralph. "The Metamorphoses of *Coriolanus.*" *Shakespeare Quarterly* 26 (1975):172-183.
Looks at various productions of the play to see how they reveal the very age and body of the time. For example, the *Comédie-Française* production in December, 1933, was understood as an attack on the Socialist government. Argues that, after World War II, productions focused on elements other than the political, in part because of "lowered social tensions." Laurence Olivier's 1938 Coriolanus was a fascist dictator in the making, reflecting the situation in Europe. His 1959 interpretation of the role highlighted the character's relationship with Aufidius. Berry regards this production as the best the play has enjoyed.

Brockman, B. A., ed. *"Coriolanus": A Casebook*. London: Macmillan, 1977.
Brockman's introduction briefly traces the play's theatrical and critical fortunes. Part 1 then presents comments by Samuel Johnson, William Hazlitt, Samuel Taylor Coleridge, Edward Dowden, Algernon Charles Swinburne, H. A. Taine, George Bernard Shaw, and T. S. Eliot. Lengthier pieces by twentieth century critics follow in the second part, beginning with A. C. Bradley, who, like his nineteenth century predecessors, focused on character but also examined the play's peculiar atmosphere. Among the other selections here is O. J. Campbell's study of the play as satire, T. J. B. Spencer's discussion of Shakespeare's vision of Rome, and A. P. Rossiter's treatment of the play's politics and its view of the historical process.

Browning, I. R. "*Coriolanus*: Boy of Tears." *Essays in Criticism* 5 (1955):18-31.
A response to D. J. Enright's "*Coriolanus*: Tragedy or Debate" (*Essays in Criticism* 4 [1954]:1-19), which treats the play as a debate revealing the limits of political partisanship and which, Browning believes, diminishes the character of Coriolanus. According to Browning, Coriolanus lacks self-knowledge. He needs public approval but despises this dependence. He also depends upon his mother's approval—he has fought to win her love. Hence, he yields to Volumnia's entreaties and is destroyed. Browning argues that Coriolanus' fall is tragic and that Enright is wrong to call the work merely a debate.

Burke, Kenneth. "*Coriolanus*—and the Delights of Faction." *Hudson Review* 19 (1966):185-202.
Claims that the play deals with class conflict. Coriolanus epitomizes patrician pride; he is noble enough to be heroic, sufficiently flawed to be sacrificed. Burke

discusses the relationship of the other characters to Coriolanus, each serving to highlight certain aspects of his behavior. Coriolanus effects catharsis in various ways: his excesses force the audience to confront class conflict; he embodies family, class, and national concerns; and his speeches express thoughts the audience represses.

Calderwood, James L. "*Coriolanus*: Wordless Meanings and Meaningless Words." *Studies in English Literature* 6 (1966):211-224.
Words lack meaning in the play. The plebeians' opening speeches signify nothing. Coriolanus tries to create a language that conveys truth, with words and symbols meaning only one thing, though he prefers silence or deeds, which are unambiguous. Calderwood sees Coriolanus' view of language as being too limited. He has no probing soliloquies because his words cannot explore his mind. He cannot accept or recognize language's ambiguity, so he cannot distinguish between true and false praise. Just as he distrusts public discourse, so he distrusts public opinion and so bases his sense of honor on his own estimation alone. Coriolanus thus divorces honor from its social context. He is great in his self-sufficiency but isolated and finally destroyed by his failure to join a society.

Daniell, David. "*Coriolanus*" in Europe. London: Athlone Press, 1980.
Looks closely at the 1978-1979 Royal Shakespeare Company production of *Coriolanus*. Daniell focuses on the play's European tour and includes interviews, journal notes, reviews, and descriptions of the performances, together with anecdotes about the tour and the theater world. Because Daniell admired the production, the book mutes negative criticism. In discussing this interpretation, Daniell provides commentary on the play. Thus, he observes that the opening line introduces the question of the "relationship between voice and action" and quotes a French review that describes the play as treating individual destiny.

Gurr, Andrew. "*Coriolanus* and the Body Politic." *Shakespeare Survey* 28 (1975):63-69.
The matter of sovereignty was hot in question as Shakespeare was writing *Coriolanus*. James I rejected the view that, in Richard Hooker's words, the law makes the king and that sovereignty resides in king and parliament joined in a body politic. In the belly fable, Shakespeare alludes to the food riots in the Midlands in 1607 and also to the political debate about sovereignty, and he points out the fallacy of the state as body. The play highlights factional antagonism, not organic unity, among different segments of society.

Hofling, Charles K. "An Interpretation of Shakespeare's *Coriolanus*." *American Imago* 14 (1957):407-435.
A psychological reading of the play. *Coriolanus* "is pre-eminently a tragedy of personality." Coriolanus is shaped by his mother; Hofling regards him as phallic-

narcissistic. Coriolanus' aversion to the plebeians arises from his seeing in them what is latent in himself, and he refuses to show them his wounds because he does not want to be subservient to anyone. He explodes in rage at the trial (III, iii) when he is called a traitor to Rome; he equates the charge with treachery against his mother, believing that he has been accused of seeking exclusive possession of her. His wife, too, plays an important role. In fact, if not for his healthy relationship with his wife, he would have destroyed his native city. The article concludes with a brief psychoanalysis of Shakespeare, linking *Coriolanus* to the death of Shakespeare's mother in 1608.

Holstun, James. "Tragic Superfluity in *Coriolanus*." *ELH* 50 (1983):485-507.
Agrees with Andrew Gurr that *Coriolanus* satirizes the metaphor of "body politic" but extends the implications to the nature of tragedy. Tragedy requires a belief in an organic society suffering through loss of a king. As Rosencrantz says in *Hamlet*, "The cess of majesty/ Dies not alone, but like a gulf doth draw/ What's near it with it." Among the tragedies, only *Coriolanus* does not deal with majesty's cess. Coriolanus is a misfit; he is not a king because Republican Rome has none, and he cannot behave as a politician. His exile leads to peace in Rome. Shakespeare presents a model of aristocratic rule through political manipulation, and that world allows not for tragedy but for satire. While the plebeians and the tribunes are objects of this satire, so is Coriolanus. He is punished, but he deserves his fate. Thus, "*Coriolanus* satirizes tragedy and the tragic affiliations of the body politic by placing a tragic king-figure within a satiric plot as its gull."

Holt, Leigh. *From Man to Dragon: A Study of Shakespeare's "Coriolanus."* Salzburg, Austria: University of Salzburg Press, 1976.
Holt believes that *Coriolanus* reflects the political and social divisions of Jacobean England. The play's hero seeks to be true to himself, and in an ideal world he would also then be true to his state. In this play, time is once more out of joint, and Coriolanus' integrity alienates him from plebeians and patricians alike; he becomes his own state, as he demonstrates when he banishes Rome. The world of the Volsci is more complex; he begins to encounter moral ambiguities. When his mother asks him to spare Rome, he confronts divided loyalties, and he seeks to win approval from the Volsci by deception. Aufidius' taunts brings Coriolanus back to his true self—isolated but with the integrity of Shakespeare's other tragic heroes.

Huffman, Clifford Chalmers. *Coriolanus in Context.* Lewisburg, Pa.: Bucknell University Press, 1971.
The play advocates a moderate aristocracy and so participates in the period's political debate. Both the tribunes who pander to the populace and the tyrannical Coriolanus represent undesirable extremes. Huffman places the work within the political context of the reign of James I and notes how Shakespeare and others

looked at the fall of the Roman Republic and also at contemporary politics. Shakespeare opposed tyranny and favored a mixed form of government. Huffman believes that *Coriolanus* moves away from the earlier Roman plays' position of endorsing republicanism and so reveals an attempt to please James, who equated democracy with misrule.

Hutchings, W. "Beast or God: The *Coriolanus* Controversy." *Critical Quarterly* 24 (Summer, 1982):35-50.
This useful article surveys criticism of the play from the early nineteenth century onwards. Hutchings regards Una Ellis-Fermor's essay on the play in *Shakespeare the Dramatist* (1961) as the best analysis of the work; that study sees Coriolanus as an idealist confronting a less-than-ideal Rome. Coriolanus joins Aufidius because he hopes that with the Volscians they can find the ideal that Rome fails to provide. Aufidius, however, also proves flawed.

Lowe, Lisa. "'Say I Play the Man I Am': Gender and Politics in *Coriolanus.*" *Kenyon Review* 8 (Fall, 1986):86-95.
Looks at feminist criticism of the play and argues that gender and politics are interrelated in *Coriolanus*. Lowe sees Roman patriarchal society, not Volumnia, as the source of Coriolanus' equation of manhood with war. Coriolanus lacks a father and hence a name; to receive the name "Coriolanus" he must submit to society and so at once become a man and be emasculated. He therefore prefers another name, "traitor," which does not require submission. He wants to be "author of himself" (V, ii, 36).

Meszaros, Patricia K. "'There Is a World Elsewhere': Tragedy and History in *Coriolanus.*" *Studies in English Literature* 16 (1976):273-285.
Critics have looked at the politics of the play or at the psychology of the hero. Meszaros combines the two by arguing that the play links the history of Rome and the fate of Coriolanus at a crucial moment in Western political thought. Coriolanus represents an older, medieval view of society, whereas everyone else is concerned with Machiavellian politics. Coriolanus thinks of a commonwealth, where all are joined by duties and rewards; the others think of a state in which each group or person seeks control. In seeking a world elsewhere, Coriolanus hopes to find in Antium the old order lacking in Rome. He fails to realize that the Volscians and Romans are alike. Coriolanus is great because he believes in a divine order, but that belief destroys him. He dies as he lived: alone. Meszaros argues that the play is a tragedy because Coriolanus is a "victim of historical forces" but also a victor over them by adhering to his view.

Oliver, H. J. "Coriolanus as Tragic Hero." *Shakespeare Quarterly* 10 (1959):53-60.
Noting that *Coriolanus* has not been popular with critics, Oliver argues that the hero is sympathetic. The play is a study of what happens to the uncompromising

aristocrat in a democratic society. The hero fails where lesser men such as Aufidius triumph. Shakespeare alters his source to make Coriolanus more attractive. In this play, Shakespeare shows that one may be good and still be destroyed.

Phillips, James E., ed. *Twentieth Century Interpretations of "Coriolanus."* Englewood Cliffs, N.J.: Prentice-Hall, 1970.
In his introduction, Phillips attributes Coriolanus' political ambition to Volumnia, and Coriolanus finally sees how much of a "boy" he has been. This recognition constitutes the tragic enlightenment that gives the play its power. Among the critics included here, G. Wilson Knight argues that the world of the play is harsh and metallic, but love triumphs. Harley Granville-Barker ranks the play below the great tragedies but argues that it remains dramatically effective and nicely balances language and action. A. A. Smirnov sees the plebeians as the play's only positive force. Brents Stirling, placing the work in its historical context, regards Shakespeare's treatment of the citizenry as "coldly cynical." A useful collection.

Poole, Adrian. *Coriolanus*. Boston: Twayne, 1988.
Opens with a discussion of the play's stage history and critical reception. Poole then offers his interpretation of the work, moving methodically through *Coriolanus* to note the effects of various episodes and the questions that they raise. Though intended for the undergraduate rather than for the scholar, this short book occasionally makes telling observations. For example, Poole notes that Volumnia, Virgilia, and Valeria twice greet Coriolanus—once when he returns in triumph from Carioles and again when he prepares to defeat Rome. The first scene with the three women is set indoors, balancing Coriolanus' reception at the house of Aufidius. Poole is especially good in treating the play's effectiveness in the theater.

Rabkin, Norman. "*Coriolanus*: The Tragedy of Politics." *Shakespeare Quarterly* 17 (1966):195-212.
More than any other of Shakespeare's tragic heroes, Coriolanus shows how a virtue can also be a vice. He is a man of principle in a world that has none, so society cannot be redeemed by his presence or his death. Argues that the play questions even his virtues, though, by suggesting that he acts not from choice but because of his conditioning. Like *Antony and Cleopatra*, this play denies the possibility of "self-fulfillment in this world" for the hero, who must create his own world and so triumph in death.

Sicherman, Carol M. "*Coriolanus*: The Failure of Words." *ELH* 39 (1972):189-207.
"In *Coriolanus*, dissociation between words and meanings . . . has become hopeless disjunction." Whereas Plutarch's Coriolanus is eloquent, Shakespeare's

speaks with difficulty; for him "action is eloquence." His distrust of language derives from Volumnia; she raised him on commonplaces that he echoes, and she has taught him to curse. He also has trouble hearing—he will isolate a word in a speech and react to it. Aufidius plays on this habit at the end of the play. Sicherman observes that, after this exploration of language as detached from meaning, Shakespeare moved to the romances, where words serve as charms, "magical symbols."

Sprengnether, Madelon. "Annihilating Intimacy in *Coriolanus.*" In *Women in the Middle Ages and the Renaissance: Literary and Historical Perspectives*, edited by Mary Beth Rose. Syracuse, N.Y.: Syracuse University Press, 1986, 89-111.
Explores the relationships between men and women in Shakespeare's tragedies generally and in *Coriolanus* particularly. In *Romeo and Juliet*, *Othello*, *Antony and Cleopatra*, and *King Lear*, the hero destroys himself in the process of uniting with a woman. In *Hamlet*, *Julius Caesar*, and *Macbeth*, the hero flees union with a woman but finally accepts the "feminine posture" of submission. Coriolanus submits to a woman but dies as a soldier, yet the fusion of the two modes of flight from and embracing of the woman leaves him "neither the dignity of a warrior nor . . . the luxury of the illusion of union in death." Sprengnether concludes that in the tragedies "union with a woman . . . is dangerous, if not fatal," but those who "pursue a counter-fantasy of ideal masculinity succumb to the contradiction inherent in the attempt to author oneself."

Vetz, John W. "Cracking Strong Curbs Asunder: Roman Destiny and the Roman Hero in *Coriolanus.*" *English Literary Renaissance* 13 (1983):58-69.
Vetz claims that Shakespeare's Roman world is Virgilian as well as Plutarchan. Like Virgil, Shakespeare sees Rome fulfilling its destiny, and those who oppose that destiny are destroyed, regardless of their heroism. Coriolanus, like Turnus, belongs to an earlier stage of history. Both are fighters in a world that is progressing to civic arts, both fight alone against a city, and both are linked to animals of prey. The play imitates Virgilian tragedy, in which "the cosmic Necessity . . . destroys a great but flawed man."

Vickers, Brian. *Shakespeare: "Coriolanus."* London: Edward Arnold, 1976.
An introduction that addresses a number of key issues. Vickers sees Shakespeare as critical of both plebeians and patricians. The tribunes seek power; the patricians hope to use Coriolanus to control the populace. Coriolanus alone has integrity. He fights for Rome, not for personal ends. He spares Rome to be true to himself, but back in Antium he begins to speak like a politician. He is quickly killed, though, leaving his corrupt world unredeemed. Aufidius' eulogy is not sincere, according to Vickers. Coriolanus' failure as a politician is his greatest virtue, and he becomes admirable because he differs from everyone else; only he is not self-serving.

Cymbeline

Brockbank, J. P. "History and Histrionics in *Cymbeline.*" *Shakespeare Survey* 11 (1958):42-49.
Traces the historical sources of the play. Brockbank sees *Cymbeline* as a historical romance that fuses English chronicles with Giovanni Boccaccio's work. The play remains superficial, transparently artificial. Argues that "we are haunted by intimations of a profound significance, but it is constantly clear that the apocalyptic destiny of Britain cannot be reconciled with the form of pastoral romance on any but the terms which Shakespeare offers." Among the serious themes explored here is the tension between primitivism and civilization.

Harris, Bernard. "What's Past Is Prologue: *Cymbeline* and *Henry VIII.*" In *Later Shakespeare*, edited by John Russell Brown and Bernard Harris. London: Edward Arnold, 1966, 203-233.
Harris begins by reviewing *Cymbeline*'s mixed critical reception from Samuel Johnson onward. Recognizing incongruities in the play, Harris re-creates the historical context; Shakespeare's audiences would have recognized the similarities between Cymbeline and James I and would have seen reflected in the work James's desire for peace. Historical perspective alone, however, does not make an audience enjoy a play; Harris also notes that the work's diversity creates true tragicomedy, lacking both tragic finality and comic confidence. The article concludes by linking the vision of *Cymbeline* with the prophecy at the end of *Henry VIII* as pleas for peace with "Rome" (that is, Catholic Spain).

Hoeniger, F. David. "Irony and Romance in *Cymbeline.*" *Studies in English Literature* 2 (1962):219-228.
Attributes incongruities in *Cymbeline* not to conventions of romance but to dramatic irony. This irony is directed not only at the evil characters but also at Imogen and Posthumus. At the end of the play, romance dispels irony to create a world of joy, and appearance yields to reality.

Hunt, Maurice. "Shakespeare's Empirical Romance: *Cymbeline* and Modern Knowledge." *Texas Studies in Language and Literature* 22 (1980):322-342.
The soothsayer first believes that a vision foretells Rome's victory. Experience teaches him that it predicted British triumph instead. In *Cymbeline*, characters learn from experience how to judge; they discover that language alone, or commonly received ideas, cannot adequately reflect reality. Even Providence can be comprehended only "by means of natural events." Shakespeare thus reveals himself as a Baconian empiricist.

Jones, Emrys. "Stuart *Cymbeline.*" *Essays in Criticism* 11 (1961):84-99.
Tries to understand how *Cymbeline*'s first audiences would have regarded the play. Shakespeare chose to write about King Cymbeline's uneventful reign because it coincided with the birth of Christ, who brings peace to the world. The references to peace praise James I's foreign policy. James took as his motto "beati pacifici" (blessed are the peacemakers), and he saw himself as another Augustus (who ruled Rome when Cymbeline ruled England). The references to Milford Haven in the play recall the landing there in 1485 of Henry, Earl of Richmond, the first Tudor king; the allusions strengthen the nationalistic theme, and Henry VII was James's great-grandfather. The attempt to create panegyric fails to produce great art here; "the whole play suffers . . . from being too close to its royal audience."

Kirsch, A. C. "*Cymbeline* and Coterie Dramaturgy." *ELH* 34 (1967):285-306.
Like others writing for the private theaters in the early 1600s, Shakespeare in *Cymbeline* creates self-conscious tragicomedy that distances the audience from characters and actions. Imogen is the one exception; though she is sympathetic, the situations in which Shakespeare places her are still as contrived as anything in the works of Francis Beaumont and John Fletcher or John Marston. Even the language is that of coterie theater.

Lawrence, J. "Natural Bonds and Artistic Coherence in the Ending of *Cymbeline.*" *Shakespeare Quarterly* 35 (1984):440-460.
The ending of the play calls attention to its artificiality, detaching audiences from the characters. Shakespeare here examines the conventions of romance, not to satirize the genre but to show that despite its contrivances it speaks to a fundamental human need. The play emphasizes the necessity of human connections, for ties that paradoxically liberate. Lawrence claims that the ending of *Cymbeline* similarly shows how the bonds of artistic convention free the writer to create something of great constancy.

Schwartz, Murray M. "Between Fantasy and Imagination: A Psychological Exploration of *Cymbeline.*" In *Psychoanalysis and Literary Process*, edited by Frederick C. Crews. Cambridge, Mass.: Winthrop, 1970, 219-283.
"*Cymbeline* is largely about a dissociated world brought back to rooted stability by the elimination of threatening forces." Schwartz offers a psychological reading of the play. "Cloten represents isolated, detached, and uncontrolled phallic wishes," and Iachimo "is Cloten in civilized dress." Posthumus matures during the play; Cymbeline, made whole by recovering his children, can yield to Caesar, and all evil is blamed on the wicked, "castrating" queen. Schwartz interprets the vision of the eagle's flight as summarizing the play's movement "from genital and anal eroticism to sublimated oral fusion which guarantees masculine virility." The good fathers become mothers. The conclusion does not, however, resolve the psychological conflicts.

Swander, Homer. "*Cymbeline* and the 'Blameless Hero.'" *ELH* 31 (1964):259-270.
In *Shakespeare's Problem Comedies* (1931), William Witherle Lawrence observes
that Posthumus' behavior should be regarded in light of the literary conventions
of the time. Lawrence sees Posthumus as a blameless hero, whose boasting,
credulity, and rage are part of the tradition. Swander disagrees, arguing that
Shakespeare alters the conventions to show flaws in Posthumus and also to
criticize the stock hero. In the fifth act, Posthumus transcends the flawed morality
of romance and so becomes worthy of Imogen.

Taylor, Michael. "The Pastoral Reckoning in *Cymbeline*." *Shakespeare Survey* 36
(1983):97-106.
Even in the romantic comedies, Shakespeare questions the conventions of pastoral. *Cymbeline* carries that probing further in its treatment of Arcadia. In the
pastoral world of the play, Imogen encounters the headless body of Cloten, and
her response to it has erotic implications. Posthumus and Imogen are sexually
naïve and behave badly to each other; even in the final scene, Posthumus unwittingly hurts Imogen. The play's last word, however, is "peace." The lovers join
in pastoral metaphor, and similar language projects Britain's regeneration.

Thorne, William Barry. "*Cymbeline*: 'Lopp'd Branches' and the Concept of Regeneration." *Shakespeare Quarterly* 20 (1969):143-159.
Looks at the folk elements of the play and notes the links with Shakespeare's
earlier romantic comedies. The folk motifs strength the play's nationalistic flavor,
its praise of Britain and her people. The young characters regenerate the world
of the play, and all are reconciled under Cymbeline's rule as family and nation
end their conflicts.

Tinkler, F. C. "*Cymbeline*." *Scrutiny* 7 (1938/1939):5-20.
Begins by looking at the versification, in which Tinkler finds a conflict between
exaggerated melodrama and the mundane. This same tension pervades the entire
play. Imogen, for example, is a supremely chaste ideal who lives "in the local
routine of homely images." Rome is grand, but Italy is corrupt. The dirges
embody stillness in the midst of activity. The play moves "towards a repose
achieved in spite of violence," but the dichotomies remain unresolved.

Warren, Roger. *Cymbeline*. Manchester, England: Manchester University
Press, 1989.
Part of the "Shakespeare in Performance" series. Warren's first chapter discusses
the theatrical issues that the play raises. For example, can a production highlight
Cymbeline's connections with Christ, born during his reign, or with James I, who
may have prompted Shakespeare's choice of this particular ruler? Warren thinks
not. Should Iachimo's trunk scene stress the dark side of the action or its humor?
The rest of the volume looks at seven productions, beginning with Peter Hall's

1957 *Cymbeline* at Stratford and ending with Hall's 1988 version at the National Theatre. Of these, Warren finds William Gaskill's 1962 production at Stratford the most successful because it focused on the text and used simple staging to highlight the acting and speeches.

Wickham, Glynne. "Riddle and Emblem: A Study in the Dramatic Structure of *Cymbeline*." In *English Renaissance Studies: Presented to Dame Helen Gardner in Honour of Her Seventieth Birthday*, edited by John Carey. Oxford, England: Clarendon Press, 1980, 94-113.
Finds analogues between the play and contemporary politics. Cymbeline is James I; the union of British Imogen and Roman Posthumus reflects James's willingness to conclude Catholic marriages for his children—his version of tribute freely granted by Cymbeline to Augustus—in return for peace with the Catholic League. The riddles exploit images that James used for himself and that other poets, such as Ben Jonson and Samuel Daniel, used for masques and pageants flattering the Stuart king. Cloten and the Queen represent the war party at court. Wickham links the play to the marriage of Sir John Hay of Scotland with the English Honora, daughter of Lord Denny, symbolizing the union of Scotland, England, and Wales. Wickham therefore dates the play no later than 1609.

Hamlet

Anthologies and Surveys of Criticism

Bevington, David, ed. *Twentieth Century Interpretations of "Hamlet."* Englewood Cliffs, N.J.: Prentice-Hall, 1968.
Still a useful collection. Bevington offers his interpretation of *Hamlet* in his introduction. Two early twentieth century studies begin part 1—A. C. Bradley's (from his 1904 *Shakespearean Tragedy*) and T. S. Eliot's. These are followed by Harley Granville-Barker's discussion of Shakespeare's use of time and space in the play; Theodore Spencer's "Hamlet and the Nature of Reality" (1938), which sets the play within the intellectual milieu of the sixteenth century view of man; D. G. James's assessment of *Hamlet* as a study in despair; Maynard Mack's excellent analysis of the play ("The World of *Hamlet*"); and L. C. Knights's vision of Hamlet as isolated. Harry Levin, Fredson Bowers, and Bertram Joseph conclude this section with pieces that remain classics. The second section presents short excerpts from seven other critics; included here are short comments by Ernest Jones on Hamlet's Oedipal conflict and C. S. Lewis' observation that Hamlet appeals to audiences as an Everyman.

Brown, John Russell, and Bernard Harris, eds. *"Hamlet."* Stratford-upon-Avon Studies 5. London: Edward Arnold, 1963.

A collection of essays written for this volume. Patrick Cruttwell, David William, and J. K. Walton defend Hamlet's obedience to the ghost's commands, seeing the specter as honest. Peter Ure treats Hamlet's character and his role and finds that by the fifth act he has ceased to be an avenger because he submits to Providence. G. K. Hunter treats "The Heroism of Hamlet" as the prince struggles to retain his humanity and control the time so out of joint. Patrick Cruttwell defends Hamlet, E. A. J. Honigmann speaks of the politics of *Hamlet*, and T. J. B. Spencer traces the play's critical fortunes in various times and places. R. A. Foakes observes that different characters reveal themselves through their language: Claudius' speeches demonstrate his lack of substance, Laertes sounds like his father, Horatio speaks plainly, and Hamlet uses language as both weapon and mask. The volume concludes with a seven-page bibliography.

Conklin, Paul S. *A History of "Hamlet" Criticism, 1601-1821*. New York: King's Crown Press, 1947.
Focuses on the way actors and critics have understood Hamlet's character over the centuries. Shakespeare's contemporaries saw Hamlet as an eloquent malcontent, an avenger in the tradition of Thomas Kyd, and mad. David Garrick highlighted Hamlet's melancholy but did not treat him as a procrastinator. The eighteenth century began the divorce of theater and text, since few actually read Shakespeare in the seventeenth century. Nicholas Rowe, Shakespeare's first eighteenth century editor, sees Hamlet as a more humane version of Orestes. After 1770, critics focus on Hamlet's procrastination, madness, and complexity: Hamlet often comes to resemble the critic. Conklin also discusses French and German views of Hamlet to 1821.

Gottschalk, Paul. *The Meanings of "Hamlet": Modes of Literary Interpretation Since Bradley*. Albuquerque: University of New Mexico Press, 1972.
Attempts to classify Hamlet criticism under the headings Evolutionist School, Elizabethan Psychology, Elizabethan Ethos, Psychological Interpretation, and Anagogical Interpretation. Gottschalk evaluates the various works that he includes in each category and notes that no single interpretation can fully account for the play. The book helps the student make some sense of the welter of material on *Hamlet* and of the vogues in literary analysis. Bernard McElroy praised the book for its ability "to bestow liveliness and intellectual vigor upon a subject that is not only vast as the Sahara but could, handled differently, be every bit as dry" (*Renaissance Quarterly* 27 [1974]:587).

Hattaway, Michael. *"Hamlet."* Atlantic Highlands, N.J.: Humanities Press International, 1987.
A study of various types of Shakespeare criticism; looks at productions and publications. The larger portion of this slim volume considers four approaches: historical and formal, romantic and psychological, philosophical, and linguistic.

Though a survey of modern criticism, Hattaway repeatedly offers his own understanding of the work. In "Part Two: Appraisal," Hattaway offers his interpretation of the play by looking at such issues as structure and Hamlet's mind. Hattaway believes that all approaches can be enlightening, but he denies that there is an authentic *Hamlet*; varying interpretations have their merits. A good introduction to the wealth of criticism on the play. Concludes with a brief bibliography of modern studies.

Leavenworth, Russell E., ed. *Interpreting "Hamlet": Materials for Analysis*. San Francisco: Howard Chandler, 1960.
A valuable collection for high school students and undergraduates. Begins with Francis de Belleforest's account (in a 1608 English translation) of *The Hystorie of Hamblet, Prince of Denmarke*. Leavenworth includes many of the most famous pronouncements on the play and characters: Johann Wolfgang von Goethe's statement in *Wilhelm Meisters Lehrjahre* that Shakespeare presents "the effects of a great action upon a soul unfit for the performance of it"; Samuel Taylor Coleridge's view that Hamlet "mistakes the seeing of his chains for the breaking of them, delays action till action is of no use, and dies the victim of mere circumstance and accident"; and A. C. Bradley's famous 1904 study. A number of selections provide insight into the stage history of the work: William Hazlitt discusses Edmund Kean's treatment of the role; John Forster looks at William Charles Macready as Hamlet; William Winter comments on Sir Henry Irving; and George Bernard Shaw discusses Sir Johnston Forbes-Robertson. The work concludes with suggestions for student papers.

Muir, Kenneth, and Stanley Wells, eds. *Aspects of "Hamlet."* Cambridge, England: Cambridge University Press, 1979.
Nine articles reprinted from *Shakespeare Survey*. The volume begins with Clifford Leech's survey of twentieth century criticism to 1955. Harold Jenkins looks more broadly at the play's theatrical and critical fortunes from Shakespeare's day to the mid-twentieth century. R. A. Foakes compares Hamlet and Vindice in Cyril Tourneur's *The Revenger's Tragedy*. The latter falls in love with his role as avenger; it is Hamlet's greatness that he exercises moral restraint. Keith Brown examines parallels in the play, such as the platform of I, i, and the stage where Hamlet's body will be displayed at the end of the play. Juliet McLauchlan's "The Prince of Denmark and Claudius' Court" sees the play as contrasting the humanistic world of Wittenberg with the opposite vision of Elsinore. Frank McCombie finds Desiderius Erasmus' influence in the play. Ralph Berry deals with the lines "A man's life's no more/ Than to say one"; Berry finds here an affirmation of life and self. Inga-Stina Ewbank examines the play's language, and Nigel Alexander compares Sophocles' Oedipus and Hamlet: both must purge corruption and both succeed, but at a terrible price that leaves audiences uncertain about how to understand these characters. Includes sixteen

photographs from modern productions. These illustrations bear no relationship to the text.

Price, Joseph G., ed. *"Hamlet": Critical Essays.* New York: Garland, 1986.
A generous sampling of some three centuries of criticism, though weighted to the twentieth century. Arranged under six headings: "The Play," "The Character of Hamlet," "Specific Scenes and Other Characters," "Language," "Hamlet on Stage," and "References to the Play in Fiction." Includes such frequently reprinted items as Maynard Mack's "The World of *Hamlet*" and Ernest Jones on Hamlet's Oedipal conflict. In addition, offers less common items, such as Sheldon P. Zitner's "Hamlet, Duellist" (1969), which relates the prince to the code of Vincentio Saviolo's *Practice* (1595) dealing with fencing and the art of quarreling.

Sacks, Claire, and Edgar Whan, eds. *"Hamlet": Enter Critic.* New York: Appleton-Century-Crofts, 1960.
Brings together a sampling of two centuries of Shakespeare criticism from Thomas Hanmer's *Some Remarks on the Tragedy of Hamlet, Prince of Denmark* (1736) to works published in the 1950s. The alphabetical arrangement, chosen to avoid imposing a pattern, is awkward, and the editors, aiming the work at undergraduates, include selections that are provocative but critically suspect. Still a good anthology, though not as complete as Claude C. H. Williamson's *Readings on the Character of Hamlet* (1950).

Williamson, Claude C. H., ed. *Readings on the Character of Hamlet.* London: George Allen and Unwin, 1950.
Includes 324 selections arranged chronologically from John Evelyn's brief comment in his diary for November 26, 1661, that he saw *Hamlet*, "But now the old plays begin to disgust this refined age" to Claude W. Sykes's 1947 effort to identify the "real" Shakespeare from the play. Illustrates that the character has inspired much throwing about of brains, prompting Williamson to ask "What sort of person are you, Hamlet, Prince of Denmark, you weak-willed and head-strong youth, melancholy and violent, dreamy and brutal, superstitious and philosophical, sensible and mad; . . . the earliest exponent of the modern mind, of romanticism and pessimism, and nihilism and neuroticism, and many other things which doubtless never entered your mind?"

Source Studies

Gollancz, Israel, ed. *The Sources of "Hamlet": With Essays on the Legend.* London: Oxford University Press, 1926.
Provides the first printed Latin text of Saxo Grammaticus' tale of Hamlet (1514) with an English translation on facing pages. Also includes Francis de Belleforest's

version from the *Histoires tragiques* (1582 edition) and the 1608 *Hystorie of Hamblet*. Gollancz's essay explores the development of the Hamlet story through Celtic and Scandinavian sources but does not speculate on an *Ur-Hamlet* that may have intervened between Belleforest and Shakespeare.

Hansen, William F. *Saxo Grammaticus and the Life of Hamlet: A Translation, History, and Commentary*. Lincoln: University of Nebraska Press, 1983.
The first written account of Hamlet dates from Saxo's *Gesta Danorum* of about 1200. Hansen regards the account as deriving from oral tradition but is related to the *Saga of Hrolf Kraki* and also the story of Lucius Junius Brutus, who feigned imbecility to save his life. Hansen compares Saxo's version with Francis de Belleforest's sixteenth century story and Shakespeare's, but he regards the *Ur-Hamlet* as Shakespeare's only source. Hansen's translation, which appears without the Latin original, is sprightly and readable, though not literal.

Malone, Kemp. *The Literary History of Hamlet: The Early Tradition*. Heidelberg: Carl Winter, 1923.
Intended as the first of a three-part study, the volume attempts to reconstruct the story of Hamlet before Saxo Grammaticus recorded it in his twelfth century *Historia Danica*. Examines early sagas such as *Beowulf* and the Hervarasaga. For the final chapter, Malone constructs what he terms "the primitive plot" based on these early accounts. In this version, Feng kills his older brother Orvendill for the latter's wife, Geruth. Feng becomes king, and Amleth, the rightful heir, feigns madness to save his own life. Vilfill, faithful to Amleth, allows him to escape Feng's attempt to kill the youth, and Amleth eventually returns to kill his uncle and assume the throne of Jutland.

Taylor, Marion A. *A New Look at the Old Sources of "Hamlet."* The Hague: Mouton, 1968.
A study of Saxo Grammaticus' *Historia Danica*, particularly concerned with Amleth's grandfather, Rorik. In her concluding chapter Taylor defends Gertrude as having been originally a good pagan who for that reason was vilified by Christian writers, including Shakespeare. Though only tangentially related to the play, this short study makes some useful comments on the ultimate source of *Hamlet*.

General Studies

Aldus, P. J. *Mousetrap: Structure and Meaning in "Hamlet."* Toronto: University of Toronto Press, 1977.
Hamlet creates a myth, which in its simplest form is the story of a king or father seeking to possess a woman. He is killed by his son or nephew who seizes the queen/mother. All the men are aspects of Hamlet. The myth is presented in the

play in a variety of ways. For example, when Hamlet says that exaggerated acting "out-Herods Herod," Aldus believes that the statement calls to mind Herod Antipas' marriage to his brother's wife, the killing of John the Baptist, and the seductive dance of Salome. Guy Hamel wrote that "every reader of *Mousetrap* is certain to find observations that enrich his understanding of *Hamlet*; every reader is equally certain to find conclusions that seem pushed too far" (*University of Toronto Quarterly* 47 [1978]: 405).

Alexander, Nigel. *Poison, Play, and Duel: A Study in "Hamlet."* Lincoln: University of Nebraska Press, 1971.
Praised by Stanley Wells as "a deeply serious and highly intelligent study of the play" (*Review of English Studies* n.s. 23 [1972]: 200), this work looks at the play's Renaissance background but also sees in it universal concerns. Alexander distinguishes between the character of Hamlet and the play, "which dramatizes a number of possible human responses to direct and indirect aggression." Pointing out the artistic unity of the play, Alexander draws on theatrical criticism, imagery, and intellectual history to comment on this elusive work. The title refers to the play's three central actions: the killing of Old Hamlet, *The Murder of Gonzago*, and the concluding duel, all of which involve poison and death. Alexander regards delay as a theatrical device that questions revenge. Hamlet acts finally because circumstances force him to, and his conscience makes him a hero far different than the stock avenger.

Alexander, Peter. *Hamlet: Father and Son.* Oxford, England: Clarendon Press, 1955.
Alexander begins by differing from Laurence Olivier's pronouncement in his 1948 *Hamlet* that the play is "the tragedy of a man who could not make up his mind." "The vicious mole of nature" that Hamlet speaks of in the first act does not refer to his own tragic flaw. According to Alexander, Oedipus, Philoctetes, and Hamlet have no tragic flaw. The Ghost represents the age of heroes, Hamlet the Renaissance in his combination of toughness and sensitivity. Alexander concludes that "the play dramatizes the perpetual struggle to which all civilization that is genuine is doomed. To live up to its own ideals it has to place itself at a disadvantage with the cunning and treacherous." Hamlet is both humane and tough, the ideal man.

Calderwood, James L. *To Be and Not To Be: Negation and Metadrama in "Hamlet."* New York: Columbia University Press, 1983.
A study of language, identity, and self-consciousness in the play. In "*Hamlet*: The Name of Action," Calderwood compares Hamlet's relationship with his father to Shakespeare's *Hamlet*'s relationship to Kyd's play. Both must be true to their parents yet earn for themselves "the names they share with their respective parents." Hamlet's procrastination results from his reluctance to sacrifice

his identity by adopting his father's cause; he must find a way to act without losing himself. The second chapter, "To Be and Not To Be; The Range of Negation in *Hamlet*," looks at language, which tends to negate itself in the play. Hence the pun is so popular here—it says and unsays at once. Again the play
· resolves the tension between opposites when it finds a way to reconcile being and not-being. In the third and final chapter, Calderwood notes how the play's structure evokes delay and calls attention to its own artifice, demanding that audiences acknowledge both Elsinore and the Globe. Mark Rose called the book "lucid and witty in style, elegant in form, and never pompous or pretentious in manner" (*Shakespeare Quarterly* 35 [1987]: 234); Sidney Homan called it one of the "major studies" of *Hamlet* (JEGP 83 [1984]:561).

Charney, Maurice. *"Hamlet's" Fictions*. London: Routledge, 1988.
A collection of ten essays that examine such issues as text, structure, the revenge tragedy tradition, and imagery. Among the observations is that Hamlet's pursuit of personal vendetta alienates the audience by the end of the fourth act, but the character regains sympathy when he places his actions in a providential context in act V. Charney regards the second quarto and the folio versions as two separate plays and prefers the latter. He sees the play as containing four rather than five divisions, and he shows that Hamlet first defeats Polonius, Rosencrantz, Guildenstern, and Osric in a comic vein before he turns to the serious business of overcoming Claudius.

_____. *Style in "Hamlet."* Princeton, N.J.: Princeton University Press, 1969.
Charney first examines imagery: warfare and weapons, secrecy and poison, corruption, limits, and the stage. In the second section, he looks at the ways in which the play communicates without words through such devices as music, properties, gesture, and costume. The book concludes with a discussion of language. Among Charney's observations here is that Claudius' language reveals a determined figure but one who masks intentions in complex syntax. Hamlet uses four styles of speech: self-conscious, witty (associated with madness), passionate (especially in soliloquies), and a simple style for narration. Though not primarily concerned with developing an interpretation of the play, Charney argues against the view that Hamlet procrastinates and notes how pervasive evil is in the play. T. H. Howard Hill called Charney's study "sane, learned, perceptive" (*Review of English Studies*, n.s. 22 [1971]:191).

Cohen, Michael. *"Hamlet" in My Mind's Eye*. Athens: University of Georgia Press, 1989.
A scene-by-scene interpretation, or interpretations, that highlights both the variety of possible meanings and the unchanging core of the play. For example, when the priest refuses to give full burial ceremonies to Ophelia, is he standing up to

court influence or is he Claudius' toadie? Is Hamlet's response to Laertes' leap into the grave a fit of madness, pretense, or an effort to show Laertes how foolish the young man is acting? Does Hamlet send Rosencrantz and Guildenstern to their deaths in self-defense, in revenge, or out of malice?

Cox, Lee Sheridan. *Figurative Design in "Hamlet": The Significance of the Dumb Show.* Columbus: Ohio University Press, 1973.
Regards the dumb show in *The Murder of Gonzago* as central to *Hamlet*. While the most obvious pantomime appears in III, ii, Cox notes that throughout the play Shakespeare has introduced various "dumb shows," which become a metaphor for "the action that makes life a hollow show." The book looks at three central images: poison poured into the ear, encrustment/confinement, beasts and traps. According to Cox, the Ghost pours poison into Hamlet's ear and the prince becomes corrupt. His life becomes a dumb show that ends in silence. Yet Cox concedes that audiences remain loyal and sympathetic to Hamlet. Dieter Mehl commented that "even if we have doubts about Professor Cox's overall assessment of the play's figurative design, we will be grateful for many incidental insights and will certainly agree that the dumb show is an important and fully integrated part of the play, not just an isolated stage-effect" (*Renaissance Quarterly* 27 [1974]:589).

Davis, Arthur G. *"Hamlet" and the Eternal Problem of Man.* New York: St. John's University Press, 1964.
Maintains that Hamlet is not mad and that he must avenge his father's death not only for personal reasons but also to bring Claudius to justice. The Ghost's injunction, moreover, should bind Hamlet, since Old Hamlet has been sent to Purgatory, not Hell, and so is not a goblin damned. Hence, his commands have a moral sanction. Hamlet shirks his responsibility, not because he is too weak but because he possesses "innate goodness." Therefore, he is flawed but also lovable.

Davidson, Peter. *"Hamlet": Text and Performance.* London: MacMillan, 1983.
The first part of this slim volume offers a critical introduction that discusses the play's continuing popularity, the text, the character of Hamlet, humor in the play, its language, and its relevance to modern audiences. Part 2 looks at five twentieth century productions, including the fascinating Charles Marowitz adaptation that eliminates Horatio and that Marowitz himself likened to a rape of the play. The other, more conventional treatments discussed are Laurence Olivier's 1948 film version, John Gielgud's 1934 and Richard Burton's 1964 productions, and Peter Hall's 1965 Royal Shakespeare Company's *Hamlet*, which sought to achieve relevance by relating the play to student unrest.

Dodsworth, Martin. *"Hamlet" Closely Observed*. London: Athlone Press, 1985.
Dodsworth sees the play as depicting a society with a debased cult of honor, and he regards Hamlet as haughty and hypocritical, "pathetic and appalling." Though viewing the play as a novel or poem rather than as a drama, Dodsworth offers sound interpretations of numerous elements. Thus, he notes how the third act abounds in staged events: Ophelia's encounter with Hamlet, Hamlet's presentation of *The Murder of Gonzago*, and the meeting of Hamlet and Gertrude in her bedroom. Dodsworth sees the work as "rhapsodic," as chaotic as the protagonist's mind.

Dollerup, Cay. *Denmark, "Hamlet," and Shakespeare: A Study of Englishmen's Knowledge of Denmark Towards the End of the Sixteenth Century with Special Reference to "Hamlet."* 2 vols. Salzburg, Austria: University of Salzburg Press, 1975.
The study begins with an examination of the story of Amleth and then looks at the treatment of Denmark elsewhere in Elizabethan literature. Dollerup also considers other sources of information about Danish matters. Believing that Shakespeare sought to make *Hamlet* as authentic as possible, Dollerup finds that the play uses Danish elements to create its atmosphere by dwelling on geography, typically Danish features such as the election of kings, language, music, and striking visual effects. The study concludes that in this play "Shakespeare embedded the ideas and notions his contemporaries had of Denmark."

Draper, John W. *The "Hamlet" of Shakespeare's Audience*. Durham. N.C.: Duke University Press, 1939.
A study of the supporting characters of the play in an attempt to see them from a perspective other than Hamlet's. For example, Draper defends Gertrude, believes that Polonius "at least had been a great prime minister," and argues that the guards' ignorance of modern Danish history indicates that they are Swiss. Rosencrantz and Guildenstern are nice young men eager to help Hamlet. Draper does look at Hamlet, too, and sees him not as melancholy but as a frustrated man of action who at length achieves his revenge. Draper likens Hamlet to Brutus, Macbeth, Coriolanus, and Antony— facing a hostile world but pursuing his goal. The volume concludes with chapters on the plot and the setting, style, and theme (the struggle of the individual against society).

Duthie, George Ian. *The "Bad" Quarto of "Hamlet": A Critical Study*. Cambridge, England: Cambridge University Press, 1941.
The first (1603) quarto is a memorial reconstruction of the true text of the play. The reporter, however, did at times compose his own blank verse to convey the meaning, though not the language, of the original. In so doing, the reporter borrowed from other plays by Shakespeare and his contemporaries. Duthie believes that the First Quarto is an edited text, another person having revised the

remembered text. The text was intended for performance in the provinces and was written down by the person who played Marcellus. Duthie rejects the possibilities that the First Quarto was actually the text of Shakespeare's play or even a draft of a revision of an *Ur-Hamlet*.

Erlich, Avi. *Hamlet's Absent Father*. Princeton, N.J.: Princeton University Press, 1977.
Essentially a Freudian reading of the play. Sees *Hamlet* as "a complicated attempt to deal with a very specific Oedipal crisis, one that has to do with an absent father, a ghostly father." Hamlet identifies with his father (not, as Ernest Jones believes, with Claudius) but recognizes that Old Hamlet was flawed. Hamlet fears growing up and would like his father—or God, a father substitute—to avenge the murder. The prince looks for other father figures from Adam to Priam to Old Fortinbras and Old Norway, but all are weak, so Hamlet retreats into near-madness. Hamlet also tries to emasculate Claudius, but he finally must face reality. Erlich argues that most of Shakespeare's plays portray weak fathers, perhaps because he grew up and began writing while a woman ruled England. The excessive insistence on Freudian readings weakens the argument. For example, when Hamlet refers to Claudius as a smiling villain, the prince (according to Erlich) uses the smile as a substitute for a vagina and so the reference represents part of Hamlet's effort to castrate Claudius.

Fisch, Harold. *"Hamlet" and the Word: The Covenant Pattern in Shakespeare*. New York: Frederick Ungar, 1971.
Compares Hamlet's confrontation with the Ghost to the revelation Moses experienced on Mount Sinai. The Ghost urges Hamlet to undertake the natural duty of punishing guilt while leaving Gertrude to heaven. Thus, the Ghost is both "goblin damned" and "spirit of health," fusing Senecan revenge with the biblical injunction of forgoing vengeance. Hamlet must find a way to "adapt grace to nature," and this duality directs the play. The Ghost has come from Purgatory to "elect" Hamlet, who moves "from revenger to redeemer." When Hamlet refrains from killing Claudius at prayer, the prince, despite his statement, fears losing his own place in heaven, and here grace defeats nature. Argues that Hamlet would have killed his mother, however, had Polonius not intervened; Polonius acts like the ram in the sacrifice of Isaac. Fisch also sees typology being used in Hamlet's apology to Laertes, which resembles the relationship between David and Jonathan. Kenneth Muir praised the study as "convincing and eloquent" (*English Language Notes* 10 [1972]:296). James H. Jones found the work "fascinating and stimulating" but disagreed with Fisch's interpretation of the nature of tragedy in the play (*Renaissance Quarterly* 26 [1973]:370-372).

Frye, Roland Mushat. *The Renaissance "Hamlet": Issues and Responses in 1600*. Princeton, N.J.: Princeton University Press, 1984.

"My purpose here is to examine the play afresh in the light of the audiences for which it was initially written, and to see it in the ambience of Elizabethan attitudes." Shakespeare's audiences might well have equated Gertrude's marriage to Claudius with Mary Stuart's hasty marriage with James Hepburn, the Earl of Bothwell, after he killed her husband. Though modern readers are sometimes troubled by Hamlet's unconcern over the fate of Rosencrantz and Guildenstern, Frye indicates that in 1600 audiences would not have been troubled by their deaths. By showing the monarchy of Denmark as elective, Shakespeare avoids the problem of deposing a hereditary monarch. Claudius, according to Frye, is justly served. A learned survey of Renaissance attitudes embodied in the play; concludes with an extensive bibliography and includes eighty-seven fine illustrations. R. A. Foakes, who found some limitations in Frye's approach, nonetheless wrote that the book offers "a mass of evidence, historical and visual, that sheds light on many aspects of the play" (*Modern Philology* 84 [1986]:71).

Ghose, Zulfikar. *Hamlet, Prufrock, and Language.* New York: St. Martin's Press, 1978.
A study of the complexities of language in a play where words and actions are divorced. Horatio's smug reliance on language is shattered in the first scene. Claudius manipulates language, as does Laertes, for personal gain. Hamlet wants to penetrate language to understand the reality that words embody; by the end of the play, he finds that words have failed him, leaving only silence. Ophelia does not think about her words: she understands neither them nor the world. Polonius understands language, both as means and end, but he always seeks practical use in language. Ghose maintains that Shakespeare and T. S. Eliot both seek vision but recognize that "words cannot be used to come to a knowledge of it. There is only silence." Stanley Wells commented that "in spite of its simplifications, its occasional imperfections of idiom, its excessive claims to originality, this book may be recommended for its economy, its eloquence, and a quality of imaginative perception" (*The Times Literary Supplement*, May 30, 1980, p. 625).

Grebanier, Bernard. *The Heart of "Hamlet": The Play Shakespeare Wrote.* New York: Thomas Y. Crowell, 1960.
Grebanier believes that *Hamlet* has been consistently misunderstood. After presenting the Aristotelian view of tragedy, the author surveys Shakespearean criticism before presenting his own view that Hamlet is not mad, does not feign madness, and does not procrastinate. Though a man of action, Hamlet must have proof of Claudius' guilt before he can kill the usurper. The play's turning point is the murder of Polonius, which denies Hamlet the ability to act as an agent of justice. Hamlet here yields to rashness and so precipitates the tragedy. Though Grebanier claims to be the first to develop this theory, it follows closely Fredson Bowers' "Hamlet as Minister and Scourge" (*PLMA* 70 [1955]:740-749).

Gurr, Andrew. *"Hamlet" and the Distracted Globe*. Edinburgh, Scotland: Sussex University Press, 1978.
Hamlet is an honest man in a corrupt world who must find a way to secure revenge that will punish the guilty; Polonius' death teaches Hamlet the means. Gurr builds on the ideas of Fredson Bowers' "Hamlet as Minister and Scourge" (1955) but blames Claudius for Polonius' death because the king has corrupted Denmark. Gurr offers a number of fascinating observations along the way, such as linking the name of Claudius to Hamlet's reference to Nero (Claudius' nephew) in III, ii, and Rosencrantz and Guildenstern to James Hepburn, the Earl of Bothwell and the murderer of the second husband of Mary, Queen of Scots.

Heilbrun, Carolyn. "The Character of Hamlet's Mother." *Shakespeare Quarterly* 8 (1957):201-206.
An early challenge to the conventional viewing of Gertrude as frail, superficial, and unintelligent. Heilbrun argues that on the contrary Gertrude is perceptive, loves her son, and is innocent of wrongdoing but that she is subject to passion that drives her to Claudius. She is most like Horatio in the play. A useful, insightful analysis.

Hoff, Linda Kay. *Hamlet's Choice*. Lewiston, N.Y.: Edwin Mellen Press, 1988.
A study of the play's religious elements. Hoff maintains that *Hamlet* was influenced by readings of *Revelation*, conflicts over biblical translations, intra-Catholic controversies, and arguments about the Immaculate Conception. Since overt reference to religious controversy would have been censored, Shakespeare treated these issues obliquely. Thus, the university elements— as well the First Quarto claim that the play was performed at the universities, where Calvinism was rife—suggest to Hoff that the play contains a religious message. Shakespeare makes Denmark a Catholic country. Hoff writes that "Claudius is the Beast of Revelation and Gertrude is the Harlot Queen," while Ophelia is the Virgin Mary. The play presents the triumph of Protestantism. An ingenious and wrongheaded reading of the play.

Jack, Adolphus Alfred. *Young Hamlet: A Conjectural Resolution of Some of the Difficulties in the Plotting of Shakespeare's Play*. Aberdeen, Scotland: Aberdeen University Press, 1950
Rejecting the view of Hamlet presented by Johann Wolfgang von Goethe in *Wilhelm Meister's Apprenticeship* and by Samuel Taylor Coleridge—that the prince cannot make up his mind—Jack proposes that Hamlet is, as the First Quarto indicates, a young man "in a position of capital difficulty." Jack sees the First Quarto, generally viewed as defective, as essentially the first version of the play, better in some ways than the Second ("Good") Quarto, though the revised version has its virtues. Gertrude appears more sympathetic, Hamlet more human. While Jack does not resolve the play's complexities, he does suggest many fascinating possibilities.

Jones, Ernest. *Hamlet and Oedipus*. London: Gollancz, 1947.
A Freudian reading that regards Hamlet as procrastinating because in his uncle's case he sees his own. Hamlet wishes that he could have killed his father and married his mother, so that he both hates and identifies with Claudius. Only after Laertes essentially kills Hamlet can the prince act against Claudius. A highly influential study of the play which first appeared in the *American Journal of Psychology* in January, 1910. Jones also suspects Shakespeare of harboring an Oedipal complex: "There must be some correspondence . . . between feelings a poet has described and feelings he has himself experienced in some form."

Joseph, Bertram L. *Conscience and the King: A Study of "Hamlet."* London: Chatto & Windus, 1953.
Seeks to interpret *Hamlet* from an Elizabethan perspective. For example, melancholy by 1600 did not necessarily imply inaction, though it did cause introspection. Revenge was not regarded as unworthy. Claudius is a villain and hypocrite, corrupt of heart, and has corrupted his kingdom. The play depicts the clash of good and evil; in the end, evil is destroyed and goodness is triumphant, but the battle takes its awful toll. The world of the play is providential, but individuals exercise free will.

King, Walter N. *Hamlet's Search for Meaning*. Athens: University of Georgia Press, 1982.
Hamlet expresses a belief in Providence, and the prince's search for meaning leads him to Christian affirmation, which he expresses in the final scene: "There's a Divinity that shapes our ends,/ Rough-hew them how we may." Throughout the play, Hamlet has been trying to understand events and God. King sees the Ghost as evil and Hamlet's procrastination as admirable. Hamlet has an Oedipal obsession but is purged of it in the bedroom scene in act III: "His encounter with Gertrude [is] therapeutic for them both." Yet King also writes that "Shakespeare left the nature of Providence mysterious, ambiguous, and problematic."

Kliman, Bernice W. *"Hamlet": Film, Television, and Audio Performance*. Rutherford, N.J.: Fairleigh Dickinson University Press, 1988.
After discussing cuts, exits, and entrances in film versions of the play, drawing heavily on Laurence Olivier's 1948 and Grigori Kozintsev's 1964 production, Kliman looks at nine television performances from 1953 to 1987 (including the 1969 Tony Richardson *Hamlet*, which first appeared as a movie). She correctly notes the pervasive influence of Olivier's film. The book concludes with a survey of silent movies and recordings. Michael Cohen called the book "careful, inclusive and readable" (*Shakespeare Quarterly* 41 [1990]:394).

Knights, L. C. *An Approach to "Hamlet."* Stanford, Calif.: Stanford University Press, 1961.

By focusing on evil, Hamlet has become paralyzed. The Ghost is a tempter; revenge is wrong. Knights sees the tragedies as moving to *King Lear*, and Hamlet fails because he lacks "a ready responsiveness to life as it comes." Knights denies any change in Hamlet and sees no virtue in the prince's "readiness is all." Knights admits that his reading of the play is intended to provoke rethinking of the work; such rethinking is likely to lead to a conclusion differing from this one. Commenting on this volume and also on Knights's *Some Shakespearean Themes* (1960), Robert Ornstein, who disagreed with Knights's reading of *Hamlet*, did conceed that his writings offer "the rare and stimulating experience . . . of contact with a mind that is passionately concerned with the humane and humanizing value of art and that is deeply responsive to the beauty and meaning of Shakespeare's plays" (*Modern Philology* 59 [1962]:288).

Levin, Harry. *The Question of "Hamlet."* New York: Oxford University Press, 1959.

Hamlet is replete with dualities: "Gothic clowns and classical allusions, Viking prowess and humanistic learning, medieval superstition and modern skepticism." Another duality, the one Levin focuses on, is that of thought and action. This duality affects the play's language, which relies on interrogation, doubt, and irony. Words are doubled, Hamlet's words have double meanings (puns), Claudius says one thing but means another, and even Rosencrantz and Guildenstern are doubles. Hamlet must learn to see his world as part of "cosmic irony." Levin finds groups of three (even three acts) in the play also. He includes in the book three pieces previously published. "The Antic Disposition" argues that Hamlet must feign madness to act as a court fool who speaks truth in the guise of folly. "The Tragic Ethos" reviews Peter Alexander's *Hamlet: Father and Son* (1955). "An Explication of the Player's Speech" looks at the speech in II, ii, about Pyrrhus.

Lidz, Theodore. *Hamlet's Enemy: Madness and Myth in "Hamlet."* New York: Basic Books, 1975.

In this fusion of psychology and literary analysis, Lidz, author of *The Family and Human Adaptation* (1963), explains *Hamlet* as depicting "the plight of a man embittered by a matricidal fury who is kept from committing the act by his father's spirit." The death of Polonius reconciles Hamlet to his own demise and so leads to his salvation. Ophelia goes mad when she, like Hamlet, loses the necessary parental support. *Hamlet* is thus a warning to parents against self-indulgence, an illustration of the dangers of passion, and a treatise on the importance of family integrity over individual desire. Lidz's linking of Hamlet's madness to the behavior of Gertrude echoes A. C. Bradley and John Dover Wilson, but Lidz provides a fuller analysis of Hamlet's family and Ophelia's.

Lundstrom, Rinda F. *William Poel's "Hamlets": The Director as Critic*. Ann Arbor, Mich.: UMI Research Press, 1984.

In the late nineteenth century, Poel rebelled against the stylized acting of his day: as director, he sought more natural presentation in speech and mannerisms. In 1881, he produced the First Quarto *Hamlet* without scene breaks on a bare stage. Thirteen years later, he organized the Elizabethan Stage Society; over the next decade, it presented forty Elizabethan plays on a stage patterned on the Fortune Theatre and using Elizabethan music and dress. Until his death in 1934, Poel remained active as actor and producer; he also wrote much about Shakespeare and the Elizabethan stage. Poel influenced such figures as Laurence Olivier, John Dover Wilson, and Harley Granville-Barker. To understand more fully Poel's ideas, Lundstrom looks at four productions of *Hamlet* that Poel directed. Sees Poel not as an antiquarian but as a pioneer in faithfully interpreting Shakespeare's text for modern audiences.

Mack, Maynard. "The World of *Hamlet*." *Yale Review* 41 (1952):502-523.

A seminal article that illuminates the play and that articulated the concept of the play as a world. *Hamlet*'s world is mysterious: the play opens with a question and appearances differ from reality, which remains indeterminate. Is Hamlet mad? Is the Ghost honest? Is Ophelia? Mortality and change pervade the work, and Mack looks at imagery that highlights this theme—infirmity, infection, and loss. In the course of the play, Hamlet comes to accept the world's limitations and his own.

Madariaga, Salvador de. *On "Hamlet."* London: Hollis & Carter, 1948.

Sees Hamlet as a Cesare Borgia—self-centered and manipulative with no desire to kill Claudius or marry Ophelia, with whom he has been having an affair. Ophelia lies to her father about Hamlet's "honorable fashion" of loving. Sees Rosencrantz and Guildenstern as innocent victims and Claudius as "a better Christian than Hamlet, who indeed is hardly a Christian at all."

Mander, Raymond, and Joe Mitchenson. *"Hamlet" Through the Ages: A Pictorial Record from 1709*. London: Macmillan, 1952.

As the title suggests, Mander and Mitchenson have assembled sketches and photographs of productions covering two and a half centuries. Some of the reproductions are too small, but, as *Theatre Arts* observed in April, 1953, that "as a record [the book] is excellent, full of curiosities, like the various attempts to do the play in modern dress, and full of opportunities to speculate on whether Hamlet was any madder than the actors who have at various times undertaken to play him (p.14)." The authors also offer their views on the play.

McGee, Arthur. *The Elizabethan "Hamlet."* New Haven, Conn.: Yale University Press, 1987.

Modern audiences agree with Hamlet that it is an honest Ghost, and most modern critics see Hamlet as a model prince who was like to have proved most royal had he been put on. McGee disagrees. The Ghost is a demon, Hamlet damned. An epilogue traces the history of Shakespearean criticism to show how readers have lost the meaning the play carried to seventeenth century audiences. McGee places *Hamlet* in the context of anti-Catholic sentiment and argues that, since censors did not question such elements as the reference to Purgatory, the play must be Protestant and the Ghost dishonest. One of those books that prompts the question "Are *Hamlet*'s critics mad or merely feigning madness?"

Mills, John A. *"Hamlet" on Stage: The Great Tradition.* Westport, Conn.: Greenwood Press, 1985.
Examines how actors from Richard Burbage to Albert Finney have performed this role. Mills sees two basic types of Hamlet: "hard-fast" and "slow-soft," though the categories are not absolute. Edmund Kean, for example, belongs to the first group but also provided a number of soft moments. Marvin Rosenberg wrote (in *Shakespeare Quarterly* 38 [1987]:271) that "Mills . . . has compiled a record that must be useful to both scholars and theatre people concerned with the realization of Shakespeare's text."

Prosser, Eleanor. *"Hamlet" and Revenge.* London: Oxford University Press, 1967.
Challenges the notion that Shakespeare favors revenge in the play, pointing out numerous Christian and classical sources opposing vengeance. She also looks at all the plays from 1562 to 1607 dealing with revenge and agrees with Thomas Nashe's Cutwolfe in *The Unfortunate Traveller* (1594) that "revenge in our tragedies is continually raised from hell." She regards the Ghost as "a goblin damned" and Hamlet as degenerating under his influence. A provocative interpretation, though not one widely held. As Prosser analyzes each scene, though, she offers thoughtful suggestions, particularly in her understanding of the "To be or not to be" speech, which she sees as the pivotal point of the play. Here Hamlet debates whether to act or not and decides that he will. Not until the fifth act will he resolve on passivity and thus become a good Christian.

Quillian, William H. *"Hamlet" and the New Poetic: James Joyce and T. S. Eliot.* Ann Arbor, Mich.: UMI Research Press, 1975.
Both Eliot and Joyce saw *Hamlet* as an artistic failure, thus rejecting the fascination and idolatry lavished on the play and its hero for the previous two hundred years. Quillian first looks at the eighteenth and nineteenth century responses to the work and then examines Joyce's 1912 lectures on the play and Eliot's 1919 review of John Mackinnon Robertson's *The Problem of Hamlet* for the *Athenaeum*. Though their views are now only historical curiosities, they do reflect the early modernist attitude and also called for a more objective approach to the play. Quillian's short book—the actual text is seventy-seven pages—would have

been more illuminating if it had explored why Eliot and Joyce responded as they did to *Hamlet*, especially since Eliot reversed his opinion in the 1940s.

Rossi, Alfred. *Tyrone Guthrie Directs "Hamlet."* Berkeley: University of California Press, 1970.
Rossi was Guthrie's assistant for the 1963 production of *Hamlet* by the Minnesota Theatre Company. This book presents Rossi's record of the rehearsals and a facsimile of the prompt script with blocking and other stage directions. Tanya Moiseiwitsch's designs for the modern costumes are illustrated as well. Useful for its insights into the play, whether one is reading the work or considering a production.

Rowe, Eleanor. *"Hamlet": A Window on Russia*. New York: New York University Press, 1976.
Alexander Petrovich Sumarokov introduced *Hamlet* to Russia in 1748, though his version differed from the original; Sumarokov conceded that "except for the monologue at the end of the third act and Claudius' falling on his knees, my *Hamlet* scarcely resembles Shakespeare's tragedy." Yet this production and Pierre Le Tourneur's 1776 translation made the Danish prince popular in Russia. Rowe traces Russian response to *Hamlet*, which has been used to comment on political developments and has influenced numerous authors who have echoed the play. She sees the treatment of Hamlet as a reflection of the society. Thus, in the 1830s and 1840s, Hamletism was associated with introspection and noble sentiments, a view stimulated by Mochalov's 1837 Moscow interpretation of the character. By the end of the nineteenth century, the perception of his hesitation made Hamlet appear superfluous in a world demanding social reform. Under the Soviets, he was portrayed as socially responsible.

Scofield, Martin. *The Ghosts of "Hamlet": The Play and Modern Writers*. Cambridge, England: Cambridge University Press, 1980.
In part 1, Scofield considers how Stéphane Mallarmé, Paul Claudel, Paul Valéry, Jules Laforgue, T. S. Eliot, James Joyce, D. H. Lawrence, Søren Kierkegaard, and Franz Kafka have used *Hamlet* in their works. From these writers' treatments, he arrives at some conclusions about modern perceptions of the play, such as the prince's dual nature of sweet prince and arrant knave. Part 2 offers Scofield's own interpretation of the play, which he sees as a quest for certainty in a world without authority, a quest that for Hamlet ends in failure. The vision of *Hamlet* is most like that of Kafka, "in which the manifestations of authority are always ambiguous, and the perceptions of the protagonist are always limited." G. P. Jones commented that "Scofield offers sound analysis of a divided and disturbed protagonist in a play especially concerned with problems of perception and self definition. Invariably suggestive are Scofield's observations on the ambiguous authority and provenance of the Ghost" (*University of Toronto Quarterly* 52 [1982]:114).

Semper, I. J. *"Hamlet" Without Tears*. Dubuque, Iowa: Loras College Press, 1946.
Six essays on such matters as Hamlet's apparent desire to destroy Claudius' soul
as well as his body and Hamlet as ideal Renaissance gentleman. Governing the
book is the view of the Ghost as an agent of justice, not a goblin damned.
Semper sees the play as Thomist and medieval in outlook, finding echoes of
Thomas Aquinas in speeches such as Marcellus' description of the Ghost's
insubstantiality. The play is thus set in a Catholic context, still familiar to an
Elizabethan audience. The Ghost enjoins divine retribution, not private revenge,
but Hamlet still hesitates because he feels personal animosity and so suffers
because of his scruples.

Senelick, Lawrence. *Gordon Craig's Moscow "Hamlet": A Reconstruction*. Westport, Conn.: Greenwood Press, 1982.
In 1912, under Gordon Craig's direction, the Moscow Art Theatre presented a
Hamlet that was a landmark in modern drama, one that Senelick says "revolutionized the staging of Shakespeare in this century." This book describes the production and discusses the events that led to it. Senelick also notes the work's influence, such as the use of unlocalized setting and Hamlet's alienation from the
world of the court. Appendix I reprints Craig's 1909 address to the actors of the
Moscow Art Theatre; appendix II offers Vlas Doroshenvich's recollections of
Craig's directing.

Stoll, Elmer Edgar. *"Hamlet": An Historical and Comparative Study*. Minneapolis:
University of Minnesota Press, 1919.
Attempts to recover Shakespeare's *Hamlet* by looking at the works of his Elizabethan contemporaries, at Greek drama, and at the changes in the text of the play.
The delay of revenge occurs because the play demands it, not because Hamlet
is melancholy. Hamlet is a worthy hero with no tragic flaw. An important study
for its rejection of the Romantic view that had made Hamlet into a Coleridgean
figure.

Todd, D. K. C. *I Am Not Prince Hamlet: Shakespeare Criticism Schools of English*.
New York: Barnes & Noble Books, 1974.
A curious book of criticism that attacks criticism as sicklied o'er with the pale
cast of thought, whereas literature belongs to the realm of non-thinking. Todd's
extended and disjointed soliloquy nevertheless interprets *King Lear* as a demonstration that Evil must be defeated by sacrifice, not by Goodness' adopting the
ways of Evil, and that the Freudian interpretation of *Hamlet* is correct but does
not go far enough—Polonius, Ophelia, and Laertes share the incestuous feeling
of the prince. Ronald Berman aptly characterized the volume as "intelligent and
tentative, too often peripheral, and finally a kind of indulgence of literacy"
(*Sewanee Review* 84 [1976]:666).

Walker, Roy. *The Time Is out of Joint: A Study of "Hamlet."* London: Andrew
Dakers, 1948.

According to Walker, "Hamlet's is the pacifist problem: how to find a course
of action that avoids the ignoble inaction of surrender and the equally ignoble
action of violence." Though he succumbs at times to evil impulses, as when he
kills Polonius and sends Rosencrantz and Guildenstern to their deaths, Hamlet's
return from his sea voyage marks his acceptance of humanity. Hamlet does not
delay; he waits for the right moment to cleanse Denmark of the poison of
Claudius, and he succeeds in purging the realm. Walker suggests that Hamlet's
death is a just punishment for the murders he has committed.

Warner, William Beatty. *Chance and the Text of Experience: Freud, Nietzsche, and
Shakespeare's "Hamlet."* Ithaca, N.Y.: Cornell University Press, 1986.

In a roundabout way, Warner interprets Hamlet in conventional terms as one who
moves from classic avenger to one who in the fifth act accepts the vagaries of
life. In the introduction, Warner argues against the dogmatism of deconstructive
and new historicist readings in favor of a middle ground that he calls Chance,
"neither an objective event in the world nor merely reducible to its textual
inscription in some personal narrative, but something which, befalling the person,
and being construed by him or her, becomes a sign of a necessity that is opaque
and resists the control of a presiding consciousness." In looking at how Sigmund
Freud, Friedrich Nietzsche, and Hamlet shape their lives, Warner suggests
Harold Bloom's Oedipal struggle with the precursor—Freud writes Wilhelm
Fliess out of the history of psychoanalysis, for example. Hamlet struggles
between his desire for ideals (such as his vision of his father) and his recognition
of a flawed world, and he finally accepts the role of chance. Warner's writing
is dense, his theoretical approach likely to appeal to the advanced graduate
student or teacher of Shakespeare, not to the undergraduate.

Watkins, Ronald, and Jeremy Lemmon. *Hamlet.* Totowa, N.J.: Rowman & Littlefield, 1974.

An attempt to recreate *Hamlet* as it appeared on the stage of the Globe in 1601.
The authors present a heavily annotated promptbook, based on a conflation of
the Second Quarto and First Folio texts, providing extensive stage directions and
explication of the lines. Some of the glosses are questionable, as when Watkins
and Lemmon maintain that "To be, or not to be, that is the question" refers to
the text that Hamlet is reading as he appears in act III. Overall, though, a
sensible approach useful to students, teachers, and producers.

Watts, Cedric. *"Hamlet."* Boston: Twayne, 1988.

As in the other volumes in this series, this book opens with a brief survey of
Hamlet's stage and critical history, followed by Watts's reading of the play. He
sees Hamlet as enigmatic; Watts believes that Hamlet is correct in saying that

he is delaying his revenge, but the audience never discovers why he delays. Hamlet is both sweet prince and arrant knave, but that combination is not an enigma, because it is common. Watts also does not find any difficulty with Hamlet's concern for his mother's sexuality: both she and Claudius have yielded to "appetite." Concludes that no one interpretation will explain the play, but that on stage many problems that trouble readers and critics disappear.

Wilson, John Dover. *What Happens in "Hamlet."* 3d ed. Cambridge, England: Cambridge University Press, 1951.
Sees Hamlet as a sympathetic hero wrongly deprived of the throne; he must operate secretly to protect family honor. Wilson examines numerous questions about the play and arrives at plausible if not convincing solutions. He maintains, for example, that Claudius is unmoved by the dumb show because the king does not see it. Hamlet wants the court to believe that ambition prompts him to kill Claudius, as he plans to do, and so not reveal the crimes that have occurred because he wants to save Gertrude's reputation. The play tests Gertrude as well as Claudius. Wilson believes that Hamlet remains a mystery but is modeled on the Earl of Essex. Though some of what Wilson says will provoke dissent, his theories are stimulating and his arguments are presented clearly.

1, 2 Henry IV

Aoki, Keiji. *Shakespeare's "Henry IV" and "Henry V": Hal's Heroic Character and the Sun-Cloud Theme.* Kyoto, Japan: Showa Press, 1973.
Chapter 1 of this short work addresses the question of the unity of *Henry IV*. Since Hal apparently reforms and is reconciled to his father in part 1, why does Shakespeare write a second part? Aoki perceptively notes that Hal does not actually reform because he never was dissolute, and he is not reconciled to his father at the end of part 1. Henry IV does not know that Hal has killed Hotspur—Falstaff claims the glory—and the king is hardly profuse in thanking Hal for driving off the Douglas. Hal intends to hide his true character until he becomes king; he conceals his heroism at Shrewsbury and returns to the tavern world in part 2. Shakespeare intended to end part 1 with the revelation of Hal's true character, but around act IV the playwright changed his mind. The second chapter addresses the character of Henry V, who seems so different from Hal, but Aoki argues that his character remains constant. He is the sun-king from his first soliloquy in *1 Henry IV*, and in *Henry V* he finally blazes forth to surprise everyone.

Bevington, David, ed. *"Henry the Fourth Parts I and II": Critical Essays.* New York: Garland, 1986.
An eclectic collection of essays covering more than two centuries of criticism,

from Carolyn Morris' 1774 discussion of Falstaff to four pieces published in the 1980s. Among the major critics represented are Samuel Johnson, A. C. Bradley, John Dover Wilson, Northrop Frye, C. L. Barber, and Jonas A. Barish. Bevington's fine introduction surveys the criticism presented here. Useful.

Jenkins, Harold. *The Structural Problem in Shakespeare's "Henry the Fourth."* London: Methuen, 1956.
In this brief monograph, Jenkins argues that Shakespeare planned originally to write only one part of *Henry IV*, at the end of which Hal would banish Falstaff. By act IV of *1 Henry IV*, Shakespeare changed his mind. As a result of adding a second part, the playwright has to duplicate Hal's demonstration of physical bravery and reformation.

McLuhan, Herbert Marshall. *"Henry IV: A Mirror for Magistrates." University of Toronto Quarterly* 17 (1947):152-160.
Discusses the three worlds of *Henry IV*: court, rebels, and tavern; all three are flawed. The court, led by Henry IV, is that of a Machiavellian usurper. The tavern, ruled by Falstaff, represents disorder and appetite. The rebels are honorable but misguided. Argues that Hal learns to avoid the errors of all three: to adopt the rebels' honor but to use it properly against England's enemies, to accept the humanity of Falstaff but not his misrule, and to be politically astute without being treacherous.

Mitchell, Charles. "The Education of the True Prince." *Tennessee Studies in Literature* 12 (1967):13-21.
Henry IV and Falstaff represent two outlooks that Hal must reconcile to become the ideal ruler. A good prince is superior to his subjects but recognizes his equality with them. Henry IV fails as a king because he rejects that equality, while Falstaff never overcomes his baseness to transcend flawed humanity. Hal fuses humility with dignity.

Morgan, Arthur Eustace. *Some Problems of Shakespeare's "Henry IV."* London: Oxford University Press, 1924.
The plays that have survived as the two parts of *Henry IV* differ greatly from the version Shakespeare wrote with Oldcastle as the original Falstaff. Morgan sees that lost play as a revision of another play no longer extant, not *The Famous Victories of Henry V*, which also derives from that original. The original Shakespeare play was in verse and focused on history, which yielded to comedy when Falstaff was introduced. Morgan's speculations remain unproved but fascinating.

Prosser, Eleanor. *Shakespeare's Anonymous Editors: Scribe and Compositor in the Folio Text of "2 Henry IV."* Stanford, Calif.: Stanford University Press, 1981.
The 1600 quarto of *2 Henry IV* is based on Shakespeare's manuscript, but the

1623 folio version differs in many places from the quarto text. Prosser accepts the 150 lines not found in the quarto, but argues that an editor and typesetter made the other changes, deleting and reassigning speeches, polishing versification, and modifying stage directions. The quarto therefore more closely reflects Shakespeare's intentions. Though W. W. Greg and George Walton Williams made some of the same suggestions, Prosser offers more support for her position, though she is not always persuasive.

Scoufos, Alice-Lyle. *Shakespeare's Typological Satire: A Study of the Falstaff-Oldcastle Problem.* Athens: Ohio University Press, 1979.
Claims that Shakespeare's plays attack the Brooke family and Lord Cobham. The satiric intent appears as early as *1 Henry VI* and continues through *The Merry Wives of Windsor* and beyond. Scoufos contends that Shakespeare hoped to block the appointment of Cobham as Lord Chamberlain and so portrayed his ancestor as a traitor and a false martyr. Her argument is not persuasive, but it does present much historical detail.

Wharton, T. F. *"Henry IV, Parts 1 and 2": Text and Performance.*London: Macmillan, 1983.
Like the other volumes in this series, this brief study first examines some central issues in the work: the kind of history *Henry IV* represents, the imagery of sickness, and Hal's character. Shakespeare presents the Tudor myth, but he also questions it; no one is a reliable historian in the two parts of *Henry IV*. Hal can be made to appear sympathetic, but he also can appear cold and ruthless. Part 2 of this study examines how four productions addressed the play: the 1964 Royal Shakespeare Company version directed by Peter Hall, the 1975 Royal Shakespeare Company under the direction of Terry Hands, Trevor Nunn's 1982 production at the Barbicon, and the BBC television version. All are good productions, but Nunn's offers the subtlest treatment of Hal. The volume concludes with a brief annotated bibliography.

Wilson, John Dover. *The Fortunes of Falstaff.* Cambridge, England: Cambridge University Press, 1943.
A response to A. C. Bradley and other critics who saw Falstaff as the real hero of the *Henry IV* plays and who found Hal's rejection of him unconscionable. Looking at the tradition of morality plays, Wilson points out Falstaff's kinship with the figures of Riot and Vice, who mislead the hero but who eventually are defeated. Falstaff is attractive—he had to be to palliate the prince's love for this sinner. Though Hal banishes Falstaff, Shakespeare does not; even at the end of *2 Henry IV*, Falstaff retains his confidence "and rejoices, like Milton's Satan, 'all is not lost.'" J. B. Leishman observed that "Professor Dover Wilson is on the whole most sensible and convincing" (*Review of English Studies* 20 [1944]:315).

Young, David P., ed. *Twentieth Century Interpretations of "2 Henry IV."* Englewood Cliffs, N.J.: Prentice-Hall, 1968.
Young's introduction makes a case for looking at *2 Henry IV* apart from, rather
than as a part of *1 Henry IV*. The second play is darker and serves as a commentary on and a reassessment of the political outlook articulated earlier, though
much comedy remains. Part 1 of this volume offers essays by L. C. Knights,
Clifford Leech, C. L. Barber, Robert B. Pierce, Harold E. Toliver, and Derek
Traversi. Part 2 offers shorter comments by A. C. Bradley, John Dover Wilson,
E. M. W. Tillyard, Harold Jenkins, A. P. Rossiter, R. J. Dorius, and A. R.
Humphreys. The essays explore the themes of kingship; examine the characters
of Henry IV, Hal, and Falstaff; and comment about the language and structure
of the work. They offer helpful guidance through the play's complexities.

Henry V

Battenhouse, Roy W. *"Henry V* as Heroic Comedy." In *Essays on Shakespeare and
Elizabethan Drama in Honor of Hardin Craig*, edited by Richard Hosley.
Columbia: University of Missouri Press, 1962.
Notes that critics differ as to whether *Henry V* is comedy, tragedy, satire, or
history. Battenhouse sees Henry V as a successful public figure but flawed;
Shakespeare reveals these flaws through ironic treatment of the main characters,
through comments by secondary characters such as Fluellen, and through parody
by Pistol and his associates. The history play thus becomes heroic comedy, and
Henry emerges as a comic hero whose pursuit of glory is foolish. Yet he remains
content with his quest.

Beauman, Sally, ed. *The Royal Shakespeare Company's Production of "Henry V"
for the Centenary Season at the Royal Shakespeare Theatre*. Oxford, England:
Pergamon Press, 1976.
The subtitle summarizes the contents: "The working text of Shakespeare's play
together with articles and notes by the director, designer, composer, actors and
other members of the Company, and comments from the critics and the audience." The 1975 Royal Shakespeare Company's *Henry V*, directed by Terry
Hands, was warmly received by critics and audiences. Beauman offers the full
text of the play, with cuts printed in italics, and Hands explains the omissions.
He also offers his view of the work: "It is Shakespeare's theatre play par excellence" and a play full of doubts. Beauman surveys the play's stage history,
interviews numerous people involved with the production in various ways,
presents brief biographies of the company's members, and includes reviews and
letters from spectators. Indicative of the overall response was the comment by
Professor Guy Butler of Rhodes University, Grahamstown, South Africa: "This
is the first time in my 25 years as an academic, whose main interest is Shake-

speare, that I have written to congratulate a producer on one of his plays." The fourteen-year-old Joanne Loftus wrote to Alan Howard, who played the title role: "I do have heroes, and I've moved David Essex to second place, just to put you at the top."

Berman, Ronald, ed. *Twentieth Century Interpretations of "Henry V."* Englewood Cliffs, N.J.: Prentice-Hall, 1968.
Berman's introduction helpfully places *Henry V* within the context of Tudor thought and Shakespeare's histories. Berman briefly surveys concerns of plot, character, imagery, and theme; for Berman, "Henry V is a hero of moderation" and "the model of a humanist prince." Lily B. Campbell's essay rejects the identification of Henry V with the Earl of Essex. Geoffrey Bullough's introduction to the play, reprinted from volume 4 of his compilation of sources, shows how Shakespeare used the accounts available to him. E. M. W. Tillyard, Charles Williams, Derek Traversi, and M. M. Reese consider Henry V's character; Una Ellis-Fermor writes on the politics of the play; and A. P. Rossiter comments on the play's double vision. The volume concludes with various shorter observations by William Butler Yeats, A. C. Bradley, Elmer Edgar Stoll, Caroline F. E. Spurgeon, Mark Van Doren, John Dover Wilson, and Paul Jorgensen. Includes a brief bibliography.

Geduld, Harry M. *Filmguide to "Henry V."* Bloomington: Indiana University Press, 1973.
A detailed study of Laurence Olivier's 1944 film of the play, providing credits, list of the cast, outline, locations of the filming, and a biography of Olivier. Discusses the origins of the film in Olivier's 1937 Old Vic performance of the role and gives a detailed account of the production. Geduld analyzes the film's aesthetics and the changes that the film made. For example, Olivier cut about half the text and simplified the characters. Geduld praises the film; Andrew M. McLean commended Geduld's study in his review "God for Harry! England and St. George" (*Literature/Film Quarterly* 1 [1973]:377-380).

Hobday, C. H. "Imagery and Irony in *Henry V.*" *Shakespeare Survey* 21 (1968):107-113.
Death imagery surrounds the figure of Henry V. Hobday argues that Shakespeare saw the king as a murderer, but he was under obligation to his company to write a play about Henry V, having promised such a work in the epilogue to *2 Henry IV*. "Faced with the demand to depict such a man as a hero, he took refuge in the irony which permeates the whole play, and constantly juxtaposed the fine talk of honour and religion with the realities of human greed and cruelty." The play satirizes combat and reflects the war-weariness of many Englishmen after more than a decade of fighting Spain. Yet Shakespeare was patriotic; stirred by the plight of the English at Agincourt, he produced the brilliant St. Crispin's speech.

1, 2, 3 Henry VI

Alexander, Peter. *Shakespeare's "Henry VI" and "Richard III."* Cambridge, England: Cambridge University Press, 1929.
Denies that *2, 3 Henry VI* were collaborative efforts of Shakespeare and others, a matter then hot in question. Also established that the 1594 quarto of *The First Part of the Contention Between the Two Famous Houses of York and Lancaster* and the 1595 quarto of *The True Tragedy of Richard Duke of York* are bad quartos of the second and third parts of *Henry VI*, recreated largely from memory by the actors who played Warwick and Suffolk-Clifford (a doubled role). Alexander suspects that these actors also had access to at least parts of the manuscript and received assistance from other actors. A landmark textual study; although Alexander's position has been challenged, it remains the orthodox view.

Berman, Ronald S. "Fathers and Sons in the *Henry VI* Plays." *Shakespeare Quarterly* 13 (1962): 487-497.
Like Greek tragedy, Shakespeare's *Henry VI* uses the family to describe trouble in the state. In *1 Henry VI*, the Talbots, father and son, fight and die united in chivalry. By *3 Henry VI*, children and fathers kill one another. Corruption, not nobility, is inherited; relatives betray one another. Henry VI as king proves a poor father to the realm. A good discussion of an important theme in the trilogy.

Brockbank, J. P. "The Frame of Disorder: *Henry VI.*" In *Early Shakespeare*, edited by John Russell Brown and Bernard Harris. London: Edward Arnold, 1961.
"The three parts of *Henry VI* express the plight of individuals caught up in a cataclysmic movement of events for which responsibility is communal and historical, not personal and immediate, and they reveal the genesis out of prolonged violence of two figures representing the ultimate predicament of man as a political animal—Henry and Richard, martyr and machiavel." Shakespeare presents the morality of the chronicles—the Wars of the Roses and the loss of France as wages of sin—but does not wholly accept that view. Misrule provides sufficient explanation for disaster in the plays. Contains much on the translation of history to the stage.

Dean, Paul. "Shakespeare's *Henry VI* Trilogy and Elizabethan 'Romance' Histories: The Origins of a Genre." *Shakespeare Quarterly* 33 (1982):34-48.
While Shakespeare was apparently the first to write serious historical drama based on the chronicles, he found precedents in romance histories—plays fusing historical figures and imaginary events—usually with comic conclusions. The *Henry VI* plays incorporate supernaturalism, love triangles, disguises, and a view of monarchy that all derive from these romance histories. These devices serve thematic functions in Shakespeare. For example, Henry VI disguises himself as

a commoner, but even as a king he did not command. His capture reveals that power determines right.

Henke, James T. *The Ego-King: An Archetype Approach to Elizabethan Political Thought and Shakespeare's "Henry VI" Plays*. Salzburg, Austria: Salzburg University Press, 1977.
Applies Jungian archetypes to the study of the *Henry VI* trilogy. The plays reveal both Shakespeare's unconscious and the "collective political consciousness" of the Elizabethan age. The three archetypes that Henke examines are shadows, the temptress, and the child. The shadow represents the heart of darkness within everyone, the temptress is the dangerous yet alluring life force that threatens the "intellectual order of conscious existence," and the child represents desire for continuity and "psychic health." In the plays, Joan of Arc, for example, appears as the archetypal temptress, as do the Countess of Auvergne and Margaret of Anjou, perhaps France itself. Whether or not Shakespeare accepted the Tudor orthodoxy, Henke argues that such a collective unconsciousness existed and underlies the trilogy, which shows an insane England. Only in *Henry V* will England regain full psychic health, as Henry V woos and wins the temptress Katherine, as the king himself fuses machiavel and christian prince.

Prouty, Charles Tyler. *The Contention and Shakespeare's "2 Henry VI": A Comparative Study*. New Haven, Conn.: Yale University Press, 1954.
Rather than seeing the quarto text of *2 Henry VI* as a garbled version of the play, Prouty argues that it represents a legitimate production, though not by Shakespeare. The folio text is Shakespeare's revision of this work. To prove his case, he looks at staging, style, characterization, structure, and sources. According to Prouty, Raphael Holinshed's work is the chief source of the folio version but not of the quarto. Since *2 Henry VI* is not by Shakespeare, Shakespeare did not write original history plays early in his career. An appendix conveniently compares quarto and folio texts on facing pages. Though Prouty offers good comparisons, his conclusions are questionable.

Ricks, Don M. *Shakespeare's Emergent Form: A Study of the Structure of the "Henry VI" Plays*. Logan: Utah State University Press, 1968.
The structure of the *Henry VI* plays resembles that of history itself, with large numbers of characters, none of whom dominate the action. Events unfold of themselves, not controlled by individuals. The second and third parts of *Henry VI* use a complementary theme to reflect on the main theme. In *2 Henry VI*, the contentious lords of the main theme cause lawlessness in society, the secondary theme. In *3 Henry VI*, the Wars of the Roses cause the breakdown in family ties. Though all three plays show skill, they reflect increasing artistry, from the artificial structure of *1 Henry VI* to the more complex *3 Henry VI* that fuses plot and design. Ricks concludes that "the variegated texture of the plays, the impres-

sion of massive inclusiveness Shakespeare attained within the allowed dramatic time of two and a half to three hours, and the sense of great forces inexorably in motion, all make these three plays resemble history apprehended in something approaching its full complexity and communicated in a form at least suggestive of, if not fully expressive of, its sweep." Argues for greater appreciation of the plays' artistry.

Riggs, David. *Shakespeare's Heroical Histories: "Henry VI" and Its Literary Tradition*. Cambridge, Mass.: Harvard University Press, 1971.
Sees the "deterioration of heroic idealism between the Hundred Years' War and the Yorkist accession." This deterioration is not bad because heroism can lead to the Machiavellian Richard III. Talbot's heroism in *1 Henry VI* is commendable, but Joan of Arc, York, and Suffolk fail as heroes. Henry VII provides the ideal, with his Christian modesty. Contains much on the antecedents of the *Henry VI* plays in other historical dramas of the period, especially Christopher Marlowe's *Tamburlaine*, and "the rhetorical training that Shakespeare would have received as a youth." According to Riggs, Shakespeare rejects Marlowe's notion of heroism. A final chapter discusses *Richard III* and *1 Henry IV*, and the volume includes a good bibliography.

Henry VIII

Berman, Ronald. "*King Henry the Eighth*: History and Romance." *English Studies* 48 (1960):112-121.
Sees *Henry VIII* as combining elements of the early history plays and the late romances. Like the former, it deals with motivation and political conflict; like the latter, "it is symbolic, less concerned with excellence of plot than with the development in its protagonists of a new consciousness." The play moves from death to birth, and the chaotic transformations of politics are ordered here through the symbolic means of the masque. Anne Boleyn becomes a Ceres and a Venus Genetrix who will bring blessing to England in the form of Elizabeth.

Berry, Edward I. "*Henry VIII* and the Dynamics of Spectacle." *Shakespeare Studies* 12 (1979):229-246.
Henry VIII reverts to earlier forms but reinterprets them. The fall of Buckingham resembles *A Mirror for Magistrates* but is more ambiguous, both in determining Buckingham's guilt and in its redeeming value. Wolsey's fall is more conventional, but his redemption smacks of Fletcherian tragicomedy, not tragedy. Katherine is innocent, and she triumphs in the promise of a heavenly crown. Cranmer does not fall; thus the pattern of the *Mirror* is broken. The play ends at a moment when the ideal is realized, but audiences know what happens later: Anne Boleyn and Cranmer are executed. The play also moves from the chaos

of antimasque to the order of masque. The opening report about the Field of the Cloth of Gold is antimasque, failing to produce peace. Cranmer's concluding prophecy, with its pastoral imagery, promises order; its biblical echoes indicate eternal peace. Berry concedes that Henry VIII remains unconvincing as a character, and the play, though "a rich one," does not please as much as *1 Henry IV* or *Richard II*.

Cespedes, Frank V. "'We Are One in Fortunes': The Sense of History in *Henry VIII*." *English Literary Renaissance* 10 (1980):413-438.
Rejecting the view that Henry VIII increases in stature during the play, Cespedes argues that the king throughout is "a thoroughly political, self-aggrandizing monarch." The play moves towards the happy reign of Elizabeth but does so through the tragedies of Buckingham, Wolsey, and Katherine. History operates according to its own amoral forces; well-meaning individuals may produce weal or woe.

Clark, Cumberland. *A Study of Shakespeare's "Henry VIII."* London: Golden Vista Press, 1931.
Shakespeare's play portrays "the doom of feudalism, the evolution of a strong constitutional monarchy, the fall of the papacy, and the establishment of the Reformed Church." Clark discusses the date of the play (1613), the authorship (a collaboration between Shakespeare and John Fletcher, the latter having created the outline to allow for the spectacles at which he excelled), use of sources (Raphael Holinshed, Edward Hall, George Cavendish, and John Foxe's *The Book of Martyrs*), historical accuracy of the work (Shakespeare did not feel compelled to adhere strictly to chronology), characterization, and the play's stage history after Shakespeare's death (it remained popular because of its spectacle, though it was altered severely in performance during the eighteenth and early nineteenth centuries).

Kermode, Frank. "What Is Shakespeare's *Henry VIII* About?" *Durham University Journal*, n.s. 9 (1948):48-55.
Links the play to the *de casibus* (the fall of princes) tradition. In this late morality play, Buckingham, a fairly just man, falls by treachery. Katherine is a good woman whose fall evokes pity and plays on the sentimental strain of the convention. Wolsey exemplifies the standard *de casibus* pattern, rising by ambition and then falling because he arouses envy and because he behaves badly. Cranmer does not fall because Henry VIII, the agent of grace, saves him. Henry unifies the play; celebrating the king as an agent of God's mercy gives the play an orthodox outlook.

Leggatt, Alexander. "*Henry VIII* and the Ideal England." *Shakespeare Survey* 38 (1985): 131-143.

In *Henry VIII*, Shakespeare evokes the age of Elizabeth through dramatic devices typical of plays during her reign: praise of the queen and the fusion of the ideal and the real. Yet the play is also Jacobean in its divided judgments: Wolsey's fall evokes "both satisfaction and unexpected pity," for example. Shakespeare sees history as complex but patterned, moving towards the reign of Elizabeth and beyond to that of James. Elizabeth's reign is ideal, but even here reality intrudes—she will have enemies, she will die. Thus *Henry VIII* "offers one more illustration of Shakespeare's abiding interest in the difficult but close relationship between what we dream of and what we are."

McBride, T. "*Henry VIII* as Machiavellian Romance." *JEGP* 76 (1977):26-39.
A number of critics are troubled by the morality of *Henry VIII*. Katherine is sympathetic but must be rejected for the new queen. The play promises a golden Tudor age but says nothing about Anne's execution and Cranmer's martyrdom. Some acquit Henry as acting according to God's providence; others condemn him as un-Christian. McBride argues that the play juxtaposes Christian and Machiavellian morality and demonstrates the impossibility of reconciling them. Buckingham and Wolsey fall because they are poor students of Niccolò Machiavelli, whose lesson Henry learns during the play. Political realism is thus an element in a play that is essentially a romance. Henry is both Machiavellian and a romantic hero. Shakespeare recognizes the value of Christian ethics but also that such ethics make poor politics.

Partridge, A. C. *The Problem of "Henry VIII" Re-opened: Some Linguistic Criteria for the Two Styles Apparent in the Play.* Cambridge, England: Bowes and Bowes, 1949.
Defends the view—now generally accepted—that *Henry VIII* shows the hands of both Shakespeare and John Fletcher. Partridge finds a number of stylistic differences between the portions assigned to each. For example, Shakespeare prefers "hath" to "has" (twenty-two to fourteen); Fletcher's sections use "hath" only twice. Fletcher uses "'em" and "ye" more often than "them" and "you" (fifty-nine to seven); in Shakespeare's scenes "them" and "you" predominate. Also, Shakespeare's syntax is more complex than Fletcher's. Though Partridge finds two authors, he does not believe that the two authors collaborated. Rather, he suggests that Shakespeare left the work unfinished and that Fletcher was asked to complete it.

Richmond, Hugh M. "Shakespeare's *Henry VIII*: Romance Redeemed by History." *Shakespeare Studies* 4 (1968):334-349.
Defends the work as "a moralized history concerned once more with what had been Shakespeare's profoundest preoccupation earlier, the nature of human justice." Henry VIII matures during the play; he frees himself from amoral statecraft. Christian Providence also intervenes to defeat Nemesis: Henry's

adultery proves fortunate for England, and the same mercifulness that pervades the romances concludes this piece as well.

Shirley, Frances A., ed. *"King John" and "Henry VIII": Critical Essays.* New York: Garland, 1988.
A collection of criticism on the plays drawn from nineteenth and twentieth century sources. Shirley provides an overview of the essays in her introduction and concludes with a bibliography of the works included. A useful compilation that includes a number of standard selections, such as the comments of E. M. W. Tillyard and Caroline F. E. Spurgeon on *King John* and William Hazlitt's observations on both plays. Alongside these familiar pieces are such selections as Adrien Bonjour's "The Road to Swinstead Abbey: A Study of the Sense and Structure of *King John*" (1951), which defends the construction of the play, and Anna Jameson's 1866 discussion of Katherine as historical figure and dramatic character in *Henry VIII*.

Wickham, Glynne. "The Dramatic Structure of Shakespeare's *Henry VIII*: An Essay in Rehabilitation." *Proceedings of the British Academy* 70 (1985):149-166.
Argues for the coherence of *Henry VIII*, a play that Wickham says was intended to rehabilitate the reputation of Katherine of Aragon. James I was pursuing a policy of Protestant-Catholic marriages; to allay English fears of Catholics, James approved a work that would show a good Catholic, Katherine, while at the same time condemning papal politics and supporting the Reformation.

Julius Caesar

Bonjour, Adrien. *The Structure of "Julius Caesar."* Liverpool, England: Liverpool University Press, 1958.
Sees *Julius Caesar* as portraying two heroes, Brutus and Caesar, with the essence of the tragedy lying in the conflict between these individuals, not in the debate between two forms of government. Despite his flaws, Caesar is sympathetic. Despite his virtues, Brutus must die for killing another. In the course of his study, Bonjour offers a useful survey of criticism of the play. James E. Phillips (in *Shakespeare Quarterly* 11 [1960]:78) called the book "illuminating and helpful in its main argument," which particularly seeks to rehabilitate Caesar from detractors.

Daiches, David. *"Julius Caesar."* London: Edward Arnold, 1976.
Shakespeare inherited two views of Rome. The medieval view extolled the empire; hence, Dante places Brutus at the bottom of Hell. The Renaissance praised Brutus for his effort to save the Republic. In its ambiguity, *Julius Caesar* draws on both traditions. Argues that the play poses morality against politics,

private virtue against public. A good introduction that follows the play's action while offering sensible commentary on plot, language, and characters.

Dean, Leonard F., ed. *Twentieth Century Interpretations of "Julius Caesar."* Englewood Cliffs, N.J.: Prentice-Hall, 1968.
A collection of eighteen pieces on the play, with an introduction by the editor, who surveys earlier approaches and notes some central concerns in the work. A number of the selections deal with the character of Brutus; others, such as those by R. A. Foakes and Sigurd Burckhardt, consider the language, which proves richer than earlier critics believed. Geoffrey Bullough addresses Shakespeare's use of Plutarch; Norman Rabkin examines the play as a revenge tragedy. Though the selections are brief, they offer a range of approaches and attitudes that highlight significant issues raised by the tragedy.

Field, B. S., Jr. *Shakespeare's "Julius Caesar": A Production Collection.* Chicago: Nelson-Hall, 1980.
As the title page states, this volume presents "comments by eighteen actors and directors in seven different productions, illustrated with 101 photographs." Arranged by act, the comments are keyed to the illustrations, the actors explaining what they hoped to convey at a particular moment captured on film. Especially useful for those involved in a production. Photographic quality varies; in figure 1, for example, many characters are hard to see in their dark robes against a dark background. Also, not all the pictures of the same episode appear together, so that "Et tu Brute" is treated in figures 27-29, 35, and 46.

Foakes, R. A. "An Approach to *Julius Caesar.*" *Shakespeare Quarterly* 5 (1954): 259-270,
Foakes approaches the play through its language. The imagery of the play includes omens, war, noise, and disease, all of which "suggest a full circle of events." The work begins with the close of one civil war— between Caesar and Pompey—and concludes with the end of another. Language also reveals a gulf between characters' ideals and reality. Caesar, Brutus, and Cassius are noble but weak, subject to self-deception. The play has neither heroes nor villains but is "a tale of frustration and disorder" leading to "civil destruction."

Green, David C. *"Julius Caesar" and Its Source.* Salzburg, Austria: Salzburg University Press, 1979.
Shakespeare creates his play by rewriting Plutarch's biographies of Caesar, Brutus, and Antony, which the dramatist read in Thomas North's English translation. Green examines Shakespeare's borrowings and alterations. For example, Plutarch blames the civil war on Antony's ambition, whereas Shakespeare blames the conspirators and makes Antony more ambiguous. Only Brutus emerges as truly admirable throughout, a hero without a flaw. An excellent study of Plutarch; not all readers will agree with Green's interpretation of Shakespeare's play.

Greene, Gayle. "'The Power of Speech To Stir Men's Blood': The Language of Tragedy in Shakespeare's *Julius Caesar.*" *Renaissance Drama*, n.s. 11 (1980):67-93.

Like Francis Bacon and Michel de Montaigne, Shakespeare recognized the corrupting power of language divorced from reality. The play presents four persuasion scenes to show how treacherously language can deceive. The comic treatment of the poets in *Julius Caesar* shows their irrelevance in such a world. Cassius and Antony, who recognize that words do not necessarily reflect external reality, succeed in their respective goals, whereas Caesar and Brutus, who die believing in the equation of word and thing, are destroyed.

Hartstock, Mildred E. "The Complexity of *Julius Caesar.*" *PMLA* 81 (1966):56-62.

Shakespeare alters Plutarch's account of Caesar, Antony, Brutus, Cassius, and the citizens of Rome, all to create ambiguity. Hartstock maintains that audience sympathy keeps shifting but that no character emerges clearly as hero or villain. She offers two explanations for the lack of resolution: Shakespeare may have sought to provoke thought about the issues that the play raises, or he may be demonstrating that truth is unknowable. Hartstock finds it significant that the poets, Cicero, and the soothsayer—those who see truth most clearly—are ignored.

Ripley, John. *"Julius Caesar" on Stage in England and America, 1599-1973.* Cambridge, England: Cambridge University Press, 1980.

Presents a wealth of detail about the stage history of the play, much of the information derived from little known, even unpublished sources, such as promptbooks and letters. In the course of this chronological survey, Ripley traces the changes in production style. Antony grows more attractive, costumes become modern, the crowd assumes a larger role because of the emphasis on ensemble acting, and directors impose their vision on the play at the expense of the text (such as in Orson Welles's fascist *Julius Caesar*). Though Ripley offers no personal interpretation of the play, he does regret the failure of modern performances to realize the play's potential. Hugh M. Richmond called this "a precise, useful, conscientious book" (*Shakespeare Quarterly* 32 [1981]:411).

King John

Braunmuller, A. R. "*King John* and Historiography." *ELH* 55 (1988):309-332.

Argues that both chronicles and history plays are factitious rather than factual; both create their accounts for special purposes. Both are restricted in some ways by facts—such as the sequence of English monarchs— but within these limits they focus on events in a certain way to promote a viewpoint. Historians and dramatists of the late sixteenth century had to beware censorship, and they wrote in the context of their age. Raphael Holinshed, Shakespeare, and Sir John Heywood, however, all manipulate sources and facts to create their texts.

Burckhardt, Sigurd. "*King John*: The Ordering of This Present Time." *ELH* 33 (1966):133-153.
The Troublesome Raigne of King John (1591), one of Shakespeare's sources, presents an ordered, hierarchical world. Shakespeare's changes reflect his rejection of this sense of degree; *King John* presents unsolvable conflicts between equally legitimate claims where no side has clear authority. As Constance declares, "He that holds the kingdom holds the law." However valid E. M. W. Tillyard's Elizabethan world picture may be for most of Shakespeare's contemporaries, the playwright saw the speciousness of that outlook. Language—because it, too, lacks external validation—loses its authority. "The play demonstrates the simultaneous disintegration of order and speech and truth." Hence the Bastard cannot find a proper idiom in the last two acts, as he seeks to create order and behave as the king's agent. Only nationalism serves as a unifying force; later Shakespeare will seek another, stronger bond in love, which "alone is hugely politic." In this play, Shakespeare becomes a modern.

Curren-Aquino, Deborah T., ed. "*King John*": *New Perspectives*. Newark: University of Delaware Press, 1989.
A collection of twelve essays followed by a brief stage history and selective bibliography. Marsha Robinson's "The Historiographic Methodology of *King John*" interprets the play as a parody of "conventional representations" of events. Guy Hamel compares Shakespeare's play with its chief source, *The Troublesome Raigne of King John*. Virginia Mason Vaughn argues that the work rejects the view of John as a proto-Protestant martyr. For both Vaughn and Phyllis Rackin, who offers a feminist perspective, the play subverts Tudor orthodoxy. Barbara Traister considers the genre of the play and the nature of John's kingship. Dorothea Kehler studies the role of Providence in the work. Joseph Candido looks at the characters' quest for purity amidst "moral pollution." The Bastard provides the focus for Michael Manheim's contribution, and Joseph A. Porter continues the examination through a study of the play's language. Carol J. Carlisle and Edward S. Brubaker discuss the play on stage, and the volume fittingly concludes with Larry S. Champion's treatment of the problematic ending.

Kastan, David Scott. "'To Set a Form upon That Indigest': Shakespeare's Fictions of History." *Comparative Drama* 17 (1983):1-16.
The world of the history plays in general, and that of *King John* in particular, lacks moral cohesion. Like drama, history is fictional, "created and preserved by human effort and will." In both areas, individuals construct "reality" to suit their needs. Through language, the Bastard creates a strong king out of John and

a strong England out of a weak, divided country, just as Shakespeare makes both men "scribbled [forms], drawn with a pen/ Upon a parchment" (V, vii).

Shirley, Frances A., ed. *"King John" and "Henry VIII": Critical Essays*. New York: Garland, 1988.
A useful collection of criticism on the plays drawn from nineteenth and twentieth century sources. Shirley provides an overview of the essays in her introduction and concludes with a bibliography of the works included. A compilation that includes a number of standard selections, such as the comments of E. M. W. Tillyard and Caroline F. E. Spurgeon on *King John* and William Hazlitt's observations on both plays. Alongside these familiar pieces are such selections as Adrien Bonjour's "The Road to Swinstead Abbey: A Study of the Sense and Structure of *King John*" (1951), which defends the construction of the play, and Anna Jameson's 1866 discussion of Katherine as historical figure and dramatic character in *Henry VIII*.

Vaughn, Virginia Mason. "Between Tetralogies: *King John* as Transition." *Shakespeare Quarterly* 25 (1984):407-420.
Shakespeare's first tetralogy does not analyze political behavior. With *King John*, he "acknowledges the complexity of political life" and notes that the varying factions have their flaws and virtues. To present this altered outlook, Shakespeare develops new dramatic techniques. He creates divided loyalties in the audience, probing questions of legitimacy and sovereignty. To foster ambiguity, he mutes the anti-Catholic, patriotic tone of *The Troublesome Raigne of King John*. The concern of *King John* is that of the second tetralogy, "the conflict between our idealized longing for the perfect ruler in the perfect commonwealth and the grim realities of power, guile, and treachery in a fallen world."

Wixson, Douglas C. "'Calm Words Folded Up in Smoke': Propaganda and Spectator Response in Shakespeare's *King John*." *Shakespeare Studies* 14 (1981):111-127.
Each act contains a debate; this form was popular in the political pamphlets of the sixteenth century. Shakespeare allows his audience to draw its own conclusions based on its knowledge of Elizabethan polemics and its observation of the play. *King John* transcends its time, though, because it addresses universal political questions without imposing particular answers.

King Lear

Textual Studies

Doran, Madeleine. *The Text of King Lear*. Stanford, Calif.: Stanford University Press, 1931.

Regards the 1608 quarto not as "bad" but as printed from a revised manuscript by Shakespeare. The shorter folio text is a better play and derives from a revised transcript of the same manuscript used to create the quarto. In 1931, the bibliographical experts generally rejected Doran's view, but it has found increasing support since, so that in 1986 Oxford University Press published the 1608 quarto and 1623 folio versions as separate plays, each text legitimate. Doran herself later abandoned her position on the legitimacy of the quarto text.

Duthie, George Ian. *Elizabethan Shorthand and the First Quarto of "King Lear."* Oxford, England: Basil Blackwell, 1949.
Argues that the folio version derives from the 1608 quarto, modified from a playhouse copy, most likely the promptbook. The 1608 quarto was created from actors' memories, not from someone's recording the play in shorthand, because Elizabethan shorthand was not sufficiently developed to allow such full transcription. Most of the book examines Willis' system of shorthand, the best available in the first decade of the seventeenth century but still inadequate, according to Duthie, to produce a usable transcript of a play.

Kirschbaum, Leo. *The True Text of "King Lear."* Baltimore: The Johns Hopkins University Press, 1945.
Reviews the debate on the text of *King Lear* to 1945 and argues that the 1608 quarto lacks authority because it is a memorial reconstruction of the text accurately represented in the First Folio. The First Folio text was printed from a corrected version of the quarto. The corrections came from someone in Shakespeare's company; therefore the folio readings are the ones to be adopted when they differ from the quarto. Where quarto and folio agree, both may err, so the editor may emend the text if necessary. Most of the book compares the two versions and argues for the folio's authority. Though orthodox in 1945, this view of the text has grown less popular, Oxford and Cambridge University Presses maintaining that both versions of the play have authority; hence, they have printed the two versions instead of a conflated text.

Stone, P. W. K. *The Textual History of "King Lear."* London: Scolar Press, 1980.
Advocates an amalgamated text. The 1608 quarto derives from a transcript made by someone who attended several performances. Neither the quarto nor the folio is the authoritative text, so a modern edition must seek to fuse the two in a "hypothetical reconstruction of a text which does not in fact exist, but which once did as the ancestor of the editions still surviving." Although Stone's argument is pessimistic in rejecting any extant text as authentic, his arguments must be considered (even if rejected) by anyone concerned with the play.

Taylor, Gary, and Michael Warren, eds. *The Division of the Kingdom: Two Versions of "King Lear."* New York: Oxford University Press, 1984.

A collection of twelve essays that endorse the view that the 1608 quarto and 1623 folio are both authoritative texts despite their differences. Shakespeare revised *King Lear* after it was published in 1608, perhaps for the opening of the Black-friars Theatre in 1609. The folio version, which is shorter, is theatrically more effective. Though Richard Knowles was not convinced that the folio version is reliable, he praised the contributions here as "challenging and thought-provoking, [exhibiting] immense learning, labor, energy, and ingenuity" (*Shakespeare Quarterly* 36 [1985]:120).

Urkowitz, Steven. *Shakespeare's Revision of "King Lear."* Princeton, N.J.: Princeton University Press, 1980.
The folio version is the better text, according to Urkowitz, but the 1608 quarto is not a flawed edition, nor should a modern editor conflate the two to create a single text. The quarto is an earlier draft, and the changes reveal much about Shakespeare's skill as a playwright. Whatever the status of the two texts, Urkowitz shows that conflating them leads to contradictions. He does not demonstrate, however, that the folio changes are necessarily authoritative. Gary Taylor called this "a landmark in the study of *King Lear*" (*Review of English Studies*, n.s. 34 [1983]:69).

Anthologies of Criticism

Adelman, Janet, ed. *Twentieth Century Interpretations of "King Lear."* Englewood Cliffs, N.J.: Prentice-Hall, 1978.
Adelman opens this fine collection of essays with an excellent introduction to the play as a whole and to the character of Edgar in particular. Seven essays follow in part 1, short excerpts from nine others in part 2. The old standards, such as A. C. Bradley and G. Wilson Knight, are supplemented with newer interpretations, such as Marvin Rosenberg's "*Lear*'s Theatre Poetry" and Stephen Booth's "On the Greatness of *King Lear*." Michael Goldman praised the anthology as "helpful to the beginner, and stimulating to the advanced student" (*Shakespeare Quarterly* 30 [1979]:421). Because even the essays in part 1 are cut, students who find a selection useful should turn to the original to read the full argument.

Bonheim, Helmut, ed. *The "King Lear" Perplex.* Belmont, Calif.: Wadsworth, 1960.
A sampling of critical commentary on the play from Nahum Tate's 1681 revision up to William R. Elton's *"King Lear" and the Gods* (1966), still unpublished when Bonheim's volume went to press. The emphasis is on twentieth century criticism. The excerpts are so short—often little more than a page—that the chief value of the book is as a selective bibliography. Concludes with a briefly annotated bibliography.

Colie, Rosalie L., and F. T. Flahiff, eds. *Some Facets of "King Lear": Essays in Prismatic Criticism.* Toronto: University of Toronto Press, 1974.
A collection of twelve illuminating essays. Sheldon P. Zitner's "*King Lear* and Its Language" sees the play as rejecting language's ability to describe the horrific events portrayed. Bridget G. Lyons agrees that "Lear's sufferings . . . cannot be accommodated by traditional formulas, moral or literary." John Reibetanz looks at Shakespeare's use of emblems, a practice Reibetanz derives from the private playhouses. Thomas F. Van Laan examines the theatrical metaphor, which reflects growing chaos in the play. The play's use of clothing imagery interests Maurice Charney, and F. D. Hoeniger looks at the work's treatment of nature and the primitive. W. F. Blissett focuses on Aristotelian *anagnorisus*, while Colie and Martha Andresen respectively consider borrowings from the Bible and other commonplaces. For Nancy R. Lindheim, the play fuses pastoral and comedy. Colie and Flahiff conclude the volume with considerations of the play's historical and political contexts. Jay L. Halio observed that "many students will be glad to have the insights and scholarship that these twelve essays . . . provide" (*Shakespeare Quarterly* 28 [1977]:107).

Danson, Lawrence, ed. *On "King Lear."* Princeton, N.J.: Princeton University Press, 1981.
A collection of eight pieces originally offered as lectures at Princeton University. Alvin B. Kernan begins the volume by looking at Shakespeare's view of history as a void requiring human community and human effort to create order, however diminished. Michael Goldman, G. E. Bentley, and Daniel Seltzer offer various slants on the play in the theater. Theodore Weiss explores the play's poetic richness, and Thomas McFarland sees the play as dealing with families. The editor considers the way *King Lear* stretches the audience "between the two abysses of Infinity and Nothingness." Thomas P. Roche sees the play's ending as bleak because the setting is pre-Christian, "in a time when there was no salvation, no revelation, no help for humanity in its fallen condition," so even Cordelia cannot redeem Lear or his world.

Muir, Kenneth. *"King Lear": Critical Essays.* New York: Garland, 1984.
A collection of comments from Samuel Johnson's 1765 observations to Muir's "Epilogue" written for this volume. Includes statements by many major critics of the play: Charles Lamb, Samuel Taylor Coleridge, A. C. Bradley, Harley Granville-Barker, G. Wilson Knight, L. C. Knights, and Maynard Mack, among others. Some unhappily are drastically abridged, such as Robert B. Heilman's *This Great Stage* (1948), which receives only four pages. Limited space also prevents the inclusion of many significant studies. Undergraduates and beginning graduate students will nevertheless find a wealth of seminal material frequently cited by other critics.

General Studies

Bickersteth, G. L. *The Golden World of "King Lear."* Oxford, England: Oxford University Press, 1946.

Bickersteth takes his title from Sir Philip Sidney's *An Apologie for Poetrie*, which says that Nature's world is brass—"the poets only deliver a golden." *King Lear*, like all great art, does not create a new world but instead faithfully shows the brazen world in such a way as to make it appear golden. *King Lear* confronts "the mystery of human nature." The play is didactic, showing that evil destroys itself and brings about goodness: Edmund, for example, repents in defeat. Yet the play seems to offer gratuitous evil, especially the death of Cordelia. Bickersteth therefore argues that the play's primary aim is artistic success, to depict nature as it is, or as Shakespeare saw it. The suffering in the play is redemptive. Cordelia's love in the world of *King Lear* is as alien as Christ in Hell; both cause disruption but also rescue and redeem.

Davis, Arthur G. *The Royalty of Lear.* New York: St. John's University Press, 1974.

A defense of the character of Lear as every inch a king and a noble individual. Davis defends the initial plan to divide the kingdom; even the twofold division that excludes Cordelia appears wise to Davis. Thus, Lear is not a foolish, fond old man. What critics treat as the love test in the opening scene Davis sees as merely a desire for reassurance. Lear does not doubt that his daughters love him, nor has he previously demanded flattery from his children. Davis also admires Cordelia, and he regards Edmund as an opportunist and the Fool as the voice of common sense. The play affirms an ordered universe disrupted for a time by evil; Shakespeare portrays "expiation, forgiveness, reconciliation and an ultimate purification of the one who did wrong." Though not overtly Christian, the play is not anti-Christian. It is "grim rather than hopeless." In the end, evil is destroyed. "The play has demonstrated that evil is potent, that it may inflict much harm on the innocent and win many victories, but that it will not survive."

Elton, William R. *"King Lear" and the Gods.* San Marino, Calif.: Huntington Library, 1966.

Challenges the interpretation that sees the play as grounded in Christian optimism. Elton first surveys Renaissance ideas about Providence, finding four attitudes in Sir Philip Sidney's *The Arcadia* and in *King Lear*: "the *prisca theologia*, or virtuous-heathen view" similar to Christian trust in faith, hope, and love; atheism; superstition; and "human reaction to the effects of hidden providence." These attitudes are represented by the various characters. Orthodox viewers of the play could see in the failure of pagan belief a statement about Christianity's superiority, while the more sophisticated could find in the play's theological doubts a mirror of their own uncertainty. In altering his sources,

Shakespeare distanced himself from a conventional Christian treatment. Clifford Leech observed that "Mr. Elton has the courage to see the play whole, and he has supported his view of it by a most thorough scrutiny of the nature of Renaissance humanism" (*Review of English Studies*, n.s. 18 [1967]:459). Edward A. Langhans found the argument persuasive, "methodical, detailed, and heavily laden with documentary proof" (*Shakespeare Quarterly* 20 [1969]:100).

Fraser, Russell A. *Shakespeare's Poetics in Relation to "King Lear."* London: Routledge & Kegan Paul, 1962.
Looks at the iconography of the play, focusing on images of Providence, kind, Fortune, anarchy and order, reason and will, appearance and reality, and redemption. Thus, in depicting Edmund, Shakespeare draws on the emblems of Aeneas and Absalom. *King Lear* depicts chaos in many ways—"Albany at the distaff, Goneril with a drum, and Regan (with) a baton, and the Duke of Cornwall put down by a peasant." Over fifty illustrations support the text. In the concluding chapter, Fraser presents an overall assessment of Shakespeare's vision, which believes in Providence, though not necessarily in poetic justice. Evil arises from attempts at self-sufficiency. Fraser sees *King Lear* as endorsing the orthodox position of the day, as exemplified in the moral commonplaces of emblematic literature.

Gardner, Helen. *"King Lear."* London: Oxford University Press, 1967.
Begins by discussing the grand scale of the action, characters, and language. The play differs from Shakespeare's other tragedies by its lack of clearly defined time and space, by the ubiquitous comic elements, and by the dual plot that seems two stories but becomes one. Though one can find support for either an optimistic or a pessimistic reading of the play, the ending is ambiguous and offers no consolation, no answers.

Goldberg, Samuel Louis. *An Essay on "King Lear."* Cambridge, England: Cambridge University Press, 1974.
King Lear cannot be explained by a single interpretation; it offers multiple visions of reality, though each character has a particular view. Goldberg concludes that "no critical 'saying' . . . can be final, because no one can experience as a coherent, final judgment all the possibilities of judgment the play evokes." Producers face great difficulty in putting on stage a play that will allow for the multiplicity of views embodied in the text. Patrick Cruttwell called this study "interesting and intelligent" (*Sewanee Review* 83 [1975]:313).

Heilman, Robert B. *This Great Stage: Image and Structure in "King Lear."* Baton Rouge: Louisiana State University Press, 1948.
Studies the play's language and images to understand the work. For example, Shakespeare draws on the dichotomies of sight and blindness, sanity and mad-

ness. Ironically, Gloucester saw least when he had his eyes and Lear's madness leads to understanding. Heilman sees Shakespeare as believing in an ordered universe; "nature" also is an important term in the play and is viewed in opposing ways. G. I. Duthie commented that "Mr. Heilman argues cogently: he is sensitive to the overtones of poetic language" (*Review of English Studies*, n.s. 2 [1951]:79). Philip Edwards, while not persuaded of the value of image-hunting, remarked that "in many ways, the student's approach to *Lear* should be the fresher for this book" (*Modern Language Review* 44 [1949]:264).

Jorgensen, Paul A. *Lear's Self-Discovery*. Berkeley: University of California Press, 1966.
Suggests that *King Lear* is "perhaps the greatest drama of self-discovery in all literature." Lear must undergo the arduous process of discovering his wretchedness so that he may attain redemption. Edgar also undergoes a journey of self-discovery; the other characters do not. In this study, Jorgensen places the play within the context of Renaissance discussions of self-knowledge and the development of other Shakespearean characters as they become thinkers. *The Times Literary Supplement* for October 26, 1967, called this a "lucid and sensible study"; F. D. Hoeniger said that it combines a number of "really striking perceptions" presented in a scholarly fashion (*Renaissance Quarterly* 21 [1968]:362).

Kozintsev, Grigori Mikhailovich. *"King Lear": The Space of Tragedy*. Berkeley: University of California Press, 1977.
Kozintsev's diary kept during the filming of his version of *King Lear*, showing his wrestling with technical problems such as a Lear with an Estonian accent or choosing the proper setting for the play. Kozintsev also examines the philosophical issues posed by the work—the play's mental landscape. Useful for those involved with the play on the page or on the stage.

Leggatt, Alexander. *"King Lear."* Boston: Twayne, 1988.
After a brief survey of the play's stage history and critical reception, Leggat turns to an examination of the work's dramatic idiom and characters. *King Lear* relies on ironic juxtapositions, on contradictions between word and action, making it a highly theatrical piece. Though characters seem to divide into good and bad, Edmund appears sympathetic at first; even at the end of the play, he exhibits a certain courtliness. Albany develops during the play; Kent grows ineffectual. Lear "gropes reluctantly towards his new life [and] ends by demonstrating his own love, and our mortal helplessness, in a manner beyond words." A good introduction to the play.

Lothian, John M. *"King Lear": A Tragic Reading of Life*. Toronto: Clark, Irwin, 1949.

The first chapter discusses the changes Shakespeare made as he adapted his sources: giving the play a tragic ending, adding the Fool, making Lear go mad, and creating the storm. The second chapter explores the meaning of the play, which records "the spiritual history or regeneration of King Lear and the tremendous wrench with which it is effected." This play thus shows man's weakness and strength, "his ridiculousness and his sublimity." The third chapter treats the Fool, who provides entertainment but also teaches wisdom to the king. Other chapters discuss Edgar and the play's structure and significance. Lear learns that chaos is the law of nature; order is the dream of humanity.

Lusardi, James P., and June Schueter. *Reading Shakespeare in Performance: "King Lear."* Cranbury, N.J.: Associated University Presses, 1991.
Uses performance as a way of understanding the text, recognizing that no single ideal production exists. The authors examine the opening scene (I, iv), the scene in which Goneril and Regan reject Lear (II, iv), the mock trial (III, vi), Gloucester at Dover Cliff (IV, vi), and the conclusion (V, iii). Two television productions receive particular attention: the BBC's 1982 version and the 1983 Granada interpretation with Laurence Olivier as Lear. An appendix presents comments by some of those involved in these productions and also some reviews. Essential for anyone contemplating staging the work and useful for students, who will find varying interpretations here. The book demonstrates that Charles Lamb erred when he said that the play could not be performed.

Mack, Maynard. *"King Lear" in Our Time.* Berkeley: University of California Press, 1965.
A highly influential study that examines the play's theatrical history, its sources, and its appeal to twentieth century audiences. Mack notes that Nahum Tate's 1681 revision of *King Lear* popularized the work and held the stage for well over a century. Mack condemns modern productions, such as Peter Brook's 1962 version, that ignore the text in favor of subtext. Though the play's printed sources are well known, Mack observes that the impetus for composing the work may have come from the efforts of two of Sir Brian Annesley's daughters to have him declared insane so that they could keep his estate; his daughter Cordell thwarted these efforts. The play seems especially relevant to modern audiences because of its concerns with endurance, suffering, death, and chaos. Nicholas Brooke observed that Mack "writes . . . with his characteristic combination of urbanity, profound insight, and careful regard for the known or knowable" (*Modern Language Review* 65 [1970]:379).

Martin, William F. *The Indissoluble Knot: "King Lear" as Ironic Drama.* Lanham, Md: University Press of America, 1987.
"In *King Lear* comic scenes are not added in order to heighten the tragic effect, as is the case in most other tragedies, but are instead *blended* with the serious

action; the result is a dramatic effect at once serious and ludicrous, or, in as word, ironic." This ironic drama best demonstrates the complexities of life and human nature. Such a play "educates us for an effective, well-integrated life." As such, it is preferable to conventional tragedy. Martin is more persuasive in noting the differences between *King Lear* and other tragedies; much of what he sees as comic will not strike all in that way.

Muir, Kenneth. *"King Lear": A Critical Study*. Harmondsworth, England: Penguin Books, 1986.
A survey of the play's sources, structure, characters, themes, and images, followed by a scene-by-scene analysis. An appendix addresses the problems of the text and the dating of the play. Muir links the play to Desiderius Erasmus' view of folly as true wisdom; the "reasonable" characters are evil. Whether or not the play accepts a Christian world, it emphasizes the need for faith, hope, and charity. Though treating timeless issues, it also examines such contemporary problems as the plight of beggars and the fascination with Revelation, a book about which King James I had written. A sound introduction that deals sensibly with the play's various issues.

Murphy, John L. *Darkness and Devils: Exorcism and "King Lear."* Athens: Ohio University Press, 1984.
Looks at Shakespeare's sources, especially Samuel Harsnett's *A Declaration of Egregious Popish Impostures* (1603), and suggests that Edgar serves as an exorcist for both Lear and Gloucester. Murphy believes that Shakespeare read Harsnett's condemnation of Jesuit exorcism with sympathy for the Catholic viewpoint and in act III showed that exorcism can purge demonic possession. John Reibetanz's review questions the specific religious viewpoint that Murphy finds in the play but notes that Murphy "does justice to the power of evil in *King Lear*: the responses demanded by his interpretation probably bring us closer to the Elizabethan spectator's awe of something so enormous and so insidious" (*Modern Language Quarterly* 46 [1985]:187).

Nameri, Dorothy E. *Three Versions of the Story of King Lear*. 2 vols. Salzburg, Austria: University of Salzburg Press, 1976.
Argues that when Nahum Tate prepared his revised version of *King Lear*, he looked not only at Shakespeare's play but also at the anonymous *King Leir* that was Shakespeare's source. Tate borrowed themes, structure, characters, and plot from the older work. Nameri even finds verbal parallels. Tate remained close to Shakespeare's text, but his changes often result from his returning to the earlier version of the play.

Reibetanz, John. *The Lear World: A Study of "King Lear" in Its Dramatic Context*. Toronto: University of Toronto Press, 1977.
King Lear is a peculiarly Jacobean play, with its reliance on episodes rather than

ordered narrative, its use of emblems, and its portrayal of Edmund, and to a lesser extent Edgar and Cordelia, as stage manager arranging the action. The subplot's echo of the main plot is Jacobean, too; Elizabethan subplots often provided only comic relief. Reibetanz's argument is shaky, but he offers many insights into the play even though these do not relate to its Jacobean ambience; for example, the play uses emblems to depict a "hostile world." Nicholas Brooke, reviewing this work for *The Times Literary Supplement* (October 27, 1978), wrote that "this is not a profoundly original book, but it is an observant one, which will be important in advancing our tenuous grip on a genuine dramatic criticism."

Rosenberg, Marvin. *The Masks of "King Lear."* Berkeley: University of California Press, 1972.
A learned study—as the thirty pages of notes and bibliography indicate—that examines the play scene by scene to find its artistic unity. Language is key, dominated by an "if" that reveals the ambiguity of the world of the play. Rosenberg never loses sight of the play on stage, referring frequently to performances that illuminate as much as critical commentary. His interpretation rejects the optimistic reading. The play affirms love, kindness, and loyalty, but "nothing is sure in this world." As David M. Bergeron observed, "One cannot fail to be informed and instructed by this book; its value is apparent" (*Shakespeare Quarterly* 25 [1974]:370).

Salgado, Gamini. *"King Lear": Text and Performance.* London: Macmillan, 1984.
Part 1 surveys varying interpretations of the play on the page, noting the paradoxes that inform the work. Lear is wiser in his madness than in his sanity. The Fool embodies wisdom. Cordelia's silence is more eloquent than her sisters' speeches. Salgado also looks at character and structure. In part 2, he examines four productions: the Old Vic 1940 presentation with John Gielgud as Lear, Peter Brook's 1962 version, Trevor Nunn's 1968 Royal Shakespeare Festival production, and Grigori Kozintsev's 1970 film. These may be described respectively as "Heroic, Humanist, Historical, and Absurdist"; Salgado admires the film version but offers fair assessments of all four, which show the problems the play presents and how one may approach these in various ways.

Sewall, Richard B. *"King Lear."* In *The Vision of Tragedy.* New and enlarged ed. New Haven, Conn.: Yale University Press, 1980.
"*King Lear* is another story of a soul in torment, a 'purgatorial' story." The play draws on Christian ethics, but Lear must win salvation without grace, and he must do so alone. Nor does he go to some celestial city at the end of the play. The promises of Christian revelation are shattered at the play's conclusion. The heaven to which Lear appeals is deaf; neither good nor evil triumphs. The hope that the play offers lies in the existence of good as well as evil and in the ability

to distinguish between the two. Lear, Cordelia, Gloucester, Edgar, and Albany have suffered, but they also become more truly human. "If the play denies the comforts of optimism, it does not retreat into cynicism. Its world is hard; evil is an ever-present wolf at the door. But man is free to act and to learn."

Thompson, Ann. *"King Lear."* Atlantic Highlands, N.J.: Humanities Press, 1988.
Graduate students and advanced undergraduates will be informed and perhaps dismayed by this brief survey of modern critical approaches to the play. Part 1 examines a number of different viewpoints, from formal, structural, and generic approaches to character analysis. This section is more objective than part 2, where Thompson incorporates modern approaches in an assessment of the play's greatness. Feminists, cultural materialists, and new historicists reject the notion of the work's universality and timeless meaning: "We can still find *King Lear* an excellent play in its own terms, but we must be aware that those terms are no longer our terms," she concludes.

Wittreich, Joseph. *"Image of That Horror": History, Prophecy, and Apocalypse in "King Lear."* San Marino, Calif.: Huntington Library, 1984.
Relates the play to the prophecies that predicted apocalypse or redemption for England after Elizabeth's death. The play allows for the latter, but salvation must be constructed; in the play, Kent, Albany, and Edgar are left to rebuild the kingdom on earth. The suffering that Cordelia, Lear, and Gloucester endure parallels the vision of Apocalypse in which the good experience hell on earth. Wittreich notes that the play was performed on St. Stephen's Day, 1606, and echoes readings appointed for that day; the deaths of Cordelia and Lear mirror that of the protomartyr. Yet the Christian references undercut themselves as the play rejects the "apocalyptic myth of providence, justice, order, tragic defeat and spiritual triumph." The play endorses secular history, not Christian eschatology. As René E. Fortin observed, "Professor Wittreich has produced an extraordinarily well-researched study that renews the reader's sense of the richness of *King Lear* and the critical tradition that it has spawned" (*JEGP* 85 [1986]:449-450).

Zak, William F. *Sovereign Shame: A Study of "King Lear."* Lewisburg, Pa.: Bucknell University Press, 1984.
Like Stanley Cavell, whose *Must We Mean What We Say?* (1969) argues that Lear harbors an unconscious flaw that provokes shame and drives him to act as he does, Zak believes that the king harbors an "unspeakable secret." Unlike Cavell, though, Zak does not see this secret as incestuous desire; moreover, Edgar, Edmund, Gloucester, and Albany suffer the same disease that afflicts Lear. Lear is ashamed of his need for love and suspects that he may be unlovable. Albany should have saved Cordelia and not fought against the French; Edgar is callous and morally wrong to disguise himself as a beggar. Cordelia,

Kent, and the Fool accept their flawed condition and so can give love to others. Shakespeare offers this salvation, though he recognizes that the self-tormented will create their own tragedy by refusing proffered love. A fresh but perverse interpretation of the play. As John Reibetanz noted, "Zak's reading deals more harshly with the well-intentioned men than with the villains" (*Modern Language Quarterly* 46 [1985]:189).

Love's Labour's Lost

Berman, Ronald. "Shakespearean Comedy and the Uses of Reason." *South Atlantic Quarterly* 63 (1964):1-9.
Likens the Academy of Navarre to François Rabelais' Academy of Paris and sees *Love's Labour's Lost* as a satire against Platonism. "The platonic ideal of intellect, the bourgeois ideal of accomplishment, and the Puritan ideal of restraint are all examined in *Love's Labour's Lost*, and they are all discarded." The play instead favors the freedom of Rabelais' Abbey of Thélème, where reason serves people and honor comes naturally. Also discusses *The Taming of the Shrew* as the triumph of madness over excessive rationality.

Bradbrook, Muriel C. *The School of Night: A Study of the Literary Relationships of Sir Walter Raleigh*. Cambridge, England: Cambridge University Press, 1936.
Accepting the existence of a "School of Night" founded by Sir Walter Raleigh, Bradbrook examines some of its tenets and interests—stoicism, astronomy, Niccolò Machiavelli. Bradbrook looks at the works of Raleigh, Christopher Marlowe, and George Chapman, who reflect the views of this school. Shakespeare took issue with this group, whose use of language prepared the way for the metaphysical poetry of the next century. *The Criterion* (16 [1937]:758) called this "an interesting and useful little study."

Carroll, William C. *The Great Feast of Language in "Love's Labour's Lost."* Princeton, N.J.: Princeton University Press, 1976.
"More than any other of Shakespeare's plays, [*Love's Labour's Lost*] deliberately explores the nature of language." Carroll first surveys the criticism—mostly negative—of the play. The first three chapters then look at style: prose, theatrical, and poetic. Chapter 4 links Shakespeare with Ovid. In chapter 5, Carroll discusses the play's dialectic, which calls for continuum rather than opposition. This idea informs chapter 6 as well, in which Carroll shows the all-embracing nature of the play's conclusion. He sees the women as commonsensical teachers of the men, who acquire a moral education in the play.

Coursen, Herbert R., Jr. "*Love's Labour's Lost* and the Comic Truth." *Papers on Language and Literature* 6 (1970):316-322.
"Like all Shakespearean comedies, *Love's Labour's Lost* exhibits a false world

gradually overtaken by truth." The men first pretend to be monks, then true lovers, but both guises are exploded by the women. The Play of the Nine Worthies repeats the theme of the larger work, as characters assume inappropriate guises, which they change for others equally false. The play within the play yields to the reality of death, as the men must face the real world as their penance before they can unite with their ladies. Their tasks fuse monasticism and love, previously divided, and now both are real, not superficial pretense. The final song repeats the play's movement from easeful spring and the folly of the cuckoo to the harsh reality of winter with the owl's wisdom.

Ellis, Herbert A. *Shakespeare's Lusty Punning in "Love's Labour's Lost": With Contemporary Analogues.* The Hague: Mouton, 1973.
Finds more than two hundred puns in the play, about a third of them previously unidentified. Using Helge Kokeritz's classification of puns in *Shakespeare's Pronunciation* (1953), Ellis first discusses semantic puns. Here he may press his reading too hard, as when he equates "nothing" with "O," "ring," "circle," and hence "vagina." The third chapter discusses homophonic puns; again Ellis strains at times. The innocent "haud credo" becomes, according to his version of Renaissance pronunciation, "hard creature." "Late edict" turns into "lated dick" (also, Eric Partridge claims that "dick" acquired its bawdy meaning in the nineteenth century). Most helpful are the observations that penetrate to the thematic significance of the puns. Thus, "academy" could be a brothel as well as a place of study, so that "Navarre could . . . be ironically portrayed as unwittingly foretelling the failure of his own unnatural resolve." Ellis also challenges the view that the play was composed for a learned coterie. The humor is broad enough to appeal to a popular audience. Stephen Booth praised this as a reference work "of general interest to students of Renaissance English" (*Modern Language Quarterly* 36 [1975]:82).

Hoy, Cyrus. "*Love's Labour's Lost* and the Nature of Comedy." *Shakespeare Quarterly* 13 (1962):31-40.
"The action of *Love's Labour's Lost* is directed at righting the balance of nature, which the proud in their simplicity would upset; it is concerned with undeceiving the self-deceived." The King of Navarre, Berowne, Longaville, and Dumain begin the play by declaring war on the senses. They must move "from the artificial to the natural" to find themselves. The penance imposed upon them by the women is designed to acquaint them with reality. The songs of spring and winter that end the play contrast human infirmities with the natural world that endures.

Montrose, Louis Adrian. "*Curious-Knotted Garden": The Form, Themes, and Contexts of Shakespeare's "Love's Labour's Lost."* Salzburg, Austria: University of Salzburg Press, 1977.
Love's Labour's Lost should be taken seriously as "a fictive critique of the ways

in which its own characters use games, rituals, myths, social institutions, and language as media by which to construct, explore, manipulate, and protect their reality." The play remains unresolved, leaving to the audience the task of fusing art and nature, a task realized in *The Winter's Tale*. An appendix addresses the question of text, the play's topicality, and its date. Montrose proposes three stages of composition—from the late 1580s or early 1590s to 1598, when the quarto edition appeared.

Taylor, Rupert. *The Date of "Love's Labour's Lost."* New York: Columbia University Press, 1932.
Argues that the play was composed in mid-1596, later than most critics place it. The Russian masque in the last act suggests to Taylor the revels at Gray's Inn for the Christmas season of 1594-1595. The heavy use of rhyme and the stanza form of *Venus and Adonis* (1593) indicate to most critics an early date, but even *Much Ado About Nothing* (c. 1598) contains *Venus and Adonis* stanzas. The French names suggest contemporary events, but if Dumain refers to the Duke de Mayenne he would not have been at the court of Henry IV (King of Navarre before 1598) until 1595. The references in the play to "necessity" echo Henry IV's references to his "necessity" in 1596. Puns on "pierce," "purse," and "penniless" suggest Nashe's *Piers Penniless* and the Gabriel Harvey-Thomas Nashe quarrel that began in 1592 but persisted for several years. Taylor conjectures a family relationship between the Greenes of Warwick and the Shakespeares and suggests that Shakespeare may have been educated in Warwick. In an appendix, Taylor speculates on the identity of Holofernes and concludes that the original is still lacking. Taylor believes that the play was composed at one time, not revised later to incorporate topical allusions.

Yates, Frances A. *A Study of "Love's Labour's Lost."* Cambridge, England: Cambridge University Press, 1936.
While denying precise correspondences between characters in the play and historical figures, Yates finds much topical satire in the play. The play was written against the Raleigh-Northumberland "School of Night" and in support of the Earls of Essex and Southampton. Shakespeare sided with the Catholics in Southampton's household, attacking Florio, Gabriel Harvey, George Chapman, and Bruno (who criticized Sir Philip Sidney's "Stella," sister of the Earl of Essex). Shakespeare also argued that life can teach more than books and satirized those who were educated but lacked intelligence. Enid Welsford wrote that "Miss Yates handles her intricate argument with ease, her book is thoroughly readable as well as scholarly, and is a real aid to the appreciation of *Love's Labour's Lost* (*Modern Language Review* 33 [1938]:68).

Macbeth

Bartholomeusz, Dennis. *"Macbeth" and the Players*. Cambridge, England: Cambridge University Press, 1969.
Examines the stage history of the play in an effort to understand the work and to show how performances have changed over the centuries, from Shakespeare's day to 1964. Bartholomeusz focuses on the portrayals of Macbeth and his wife and judges productions on their ability to demonstrate the dual natures of these characters: Macbeth as sensitive but evil, Lady Macbeth as beautiful and terrible. The book concludes that David Garrick and Laurence Olivier offered the two most successful renditions of Macbeth and that Sarah Siddons was the best Lady Macbeth because they "combined grandeur without pomp and nature without triviality, and they illuminated the text with a rare brilliance." This survey demonstrates how modern audiences and readers have been affected by the vision of actors, such as Helen Faucit's playing of Lady Macbeth as a devoted wife.

Brown, John Russell, ed. *Focus on "Macbeth."* London: Routledge & Kegan Paul, 1982.
A collection of eleven essays with an afterword by the editor. R. A. Foakes considers *Macbeth* as Shakespeare's "most searching analysis of the effects of ambition." Brian Morris dissents, seeing the play as dealing with guilt. D. J. Palmer analyzes the visual repetitions, facial expressions, and gestures that abound in the play; he also discusses what is not shown, such as Duncan's death. Marvin Rosenberg and Gareth Lloyd Evans examine aspects of stage history, the former surveying the treatment of Macbeth and his wife in the eighteenth and nineteenth centuries, the latter examining eight postwar productions at Stratford-upon-Avon. Robin Grove discusses the ambiguous treatment of nature. Michael Goldman explains how language in the play makes evil fascinating. The play's political concerns are the subject of Michael Hawkins' contribution, witchcraft the topic that Peter Stallybrass explores. Derek Russell Davis psychoanalyzes Macbeth and Lady Macbeth. The anthology concludes with Peter Hall's insights into the play. Brown summarizes the essays by noting *Macbeth*'s depth and complexity and observing that in its ambiguity it moves beyond a compliment to King James. Maurice Charney wrote that "The collection is exciting in its exploration of the continued vitality of this puzzling play" (*Modern Philology* 82 [1985]:420).

Calderwood, James L. *If It Were Done: "Macbeth" and Tragic Action*. Amherst: University of Massachusetts Press, 1986.
Looks at *Macbeth* as *Hamlet*'s antithesis. Time stretches out in *Hamlet* as the prince delays. In *Macbeth*, time contracts as the protagonist acts quickly. Hamlet explores his conscience; Macbeth suppresses his. Hamlet flees reality into imagination; Macbeth's imagination leads to reality. Hamlet ponders being,

Macbeth acting. In his interpretation of *Macbeth*, Calderwood draws on numerous approaches. From psychology, for example, he takes his reading of the murder of Duncan as an Oedipal act and a rite of passage into manhood. The study concludes with seven brief essays on such matters as the catalog of dogs in III, i, and Banquo's ghost in III, iv. R. A. Foakes called the book "heady stuff, sometimes verging on silliness, but frequently stimulating in its play of intelligence" (*Review of English Studies*, n.s. 39 [1988]:293).

Clark, Arthur Melville. *Murder Under Trust: Or, The Topical "Macbeth" and Other Jacobean Matters*. Edinburgh: Scottish Academic Press, 1981.
Argues that *Macbeth* reveals intimate knowledge of Scottish law and politics. Links the play to the Gowrie conspiracy of 1600, in which James was lured to the Gowrie castle, where the brothers tried to murder him. In 1587, the Scottish Parliament defined treason as "murder under trust," that is, the murder of a guest by his host. The relationship between Macbeth and his wife derives, according to Clark, not from Raphael Holinshed but from William Stewart's *Buik of the Croniclis of Scotland*, not published until 1858, but James had a manuscript copy, which Shakespeare consulted in Scotland in 1601. Shakespeare had gone north in the wake of his involvement with the Essex conspiracy. James commissioned the play to celebrate his escape from the Gowrie plot. The study brings together much information about Scotland, but its conclusions concerning *Macbeth* are highly questionable. Despite the book's publication date, Clark apparently consulted only one work printed after 1950; this reliance on older scholarship and Clark's fondness for wild surmise weaken the argument.

Elliott, George Roy. *Dramatic Providence in "Macbeth": A Study of Shakespeare's Tragic Theme of Humanity and Grace*. Princeton, N.J.: Princeton University Press, 1958.
Macbeth exemplifies the tragedy of self-reliance and rejection of God's grace. Evil and goodness are both supernatural, and even the worst person can be saved through grace. Duncan and Banquo extend that grace to Macbeth, but in IV, i, he chooses the witches and so embraces evil. On stage, the play loses much of its metaphysical dimension. A thoughtful but sometimes forced interpretation. Robert G. Shedd called this "an extremely valuable study [with] surprising and fresh insights, many provocative enough to send the reader back to the text for a corrobative second look" (*JEGP* 59 [1960]:572/575).

Fawkner, H. W. *Deconstructing "Macbeth": The Hyperontological View*. London: Associated University Presses, 1990.
Macbeth seeks perfection and certainty "but gets doubt and anguish. . . . For the entire duration of the play, Macbeth continues to participate in the dialectical equivocation he has sought to end." At the conclusion of the play, Macbeth triumphs and is defeated. Macbeth is presented as an extraordinary figure who

cannot accommodate himself to the ordinariness of Duncan and his world. A dense book that offers numerous fascinating insights if one can penetrate the jargon; the glossary at the end of the volume offers little help and seems a deconstructionist joke. Among the observations here is that Macbeth assumes the guise of Lady Macbeth's child (John Bayley makes this point in his 1981 *Shakespeare and Tragedy*) and that she uses various fluids to control his world (drugged drink, for example). She seeks to rule Macbeth—hence she makes him kill Duncan and does not do the deed herself—but she loses him.

Hunter, G. K. "*Macbeth* in the Twentieth Century." *Shakespeare Survey* 19 (1966):1-11.
A survey of critical responses to the play. Editors have come to accept all but the Hecate scenes as Shakespeare's; critics have found numerous topical references and various sources in addition to Raphael Holinshed's *Chronicles*, which provides the main outline of the play. The witches continue to fascinate and trouble students of the work. Some writers have tried overhard to Christianize *Macbeth*; others have provided helpful studies of themes and images. Macbeth himself tends to fare poorly; whereas the nineteenth century admired him, more modern critics have not. Altogether, Hunter discusses forty-four books, twenty-eight articles, and twelve editions. Very useful.

Jorgensen, Paul A. *Our Naked Frailties: Sensational Art and Meaning in "Macbeth."* Berkeley: University of California Press, 1971.
In *Macbeth*, an audience sees its own potential for evil. The play is religious; it demonstrates Thomas Aquinas' notion of condign justice and Pope Innocent's statement that sin breeds its own punishment. Yet the focus is on the human loss, which evokes pity for the hero's lack of insight that could also be the viewer's. Much good discussion of character and imagery as well as earlier criticism of the play.

Long, Michael. "*Macbeth.*" Boston: Twayne, 1989.
As in all these Twayne volumes, stage history and critical reception precede a discussion of the play, and the book concludes with a brief bibliography. Chapter 1 looks at visual and verbal features of the play, such as the feasting table, the cauldron, and Birnam Wood. Chapter 2 compares Macbeth to other literary characters such as Satan, Woton, and Alberich. In chapter 3, Long relates the play to the cycle of life, and chapter 4 looks at the play scene by scene. The last chapter examines the type of tragic experience *Macbeth* offers; Long sees the hero as "endlessly pitiful"—more so than Lear, Othello, or Timon—because Macbeth is isolated from the human community, like Jacques in *As You Like It*. *Macbeth* is at once Shakespeare's most Christian and most classical play.

Muir, Kenneth, and Philip Edwards, eds. *Aspects of "Macbeth."* Cambridge, England: Cambridge University Press, 1977.
A collection of essays drawn from *Shakespeare Survey*. G. K. Hunter leads off the volume with his 1966 survey of twentieth century criticism. Muriel C. Bradbrook discusses the sources of the play: Raphael Holinshed, of course, but also events in James I's life, the king's concern with witches, and Shakespeare's *The Rape of Lucrece*. Robert Heilman examines the problem of having a criminal as tragic hero and concludes that Macbeth retains the audience's sympathy, but at the price of diminishing his heroic nature. Glynne Wickham notes the parallels between the porter scene and the medieval "The Harrowing of Hell," which may have served as a model for the play. Lady Macbeth is the subject of W. Moelwyn Merchant's article, and Inga-Stina Ewbank compares Lady Macbeth to the Medea of Seneca. Muir and V. Y. Kantak conclude the volume with studies of the play's imagery. Includes a number of illustrations, most of them of productions of *Macbeth*, though the first four relate to Wickham's essay.

Paul, Henry N. *The Royal Play of "Macbeth": When, Why, and How It Was Written by Shakespeare*. New York: Macmillan, 1948.
A classic study of the play. Locates the first performance at Hampton Court on August 7, 1606, for a royal visit by James I's brother-in-law, King Christian IV of Denmark. This visit explains Shakespeare's removal of all references to Danish invasions, though Raphael Holinshed's account mentions two. Paul notes that, in addition to Holinshed, Shakespeare used material from James's *Basilikon Doron* and *Daemonology* and from George Buchanan's *Rerum Scoticarum historia*; Buchanan had been James's tutor. Paul glosses a number of contemporary allusions.

Ramsey, Jarold. "The Perversion of Manliness in *Macbeth*." *Studies in English Literature* 13 (1973):285-300.
The play asks "what is a man?" Macbeth initially fuses manliness and humaneness, but the two become divorced in the course of the work, culminating in Macbeth's cold response to his wife's death in V, v. At the end of the play, Macbeth recovers some of his human qualities. Shakespeare approves of humane behavior, but he also recognizes the need for ruthlessness at times, as when Malcolm and Macduff purge Scotland of Macbeth; young Seward, who unites manliness and selflessness, is killed. The audience recognizes "man's undefinable limits and capabilities" by observing the consequences of failing to fuse manliness with human sympathy.

Rosenberg, Marvin. *The Masks of "Macbeth."* Berkeley: University of California Press, 1978.
A detailed scene-by-scene analysis drawing on performance history and critical responses, including Rosenberg's own interpretation. *Macbeth* offers no simple

moral: nothing is certain; evil and good people suffer similarly; and chaos is bad, but the order that replaces it may be also. This equivocation appears in language and spectacle. Carol J. Carlisle remarked that Rosenberg stimulates the reader "to respond imaginatively to *Macbeth* and its seemingly inexhaustible possibilities" (*Shakespeare Quarterly* 30 [1979]:100).

Schoenbaum, Samuel, ed. *"Macbeth": Critical Essays*. New York: Garland, 1991. An eclectic gathering of essays from Samuel Johnson and William Hazlitt to Carol Asp's feminist reading of the play. Among the standard pieces here are Thomas De Quincey's "On the Knocking at the Gate in *Macbeth*" and L. C. Knights's send-up of spurious character analysis, "How Many Children Had Lady Macbeth?" Caroline F. E. Spurgeon's treatment of the play's imagery is included as well. More modern scholarship includes Marvin Rosenberg's and Schoenbaum's discussions of the porter scene (II, iii) on stage and page. Joseph Price, the general editor of this Garland series, states that its aim is to "represent the collective wisdom of foremost Shakespearean scholars throughout the world." To the extent that one volume can accomplish that goal, this book succeeds.

Scott, William O. "Macbeth's—and Our—Self Equivocations." *Shakespeare Quarterly* 37 (1986):160-174.
Macbeth constantly equivocates. "His imaginings impel him onward, yet he must refuse their actuality as they lead him." He destroys himself while denying that he does so. Lady Macbeth initially helps him in this matter; he can pretend that she is the force compelling him to act. Later he becomes more honest about his villainy, though he still refuses to accept its self-destructive nature. The audience, too, is taken in by language and deceives itself; in Macbeth's denial of life's reality, the audience finds affirmation. The play thus warns the audience against self-delusion yet invites self-deception.

Sinfield, Alan. "*Macbeth*: History, Ideology, and Intellectuals." *Critical Quarterly* 28 (1986):63-77.
Macbeth can be read as a vindication of the distinction James I made in *Basilikon Doron* (1599) between the legitimate monarch, who rules well, and the usurping tyrant, who rules badly. Macbeth's fall seems to result from supernatural intervention, and he appears to rule for only a short time. Both of these elements ease the qualms of those who opposed resistance even to a bad ruler. Yet one may also read the play not as an endorsement of James's view but of George Buchanan's, whose 1582 history of Scotland, one of Shakespeare's sources, justified the 1567 overthrow of Mary, Queen of Scots, who was a lawful ruler but a tyrant.

Walker, Roy. *The Time Is Free: A Study of "Macbeth."* London: Andrew Dakers, 1949.
A systematic study of the play. Finds that "the kingdom in *Macbeth* shadows

forth the kingdom of heaven on earth, obscured for a time by a blanket of the dark but never sundered from heaven." Finds much religious symbolism: Duncan eats a Last Supper with the man who betrays him, Macduff must sacrifice his son, and his flight into England leads to the Slaughter of the Innocents. Along with the theological reading, Walker offers a number of insights: Lennox is prudent rather than brave; Shakespeare announces the treachery of Cawdor in I, i, so that the news will not distract the audience from Macbeth's response in I, iii; and the third murderer is "the dramatic personification of Macbeth's guilt."

Willbern, David. "Phantasmagoric *Macbeth*." *English Literary Renaissance* 16 (1986):520-549.
"Macbeth seeks futilely to establish boundaries in a world where things won't stay put." Illusion and reality, masculine and feminine, fuse. Audiences remain in doubt about Lady Macbeth's child, about the dagger, and about the witches, and so partake of Macbeth's disorientation. Yet the audience can also use the experience to test its "own capacities for fantasy, positive or negative." A complex, fascinating analysis.

Williams, Gordon. *"Macbeth": Text and Performance*. London: Macmillan, 1985.
Part 1 examines Macbeth as a Machiavellian hero. The play posits a medieval vision of order but then shows how precarious, perhaps even false, such a view is. Williams also considers the destructive love between Macbeth and "his fiend-like queen" (V, vi), and the book treats the famous porter scene. Part 2 looks at a number of productions, particularly the 1972 Roman Polanski/Playboy film, the 1976 Royal Shakespeare Company version directed by Trevor Nunn, the National Theatre's 1978 production under Peter Hall and John Russell Brown, and Harold Davies' 1982 Royal Shakespeare interpretation. Williams admires Ian McKellen's ability as Macbeth to "yoke together those warring opposites of sensitivity and violence, deep depression and coarse brutality." Williams also praises Nunn's handling of the witches.

Measure for Measure

Bache, William B. *"Measure for Measure" as Dialectical Art*. Lafayette, Ind.: Purdue University Press, 1969.
"In *Measure for Measure* the Shakespeare ethic of love and duty operates on dark, brutal life. Each character begins with a selfish attitude towards the world and the ways of the world, and the Duke in the guise of Friar tries, and is made to try, to do what he can to preserve life so that it may become human." Argues that the play explores how to live and how to govern. Surveys the play from opening to conclusion, offering a sound interpretation of the language and action.

Bennett, Josephine Waters. *"Measure for Measure" as Royal Entertainment*. New York: Columbia University Press, 1966.

Performed before the king during the Christmas season of 1604, *Measure for Measure* depicts the ideal ruler in Duke Vincentio, who is patterned on James's ideas about government. Angelo reflects James's notions of tyranny, and Lucio plays upon James I's concern about being libeled. Bennett believes that Shakespeare played the part of the Duke (also Theseus in *A Midsummer Night's Dream* and Prospero in *The Tempest*), thus assuming the role of author, actor, and director of the action. Bennett sees the work as comic throughout; Claudio's plea for his life and his sister's reaction are sources of merriment. Bennett likens the play to W. S. Gilbert and Arthur Sullivan's *The Mikado*. Yet it has serious undertones, the Duke signifying divine Providence, for example. Stanley Wells wrote that "Bennett makes her case lucidly, even eloquently, and with real learning" (*Review of English Studies*, n.s. 19 [1969]:68).

Cox, John D. "The Medieval Background of *Measure for Measure*." *Modern Philology* 81 (1983):1-13.

"While Shakespeare derived his plot from Italian novelle and from Whetstone's attempt to treat the Italian material as neoclassical comedy, his own treatment of it is in fact unique in introducing a definable group of features that also characterize plays about sexual sin in medieval religious drama." Looks particularly at the N-Town plays *Joseph's Return*, *The Trial of Mary and Joseph*, *The Woman Taken in Adultery*, and plays about Mary Magdalene, with their conflict between the Old Law and the New Law. Cox sees the Duke as human, as one who learns from his experience; he is neither divine nor Machiavellian.

Geckle, George L., ed. *Twentieth Century Interpretations of "Measure for Measure."* Englewood Cliffs, N.J.: Prentice-Hall, 1970.

In his introduction, Geckle discusses the ethical testing that underlies the play. Kenneth Muir discusses the play's sources generally, while J. W. Lever focuses on portraits of disguised rulers. G. Wilson Knight examines the play's relationship to the Gospels; Elizabeth Marie Pope places the work in its historical context. Francis Fergusson looks at how the play balances justice and mercy as it explores the nature of government. Antony Caputi notes that the play contains a number of debates in which nothing is resolved, but the work finally affirms civilization despite its precariousness. The section on interpretation concludes with E. M. W. Tillyard's objections to the second half of the play as less engaging stylistically and less interesting in terms of its characters and action. Brief comments by five other critics and a selective bibliography conclude the volume.

Gless, Darryl J. *"Measure for Measure," the Law, and the Covenant*. Princeton, N.J.: Princeton University Press, 1979.

Lucio, Isabella, Angelo, and Claudio "precisely enact the sin specifically prohibited by the measure-for measure text. All therefore manifest in their judgments the carnality they betray . . . in other prominent ways." Isabella, for example, is guilty of spiritual carnality. The play leads the main characters from the Old Law and its contentions "to the tranquil joy that follows love's true essence." Gless reads the play as decidedly Christian and coherent. The first two chapters examine the intellectual background that informs the play, including the reading of the biblical text that gives the play its title, Renaissance ideas about law, and satires against monks. The other four chapters look at the play more closely in the light of this information. An appendix briefly addresses the question of the play's sources.

Hawkins, Harriet. *"Measure for Measure."* Boston: Twayne, 1987.
Discusses three major issues in the play: the relationship between sex and sin, justice versus mercy, and modes of characterization and dramatic structure. Hawkins does not resolve the dilemmas that the play introduces but instead notes various possible interpretations. He writes that "it may be impossible to arrive at a critical consensus about *Measure for Measure* because of the differing appetites it arouses, and satisfies, and frustrates, in differing individuals." This nihilism seems especially appropriate for a discussion of this play. An appendix notes how the conflict among Isabella, Angelo, and Claudio has been treated in various guises over the centuries by writers such as William Davenant, Guy de Maupassant, and even by the television series *Dallas*.

Lascelles, Mary. *Shakespeare's "Measure for Measure."* London: Athlone Press, 1953.
In 1954, Harold Jenkins called this "the fullest—and unquestionably the best—study" of *Measure for Measure* (*Review of English Studies*, n.s. 5 [1954]:409). Lascelles first looks at the analogues of the story of the play, the monstrous ransom. Shakespeare altered the accounts in a variety of ways; the Duke, for example, plays a larger role here. Shakespeare develops the conflict of justice versus mercy, and he presents characters who gain self-knowledge through their experiences. The play has flaws—Isabella's fading into a secondary role, subordinate to the Duke, for example, or Mariana's unpromising marriage to Angelo. The Duke also seems too detached from the action. Lascelles writes that "the play leaves many questions unanswered at the close," but the work's complexity reflects its integrity. The play is tragicomic, not real comedy.

Leavis, F. R. "The Greatness of *Measure for Measure*." *Scrutiny* 10 (1942):234-247.
Responds to L. C. Knights's essay "The Ambiguity of *Measure for Measure*" in the same volume of *Scrutiny*. Leavis dissents from Knights's opinion that the play is unsatisfactory. For Leavis, the play is complex but not contradictory, a

masterpiece that acknowledges the need for law but also warns against judging others. According to Leavis, Angelo is the Everyman of the play, the figure with whom the audience must identify in recognizing its own darkest potential.

Miles, Rosalind. *The Problem of "Measure for Measure": A Historical Investigation.* New York: Barnes & Noble Books, 1976.
A survey of criticism and stage history since 1604. John Dryden found the play "grounded upon impossibilities" and "meanly written." In the eighteenth century the play was seen as a failure and various objections were offered. G. Wilson Knight contributed greatly to rehabilitating the play in *The Wheel of Fire* (1930) when he shifted attention from plot and character to theme. Miles also places the work within its dramatic context, noting how Shakespeare develops such stock figures as the disguised ruler and stock situations such as the bed-trick. Sees the play as powerful and vital but not totally successful.

Nicholls, Graham. *"Measure for Measure": Text and Performance.* London: Macmillan, 1986.
Part 1 interprets the play by examining the role of the Duke, which Shakespeare expanded greatly from his sources. The Duke moves "from ineffectual impotence to agile, pragmatic manipulator." The play reveals the inadequacy of absolute judgments of Angelo and Isabella and shows that, in a flawed world, justice itself may be ambiguous. Part 2 studies the 1970 and 1978 Royal Shakespeare Company productions at Stratford-upon-Avon, Charles Marowitz's 1975 adaptation, and the BBC television version. This last production lets the play speak for itself but offers the audience little direction. Perhaps the most effective was the 1978 Royal Shakespeare production, which treats the characters kindly and offers a sense of progression and hope.

Soellner, Rolf, and Samuel Bertsche, eds. *"Measure for Measure": Text, Source, and Criticism.* Boston: Houghton Mifflin, 1966.
A casebook for undergraduates. Presents the text, followed by discussions of genre, character, and general criticism. Concludes with suggestions for essays. Among the critical pieces included is William W. Lawrence's *"Measure for Measure* and Lucio,"* which notes that this minor character serves as an antiromantic commentator and becomes a clown at the end of the play. The casebook also presents commentary by Eileen Mackay, Arthur Quiller-Couch, R. W. Chambers, Muriel C. Bradbrook, G. Wilson Knight, E. M. W. Tillyard, and Ernest Schanzer, together with some nineteenth century criticism. Still a good source for its intended audience.

Stevenson, David Lloyd. *The Achievement of "Measure for Measure."* Ithaca, N.Y.: Cornell University Press, 1966.
Begins with a discussion of the play's structure, followed by a scene-by-scene

analysis. The third chapter looks at critical response to the play from the seventeenth century to the twentieth. The fourth chapter examines theological interpretations, which Stevenson rejects, and the fifth chapter presents his reading of the play, which he sees as posing moral dilemmas that it never resolves. It is an intellectual rather than a romantic comedy. The play probes sexuality, moving beyond conventional views. The ironies of the work force audiences to confront the evil within themselves. Though Stevenson rejects the view that historical recreation will unlock the play's mysteries, he adds an appendix (which originally appeared in *ELH* 26 [1959]:188-208) treating the presentation of James I's political views in *Measure for Measure*, which echoes the king's ideas in many ways. Stevenson regards the play as "a brilliant, self-contained achievement which carries its meaning within its own dramatic design." It is also Shakespeare's greatest and "most ingeniously constructed comedy." As Peter Alexander commented, "Stevenson has contributed in important ways to our knowledge of the circumstances in which the play was produced. In addition, he has provided a sane, well-balanced interpretation of its dramatic import" (*Modern Language Quarterly* 28 [1967]:478).

The Merchant of Venice

Barnet, Sylvan, ed. *Twentieth Century Interpretations of "The Merchant of Venice."* Englewood Cliffs, N.J.: Prentice-Hall, 1970.
Barnet's introduction discusses the play in terms of generosity versus the selfishness of Shylock. This piece is followed by five lengthy essays. C. L. Barber's study of the play, drawn from *Shakespeare's Festive Comedy* (1959), notes Shylock's mechanical responses and his lack of a sense of community. Barber concludes that the play ends in unambiguous harmony. Barbara K. Lewalski, in "Biblical Allusions and Allegory in *The Merchant of Venice*," examines how the play treats Christian ideas of love, the Old Law and the New, as Shakespeare operates on two levels of meaning. For Harley Granville-Barker, "*The Merchant of Venice* is a fairy tale." John Russell Brown considers "love's wealth" and possessiveness in the play. The contrasting worlds of Belmont and Venice interest G. Wilson Knight. The second part of the book presents brief comments by Frank Kermode, A. D. Moody, Neville Coghill, and W. H. Auden. Like other volumes in this series, a useful compilation, especially for undergraduates.

Burckhardt, Sigurd. "*The Merchant of Venice*: The Gentle Bond." *ELH* 29 (1962):239-262.
"*The Merchant* . . . asks how the vicious circle of the bond's law can be transformed into the ring of love. And it answers: through a literal and unreserved submission to the bond as absolutely binding." Venice represents a closed, legalistic, and public realm, Belmont an open, private world based on love, but

the two worlds are bound to each other. Sees the Jessica-Lorenzo subplot as commenting on the Portia-Bassanio relationship; the former, free and bondless, is less satisfactory than the latter. Similarly, Shakespeare changed the inscription on the lead casket from what he found in his source so that he could focus on the risks and rewards of a bond. Burckhardt also looks at Shylock's language, which prevails in the play but is transformed through love.

Charlton, H. B. *Shakespeare's Jew*. Manchester, England: Manchester University Press, 1934.
The Merchant of Venice panders to anti-Semitic sentiments of the 1590s and seeks to present Shylock "as an inhuman scoundrel, whose diabolical cunning is bent on gratifying a satanic lust for Christian flesh." Shakespeare's unconscious genius did not allow such a simplistic portrait, though, just as John Milton unconsciously sympathizes with Satan. Charlton concludes that "Shylock, Antonio, Portia and Jessica do not stand forth as they were meant to do. . . . The emergence of the new Shylock is undeniable evidence of the incalculable value of the artist's intuition in helping humanity to reach the vital truths which in the end are revealed only through sympathy and on which the world's future welfare is indubitably to be built." If one dismisses the mysticism of the approach, then one finds here an understanding of Shylock's dual nature that makes him a character too complex for the play to contain.

Danson, Lawrence. *The Harmonies of "The Merchant of Venice."* New Haven, Conn.: Yale University Press, 1978.
Begins by surveying the criticism, which divides into "ironic" and "idealistic" readings. Danson chooses the latter approach and sees the play as concluding harmoniously. The play presents opposing values, particularly friendship versus love and justice versus mercy. In the trial scene of the fourth act, Portia resolves these dichotomies; Lorenzo's speech about heavenly harmony and Portia's return of the ring in the fifth act reenforce this resolution. According to Danson, Shylock declines throughout the play; Antonio's melancholy derives from his inability to love Shylock while hating usury. The resulting sadness is an "emotional response to a moral failure." Danson rejects the reading of Antonio as sexually attracted to Bassanio and sorrowing at the loss of his friend to Portia. Richard Dutton remarked that Danson's study "provides a sane and well-written analysis of a notoriously contentious play, one which will help rather than hinder our attempts to focus on the play" (*English Studies* 62[1981]:63).

Geary, Keith. "The Nature of Portia's Victory: Turning to Men in *The Merchant of Venice*." *Shakespeare Quarterly* 37 (1984):55-68.
The play treats the question of love versus friendship, with Antonio and Portia vying for Bassanio's love. Portia and Nerissa must assume masculine disguises to win their husbands from the all-male world of Venice. Portia insists on her

bond with Bassanio, and the ring episode highlights the marriage contract. In giving Portia's ring to Balthazar, Bassanio places Antonio before his wife, but by getting the ring Portia triumphs by fastening "the homoerotic tendency of Bassanio's sexuality and the obligations of masculine friendship on to herself."

Gollancz, Israel, Sir. *Allegory and Mysticism in Shakespeare: A Medievalist on "The Merchant of Venice."* London: G. W. Jones, 1931.
This slim volume presents the essence of three lectures given by Gollancz between 1916 and 1922. In the first, Gollancz argues for *The Merchant of Venice* as an allegorized treatment of the story of the crucifixion. He suggests that Peter Morwyng's translation of pseudo-Josephus provided the names of Shylock and Antonio and that Christopher Marlowe's *The Jew of Malta* and Thomas Kyd's *The Spanish Tragedy* provided some of the ideas of the play. Portia is Mercy, one of the four daughters of God. Shylock is evil, but he is formed by the scorn of Antonio and the betrayal of his own daughter. The second and third lectures largely repeat the first. Useful for its discussion of biblical analogues.

Grebanier, Bernard. *The Truth About Shylock.* New York: Random House, 1962.
The Merchant of Venice is not about the conflict between Jew and Christian but rather about the confrontation of the materialist and those who believe in love and mercy. Shylock is a villain because he is a usurer, not because he is Jewish; Grebanier denies that Shylock is either heroic or comic. Despite some objections, Clayton Garrison called this "a stimulating and vital contribution to Shakespeare studies" (*Educational Theatre Journal* 16 [1964]:183).

Lelyveld, Toby. *Shylock on the Stage.* Cleveland: Western Reserve University Press, 1960.
A survey of how actors have portrayed Shylock in the theater. The records of early performances are scanty, though Shylock probably was played in a red beard. In the mid-eighteenth century, Charles Macklin created a serious Shylock but one that Lelyveld declares was "something of a monster." Edmund Kean in the next century made the character more sympathetic. Edwin Booth's Shylock was motivated by greed and vengeance, whereas Henry Irving described the character "as the type of a persecuted race; almost the only gentleman in the play and the most ill-used." This book reveals the ambiguity of the text and the ability of actors to transform the play. Lelyveld is less successful in relating the portrayal of Shylock to society's attitude towards Jews.

Lyon, John. *"The Merchant of Venice."* Boston: Twayne, 1988.
After a brief survey of the play's stage history and critical reception, this introduction seeks to stimulate thought rather than to resolve dilemmas. How worried is Jessica about Lorenzo's fidelity? Does Portia help Bassanio choose the right casket? The work remains ambiguous, "a play of extraordinary fine moments

rather than the larger coherence of a well-made play—a collage rather than a painting." A provocative reading that serves its function of sending one back to the play.

Midgley, Graham. "*The Merchant of Venice*: A Reconsideration." *Essays in Criticism* 10 (1960):119-133.
Sees the play as "a twin study in loneliness." Shylock is an outsider in Venetian society, Antonio a stranger to the world of love and matrimony. Both are defeated, Shylock in act IV and Antonio by that defeat in act V. Ironically the two lonely men meet only in conflict, and both lose the only thing that might help them: Shylock's money provides his only entry into Venetian society, and Bassanio's love is Antonio's only stay against isolation. By the end of the play, both have been stripped of these elements.

Moody, A. D. *Shakespeare: "The Merchant of Venice."* London: Edward Arnold, 1964.
Sees the play as ironic. Portia is trivial, Gratiano inane, Belmont a fool's paradise. The play depicts "the manner in which the Christians succeed in the world by not practicing their ideals of love and mercy. . . . The play does not celebrate the Christian virtues so much as expose their absence." Audiences are challenged to examine their values; the play would qualify as "unpleasant" in George Bernard Shaw's terms. Though Moody's interpretation was even more unconventional in 1964 than in the 1990s, earlier critics cited at the end of the volume already noted incongruities in the idealistic viewpoint.

Overton, Bill. *"The Merchant of Venice."* Atlantic Highlands, N.J.: Humanities Press, 1987.
The first part of this thin volume examines some complexities of the text. Although Belmont and Venice appear to be opposites, Portia's prejudice against her foreign suitors resembles the anti-Semitism prevalent in the city. If Bassanio is right not to judge the caskets by their exterior, what about his choosing Portia for her wealth and beauty and Portia's rejection of Morocco because of his complexion? Shylock begins as a stock stage Jew and villain, but he grows increasingly complex. The play also questions women's role in society. Altogether, the play is more troubling than pleasant. Part 2 examines five productions: the 1970 National Theatre presentation with Laurence Olivier as Shylock, the 1978 Royal Shakespeare Company studio production, the 1980 BBC television version, a 1981 Royal Shakespeare Company production with David Suchet as Shylock, and the same company's 1984 rendition with Ian McDiarmid in the role of the Jew. All five reveal the problems inherent in the text, but the first two are the most successful in dealing with a difficult script.

Silverman, Rita H. *Suffrance Is the Badge of All Our Tribe: A Study of Shylock in "The Merchant of Venice."* Lanham, Md.: University Press of America, 1981.
According to Silverman, Shakespeare inherited and presented anti-Semitic stereotypes in his portrayal of Shylock, but he humanized the figure. She believes that Shylock intended his contract with Antonio to be a joke—until Jessica elopes with Lorenzo; then his desire for revenge overrules his better nature. Shylock's defeat in the Venetian court can be seen as a satire of Christian justice. Finally the character evokes more sympathy than hatred. A thoughtful response.

Spencer, Christopher. *The Genesis of Shakespeare's "Merchant of Venice."* Lewiston, N.Y.: Edwin Mellen Press, 1988.
An examination of the play's sources and Shakespeare's modifications. Chapter 2 discusses the bond plot, chapter 3 the other plot elements. In chapter 4, Spencer looks at the characters Shakespeare added, and chapter 5 considers the play's structure. Shylock is the focus of the next three chapters; Spencer argues that the character partakes of both victim and villain. Shakespeare's audience would not have been shocked by a forced conversion. Includes a useful survey of criticism and dramatic interpretations of Shakespeare's Jew. Spencer concludes by warning against trying to discover Shakespeare's sympathies or to find a message in the work. A learned, reasoned study.

The Merry Wives of Windsor

Barton, Anne. "Falstaff and the Comic Community." In *Shakespeare's "Rough Magic": Renaissance Essays in Honor of C. L. Barber*, edited by Peter Erickson and Coppélia Kahn. Newark: University of Delaware Press, 1985.
The hero of *The Merry Wives of Windsor* is the town, which contrasts with Falstaff's world of Eastcheap. The values of Windsor triumph; Falstaff is defeated. Falstaff's descendants—Sir Toby Belch (*Twelfth Night*), Lucio (*Measure for Measure*), and Parolles (*All's Well That Ends Well*)—are similarly overcome. Only Autolycus (*The Winter's Tale*) succeeds and in the process redeems the world of the play.

Bracey, William. *"The Merry Wives of Windsor": The History and Transmission of Shakespeare's Text*. Columbia: University of Missouri Press, 1952.
A study of the 1602 quarto and First Folio texts of the play. Rejects the idea that the quarto was based on shorthand transcription, memorial reconstruction, or pirated version and argues instead that the text was an actual stage version adapted for a performance. Notes that the quarto presents a coherent play, with fewer characters, shorter speeches, and streamlining of the action. Bracey believes that the play was written for the Garter Festival at Windsor in 1597 and suggests Barnabe Rich's "Of Two Brethren and Their Wives" (1581) as a source, together with Richard Tarlton's "Two Lovers of Pisa" (1590).

Carroll, William C. "'A Received Belief': Imagination in *The Merry Wives of Windsor.*" *Studies in Philology* 74 (1977):186-215.
An attempt to rehabilitate the play from adverse criticism. Argues that "the play first qualifies and then vindicates the power of the imagination to shape, even to transform 'reality,' and identifies this power with the more obvious power that every dramatist wields." This concern with imagination is evident in the Falstaff-Ford relationship, the play's style, and its use of metaphors of acting. The work demonstrates how imagination, especially Ford's, can lead to self-deception. Falstaff in this play differs from the character in *Henry IV*, but his diminished success reflects his constant changing. Also, Shakespeare uses him here to point out the dangers of delusion.

Green, William. *Shakespeare's "The Merry Wives of Windsor."* Princeton, N.J.: Princeton University Press, 1962.
Agrees with Leslie Hotson that the play was written to celebrate the Feast of the Garter in April, 1597. The text in the First Folio is fairly reliable; the 1602 quarto version is based on memorial reconstruction for a provincial touring company. The actor who recreated this script had played the Host, and he deleted the Garter references. The closest one can come to the 1597 text, though, is to blend quarto and folio versions. Ford's alias should be Brooke, as given in the quarto, not Broome (folio reading), but Brooke was also the name of Lord Cobham, who had objected to the use of the name of Oldcastle in *1 Henry IV*. Cobham had died, but to avoid danger the players in rehearsal changed the name to Broome in 1597. The "Duke of Jarmany" refers to the Duke of Wurftemberg, elected to the Order of the Garter in 1597, and this allusion explains the horse-stealing episode of IV, iii, and IV, v. An important, well-written study.

Hotson, Leslie. *Shakespeare Versus Shallow*. Boston: Little, Brown, 1931.
Argues that Justice Shallow is not a satiric portrait of Sir Thomas Lucy but rather of William Gardiner, a London justice of the peace who annoyed Shakespeare. The first production of *The Merry Wives of Windsor* occurred on April 23, 1597, so *2 Henry IV* must date from 1596-1597. Hotson carefully examined many contemporary documents, which he reproduces in an appendix that makes up most of the volume. He also concludes that Abraham Slender derives from Gardiner's stepson, William Wayte. The book adds information about Shakespeare's life and enhances the reading of *The Merry Wives of Windsor* as well as of *2 Henry IV*; his dating of the play has been generally accepted.

Hunter, George K. "Bourgeoise Comedy: Shakespeare and Dekker." In *Shakespeare and His Contemporaries: Essays in Comparison*, edited by E. A. J. Honigmann. London: Manchester University Press, 1986.
Compares Thomas Dekker's *The Shoemaker's Holiday* with *The Merry Wives of Windsor*, particularly Simon Eyre and Falstaff. Both use language to manipulate,

but Eyre fuses the workaday world and holiday, whereas Falstaff is parasitic and his advancement must come at another's expense. Dekker reveals social change; Shakespeare celebrates social stability. In Dekker, class struggle is avoided only rhetorically, whereas Shakespeare sees class conflict as unnecessary.

Roberts, Jeanne Addison. *Shakespeare's English Comedy: "The Merry Wives of Windsor" in Context*. Lincoln: University of Nebraska Press, 1979.
Surveys the criticism, the compositional and textual history of the play, analyzes the work, and places it within the framework of Shakespeare's development. Roberts agrees with earlier critics who see the quarto version as a botched recreation of the text that appears in the First Folio, and she assigns April 1596-1597 as the play's date. She relates the work to *The Comedy of Errors* and *The Taming of the Shrew* in its celebration of marriage, and she finds Falstaff here not unlike the character in *1 Henry IV*, a lord of misrule who ultimately can be controlled. Ralph Berry observed that "Roberts has written a patient, encompassing, and sensible account of the play as we know it" (*JEGP* 79 [1980]:247).

A Midsummer Night's Dream

Briggs, Katherine M. *The Anatomy of Puck: An Examination of Fairy Beliefs Among Shakespeare's Contemporaries and Successors*. London: Routledge & Kegan Paul, 1959.
When Shakespeare introduced his English fairies to the woods outside Athens, he was drawing on a folk tradition that was widespread in the sixteenth and seventeenth centuries. Briggs examines this fairy lore and devotes a chapter to Shakespeare's treatment of the subject, noting the playwright's innovations. The book also examines other literary treatments of the subject and includes a discussion of ghosts, mermaids, monsters, angels, and devils. Appendices provide brief biographical sketches of various creatures, such as the evil Redcap or the half-human Urisk; a list of fairy tales cited in the text; additional descriptions of fairies, spells, and charms; and a bibliography. Especially useful are the dozen illustrations, which include a fairy ring and a ghost. Excellent for explaining the context not only of *A Midsummer Night's Dream* but also of Mercutio's speech on Queen Mab (*Romeo and Juliet*) or the Ghost in *Hamlet*.

Dent, R. W. "Imagination in *A Midsummer Night's Dream*." *Shakespeare Quarterly* 15 (1964):115-129.
"The heart of the comedy . . . is the partially contrasting role of imagination in love and in art." Theseus links the lover and the poet as victims of imagination, but Shakespeare shows the difference. In love, imagination often opposes "discretion," whereas poetic art employs discretion. Lovers become ridiculous when imagination rules reason, but the artist creates the ridiculous by choosing to unite reason and imagination. The play defends poetry.

Fender, Stephen. *Shakespeare's "A Midsummer Night's Dream."* London: Edward Arnold, 1968.

Objects to the tendency among critics and producers to simplify the play by ignoring subtleties, which are expressed largely through language. The lovers are intentionally indistinguishable because love makes everyone behave in the same way and, as Bottom's translation demonstrates, can turn people into caricatures. Yet love can beautify the ugly, too, so that "doting love [appears] ambivalent: a laughable delusion or an intimation of something truer than the literal world." The fairies, too, are ambivalent, with potential for good or evil. The play raises questions that remain unresolved: Is the vision in the woods a fantasy (Theseus), a profound vision (Bottom), or something in between (Hippolyta)? Is the anarchy of the woods preferable to the Athenian world, or could it produce a serious *Pyramus and Thisbe*? Are plays nonsense? A good introduction.

Fisher, Peter F. "The Argument of *A Midsummer Night's Dream*." *Shakespeare Quarterly* 8 (1957):307-310.

Four worlds meet in the woods outside Athens and emerge properly aligned. The four human lovers represent passion, Theseus and Hippolyta rational order. The rude mechanicals belong to the grotesque, matter-of-fact world; the fairies represent the fantastic. These four worlds have distinct languages: Bottom and Peter Quince speak in prose; Theseus and Hippolyta use blank verse, the lovers couplets; and the fairies sing. At the end of the play, reason is in control in the guise of Theseus and Hippolyta, and "the world of common life and activity disports itself for their amusement and approval." Imagination lingers "as the undercurrent which ends the play."

Herbert, T. Walter. *Oberon's Mazed World: A Judicious Young Elizabethan Contemplates "A Midsummer Night's Dream" with a Mind Shaped by the Learning of Christendom Modified by the New Naturalist Philosophy and Excited by the Vision of a Rich, Powerful England.* Baton Rouge: Louisiana State University Press, 1977.

What thoughts would have come to "a skeptical Cambridge graduate" as he sat through a performance of *A Midsummer Night's Dream* in 1595? In other words, what is the intellectual background from which Shakespeare drew for the play? Told in the first person by the imaginary young man from Cambridge, Herbert's account ranges widely, and perhaps excessively, over the realm of Elizabethan thought. The names Hippolyta, Philostrate, Theseus, and Egeus suggest Geoffrey Chaucer's *The Knight's Tale*, while Helena and Hermia call up memories of Ovid. Lysander, which sounds like Alexander, another name for Paris, reminds the spectators of Homer. A fascinating source study, though when Pyramus thanks Wall, one doubts that Shakespeare (or anyone else) associated this episode with arguments about an animist universe.

Olson, Paul A. *"A Midsummer Night's Dream* and the Meaning of Court Marriage. " *ELH* 24 (1957):95-119.
Theseus represents reason, Hippolyta passion; according to Olson, their marriage represents the ideal order, with male/reason joining, but also ruling, female/passion. The movement to the woods represents a yielding to madness; Athens signifies reasonable love, the woods its opposite. In the forest, Oberon does not master Titania. Yet Oberon is the higher form of love, while Titania is sensuality. Oberon places sensual love in its proper perspective, and harmony is restored in the forest. Oberon also sorts out the straying lovers. The play about Pyramus and Thisbe shows the consequences of passion unruled by reason. *A Midsummer Night's Dream* thus teaches how love and marriage should be—unselfish and reasonable.

Robinson, J. W. "'Palpable Hot Ice': Dramatic Burlesque in *A Midsummer Night's Dream."* *Studies in Philology* 61 (1964):192-204.
Seeks the targets of the burlesque *Pyramus and Thisbe.* The title of this play ridicules overelaborate titles such as that of *Cambises,* which advertised itself as a "lamentable tragedy mixed full of pleasant mirth." The occupations of the amateur actors alludes to the titles assumed by actors earlier in the century to avoid being treated as vagrants. For example, George Maller, who performed during the reign of Henry VIII, called himself a glazier. The characters Wall and Moonshine mock personifications in earlier plays. The prologues mock too-detailed introductions. Shakespeare thus parodies the state of the drama a generation earlier, ridiculing works and modes that audiences would have remembered and that lingered into the 1590s.

Robinson, James E. "The Ritual and Rhetoric of *A Midsummer Night's Dream."* *PMLA* 83 (1968):380-391.
The magical aspects and concluding marriage focus on ritual, while the play's comments on love and experience are rhetorical. Robinson explores how these two seemingly contradictory elements fuse in *A Midsummer Night's Dream.* This duality is evident in the play's development, which proceeds logically, like an argument, and at the same time magically, through the intervention of the fairies. So, too, the play presents the social world of Athens and the natural world of the woods, and the varying style also reflects this modulation between two worlds. The concluding play-within-the-play parodies the four acts that have preceded it, but it also sustains the comic rhythm.

Schanzer, Ernest. "The Moon and the Fairies in *A Midsummer Night's Dream."* *University of Toronto Quarterly* 24 (1955):234-246.
Shakespeare introduces three kinds of fairies: the malicious Puck; the diminutive, busy, courtly attendants on Oberon and Titania; and the adult-size rulers of fairyland. The moon provides atmosphere; Shakespeare largely ignores its

association with chastity, madness, or inconstancy. Titania, however, to an extent fuses with the moon. Schanzer argues for a nighttime setting for the opening scene. The anatomizing of the fairies seems overprecise, the dismissal of lunar associations too facile, since madness and change dominate the night scenes.

Selbourne, David. *The Making of A Midsummer Night's Dream: An Eye-Witness Account of Peter Brook's Production from First Rehearsal to First Night*. London: Methuen, 1982.
In the introduction, Simon Trussler surveys Brook's career and the critical response to his 1970 version of the play. Selbourne then presents a brief plot summary before he discusses the rehearsals week by week. Scattered throughout are Brook's comments about the play. For example, he remarks that "a micro-cosm of the play as a whole is to be found in the mechanicals' play-acting. It raises questions as to the nature of 'reality' and the nature of 'acting.'" A detailed account of the creation of a major production, useful for anyone involved in staging the play or wishing to learn how a production evolves.

Warren, Roger. *"A Midsummer Night's Dream": Text and Performance*. London: Macmillan, 1983.
The first part examines the text, offering helpful glosses on speeches and allusions. In the second part, Warren looks at the work of four directors: Peter Hall, Peter Brook, Robin Phillips, and Elijah Moshinsky. The volume offers a number of opinions about the play: the fairies should be powerful rather than ethereal, and the young lovers are silly but should be rendered sympathetically. Of the productions treated, Warren regards Hall's as the "most illuminating modern" interpretation. Despite the great critical acclaim for Brook's version, Warren objects to it, and Moshinsky fails to tie together the worlds of court, fairies, mechanicals, and lovers.

Weiner, Andrew D. "Multiforme Uniforme: *A Midsummer Night's Dream*." *ELH* 38 (1971):329-349.
Weiner claims that the play anatomizes marriage. Theseus and Hippolyta comple-ment each other. Lysander, Demetrius, Hermia, and Helena reveal the need for both reason and passion. Oberon and Titania demonstrate how marriage can fail when responsibilities are ignored, and Pyramus and Thisbe show the conse-quences of unbridled passion. The drama thus expounds on the mysteries of matrimony, uniting disparate elements into something of great constancy.

Young, David P. *Something of Great Constancy: The Art of "A Midsummer Night's Dream."* New Haven, Conn.: Yale University Press, 1966.
A Midsummer Night's Dream unites diverse and discordant elements into a coherent whole. The first chapter of this study discusses the variety of sources that Shakespeare drew upon, not only literary predecessors (though these are

many) but also folklore, theatrical conventions, and nature. The second chapter examines style and structure, where again Young finds diversity leading to unity. For example, Theseus speaks in blank verse, Puck in trochaic tetrameter, the lovers in couplets, and the mechanicals in prose. Yet all create panoramas and rely on amplification and concrete imagery, so that "the stylistic effects are harmonized; they form a concord, and that concord joins the larger whole that is the play." In the final chapter, Young argues for serious implications of the comedy, which he views as examining the not necessarily conflicting claims of illusion and reality, imagination and reason. Stanley Wells called this "a well-balanced, serious, yet unportentous book" (*Modern Language Review* 63 [1968]: 180).

Much Ado About Nothing

Allen, John A. "Dogberry." *Shakespeare Quarterly* 24 (1973):35-53.
Although Dogberry is comic, he does not differ much from the more serious characters. He is full of self-importance and self-love, but so are his betters. His laissez-faire attitude towards crime to avoid contamination resembles that of Claudio and Don Pedro towards the slandered Hero. Like Leonato he seeks revenge for his offended dignity. According to Allen, the play satirizes fashion and notes how all can behave poorly and ignorantly, yet the work also accepts human nature and urges charity. *Much Ado About Nothing* finally proves tolerant of human folly.

Berger, Harry L. "Against the Sink-a-Pace: Sexual and Family Politics in *Much Ado About Nothing*." *Shakespeare Quarterly* 33 (1982):302-313.
The play examines sexual roles in society. Argues that marriage disrupts male bonding, so men shy away from it. Also, men fear that women will live down to the image men paint of them. At the end of the play, neither Hero nor Claudio has changed; though Hero finds Beatrice's rebellion attractive, Hero cannot participate in it finally. Still, she has come to recognize how male-oriented the world of Messina is.

Cook, Carol. "'The Sign and Semblance of Her Honor': Reading Gender Difference in *Much Ado About Nothing*." *PMLA* 101 (1986):186-202.
Dissents from interpretations that argue for the triumph of feminist values in the play. Cook maintains that the ending is ambiguous. Men fear loss of control, loss of masculinity. They preserve their masculinity through jokes and by reducing women to ciphers, the "nothing" of the play's title. Hero says little and takes her identity from others. Beatrice has a character of her own, but even she supports masculine values by adopting them for herself; she can become passive like Hero and do nothing, or she can become manly. She thus offers no positive alternative female model. The play ends with "Messina's masculine ethos . . . unchanged."

Davis, Walter R., ed. *Twentieth Century Interpretations of "Much Ado About Nothing."* Englewood Cliffs, N.J.: Prentice-Hall, 1969.
Davis' introduction briefly examines language, society, and appearance versus reality in the play. Eight longer essays follow in part 1, with brief comments by ten other critics presented in part 2. Among the essays is John Crick's anatomy of the aristocratic, urban, and corrupt world of Messina. Robert G. Hunter argues that Claudio is neither villain nor innocent but a frail human being who falls prey to hatred and is redeemed by repentance. Virgil Thomson, who wrote the music for the 1957 Stratford, Connecticut, production, discusses the selection of Mexican and American Southwest tunes he used. The shorter comments include W. H. Auden's observations about the song in II, iii, and James Smith's comparison of Dogberry to Bottom and Falstaff.

Everett, Barbara. *"Much Ado About Nothing." Critical Quarterly* 3 (1961):319-335.
Relates the play to the Shakespearean comedies that preceded it. *Much Ado About Nothing* is the first play that portrays the triumph of female values over masculine ethos. The beginning of the play focuses on Hero and Claudio, a typical romantic situation with the male in control. After the church scene, when Benedict deserts his male companions for Beatrice and Hero, the masculine world loses to the values of Beatrice. Her values include a humane outlook, generosity, and constancy—the qualities absent from the masculine world of the tragedies. Benedict and Beatrice may be seen as Shakespearean fools, but the fools in Shakespeare's plays always express wisdom.

King, Walter N. *"Much Ado About Nothing." Shakespeare Quarterly* 15 (1964):143-155.
The play is a comedy of manners, "the critical inspection of a leisure-class grown morally flabby by thoughtless acceptance of an inherited social code. . . . In the denouement the proper norm is finally established, with the excesses of the major characters brought to a point of manageability or total cure." Natural responses have been reduced to a code in the aristocratic world of Messina. Even Beatrice and Benedict, despite their criticism of others, are flawed, fools of language if not of love at the beginning of the play. These two are cured by the fifth act and become the norm. The other characters do not change but become manageable.

Mulryne, J. R. *Shakespeare: "Much Ado About Nothing."* London: Edward Arnold, 1965.
The play moves from "love begun" to "love challenged" to "love triumphant in marriage." Evil is controlled and removed without permanently injuring society. Claudio learns to trust; Benedict and Beatrice begin as self-centered but become "mutually self-giving lovers." The play examines the role of illusion in love and finds that illusion is beneficial. Yet the play recognizes discordant forces that could lead to tragedy, as illusion does in *Othello* and *King Lear*. The play also

suggests *The Winter's Tale*, in which Leontes, like Claudio, learns to become a worthy husband; to reach that play, however, Shakespeare would need another decade and the experience of the tragedies.

Prouty, Charles T. *The Sources of "Much Ado About Nothing": A Critical Study, Together with the Text of Peter Beverley's "Ariodanto and Ienerva. "* New Haven, Conn.: Yale University Press, 1950.
Prouty first discusses Shakespeare's dramatic and nondramatic sources and looks at how Shakespeare adapted these. For example, the villain in other accounts is a friend of the Claudio figure and a lover of Hero, as in *The Two Gentlemen of Verona*. Shakespeare found this device contrived; also, he wanted only one lover of Hero so that the plot would be simpler. Shakespeare makes Leonato governor of Messina to enhance Hero's status, which thus ceases to be a reason for Claudio to reject her. Throughout his study, Prouty notes how Shakespeare's artistry shapes his material into something rare and strange. The book includes a reprint of the unique copy of Beverley's *Ariodanto and Ienerva*, one of the sources of *Much Ado About Nothing*.

Rose, Stephen. "Love and Self-Love in *Much Ado About Nothing*." *Essays in Criticism* 20 (1970):143-150.
Beatrice discovers that she is not self-sufficient, that she needs Benedict, if only to kill Claudio. Benedict discovers that he needs Beatrice, even more than he needs his best friend, Claudio. Rose claims that, because Beatrice and Benedict love each other from the beginning of the play, the plotters' task to ensnare them is an easy one. Similarly, since Claudio and Hero do not love each other, the plotters easily separate them. The happy ending lies in the marriage of Beatrice and Benedict; the union of Claudio and Hero does not dispel the darker tones of that relationship.

Stafford, T. J. *"Much Ado* and Its Satiric Intent.*" Arlington Quarterly* 2 (1970):164-174.
As he had done in the sonnets and earlier comedies, Shakespeare in *Much Ado About Nothing* satirizes the inflated rhetoric of courtly love, thereby showing the hollowness of Claudio's feelings. Benedict's prose, on the contrary, demonstrates his truthfulness and reliability; he cannot write a poem, though he tries, and must rely on action. Dogberry's malapropisms further emphasize the emptiness of Claudio's speech, which Dogberry parodies. Hero's silence "flouts Claudio's talkativeness," and Leonato also distrusts excess in language.

Othello

Adamson, Jane. *"Othello" as Tragedy: Some Problems of Judgment and Feeling.*
Cambridge, England: Cambridge University Press, 1980.
Critics generally have either condemned or praised Othello, seeing him as noble
(A. C. Bradley) or as a brutal egoist (F. R. Leavis). Adamson believes that both
views are half-right. Othello, like everyone else in the play, engages in self-
definition in a way that will avert pain. "The play searches out the varied
grounds on which people really need to console themselves. . . . More than that,
it also searches out how and why, in the longer run, most attempts to do so
inevitably fail." Characters seek certainty; Othello's need drives him to kill
Desdemona and then himself. The play reveals how love can cause pain and how
seeking to avoid pain leads to disaster. One must accept the doubt that is often
impossible to live with. Audiences seeking a definite solution to the play themselves suffer the flaw of Desdemona and Othello, the desire to avoid ambiguity.
In his generally unfavorable review, Norman Rabkin conceded that Adamson
offers "some valuable insights, some of them gracefully credited to previous
critics and many of them original." Rabkin praised the treatment here of Brabantio, Cassio, and Desdemona (*Modern Language Review* 78 [1983]:898).

Calderwood, James L. *The Properties of "Othello."* Amherst: University of Massachusetts Press, 1989.
A lively deconstructionist approach that examines many facets of the play. The
concept of property has numerous meanings, not only possessions but also
distinctions of all sorts. Threats to property include love, which transgresses
boundaries. Othello seeks self-definition through Desdemona, a marital property,
and so becomes vulnerable to Iago's machinations. When he loses his faith in
his wife, Othello loses himself. Iago may be viewed as the id of civilization,
repressed only to resurface in ways that menace Othello and his world. Iago may
also be viewed as playwright and director.

Draper, John W. *The "Othello" of Shakespeare's Audience.* Paris: Marcel Didier,
1952.
Places the work within its historical context. Although set in Venice, *Othello* in
many ways is English; Cassio behaves more like an Englishman than a Floren-
tine, for example. Even Desdemona, though she comes to resemble the heroine
in Giraldi Cinthio's *Hecatommithi* (III,7), the major source of Shakespeare's play,
begins by behaving as an English lady. Draper regards Iago as a villain but an
understandable one who sees Othello as having ruined his (Iago's) marriage and
career. Othello falls "by forces of heredity and environment and social conditions
of the age, that he could not overcome." The last three chapters discuss setting;
verse, style, and tempo; and plot and theme. Appendix A briefly treats the role
of astrology in the play.

Elliott, George R. *Flaming Minister: A Study of "Othello" as a Tragedy of Love and Hate*. Durham, N.C.: Duke University Press, 1953.
The play portrays pride, not jealousy. Othello loves his wife but does not understand her; hence his love is shallow and self-centered. Desdemona loves selflessly but feels so confident that she knows Othello that she will not react to his jealousy and so aggravates it. Cassio contributes to the tragedy because he is too proud to acknowledge his fault and instead appeals to Desdemona. Iago is a good hater, but he is caught in the trap he lays; he does not want anyone to die, yet he must yield to Othello's vengeance. In the last scene, the characters finally recognize the truth. Elliott divides the play into three phases and constantly shows what is happening on the stage. This book will therefore benefit the student and the actor.

Elliott, Martin. *Shakespeare's Invention of "Othello": A Study in Early Modern English*. New York: St. Martin's Press, 1988.
After a brief survey of twentieth century criticism, Elliott presents a close reading of the text. Othello feels uncomfortable being in love, and early in the play he denies Desdemona's right to her own mind. His jealousy arises from this condition of discomfort. Emilia and Bianca suffer rejection from men, too. Othello sees himself as an agent of Fate, subject to influences outside himself. He is an idealist, and he is given to self-advertisement. A rich, rewarding, far-ranging study.

Flatter, Richard. *The Moor of Venice*. London: Heinemann, 1950.
A study of the play's characters. Iago is spiritually blind and seeks to reduce others to his low level. Roderigo is "the most lonely, most muddleheaded, completely friendless and wretched . . . figure in Shakespeare's portrait gallery." Emilia neither loves nor hates her husband, so she can denounce him in the last scene but also secure the handkerchief for him. Cassio is handsome but vapid. Desdemona's belief in her husband's love endears her to audiences and redeems the play, restoring faith in humanity. Othello rises from his fall and dies nobly. He loves Desdemona and would save her soul even when he kills her. When he learns the truth about Desdemona "he regains the moral strength to unite himself with his wife, though it is a reunion in death." Flatter sees Othello and Desdemona as unrivaled in their heroic passion.

Gardner, Helen. "*Othello*: A Retrospect, 1900-1967." *Shakespeare Survey* 21 (1968):1-11.
Surveys Shakespearean criticism of the play. A. C. Bradley established a twentieth century tradition of uneasiness with the play, which he recognized as a masterpiece but not one on the same level as *Hamlet*, *Macbeth*, and *King Lear*. Harley Granville-Barker and G. Wilson Knight found the play unsettling. Bradley saw Othello as heroic, but F. R. Leavis disagreed, and Leavis' view prevailed

for a time, though by 1960 Bradley's reading had been reaffirmed. Gardner concludes that the play embodies "the tragic sense that there is something in the very nature of our temporal existence that defeats our highest human needs and aspirations. . . . It is perilous to garner up one's heart in the heart of another human being, and whoever does so loses control of his own destiny."

Grennan, Eamon. "The Women's Voice in *Othello*: Speech, Song, Silence." *Shakespeare Quarterly* 38 (1987):275-292.
Othello is a play about voices, and Grennan examines how women's voices function in the work. Desdemona's speeches provide the moral center of the play; her husband suffocates her and thereby takes away her speech, equating loss of life and loss of language. In the play, the women seek and give speech, the men deny it. Desdemona's last speech is an attempt to protect Othello. Emilia dies asserting the truth, refusing her husband's command of silence. Grennan makes a good case for the centrality of women in the work.

Hankey, Julie, ed. *"Othello": Plays in Performance*. Bristol, England: Bristol Classical Press, 1987.
The lengthy introduction traces the play's stage history. Barton Booth in the early eighteenth century played Othello as solemn and utterly tragic. The role apparently eluded David Garrick, who never played it after 1746. The volume presents the text of the work on the left-hand side of the page; on the right are generously annotated stage directions. In I, ii, for example, Hankey notes that Charles Albert Fechter entered leaning on Iago. Laurence Olivier first appeared smelling a rose and laughing to himself. Ben Kingsley made a dramatic entrance clad in white against a backdrop of black stage and black-clad actors. Valuable for visualizing and interpreting the play.

Heilman, Robert B. *Magic in the Web: Action and Language in "Othello."* Lexington: University of Kentucky Press, 1956.
The magic of the web is the pattern of images that defines character and action in the play. Heilman looks first at Iago, who often uses the word "honest," speaks of appearance and reality, and talks like an economist and physician. Iago reduces people to animals in his choice of metaphors. As Iago's influence grows, his language spreads to the other characters. Heilman argues that Iago succeeds because Othello is flawed, guilty of the sin of pride. Othello deceives himself, casts himself in roles that are inappropriate, and never understands Desdemona or true love. Iago and Desdemona represent the polarities of hate and love. Winifred M. T. Nowottny called the book "a rich mine of observations" (*Modern Language Review* 52 [1957]:587).

Hyman, Stanley Edgar. *Iago: Some Approaches to the Illusion of His Motivation*. New York: Atheneum, 1970.

Looks at Iago from five perspectives that together explain more about the character than any single approach would. Genre criticism sees Iago as a descendant of the Vice figure at war with love and goodness. The theological reading sees Iago as Satan, Desdemona as the Christ figure, Othello as Judas, and Emilia as the repentant thief Dismas. The "symbolic action criticism" of Kenneth Burke looks at Iago as playwright-director, manipulating characters. According to a psychological reading, Iago is a latent homosexual; his love for Cassio and Othello is transformed into hatred. In terms of the history of ideas, Iago is a machiavel—ruthless, eager for power. Hyman prefers the theological reading. An appendix by his wife, Phoebe Pettingell, discusses Giuseppe Verdi's Iago in *Otello*. This operatic character is simplified, a Satanic machiavel with no homosexual tendencies.

McLauchlan, Juliet. *Shakespeare: "Othello."* London: Edward Arnold, 1971.
McLauchlan first briefly touches on the date (c. 1604), texts, and language of the play. Images of storm and of heaven and hell are significant. The brawl scene (II, iii) provides a key to Othello's nature. The study then considers the handkerchief's part in the tragedy and concludes by examining the contrast between Iago's fast-paced speeches and Othello's "ordered harmonies" that give way to chaos as Othello yields to Iago's poison. Othello kills Desdemona because he believes in revenge; had he not, even real guilt would not have caused her death. Appendices address the question of double time in the play, Shakespeare's handling of his sources, the differences between *Othello* and that other play of groundless jealousy *The Winter's Tale*, and Othello as Shakespearean lover.

Matteo, Gino J. *Shakespeare's "Othello": The Study and the Stage 1604-1904.* Salzburg, Austria: Salzburg University Press, 1974.
A study of the play's theatrical and critical history. The play enjoyed great popularity in the seventeenth century, Thomas Rymer's 1692 attack being an exception to the general reaction. In the eighteenth century, critics found more to dislike, but late in the century Samuel Johnson and Richard Hole added to the appreciation of Othello and Iago as characters. The Romantics continued this tendency. In this period, the problem of Othello's race led to altering his color in some cases. Matteo notes how A. C. Bradley inherited and developed the ideas of nineteenth century criticism, and Matteo attributes the play's enduring popularity to its display of passion.

Rosenberg, Marvin. *The Masks of "Othello."* Berkeley: University of California Press, 1961.
A survey of the play's theatrical and critical history with an emphasis on the former. Rosenberg examines the various modes of presentation from 1610, when the work moved audiences to tears. In the Restoration, decorum became a criterion. The nineteenth century wanted passion without what it regarded as

indecency (such as the use of the word "whore"). Rosenberg interviewed Earle Hyman, Sir Laurence Olivier, Anthony Quayle, Paul Robeson, Abraham Sofaer, Wilfred Walters, and Sir Donald Woffit to get these actors' perspectives. The last section looks at critical response to Othello, Iago, Desdemona, and the play in general. According to Rosenberg, *Othello* is driven by sexual jealousy. Rosenberg sees Othello as a passionate, noble outsider who is betrayed by his friend. Iago represents the evil in everyone, while Desdemona is strong-willed. The play is not a morality but a depiction of life. In weeping for Othello and Desdemona, audiences are weeping for themselves. Valuable not only for its theater history but also for its examination of the play's central issues.

Snyder, Susan, ed. *"Othello": Critical Essays.* New York: Garland, 1988.
A good collection of responses to the play from the eighteenth century to 1986. Among the most rewarding pieces is a transcript from Edwin Booth's response to H. H. Furness' request for Booth's thoughts on Iago and Othello; the portion included here treats III, iii. F. R. Leavis' important essay attacking the character of Othello and the play is reprinted, as is Helen Gardner's response, "The Noble Moor." Kenneth Burke's "*Othello*: An Essay To Illustrate a Method" treats the question of ownership of Desdemona; Othello possesses her, but Iago warns of possible loss. This sense of women as property informs both Edward A. Snow's "Sexual Anxiety and the Male Order of Things in *Othello*" and Peter Stallybrass' "Patriarchal Territories: The Body Enclosed." Snow points out that Othello behaves like Brabantio, both enraged by Desdemona's sexuality. Both essays see Desdemona as the victim of a patriarchal/masculine society.

Vaughn, Virginia Mason, and Kent Cartwright, eds. *Othello: New Perspectives.* Rutherford, N.J.: Fairleigh Dickinson University Press, 1991.
Twelve essays on the play. The collection opens with Thomas L. Berger's argument for some textual authority for the 1630 quarto, which Berger maintains, reflects the theatrical tradition of the period. Thomas Moisan and Joseph A. Porter examine the language of the play; both find inherent contradictions in the speeches. David Pollard looks at Iago's sadomasochism. Evelyn Gajowski offers a feminist reading; and Michael Mooney, James Hirsch, and Cartwright consider the play in performance. The play's physical properties are the subject of Frances Teague's contribution. B. A. Kachur looks at Beerbohm Tree's 1912 production that concentrates on Othello as a husband rather than a general; Barbara Hodgson critiques various treatments, drawing on feminist perspectives for her analysis. The volume concludes with reader-response criticism as Martha Tuck Rozett tells of her students' reactions to the play.

Wine, Martin L. *"Othello": Text and Performance.* London: Macmillan, 1984.
Begins by examining some central problems of the play: Is Othello a fool or hero? Is his suicide a triumph? What moral may be drawn from the play? How

does one account for Othello's transformation in III, iii? Is Othello's final speech sincere? Part 2 looks at modern stage interpretations by Laurence Olivier, Paul Robeson, Brewster Mason, and James Earl Jones. Wine also examines the Iagos and Desdemonas who appeared with these Othellos. He discusses the 1981 BBC version with Anthony Hopkins as Othello, Bob Hoskins as Iago, and Penelope Wilson as Desdemona. This was a beautiful production but too restricted in scope because of the medium.

Pericles, Prince of Tyre

Cutts, John P. "Pericles' 'Downright Violence.'" *Shakespeare Studies* 4 (1968):275-293.
Pericles is flawed, guilty of rashness, impetuousness. Shakespeare reveals these failings through Pericles' repeated shattering of musical harmony. Marina finally causes him to feel sympathy for another; the recognition scene leads to Pericles' redemption. Gower's presence supports the interpretation of the play as moral exemplum to help "frail mortality to know itself" (I, i). The show of the five knights indicates Pericles' fallen state; his withered branch still green on top reflects his ruined life that still can be redeemed.

Dunbar, Mary Judith. "'To the Judgement of Your Eye': Iconography and the Theatrical Art of *Pericles*." In *Shakespeare, Man of the Theatre*, edited by Kenneth Muir, Jay L. Halio, and D. J. Palmer. Newark: University of Delaware Press, 1983.
A study of the verbal and dramatic imagery, which reveals the play's message. For example, Pericles' branch, green at the top (II, ii), represents his rejuvenation after his shipwreck. In V, i, he appears dumb as the emblem of grief. In that scene, Marina's position, aloof from Pericles, turns her into the model of patience that Pericles describes. Dunbar sees these emblems as suggesting divine Providence at work in the play.

Ewbank, Inga-Stina. "'My Name Is Marina': The Language of Recognition." In *Shakespeare's Styles: Essays in Honour of Kenneth Muir*, edited by Philip Edwards, Inga-Stina Ewbank, and G. K. Hunter. Cambridge, England: Cambridge University Press, 1980.
Shakespeare's recognition scenes usually avoid language, favoring music, silence, or spectacle, because speech generally destroys intimacy. In *Pericles*, Marina and her father do speak, using simple words that particularize them. Knowledge in Shakespeare's romances moves towards the specific, and the recognition scene here operates in that way. Ewbank notes the similarity between *Pericles* and *King Lear*: in each, a daughter leads her father back from madness, and the recognition scenes are also alike.

Felperin, Howard. "Shakespeare's Miracle Play." *Shakespeare Quarterly* 18 (1967):363-374.
The introduction of Gower at the opening of the play alerts the audience to the archaic nature of the work. *Pericles* looks back to medieval allegory and miracle plays, with the title character here an Everyman figure. Felperin sees Christian eschatology becoming reality in the play. "The salvation that Marina and Thaisa bring to Pericles is absolute and enduring, a beatific love-vision realized on earth, while the gods, previously indifferent, hostile, or non-existent in Shakespeare, become benevolent." The plays after *Pericles* return to a more naturalistic mode, abandoning obvious allegory.

Flower, Annette C. "Disguise and Identity in *Pericles, Prince of Tyre*." *Shakespeare Quarterly* 26 (1975):30-41.
Pericles, Thaisa, and Marina adopt disguises. Pericles' disguises teach him about life. From Antiochus and his daughter, Pericles learns about hypocrisy. Later he assumes the guise of sufferer. When he recognizes his daughter, he also finds himself. In her suffering, Thaisa is Pericles' feminine self, while Marina represents his more astute side. Lipimachus accepts Marina's value as Simonides comes to recognize Pericles' worth.

Greenfield, Thelma N. "A Re-Examination of the 'Patient' Pericles." *Shakespeare Studies* 3 (1967):51-61.
Shakespeare follows Plutarch's portrayal of Pericles as scholar and wit; like Odysseus and Oedipus he is an adventurer and solver of riddles. Critics who focus on his patience ignore his other, more important skills. Marina, too, is a survivor, and she resembles her father. She also differs from him because she believes in the gods, whereas Pericles submits without trusting them. Argues that Marina is the more patient of the two.

Hoeniger, F. David. "Gower and Shakespeare." *Shakespeare Quarterly* 33 (1982):461-479.
Hoeniger maintains that Shakespeare wrote the entire play. Stylistic differences between the first two acts and the last three result from the playwright's experimentation, allowing Gower to proceed in his medieval narrative fashion before Shakespeare reasserts his more vigorous dramatic style. John Heminge and Henry Condell feared that future audiences would not understand the play's technique and so omitted the work from the First Folio. For a response to this article, see Sidney Thomas' "The Problem of *Pericles*" in *Shakespeare Quarterly* 34 (1983):448-450.

McIntosh, William A. "Musical Design in *Pericles*." *English Language Notes* 11 (1973):100-106.
Shakespeare uses music throughout the play. McIntosh sees three types of music,

related to the categories of Boethius' *De Institutione Musica*. *Musica instrumentalis* shows Antiochus and his daughter are evil, Simonides and his daughter good characters. Marina's healing song demonstrates the power of *musica humana*, and at the end of the play Pericles hears the music of the spheres, *musica mundana*.

Thorne, W. B. "*Pericles* and the 'Incest-Fertility' Opposition." *Shakespeare Quarterly* 22 (1971):43-56.
Shakespeare treats the stock comic concern with fertility in this play but transforms it. Sees the problem lying not in the opposition between aged father and young suitor but in a father's incestuous desire. The daughter of Antiochus appears to embody fertility but actually represents death. Pericles must atone for his desire, which he does during the play, and at the end he creates a new order. According to Thorne, Spring and fertility triumph.

Welsh, Andrew. "Heritage in *Pericles*." In *Shakespeare's Last Plays: Essays in Honor of Charles Crow*, edited by Richard C. Tobias and Paul G. Zolbrod. Athens: Ohio University Press, 1974.
Welsh discusses Shakespeare's use of four types of heritage: "the telling of the tale, the riddles, . . . the tradition of capital sins," and the devices of the knights at the court of Simonides. The first three derive from the story by Apollonius, the last from emblem books. Gower, too, serves as an emblem in the play.

Richard II

Berger, Harry, Jr. *Imagining Audition: Shakespeare on Stage and Page*. Berkeley: University of California Press, 1989.
Berger devotes the first two chapters to attacking the new historicism and theater-centered interpretations of Richard Levin and Gary Taylor. In the second part, Berger offers his own method of understanding the play; this approach involves examining a speech's effect on the speaker as well as on the listener. Employing this approach, Berger finds that Richard wills his own downfall but also defeats Bolingbroke. This book will prove heavy going for undergraduates but provocative for more advanced students and scholars.

Cubeta, Paul M., ed. *Twentieth Century Interpretations of "Richard II."* Englewood Cliffs, N.J.: Prentice-Hall, 1971.
Cubeta's introduction discusses the play in terms of Richard's political defeat and spiritual awakening and triumph. Ten essays follow. Irving Ribner provides a brief historical background and discusses the play's political outlook; according to Ribner, the work favors efficiency over legitimacy. E. M. W. Tillyard analyzes the play in terms of a medieval Richard and Renaissance Bolingbroke.

Among the other pieces are Richard Altick's exploration of the play's rich language and Peter Ure's examination of Richard II's "inwardness." Jan Kott argues that the play shows the conflict between action and morality that represents "human fate," and Alvin B. Kernan concludes the volume with a piece on Richard II's loss of identity and the recognition that "he . . . has no stable identity certified by the order of things immutable."

Hakola, Liisa. *In One Person Many People: The Image of the King in Three RSC Productions of William Shakespeare's "King Richard II."* Helsinki, Finland: Suomalainen Tiedeakatemia, 1988.
Examines the productions of John Barton (1973-1974), Terry Hand (1980-1981), and Barry Kyle (1986-1987). The opening unit discusses the play's text, imagery, and stage history, as well as the evolution of the Royal Shakespeare Company. Following this prologue, Hakola places the three productions within the play's theatrical tradition. The focus here is on the treatment of the title role. Of the three versions, Hakola finds Barton's the most challenging and rewarding, but even it does not exhaust the possibilities of the work. A good survey, especially useful for anyone involved in producing the play.

Hockey, Dorothy C. "A World of Rhetoric in *Richard II*." *Shakespeare Quarterly* 15 (1964):179-191.
In *Shakespeare's History Plays* (1944), E. M. W. Tillyard argues that Richard II speaks poetically, Bolingbroke plainly, thus revealing the contrast in their characters. Hockey disagrees. Both use a number of rhetorical devices such as repetition and inverted word order. Only Richard, though, is a "poetic visualizer [who] can rise and fall by the power of imagination alone." A good survey of the play's language, though the argument against Tillyard in a sense confirms his view that Richard and Bolingbroke do reveal different worldviews through their speech.

Humphreys, Arthur R. *Shakespeare: "Richard II."* London: Edward Arnold, 1967.
The play concerns good rule. *Richard II* derives from the chronicles of Edward Hall and Raphael Holinshed, Samuel Daniel's *The Civile Warres*, and various other plays and poems, among them Christopher Marlowe's *Edward II*. Humphreys examines the play's rich and varied style and its reputation, and he offers an interpretive introduction to the work. According to Humphreys, Richard wills his own fall and believes that words have power. In the end, Richard gains humanity and valor. Bolingbroke remains an enigma.

Page, Malcolm. *"Richard II": Text and Performance.* Atlantic Heights, N.J.: Humanities Press, 1987.
The first part surveys the play, seeing Richard II as an actor playing the role of king. Bolingbroke is efficient but comes to power improperly. The reading here

is conventional. Page also discusses the nature of the history play and observes that the work at once treats the sweep of events and the tragic fall of one person. He also draws parallels between the play and twentieth century events that testify to the continued relevance of the work. The second part examines a number of productions and concentrates on four: John Barton's Royal Shakespeare Company version, Zoe Caldwell's Ontario production, Terry Hands's Royal Shakespeare Company interpretation, and the Theatre du Soleil rendition that set the work in Japan. Of the four, Page sees Caldwell's as least successful because it was too static. The Japanese interpretation also focuses on ritual.

Phialas, Peter G. "*Richard II* and Shakespeare's Tragic Mode." *Texas Studies in Literature and Language* 5 (1963):344-355.
    Richard II marks the turning point in Shakespeare's dramatic career as he presents for the first time a character who achieves understanding through suffering and who falls because of his own actions. The soliloquy at Pomfret Castle highlights Shakespeare's artistic development. As Phialas writes, *Richard II* "is the first Shakespearean play in which the hero's attitude towards his tragic predicament changes significantly in the course of that action." In prison, Richard achieves tragic recognition, and his acceptance of responsibility becomes the pattern of the great tragedies to follow.

Reed, Robert Rentoul, Jr. "*Richard II*": *From Mask to Prophet*. University Park: Pennsylvania State University Press, 1968.
    Richard II anticipates Shakespeare's tragic heroes in his psychological complexity and in his confrontation with a hostile world. Drawing on Freudian psychology, Reed interprets Richard as directing his destructive impulses against himself. At Pomfret Castle, he comes to understand himself and his humanity, and he achieves true kingship and salvation. Reed looks at Shakespeare's sources and at Richard II's view of the divine right of kings, a view that even writers such as John Wycliffe saw as revocable when a king behaves improperly, as Richard does.

Talbert, Ernest W. *The Problem of Order: Elizabethan Commonplaces and an Example of Shakespeare's Art*. Chapel Hill: University of North Carolina Press, 1962.
    In part 1, Talbert presents sixteenth century political theories, and in part 2 he shows how these manifest themselves in various works. Elizabethans inherited a variety of sometimes conflicting ideas about kingship. Much as they deplored rebellion, they also recognized that bad rulers could be deposed and that sovereignty resided not with the monarch alone but rather with the king in Parliament. *Richard II* offers diverse views of Bolingbroke and Richard. The former expresses the Lancastrian perspective, the latter the Yorkist view of Bolingbroke as usurper, Richard as martyr-victim. The same ambivalence informs the deposi-

tion scene, omitted (probably voluntarily) from the 1597 quarto and called "the Parliament scene" in the 1608 version to show that Parliament held power. Richard serves as a model of bad rule; he never understands the nature of the commonwealth. Though Shakespeare uses Christ imagery is association with Richard, in fact the king never becomes Christ-like. According to Franklin M. Dickey, "Anyone interested in the history play and in Elizabethan political theory will want to pay close attention to Professor Talbert's work" (*Shakespeare Quarterly* 15 [1964]:436).

Richard III

Textual Studies

Patrick, David Lyall. *The Textual History of "Richard III."* Stanford, Calif: Stanford University Press, 1936.

Argues that the 1597 quarto has no authority, being an acting version that the players put together from memory for a prompt copy and then revised for a smaller cast when the company toured the provinces in the summer of 1597. Alice Walker commented that the "primary case for the memorial transmission of Q (the quarto version) is cogently argued and exhaustively illustrated, and readers will find much that is clarifying and refreshing in the sound common sense [Patrick] brings to bear on the general and individual problems presented by its variants" (*Review of English Studies* 14 [1938]:469). Oscar James Campbell, who disagreed with Patrick's conclusions, regarded the wealth of detailed comparison as "indispensable to all students who from now on try to understand the puzzling relationship between the quarto and folio texts of *Richard III*" (*Modern Language Notes* 53 [1938]:394). Patrick maintains that the folio represents Shakespeare's original text and should serve as the basis of modern editions, though the folio's printer occasionally nodded and omitted material in the quarto that should be part of the final version.

Smidt, Kristian. *Inurious Impostors and "Richard III."* New York: Humanities Press, 1964.

Disagrees with David Lyall Patrick and maintains that the 1597 quarto as well as the folio have authority. The quarto was not reconstructed from memory but probably was based on Shakespeare's manuscript, though most likely a "pretheatrical" version. The folio offers Shakespeare's revisions, together with later changes by John Heminge and Henry Condell, or someone acting for them. Smidt later revised his theory.

_____. *Memorial Transmission and Quarto Copy in "Richard III": A Reassessment.* New York: Humanities Press, 1970.

Revising his theory somewhat, Smidt concedes that the 1597 quarto may be based in part on memory but that it had written authority. Since the subsequent quartos do not represent marked improvements, the 1597 version must have satisfied Shakespeare. In the second part of this study, Smidt examines the creation of the folio version, which he believes derives primarily from a manuscript together with the third and sixth quarto editions, all of which were used to create a transcription that the printer used for the folio copy.

Walton, James Kirkwood. *The Copy for the Folio Text of "Richard III": With a Note on the Copy for the Folio Text of "King Lear."* Auckland, New Zealand: Auckland University College Press, 1955.
Argues that the folio text of *Richard III* was not, as is generally agreed, printed from a corrected version of the sixth quarto edition of 1622 but rather from a poorly corrected copy of the third quarto edition of 1602. The folio text of this play varies from the quarto more than any other play copied from an earlier printed version, but these differences do not indicate accurate collation with a manuscript. Walton also discusses the printing of the folio text from a corrected quarto of *King Lear*, where, again, differences are significant. The great bibliographer Fredson Bowers supported Walton's conclusions about the copy text of *Richard III* but not the way Walton reached them (*Shakespeare Quarterly* 10 [1959]:91-96). The issue remains unresolved. The 1986 Oxford edition drew on both the third and sixth quartos to create its version of the play.

General Studies

Churchill, George B. *"Richard III" up to Shakespeare.* Berlin: Mayer and Muller, 1900.
Examines the material available to Shakespeare as he wrote his play. The first part discusses the chronicle histories such as those of Sir Thomas More, Polydore Vergil, Edward Hall, Richard Grafton, Raphael Holinshed, and John Stow, which develop the story of Richard as evil ruler. The second section deals with literary treatments of Richard III in *A Mirror for Magistrates* and other works, including Thomas Legge's *Richardus Tertius* and the anonymous *The True Tragedy of Richard III*. The volume concludes with a useful table, arranged by scene, noting the sources for various elements in the play.

Clemen, Wolfgang H. *A Commentary on Shakespeare's "Richard III."* Translated by Jean Bonheim. London: Methuen, 1968.
A revised version of Clemen's *Kommentar zu Shakespeares Richard III* (1957), this study offers a scene-by-scene analysis of such matters as language, irony, psychology, theme, structure, and dramatic precedents. For example, he compares the opening soliloquy with similar practices by Seneca and Christopher Marlowe. Clemen regards *Richard III* as a key work in Shakespeare's develop-

ment; for the first time, a play successfully combines realism and the supernatural. Mark Eccles called this "the most masterly study of a Shakespearean play published in 1968" (*Studies in English Literature* 9 [1969]:357); E. A. J. Honigmann described it as "richly rewarding" (*Modern Language Review* 64 [1969]:872).

Garber, Marjorie. "Descanting on Deformity: Richard III and the Shape of History." In *Shakespeare's Ghost Writers: Literature as Uncanny Causality*. New York: Methuen, 1987.
In the play, "Richard . . . develops what is in effect a rhetoric of deformation, calling attention to the novelties of his physical shape and the ways in which that shape liberates him from the constraints of conventional courtly deportment." His play, too, presents a deformed view of history that serves a particular ideology, not historical truth, but it does so self-consciously; it is "the dramatization of the power of deformity inherent in both tragedy and history."

Hankey, Julie, ed. *"Richard III": Plays in Performance*. London: Junction Books, 1981.
The eighty-three-page introduction traces the play's theatrical history from 1593 to 1980. The text follows, with glosses on how various actors and producers have dealt with scenes and lines. According to Hankey, Shakespeare envisioned Richard III as agent of "historical Nemesis." Colley Cibber's popular adaptation shifted the play's focus to Richard as character, and even after Shakespeare's version regained the stage in the 1870s the transformation of the play continued. The 1963-1964 Royal Shakespeare Company production succeeded in restoring the play's balance. Hankey created her own text of the play; many will object to this edition.

Hassel, R. Chris, Jr. *Songs of Death: Performance, Interpretation, and the Text of "Richard III."* Lincoln: University of Nebraska Press, 1987.
Chapter 1 compares the highly influential Laurence Olivier film version (1955) with the more modern BBC production (1982); despite its great success, Olivier's movie oversimplifies Shakespeare's play. Chapters 2 through 5 examine a number of critical issues. In chapter 2, Hassel considers the portrayal of Richmond, which this study sees as positive. Richmond emerges as a good speaker and soldier, better than Richard even before the final battle. Chapter 3 argues for Elizabeth's significance; she is a worthy opponent to Richard. Chapter 4 looks at Richard's gulling of the citizenry; Hassel maintains that the populace is prudent, not deceived. Chapter 5 argues for a providential reading of the play, and chapter 6 looks at textual problems and the effects of different readings. An epilogue praises the 1984-1985 Royal Shakespeare Company production as being faithful to Shakespeare's text and also excellent theater.

Richmond, Hugh M. *"King Richard III."* Manchester, England: Manchester University Press, 1989.
The first chapter considers the historical and ethical dimensions of the play and notes dramatic precedents, Thomas Legge's *Richardus Tertius* performed at Cambridge and the anonymous *The True Tragedy of Richard III*, published in 1594. The next two chapters trace the play's stage history from Richard Burbage to Laurence Olivier. Richmond devotes a chapter each to the 1964 Royal Shakespeare production, the BBC version for television, and Antony Sher's much praised 1984 rendition, which Richmond finds "rather facile politically, intellectually, even morally." Richmond concludes that the best productions have relied not on spectacle but on language and on "compelling congruency of appearance and behavior with the spoken sense of the script."

Wood, Alice I. P. *The Stage History of Shakespeare's "Richard III."* New York: Columbia University Press, 1909.
Traces the theatrical fortunes of *Richard III* from Elizabethan times to 1897 in England and the United States, noting "the conditions of staging, the use of scenery, properties, and costume, the methods of actors, . . . and the attitude of the audience in successive periods and under varying conditions." Since little information was available to Wood on the Elizabethan productions of the work, her opening chapter relates *Richard III* to other historical dramas of the time, and the second chapter uses that material to reconstruct what Shakespeare's audiences would have seen. Especially useful for its discussion of stage conditions and for the contributions of Colley Cibber, David Garrick, Henry Irving, and Edwin Booth.

Romeo and Juliet

Cole, Douglas, ed. *Twentieth Century Interpretations of "Romeo and Juliet."* Englewood Cliffs, N.J.: Prentice-Hall, 1970.
Cole's introduction surveys the play's sources and Shakespeare's alterations, the language in the work, its structure and themes, and the role of fate and coincidence. Six essays follow in part 1. Harley Granville-Barker finds Shakespeare still an immature artist but notes how he effectively speeds up the action throughout. Elmer Edgar Stoll examines the two lovers and argues that they reveal love's triumphs over hatred in death. For H. B. Charlton, the play is "Shakespeare's Experimental Tragedy," rejecting Providence for Fate; the experiment does not succeed for Charlton. Caroline F. E. Spurgeon examines the imagery of light and darkness. Wolfgang H. Clemen finds both older, conventional writing and a more mature style in the play, making this a transitional work. James Sutherland comments on the dialogue, Harry Levin on the way Romeo and Juliet express their individuality against the formal, stylized pattern of the rest of the play. Part

2 offers short comments by John Dover Wilson, Franklin M. Dickey, Winifred
Nowottny, T. S. Eliot, John Wain, E. C. Pettet, Bertrand Evans, and Neville
Coghill.

Evans, Robert. *The Osier Cage: Rhetorical Devices in "Romeo and Juliet."* Lexington: University of Kentucky Press, 1966.
After a discussion of rhetoric in the Renaissance and in Shakespeare, Evans looks
at the device of oxymoron in the play. Romeo's use of this rhetorical element
displays his wit and poetic abilities; also, the device mirrors the conflicts in the
play—true love (Juliet) versus false (Rosaline), love versus hate, light versus
dark, and youth versus age. The whole play is a paradox, for which the oxymoron is especially suited. The next chapter considers Friar Laurence, whose worn
phrases show him to be not worldly wise or a wit. He can deceive, as his calling
a willow basket an "osier cage" indicates, so he can contrive the trick of the
sleeping potion. Still, he misunderstands Romeo and love. Unlike most critics,
Evans sees Mercutio's "Queen Mab" speech (I, iv) as integral to the play,
revealing Mercutio's character and contrasting love and money, the world of
Romeo and Juliet and that of mercantile Verona. The reference to cut throats in
that speech foreshadows the deaths of Tybalt, Mercutio, Paris, and the lovers.
The last chapter draws together these conclusions based on rhetorical analysis
to claim that the play ends with fulfillment, and the tragedy emerges from
character, not circumstance or fate.

Hoppe, Henry R. *The Bad Quarto of "Romeo and Juliet": A Bibliographical and
Textual Study.* Ithaca, N.Y.: Cornell University Press, 1948.
Looks at the printing of the first quarto (chapter 1), explanations of the quarto's
origin (chapter 2), Hoppe's view of the quarto as memorial reconstruction
(chapter 3), and the identity of creators of this version. According to Hoppe, the
1597 quarto of *Romeo and Juliet* is a reconstruction from actors' memories of
the play, which is presented accurately in the 1599 edition. In 1597, Gabriel
Spencer and William Bird left Shakespeare's company for Lord Pembroke's; they
probably supplied the copy, which omits scenes, assigns speeches to the wrong
characters, shifts passages, lines, and words, introduces bits from other plays,
and anticipates words and phrases. A careful and well-reasoned textual study,
though one may dispute Hoppe's contention that the 1597 quarto draws on an
abridgement of the authentic text.

Kahn, Coppélia. "Coming of Age in Verona." *Modern Language Studies* 8 (1977-
1978):5-22.
The stars that cross the lovers are their fathers, who maintain a patriarchal
society even at the price of life itself. The two lovers are impulsive, reckless,
and self-absorbed, but their tragedy results from their society's failure to recognize "their natural needs and desires." They cannot escape from their parents'

feud. In III, i, Romeo must choose between two visions of manhood: the patriarchal view of aggression or a vision shaped by love. In this world, most of the characters define their relationships with women as violent and aggressive. Mercutio's Queen Mab speech reveals his attempt to reject both women and fancy. The end of the play resolves the conflict of love and death by combining these two opposing forces. Kahn writes that "Romeo and Juliet die as an act of love, in a spiritualized acting out of the ancient pun." Their death represents their triumph over the feuding world that would have separated them. They reject the patriarchal world, as Romeo dies in the Capulets' tomb and as Juliet uses Romeo's dagger, a male weapon, to kill herself. Feminist criticism at its best.

Levenson, Jill L. *"Romeo and Juliet": Shakespeare in Performance.* Manchester, England: Manchester University Press, 1987.
A study of six productions, beginning with the Elizabethan version. This section contains much speculation, as indicated by the "must have"s. Levenson then looks at David Garrick's eighteenth century version, modified to suit neoclassical tastes, and Charlotte Cushman's handling of the role of Romeo in the nineteenth century. Three twentieth century productions receive most of the book's attention: John Gielgud's 1935 performance, Peter Brook's 1947 version, and Franco Zeffirelli's handling of the play on stage and on screen. Though each reflects its age, both Gielgud and Brook revolutionized performance of the play.

Moore, Olin H. *The Legend of Romeo and Juliet.* Columbus: Ohio State University Press, 1950.
Traces the development of the story before it reached Shakespeare. Dante was the first to treat the Montecchi and the Cappelletti together. Giovanni Boccaccio's *Il Filocolo* and *Decameron*—with their presentation of premature burial, a sleeping potion, and a corrupt abbot—are important sources for the play, as are Matteo Bandello and Arthur Brooke, among others. Luigi da Porto's "Giulietta e Romeo" played an especially important part in shaping Shakespeare's play; Shakespeare could read the work in the original Italian, according to Moore; and C. T. Prouty praised the study as "thorough" and "well-written" (*Modern Language Notes* 68 [1953]:274).

Porter, Joseph A. *Shakespeare's Mercutio: His History and Drama.* Chapel Hill: University of North Carolina Press, 1988.
In Shakespeare's chief source for *Romeo and Juliet*, the poem by Arthur Brooke, Mercutio appears only briefly and as Romeo's rival. Shakespeare expands the character's role, drawing on classical, medieval, and Renaissance ideas about Mercury. Chapters 4 through 6 examine Mercutio as a character. He is both marginal and central, mirroring Shakespeare's sense of alienation from and absorption within London, his movement from poet to playwright. Mercutio is also Christopher Marlowe to Shakespeare's Romeo, and Marlowe's homosex-

uality surfaces in Mercutio's desire to lure Romeo away from female love to male-male friendship. Chapter 7 discusses adaptations and performances; the work concludes that the treatment of Mercutio on stage and by critics reflects Shakespeare's fortunes. Ingenious but jargon-ridden; suited to the advanced graduate student.

The Taming of the Shrew

Brooks, Charles. "Shakespeare's Romantic Shrews." *Shakespeare Quarterly* 11 (1960):351-356.
Brooks maintains that Shakespeare's shrews are curst for policy; they are not monstrous but rather suffer uncertainty about their feelings. Looks at Adriana in *The Comedy of Errors* and Kate in *The Taming of the Shrew*. They have strong wills, are intelligent, self-reliant, sensitive, passionate, and witty. According to Brooks they embody the need to dominate and the need to submit; the former is essential to courtship, but in marriage the latter must prevail. Brooks's defense of these women seems pallid in an age of female liberation and feminist criticism. Yet if one reads *The Taming of the Shrew* as ending not in submission but in equality, with Kate's knowingly playing a game, the comments here about shrews become more acceptable.

Daniell, David. "The Good Marriage of Katherine and Petruchio." *Shakespeare Survey* 37 (1984):23-31.
The Taming of the Shrew deals with marriage as well as courtship. Like Beatrice and Benedict in *Much Ado About Nothing*, Katherine and Petruchio are not tamed. They remain forceful and spirited and are therefore a good match. Sly in the Induction does not change, nor do Kate and Petruchio, but they discover ways of acting that are mutually helpful and that promise a successful union.

Greenfield, Thelma N. "The Transformation of Christopher Sly." *Philological Quarterly* 33 (1954):34-42.
The Induction, like the main play, deals with transformation, with moving from one world to another. Greenfield notes that, in its organic relationship to the main play, Shakespeare's Induction is unusual. The article details the differences between the Induction of *The Taming of the Shrew* and *The Taming of a Shrew* itself. Because Shakespeare's Induction leaves Sly in I, i, the audience cannot determine what becomes of him, whether he returns to his old life or changes.

Haring-Smith, Tori. *From Farce to Metadrama: A Stage History of "The Taming of the Shrew," 1594-1983*. Westport, Conn.: Greenwood Press, 1985.
A chronological survey through the early twentieth century and a generic survey thereafter. From 1660 to 1844, Shakespeare's play yielded various adaptations,

such as John Lacy's *Sauny the Scot* (1667), a much harsher treatment of both Petruchio and Katherine (Margaret in Lacy's work). David Garrick's *Catherine and Petruchio*, immensely popular, treated only the main plot, which it converted into farce. Augustin Daly's 1887 production brought Shakespeare back to the stage but modified it to reveal Victorian ideals about marriage. Among modern productions, Haring-Smith prefers those of Trevor Nunn and John Barton, which focus on the metadrama of the work, treating the Katherine and Bianca plots as a play-within-a-play (as they are in Shakespeare's original). Such an interpretation retains the play's humanity while allowing audiences to dismiss as irrelevant any displeasing elements. Haring-Smith concludes that "*The Shrew* is most interesting when [it] becomes a statement about theatrical illusion or about the tensions within Renaissance society."

Kehler, Dorothea. "Echoes of the Induction in *The Taming of the Shrew.*" *Renaissance Papers* (1986):31-42.
Sly, the Hostess, and Kate learn the price of love. The debate in the Induction about the best dog resembles the debate in act V about the best wife. The play's imagery shows that Kate is no more than a horse or dog to her husband. Kate is subdued, no matter how one looks at her long speech about obedience. Kehler nevertheless finds a subversive subtext that shows how women's behavior is conditioned only by societal expectations. The play also demonstrates how badly women are treated by society.

Newman, Karen. "Renaissance Family Politics and Shakespeare's *The Taming of the Shrew.*" *English Literary Renaissance* 16 (1986):86-100.
The Taming of the Shrew depicts patriarchal orthodoxy, but its very representation subverts that viewpoint. In the Induction, Sly assumes a proper patriarchal role towards servants and women, just as in the play Kate is tamed. Both representations demonstrate the synthetic nature of these arrangements. Also, because she continues to speak and so rejects the role of the silent female, Kate emerges triumphant at the end of the play.

Roberts, Jeanne Addison. "Horses and Hermaphrodites: Metamorphoses in *The Taming of the Shrew.*" *Shakespeare Quarterly* 34 (1983):159-171.
Argues that an inversion of Ovidian metamorphosis underlies the play. In Ovid, people become animals; here, animals become people. Christopher Sly is transformed from a beast into a lord; Kate and Petruchio progress through various animal metaphors to become fully human in marriage. Especially important is the image of the horse. At the end of the play, Petruchio and Kate drop their animal figures of speech, revealing their metamorphosis.

Seronsy, Cecil C. "'Supposes' as the Unifying Theme in *The Taming of the Shrew.*" *Shakespeare Quarterly* 14 (1963):15-30.

George Gascoigne's *The Supposes* (1566), a translation of Ludovico Ariosto's *I Suppositi*, has long been recognized as an influence on the subplot of the wooing of Bianca. Seronsy argues that Gascoigne's play also affects the Induction and taming of Katherine, especially in the sense of "suppose" as Gascoigne defines it in his prologue, "mistaking of one thing for another." By fusing this misprision with the action of *The Taming of the Shrew*, Shakespeare created a play richer and more coherent than its source. Seronsy also notes that the play offers three visions of love: Sly's totally sensual attraction, the romantic infatuation of the subplot, and the marriage of true minds of Kate and Petruchio.

Slights, Camille Wells. "The Raw and the Cooked in *The Taming of the Shrew*." *JEGP* 88 (1989):168-189.
"In *Shrew* . . . Shakespeare is less interested in suggesting the proper distribution of power between men and women than in exploring the comedy inherent in the human desire for both individual freedom and fulfillment as a social being. The play is built on a contrast not between men and women but between civilized and uncivilized behavior." The Induction deals with this opposition by contrasting the civilized lord with the drunken Sly, who must learn proper social behavior. In the main play Petruchio and Katherine, like Sly, adopt new roles that please them better than their old ones. At the end of the play all the characters gain their desires by recognizing and then asserting their control over society's rules.

The Tempest

Brooks, Harold F. "*The Tempest*: What Sort of Play?" *Proceedings of the British Academy* 64 (1978):27-54.
Sees the happy ending of *The Tempest* as neither facile nor qualified. The play describes the cosmic order of fall, suffering, repentance, reconciliation, and pardon. Prospero exemplifies true sovereignty, the platonic ideal of philosopher-king. The play partakes of "the delight of romance" but also offers a serious commentary on the nature of life and reality.

Brown, John Russell. *Shakespeare: "The Tempest."* London: Edward Arnold, 1969.
Brown first discusses early performances and the First Folio printing of the play, where it appears as the opening work; it apparently was printed with particular care. Chapter 2 treats sources, characters, setting, form, and style. In the third chapter, Brown examines the image of nature in the play, and he concludes this short study with some thoughts on how to produce, or how to imagine, a performance of *The Tempest*. Brown notes how Shakespeare transforms elements from earlier plays throughout. A sensible introduction for the beginning student.

Egan, Robert. "'This Rough Magic': Perspectives of Art and Morality in *The Tempest.*" *Shakespeare Quarterly* 23 (1972):171-182.
The Tempest contains Shakespeare's most extended examination of art. Prospero uses art to moral ends: to lead Caliban to goodness; Alonso, Antonio, and Sebastian to self-knowledge; and Ferdinand to pure love. Before he can redeem his world, though, Prospero must accept and love fallen humanity. He restores order by forgiveness. The epilogue asks the audience to join in the world of the play through mercy, fusing the world of art and reality in a bond of common humanity.

Hamilton, Donna B. *Virgil and "The Tempest": The Politics of Imitation.* Columbus: Ohio State University Press, 1990.
Studies the art and politics of *The Tempest* in relation to its period and the *Aeneid*. Shakespeare in effect rewrote books 1 through 6 of the *Aeneid* to comment on three political concerns of the time: the royal children; colonizing efforts in America and Ireland; and, most important, the royal prerogative. Shakespeare supports a constitutional rather than an absolute form of government. Though his view conflicts with James I's political philosophy, Shakespeare presents his arguments in a way that praises rather than criticizes the king. For example, various royal figures in the play "subject themselves to discipline, regret that they once usurped power, and desire to relinquish it." One may question whether *The Tempest* is as consciously modeled on the *Aeneid* as Hamilton argues, but the parallels she points out are fascinating and illuminating.

Hillman, Richard. "*The Tempest* as Romance and Anti-Romance." *University of Toronto Quarterly* 55 (1985/1986):141-160.
The Tempest subverts the conventions of romance. The opening storm is a romantic commonplace, but the audience quickly recognizes that this storm is under Prospero's control. Characters here are more realistic than is customary in romance, and the unities bar the typical play of time; what takes sixteen years in *The Winter's Tale* occupies only a few hours in *The Tempest*. Prospero resembles the magician of romance but is self-deluded, seeking to return to the past. Romance seeks to place characters in harmony with time, but Prospero avoids time. Argues that the play thus rejects the illusions of romance.

Hirst, David L. "*The Tempest*": *Text and Performance.* London: Macmillan, 1984.
Part 1 surveys a number of issues in the play. Hirst sees the work as addressing the same question of power that underlies the two history tetralogies: the conflict between political realist and philosopher. In the histories, the pragmatist triumphs, but Prospero fuses both elements to rule properly. Like the other late romances, the play contrasts nature and art but does so ambiguously. Caliban is brutish, but he is better than some of the civilized characters, and the evil Antonio is "unnatural." Hirst also examines the various uses of magic in the

play. Part 2 discusses four interpretations: Jonathan Miller's 1970 version, Peter Hall's 1974 National Theatre production, a Milan production of 1978, and Derek Jarman's 1980 film version. Hall's is the most conventional.

Homan, Sidney R. "*The Tempest* and Shakespeare's Last Plays: The Aesthetic Dimensions." *Shakespeare Quarterly* 24 (1973):69-76.
Shakespeare's final romances present a "consistent aesthetic statement," one that becomes increasingly profound. This statement recognizes the dual nature of art. "Things base and vile, holding no quality/ [Art] can transpose to form and dignity" (*A Midsummer Night's Dream*, I, i). Yet one finds even Prospero dismissing his art as "vanity," and even he cannot completely control the world of the play. Prospero recognizes that his pageant will vanish and leave not a wrack behind. This divided attitude informs even early plays like *Love's Labour's Lost* and coincides with Renaissance views.

Hunt, John Dixon. *A Critical Commentary on Shakespeare's "The Tempest."* London: Macmillan, 1968.
The first part of this concise study traces the action of the play. Hunt finds in Prospero a desire for revenge that must at last be overcome by Ariel's response to suffering. Prospero renounces his art as a sign of his return to humanity. In "Retrospect," the book's second section, Hunt explores the themes of Providence, redemption, grace, music, government, colonization, the pastoral, and art. A good overview of the play.

James, David Gwilyn. *The Dream of Prospero*. Oxford, England: Clarendon Press, 1967.
Argues that *The Tempest* is a commentary on *King Lear* and that *King Lear* glosses *Hamlet*. *Hamlet* is "a tragedy of the arrested mind"; *King Lear* presents "a tragedy of uninhibited action." *The Tempest* retains a tragic sense of life but offers hope with Ferdinand and Miranda. Chapters 3 and 4 provide useful background on Renaissance attitudes towards magic and the New World, and in chapter 5 James posits that the play is a dream of a man who never left Milan. James sees the play as depicting the intellectual moment in European civilization when faith in magic disappeared. Gates K. Agnew called this study "a thoughtful and instructive work with respect to several of the topics it addresses and a moving exposition of its author's humane convictions" (*Shakespeare Studies* 5 [1969]:334).

Jewkes, W. T. "'Excellent Dumb Discourse': The Limits of Language in *The Tempest*." In *Essays on Shakespeare*, edited by Gordon Ross Smith. University Park: Pennsylvania State University Press, 1965.
"*The Tempest* can be called [Shakespeare's] most delicate and final disclosure of the essential difference between speech and communication." Language cannot

describe miracle, cannot command or educate. Silence, music, cries, noise, and action become primary means of communication, "expressing/ (Although they want the use of tongue) a kind/ Of excellent dumb discourse."

Nuttall, Antony David. *Two Concepts of Allegory: A Study of Shakespeare's "The Tempest" and the Logic of Allegorical Expression*. New York: Barnes & Noble Books, 1967.
Nuttall maintains that his aim is to redeem allegorical poetry from the stigma that C. S. Lewis attached to it when he distinguished between allegory, lacking a metaphysical element, and symbolism. Nuttall prefers such nineteenth century critics as Victor Hugo and James Russell Lowell, who sought allegorical interpretations of Shakespeare. Most of the book is devoted to the subject of allegory generally. In the penultimate chapter, Nuttall looks at the sonnets, with their view of love as a stay against time, chance, and mortality, a theme that informs the tragedies and romances. The last chapter analyzes *The Tempest* as allegory without dogma, open to a variety of interpretations but hinting at ideas beyond the world of the play. Frank Kermode praised this study and called Nuttall's comments on *The Tempest* "original, judicious, and argumentative" (*English Language Notes* 6 [1968]:134).

Schmidgall, Gary. *Shakespeare and the Courtly Aesthetic*. Berkeley: University of California Press, 1981.
Concentrates on *The Tempest* but discusses all the late plays in the light of the artistic expectations of the Jacobean court, such as the delight in masques. Prospero represents the ideal Jacobean ruler, and his domination of Caliban depicts the triumph of Jacobean art over the forces that would destroy it. Whether the aesthetics portrayed here are uniquely Jacobean is unclear, but Schmidgall discusses the play well and offers important new sources for it, notably the Spanish romance *Primaleon of Greece* (1534).

Smith, Hallett, ed. *Twentieth Century Interpretations of "The Tempest."* Englewood Cliffs, N.J.: Prentice-Hall, 1969.
Smith's introduction surveys a number of issues in the play: appearance versus reality; the role of music; forgiveness; and time, art, and nature. Part 1 contains a variety of interpretations. Among these is G. Wilson Knight's "Myth and Miracle" from *The Crown of Life* (1947), which sees the play as Shakespeare's self-analysis. Knight calls the play "the most perfect work of art and the most crystal act of mystic vision in our literature." E. E. Stoll disagrees. Sir Arthur Quiller-Couch, John Dover Wilson, Theodore Spencer, Bonamy Dobree, Northrop Frye, Don Cameron Allen, and A. D. Nuttall also present essays in this section. Part 2 contains brief comments by seven other critics, including A. C. Bradley, Frank Kermode, and Harry Levin.

Sringley, Michael. *Images of Regeneration: A Study of Shakespeare's "The Tempest"
and Its Cultural Background*. Uppsala, Sweden: Uppsala University, 1985.
Drawing on "various images of regeneration" in alchemy and initiation rites (both
Christian and pagan), Sringley shows how *The Tempest* serves as an allegory of
rebirth. Less conventionally, Sringley links the play to apocalyptic visions
prevalent around 1610, maintains that the play was written to celebrate the
marriage of Elizabeth Stuart and Frederick V, and argues that Prospero (who may
be modeled on Rudolf II, the Holy Roman Emperor) practiced a type of magic
that James I would have censured, hence the abjuration of magic at the end of
the play. Hugh Ormsby-Lennon praised the book as constituting "a rich and
persuasive reading of *The Tempest*, one which articulates much in the play that
has remained enigmatic heretofore" (*Modern Philology* 85 [1988]:322).

Vaughn, Alden T., and Virginia Mason Vaughn. *Shakespeare's Caliban: A Cultural
History*. Cambridge, England: Cambridge University Press, 1991.
The authors examine the origins of Shakespeare's Caliban and the way that he
has been seen since he first appeared in 1611. The study notes various historical
and literary sources that may have supplied Shakespeare with ideas for his
monster; among these are the Caribbean Indians, the traditional Wild Man of
English folklore, the anti-masque, and *commedia dell'arte's selvaggi*. The First
Folio describes Caliban as a "savage and deformed slave." The authors observe
that the seventeenth and eighteenth century focused on his deformity, the nineteenth on his savageness, and post-World War II criticism on his status as slave.
A useful guide to the varying responses that Caliban has elicited and hence to
interpretations of *The Tempest*.

Yachnin, P. "'If By Your Art': Shakespeare's Presence in *The Tempest*." *English
Studies in Canada* 14 (1988):119-134.
Accepts the view that *The Tempest* is Shakespeare's valedictory, but the play is
a dark rather than a clear allegory, consistent with the playwright's increasing
ambiguity that requires the audience to find the drama's meaning. Yachnin
comments that "in thus manipulating his audience towards a full imaginative
participation in and commitment to the dramatic vision of his later plays, Shakespeare developed to the top of its bent the principle of audience enactment which
is inherent in the dramatic form itself" and which draws on the medieval English
dramatic tradition.

Timon of Athens

Bradbrook, Muriel C. *The Tragic Pageant of "Timon of Athens."* Cambridge,
England: Cambridge University Press, 1966.
Focuses on the pageant of Timon, which Bradbrook sees as deriving from

interludes and morality plays as well as Jacobean masques. The play traces the cycle of the seasons, but because this work is a tragic pageant, it ends in the tomb, not in regeneration. The move of his company to the Blackfriars may have prompted Shakespeare to experiment with this new form of drama, and if the play is not totally successful it remains "a work of most heroic endeavour."

Brill, Lesley W. "Truth and *Timon of Athens*." *Modern Language Quarterly* 40 (1979):17-36.
Critics cannot agree on the meaning of *Timon of Athens* because the play defies a single interpretation. Timon's life is contradictory—he even has two epitaphs. Argues that the images of animals and sickness that pervade the play demonstrate that in this fallen world moral categories are ambiguous. Only art can approach the truth in such a world.

Butler, Francelia. *The Strange Critical Fortunes of "Timon of Athens."* Ames: Iowa State University Press, 1966.
Observes how critics differ over interpretations of the play in matters of structure, character, theme, authorship, success, and completeness. Butler perceptively notes that structuralists find the play unsatisfactory and question Shakespeare's authorship, whereas thematic critics praise the work as experimental. Butler offers her own view of *Timon of Athens* as "a dramatization of issues"; hence it does not lend itself to the development of characters. Butler is better on earlier critics than on those after World War II, and reviewers have objected to her representation of some of the critics she cites. References, too, are not always accurate. A useful bibliography, but one should not rely on Butler's summaries.

Collins, A. S. "*Timon of Athens*: A Reconsideration." *Review of English Studies* 22 (1946):96-108.
Reads the work as a medieval morality play. Timon is the idealist, Alcibiades the realist. The corrupt world drives Timon to rage, madness, and death. When the Athenian Senate condemns Alcibiades' friend, Alcibiades, too, reacts angrily; as a realist, however, he uses common sense and moderation to redeem the city. Collins hoped that his interpretation would encourage greater study and appreciation of the play.

Handelman, Susan. "*Timon of Athens*: The Rage of Disillusion." *American Imago* 36 (1979):45-68.
A feminist psychological study. Timon cannot accept loss; the play, by excluding females, reflects this view, since women are linked to loss. Timon rejects a divided world, but in so doing he creates a division within himself to be both self and other. He tries to unite people through money; his extravagance is a form of art. At the end of the play, order is restored through justice, but the only true bonds that can hold society together are the feminine qualities of love and mercy.

In *Antony and Cleopatra*, the female principle transforms the world of the play, but in *Timon* no such transformation occurs.

Merchant, W. M. "*Timon* and the Conceit of Art." *Shakespeare Quarterly* 6 (1955):249-257.
The opening debate between the artist and the poet is significant for introducing the question of illusion versus reality, as well as humanity's subservience to Fortune and the status of the respective crafts. The issue of appearance versus reality is reenforced through biblical allusions. Timon redeems Ventidius from prison by sending five talents, and Timon expects Ventidius to follow the biblical model by returning twice the money, but Timon's friends prove to be Judases. Even Timon, however, is not what he seems. He, too, only appears to be generous; actually, he is vain and wasteful. Timon rejects art and poetry in the fourth act because he sees all human endeavors as false. Merchant sees the fifth act as moving beyond aesthetic arguments to anticipate the themes of nothingness and despair in *King Lear*.

Muir, Kenneth. "*Timon of Athens* and the Cash Nexus." *Modern Quarterly Miscellany* 1 (1947):57-76.
In *Political Economy and Philosophy* (1844), Karl Marx refers to *Timon of Athens* in his critique of capitalist society. Muir argues that Shakespeare is not a Marxist but that Marx is a Shakespearean in his concern for the effects of commodity, an issue raised by Falconbridge in *King John*. After 1600, Shakespeare grew increasingly concerned with the conflict between order and authority in a society where everything, including love, has its price, and where people are bound to each other only by a cash nexus. *Timon of Athens* explores what happens in such a world.

Nuttall, A. D. "*Timon of Athens.*" Boston: Twayne, 1989.
Nuttall suggests that this play is a dark version of *The Merchant of Venice*. At the beginning, Timon, like Antonio, gives all to others. The others here are, however, "selfish and ungrateful," incapable of love. Society's ingratitude shocks the innocent Timon, who retreats into the wilderness. Yet he finds no resolution there, no self-discovery. He moves "from invective through the defeat of language to unbeing." Only the sea remains, perhaps as the sign of grace. Nuttall also places the work within the context of an increasingly debt-ridden aristocracy and suggests that, while Timon may be extravagant, he is noble in his generosity.

Parrott, Thomas Marc. *The Problem of "Timon of Athens."* Oxford, England: Oxford University Press, 1923.
For Parrott, the problem is how much of the play is by Shakespeare; Parrott also wonders why Shakespeare wrote what he did of *Timon of Athens*. Parrott accepts the then fashionable theory that George Chapman wrote much of the play and

apportions sections to the two authors. This study concludes that Shakespeare began the play but did not finish it. Chapman was asked to prepare it for the stage, and the two writers then worked on it. Scholars agree that the play as it exists was unfinished; the notion that other hands than Shakespeare's are present in the play has not enjoyed widespread support.

Soellner, Rolf. *"Timon of Athens": Shakespeare's Pessimistic Comedy*. Columbus: Ohio State University Press, 1979.
Rejects the views that regard the play as textually flawed, as an autobiographical work suggesting neurosis, or as a special kind of play—satire, morality, domestic drama, or pageant. G. Wilson Knight goes too far in the other direction, though, in praising it as the greatest of Shakespeare's works (*Shakespeare's Dramatic Challenge*, 1977). The play belongs to the *contemptus mundi* tradition, in the manner of Pierre Boaistuau's *Theatrum Mundi* and Richard Barkley's *A Discourse on the Felicity of Man*. Timon's misanthropy results from his recognition of society's evils; his tragedy lies in his inability to live with the knowledge. Gary Jay Williams has contributed a fine essay on the stage history of the play.

Walker, Lewis. *"Timon of Athens* and the Morality Tradition." *Shakespeare Studies* 12 (1979):159-177.
Supports the view that the play draws on the morality tradition. Timon's early career in the play resembles that of Mankind's power and prosperity. Even the use of music here would suggest the morality play to the audience. The masque in *Timon of Athens* celebrates the five senses. Like the moralities, too, the play exposes societal corruption. Timon transcends Mankind, though, because his character contains much that is kind and generous.

Titus Andronicus

Charney, Maurice. *"Titus Andronicus."* Hemel Hempstead, England: Harvester Wheatsheaf, 1990.
Begins with a brief survey of the play's stage history and critical reception. It then offers an act by act analysis framed by an introduction and conclusion. Charney links the play to *King Lear*, sees Titus as "driven beyond his ability to endure injustice," and argues that the play has merit, especially in performance, though it lacks the artistry and power of the later tragedies. A sound introduction and useful corrective to the view of the play as unworthy of Shakespeare.

Metz, G. Harold. "The Stage History of *Titus Andronicus*." *Shakespeare Quarterly* 28 (1977):154-169.
Although "among the least frequently produced Shakespearean plays," *Titus Andronicus* has enjoyed four periods of popularity: from 1594 to 1620, during

the Restoration and early eighteenth century (in Edward Ravenscroft's 1678 adaptation), from 1839 to 1860, and from 1951 to 1974. Metz examines the productions and audience response. The play's enduring appeal—together with excellent renditions by the Royal Shakespeare Company, under Peter Brook in 1955, and by the New York Shakespeare Festival, under Joseph Papp in 1967—demonstrates "that this first fruit of Shakespeare's tragic muse has something to say to the contemporary world."

Palmer, D. J. "The Unspeakable in Pursuit of the Uneatable: Language and Action in *Titus Andronicus.*" *Critical Quarterly* 14 (1972):320-339.
Defending the play, Palmer shows how carefully structured it is, how it repeatedly invokes ritual in language and action. Though *Titus Andronicus* is more ingenious than moving, it demonstrates Shakespeare's control over his material and his willingness to take risks. For example, he introduces farcical elements at solemn moments, as at the end of III, i, when Lavinia exits with Titus' hand in her mouth.

Parker, Douglas H. "Shakespeare's Use of Comic Conventions in *Titus Andronicus.*" *University of Toronto Quarterly* 56 (1987):486-497.
Another defense of the play, which Parker sees as an experiment in using comic devices for tragic effect. The article notes four comic motifs in the work: "discord followed by resolution and reconciliation"—in the first act conflicts apparently end but are not resolved; the use of the green world, which here is the scene of death and dismemberment rather than regeneration; the image of birth, here linked to death; and feasting, serving up revenge in the tragedy.

Tricomi, Albert H. "The Aesthetics of Mutilation in *Titus Andronicus.*" *Shakespeare Survey* 27 (1974):11-20.
"In the play's spectacularly self-conscious images that keep pointing at the inventive horrors in plotting, in its wittily-obsessive allusions to dismembered hands and heads, and in the prophetic literalness of its metaphors, *Titus Andronicus* reveals its peculiar literary importance." Treats the play as an experiment in language, as an attempt to surpass both Seneca and Ovid in horror, and as an effort to exploit the metaphoric significance of the stage.

Troilus and Cressida

Adamson, Jane. *"Troilus and Cressida."* Boston: Twayne, 1987.
Following a brief summary of the play's stage history and critical reception, Adamson's first chapter notes the variety of conflicts that constitute the play. The most obvious is the quarrel between the Greeks and Trojans, but even parts of

words "clash against each other"; syntax and structure also reveal antagonistic forces at work. Chapters 2 through 4 follow the play's development, treating language, character, structure, "changing moods and emphases," and *Troilus and Cressida*'s relationship to other Shakespearean plays. Adamson maintains that the nihilism here demands from the audience "a resistant counter-energy of desire."

Campbell, Oscar James. *Comicall Satyre and Shakespeare's "Troilus and Cressida."* San Marino, Calif.: Huntington Library, 1938.

On June 1, 1599, the bishops of England ordered many satires burned. Ben Jonson and John Marston at once sought to create plays that would serve the same purpose as the banned works. The first of Jonson's efforts in this new style was *Every Man out of His Humour.* Campbell looks at this piece, *Cynthia's Revels*, *Poetaster*, Marston's early satiric plays, and, finally, *Troilus and Cressida*, which he treats as Shakespeare's only contribution to this genre. Anomalies in the play arise from the demands of satire, which is ethical rather than social. The first two chapters discuss the nature of satire and its forms in England from 1588 to 1599.

Foakes, R. A. "*Troilus and Cressida* Reconsidered." *University of Toronto Quarterly* 32 (1962-1963):142-154.

Sees the play as open-ended, as neither comic nor tragic but realistic in its portrayal of how people behave. The less-than-heroic actions depicted in the play must, however, be weighed against the enduring myth that Shakespeare's audiences knew—not to destroy the vision of heroism but to reflect the polarities of life. The double ending of the play, with speeches by idealistic Troilus and practical Pandarus, reflects the dual nature of the work and its double vision.

Greene, Gayle. "Language and Value in Shakespeare's *Troilus and Cressida*." *Studies in English Literature* 21 (1981):271-285.

Argues that the play's treatment of language reflects the late Renaissance recognition of the disjunction between language and reality. Values and words have become relative; no absolutes exist. This failure of words to represent actuality mirrors and contributes to the chaos of the play, which in turn comments on the Jacobean world.

Kimbrough, Robert. *Shakespeare's "Troilus and Cressida" and Its Setting.* Cambridge, Mass.: Harvard University Press, 1964.

Seeks to understand the play by examining the work within the context of its sources, contemporary drama, and the theatrical situation of the time. The first chapter looks at the play's origins. Kimbrough then examines the "matter of Troy" as a literary and theatrical subject, the plot and structure of *Troilus and Cressida*, and the play's treatment of love and lust, war and honor, order and chaos. Kimbrough links the play to the War of the Theatres and sees it as an effort to win back audiences to the public playhouses. He claims that the play is artistically a success but theatrically a failure. While Kimbrough is not convincing in his argument that the play was written for the public stage or that it is not good theater, he does present a useful survey of the work's context. Ernest Schanzer expressed many reservations but called this a "well-informed and lively study of one of Shakespeare's most controversial plays" (*Review of English Studies*, n.s. 17 [1966]:198).

McAlindon, Thomas. "Language, Style, and Meaning in *Troilus and Cressida*." *PMLA* 84 (1969):29-43.
The language of the play is florid and Latinate. McAlindon rejects explanations that Shakespeare was tailoring the speeches to a learned audience or exploring linguistic possibilities. Rather, the playwright wants the language to sound inappropriate, dissonant; it violates decorum to emphasize the other defects of the Greeks and Trojans. Connects the play with *Love's Labour's Lost* and *Hamlet*, where violations of decorum in language reflect more serious flaws.

Martin, Priscilla, ed. "*Troilus and Cressida*": *A Casebook*. London: Macmillan, 1976.
This collection of criticism begins with John Dryden's 1679 observation that the play starts well but degenerates into "a confusion of drums and trumpets, excursions and alarms." Most of the volume presents more modern interpretations, such as Una Ellis-Fermor's praise of the work's portrayal of the collapse of civilization and its ideals. Among the critics represented here are Clifford Leech, Jan Kott, Northrop Frye, and John Bayley. In her introduction, Martin presents a helpful overview of the critical responses to the work.

Oates, J. C. "The Ambiguity of *Troilus and Cressida*." *Shakespeare Quarterly* 17 (1966):141-153.
The movement from ritual to realism, the fusion of comic with tragic elements, and the character of Troilus contribute to the difficulty of classifying the play. Oates sees Troilus as a tragic hero, but the play fails to offer hope. It remains, therefore, an aborted tragedy that exhibits "ethical nihilism."

Presson, Robert K. *Shakespeare's "Troilus and Cressida" and the Legends of Troy.* Madison: University of Wisconsin Press, 1953.
Looks at Shakespeare's sources for the play. George Chapman's *Iliad* (1598), containing eight of the twenty-four books of Homer's epic, proved more influential than the medieval accounts by John Lydgate and William Caxton (the latter reissued in 1596). Chapman's humanism also provided the central theme: the conflict between passion and reason. For the love story, Shakespeare turned to Geoffrey Chaucer, whose *Troilus and Criseyde* had been newly edited by Thomas

Speght in 1598. Presson sees Achilles as a tragic hero; indeed, he is "the first of Shakespeare's *principal* tragic heroes afflicted grievously by passions." The play is one of the major tragedies of the first decade of the seventeenth century. Troilus resembles Othello, Lear, Macbeth, Coriolanus, and Antony in being led astray by love.

Twelfth Night

Draper, John W. *The "Twelfth Night" of Shakespeare's Audience.* Stanford, Calif.: Stanford University Press, 1950.

To understand the play properly, one must look at it from an Elizabethan rather than from a modern perspective, and that approach in turn requires a knowledge of the literature and worldview of Shakespeare's audiences. For example, according to Draper, the play does not seek to provide love matches for the Duke and Olivia because in the Renaissance aristocratic marriages were concerned with "social security." Draper notes, too, how familiarity with dueling codes turns the Viola-Sir Andrew encounter into "a romping travesty," but the comparison between the knights of the play and Chaucer's knight highlights the decline of chivalry. Good on background.

Everett, Barbara. "Or What You Will." *Essays in Criticism* 35 (1985):294-314.

"*Twelfth Night* is . . . neither of the boisterously festive . . .nor of that elegiac wistfulness which modern productions often create, but of something that rises above and masters both." Contains much on music in the play. The work celebrates wholeness that comes from true love. In his chapter on the middle comedies in *Shakespeare: A Bibliographical Guide* (1990), R. L. Smallwood called this "an excellent essay, acutely responsive to the verbal precision and subtlety of the play and communicating that response sharply and tellingly to its readers. One does not ask for more in Shakespeare criticism."

Hartwig, Joan. "Feste's 'Whirligig' and the Comic Providence of *Twelfth Night*." *ELH* 40 (1973):501-513.

The play repeatedly pits individual will against benevolent design. Olivia asks Fate to grant her Cesario, but Sebastian replaces the "page" and thus provides the fulfillment that Cesario could not offer. Orsino wants to replace Olivia's brother in her heart; at the end of the play, they become brother and sister by marrying siblings. The play's subtitle, "What You Will," is realized, but not as the characters anticipate. In the subplot, Malvolio suffers through human will, showing that revenge destroys; love, endorsed by Providence, redeems. Feste's epilogue invites audiences "to recognize their own desire for humanly willed happiness," and it holds out hope for further pleasure.

Hollander, John. *"Twelfth Night and the Morality of Indulgence." Sewanee Review* 67 (1959):220-238.

The opening lines of *Twelfth Night* indicate the progress and purpose of the play. The aim of revelry is to allow indulgence to die of excess and so permit a return to the mundane and the reasonable. Here, too, excess predominates for a time, but at the end the real world returns. The priest refers to time, and Sir Toby tires of tormenting Malvolio. Malvolio, who never partakes of revelry, cannot find a place in the play, but all the other characters abandon their delusions. Finally only Feste, the pure spirit of feasting, remains to sing the summation of the play. *Twelfth Night* is as moral as Ben Jonson's comedies of humours but presents its ethical views dramatically rather than in Jonson's static manner.

Hotson, Leslie. *The First Night of "Twelfth Night."* New York: Macmillan, 1954. Winner of the Modern Language Association Macmillan Award, this study claims that *Twelfth Night* was written quickly to be performed for Don Virginio, Duke of Bracciano, on Twelfth Night, 1601. Identifies several characters as representing members of Elizabeth's court. Lady Olivia, for example, is the queen herself as a younger woman; Orsino is Don Virginio. Hotson does strain at times to make the play topical, as when he sees Aguecheek as a joke aimed at the Spanish for their "little wit." A very good discussion of the play's setting, language, themes, and characters. Hotson also imagines the first presentation of the work.

Jenkins, Harold. "Shakespeare's *Twelfth Night." Rice Institute Pamphlet* 45 (1959):1942.

The primary sources for this play are *The Comedy of Errors* and *The Two Gentlemen of Verona*. In *The Comedy of Errors*, though, lovers had to overcome external confusion, whereas in *Twelfth Night* the characters must conquer their own uncertainties before true love prevails. "Orsino and Olivia," Jenkins observes, "come to their happy ending when they have learnt a new attitude to others and to themselves." Viola is the agent of this transformation. Jenkins notes that Malvolio's delusions of love parody his mistress' mistaking Viola for a man. Malvolio, sick of self love, cannot change the way Olivia can. Hence he is punished, she married. The play suggests that reason may be the greatest folly; the foolish seeking of an ideal can prove true wisdom. Jenkins believes that *Twelfth Night* makes no final judgments.

Logan, Thad Jenkins. *"Twelfth Night*: The Limits of Festivity." *Studies in English Literature* 22 (1982):223-238.

Acknowledging the festive world of *Twelfth Night*, Logan sees celebration here as having "lost its innocence." The main plot focuses on sex, the subplot on revelry; the play invites participation in a Saturnalia. Malvolio's banishment at the end of the play indicates a lack of resolution; festivity will reign in Illyria and hence order cannot be restored. The play warns the audience, which approves of the action, that what it wills can be "dark and dangerous." A strained but challenging interpretation.

Potter, Lois. *"Twelfth Night."* London: Macmillan, 1985.
Potter first examines some issues of the text: the meaning of the title, the language and action in the play, and V, i. *Twelfth Night*'s title suggests the passing of time; it is both a holiday and the end of the holiday season, and the play warns against wasting one's youth. Potter notes how actions in the play are repeated. Orsino and Viola echo each other, for example. Potter finds in the ending a resolution of the isolation that pervades the earlier part of the play. This section concludes with a brief survey of the play's theatrical history. Part 2 looks at four productions: John Barton's for the Royal Shakespeare Company (1969-1971); Peter Gill and the Royal Shakespeare Company (1974-1975); the Haymarket Theatre version under Robin Midgley (1979); and the Berkeley Shakespeare Festival rendition, directed by Julian Lopez-Morillas. Potter likes all four, different as they are, and notes that they do agree in finding pathos as well as comedy in the play.

Salinger, Leo. "The Design of *Twelfth Night.*" *Shakespeare Quarterly* 9 (1958):117-139.
Misrule dominates the play. In the subplot, Sir Toby turns night into day; in the main plot, women woo, and men and women change roles. All this disorder stems from love, which other Renaissance writers also see as a source of folly and subversion of order. The play shows love's folly but also "its life-giving power." Antonio and Malvolio are men of principle who do not fit into the comic world. Feste links the play and real world, the views of the lovers and men of principle, by recognizing that comedy is only that, that misrule must end, but that one also needs periodic release to survive. Plot and subplot thus cohere.

Tilley, Morris P. "The Organic Unity of *Twelfth Night.*" *PMLA* 29 (1914):550-566.
"*Twelfth Night* is a philosophical defence of a moderate indulgence in pleasure, in opposition on the one hand to an extreme hostility to pleasure and on the other hand to an extreme indulgence," but the view "that would banish all indulgence" is regarded as worse. The play attacks Puritans through Malvolio and Olivia; Sir Andrew and Sir Toby represent the opposite extreme, while the proper approach to life appears in Viola and Feste, the golden mean. The concluding song repeats this vision of moderation.

Wells, Stanley, ed. *"Twelfth Night": Critical Essays.* New York: Garland, 1986.
Wells's introduction surveys the volume's contents, which samples a wide range of approaches over time. Some of the selections focus on particular productions, such as Max Beerbohm's examination of Herbert Beerbohm Tree's *Twelfth Night*, but even these move beyond the specific to comment on the work. Beerbohm

regards Malvolio as an egotist and sees the play as consisting "mainly of hack-work." Other pieces deal primarily with the text. L. G. Salinger's "The Design of *Twelfth Night*," for example, considers the ways in which Shakespeare handled his sources. A. S. Leggatt, in his examination of structure, language, and action, discusses the limited success of the characters in forming relationships. Karen Greif sees every character as "either an agent or a victim of illusion." A useful anthology.

The Two Gentlemen of Verona

Brooks, H. F. "Two Clowns in a Comedy (To Say Nothing of the Dog): Speed, Launce (and Crab) in *The Two Gentlemen of Verona*." *Essays and Studies*, n.s. 16 (1963):91-100.

Argues for the unity of the play. The clowns and dog are introduced not only for comic effect but also to comment on the themes of love and friendship central to the play. Sometimes the clowns' actions parallel those of the other characters; sometimes they burlesque elevated sentiments to reflect on the courtly love tradition. For example, "The want of sensibility to old ties and to his friend Launce's feelings which Crab is alleged to show at parting from home, is ominous as a parallel to Proteus' parting from Julia and impending reunion with Valentine." As Launce's love saves Crab, so the friendship of Valentine and love of Julia save Proteus. A classic study of the play.

Cole, Howard C. "The 'Full Meaning' of *The Two Gentlemen of Verona*." *Comparative Drama* 23 (1989):201-227.

Taking his title from T. S. Eliot's statement that "the full meaning of any of [Shakespeare's] plays is not in itself alone" but in the context of all the works, Cole examines *The Two Gentlemen of Verona* "against other early plays, against its own sources, and against the traditions those sources bespeak." He finds the play a serious but unconventional comedy that shows the incompatibility of love and friendship. He argues that *The Two Gentlemen of Verona* predates *The Comedy of Errors* and *The Taming of the Shrew*. Cole finds much awkwardness in the handling of the story but argues for unity of plot and subplot: the subplot comments comically but not negatively on the lovers.

Danby, John F. "Shakespeare Criticism and *The Two Gentlemen of Verona*." *Critical Quarterly* 2 (1960):309-321.

Despite the story's triviality, the characters' lack of substance, and the absence of drama, the play presents an integrated, comic worldview and an optimistic outlook on life. Danby's weak defense of the play is less interesting than his opening discussion of how to read Shakespeare—he offers a valuable five-part process—and his relating the work to the sonnets.

Holmberg, Arthur. *"The Two Gentlemen of Verona*: Shakespeare's Comedy as a Rite of Passage." *Queen's Quarterly* 90 (1989):33-44.
Largely a celebration of a student production of the play in Edinburgh and a discussion of how Shakespeare should be staged. Holmberg does observe, though, that the work moves "from adolescence into maturity." Valentine and Proteus leave their native city and families to find themselves. Even the journey into the wilderness can be seen as a traditional initiation motif. The end of the play celebrates their reintegration into society as adults for whom events have become experiences.

Kiefer, Frederick. "Love Letters in *The Two Gentlemen of Verona.*" *Shakespeare Studies* 18 (1986):65-85.
The play has more letters than any other Shakespearean comedy; these letters "advance the plot, reveal character, generate laughter, and evoke emotions in the audience ranging from shock to pathos." They also examine the relationship between language and love. Proteus can write passionately to two different women and so reveal that words can deceive when divorced from feeling. The play does not renounce language but warns of its potential insincerity. In V, iv, Sylvia tells Proteus to "read over Julia's heart," showing that one must seek truth beyond the written word. Yet letters can provide stability and recreate emotion.

Rossky, William. *"The Two Gentlemen of Verona* as Burlesque." *English Literary Renaissance* 12 (1982):210-219.
Likens the play to a W. S. Gilbert and Arthur Sullivan operetta. The bandits turn out, like the pirates of Penzance, to be gentlemen; the supposedly valiant Sir Eglamour flees at the first hint of danger; the Duke of Milan proves less intractable than he seemed. The ending is pure farce, not an analysis of the values of love and friendship. To support this reading, Rossky notes how Shakespeare alters the story of Titus and Gissipus, an important source for the Valentine-Sylvia-Proteus triangle. Other popular tales of love and friendship also differ from Shakespeare's treatment. Shakespeare thus highlights the absurdity of Valentine's mindless adherence to a ridiculous code.

Slights, Camille Wells. *"The Two Gentlemen of Verona* and the Courtesy Book Tradition." *Shakespeare Studies* 16 (1983):13-31.
Noting the almost universal condemnation of Valentine's offer of Sylvia to Proteus, Slights seeks to understand that behavior and the rest of the play in the light of Renaissance literature dealing with proper gentlemanly conduct. She notes the play's borrowings from such works and shows how Shakespeare undercuts the self-fashioning that they promote. The play argues that true courtesy requires more than following a standard code. Valentine's behavior in act V serves as part of this exposure of the facile "cult of the gentleman" that ignores reality.

Wells, Stanley. "The Failure of *The Two Gentlemen of Verona.*" *Shakespeare Jahrbuch* 99 (1963):161-173.
Critics have found much to dislike in the play. Wells agrees that the organization is defective, but he finds skill in wordplay and imagery, in characterization, and in the creation of scenes that hold audience attention. Obviously an apprentice piece, *The Two Gentlemen of Verona* still shows "how marvelously creative Shakespeare's imagination already was."

The Two Noble Kinsmen

Abrams, Richard. "Gender Confusion and Sexual Politics in *The Two Noble Kinsmen.*" In *Drama, Sex, and Politics.* Vol. 7 in *Themes in Drama.* Cambridge, England: Cambridge University Press, 1985.
In Shakespeare's other play of Theseus and Hippolyta, *A Midsummer Night's Dream*, Helena and Hermia, Lysander and Demetrius, exchange roles. In *The Two Noble Kinsmen*, gender, too, is confused. Emilia has both lesbian and masculine tendencies; Palamon can appear feminine and claims to have the heart of a virgin. The world of the play is ruled by the patriarchal Theseus, who rejects any deviation from a monogamous marriage for Emilia and turns her into a prize for the tournament's victor. Shakespeare undercuts the heroic tone of Geoffrey Chaucer's *The Knight's Tale* and shows Emilia's superior ethic but Theseus' greater power.

Bertram, Paul. *Shakespeare and "The Two Noble Kinsmen."* New Brunswick, N.J.: Rutgers University Press, 1965.
Argues that Shakespeare wrote all of *The Two Noble Kinsmen*; the orthodox view is that he collaborated with John Fletcher. This study, while provocatively challenging the metrical tests used to assign various scenes to Fletcher, fails to explain the work's exclusion from the First Folio and the attribution of the play in 1634 to two authors rather than only Shakespeare. In a long chapter on the printing of the 1634 quarto, Bertram maintains that the quarto derives from Shakespeare's fair copy, annotated to serve as a promptbook. This book was missing in 1623, and so the play was omitted from the folio. To bolster his argument, Bertram looks at *Henry VIII*, where he also rejects Fletcher's collaboration, a view more popular than this argument for the single authorship of *The Two Noble Kinsmen*.

Edwards, Philip. "On the Design of *The Two Noble Kinsmen.*" *Review of English Literature* 5 (October, 1964):89-105.
Critics who dislike the play and wish it had no Shakespearean connection fail to appreciate its intellectual outlook, its dark vision of people who move blindly through life. Edwards sees the play as showing the futility of resolutions and the

movement from youthful innocence to maturity. This work approaches the cynicism of *Troilus and Cressida*.

Frey, Charles H., ed. *Shakespeare, Fletcher, and "The Two Noble Kinsmen."* Columbia: University of Missouri Press, 1989.
Ten essays on the play, framed by Frey's brief introduction and a useful annotated bibliography prepared by Will Hamlin. Paul Werstine leads off the study with an examination of the text, which he believes was prepared by two typesetters using a theatrical transcript. Because managers, scribes, and typesetters intervene between the author's manuscript and the printed text, attribution of specific parts to Shakespeare and Fletcher is impossible. This question of authorship interests Frey, Donald K. Hendrick, and Michael D. Bristol. Barry Well looks at the play's treatment of friendship and marriage. Frey's second essay discusses love in the play. Susan Green sees the jailer's daughter as "the play's most potent figure of desire" in her quest for sensual enjoyment. For Jeanne Roberts, the play challenges patriarchy. Richard Abrams argues that nobility and heroism are questioned by the work. Hugh Richmond concludes these essays by examining the play's stage history. A valuable collection of pieces on a play too long neglected.

Hart, Alfred. "Shakespeare and the Vocabulary of *The Two Noble Kinsmen*." *Review of English Studies* 10 (1934):274-287.
On the basis of vocabulary, Hart argues for Shakespeare's authorship of act I; act III, scene i; and act V (except for the second scene). He thus assigns 1,091 lines to Shakespeare and 1,681 to John Fletcher. In the course of his analysis, Hart discusses Shakespeare's fondness for neologisms, compounds (like "fair-eyed"), and nouns used as verbs or turned into participles. A useful though technical study of Shakespeare's language not only in *The Two Noble Kinsmen* but throughout his career as well.

Holland, P. "Style at the Swan." *Essays in Criticism* 36 (1986):193-209.
Discusses *The Two Noble Kinsmen* and Ben Jonson's *Every Man in His Humour*, the two plays that opened the new Swan Theatre at Stratford-upon-Avon. Holland describes the Shakespearean performance as "Samurai Shakespeare," and while he does not object to transporting the play to Japan, he finds certain problems with the theater that demand recognition by a director. Holland notes that IV, ii, could be cut because Fletcher failed to grasp Shakespeare's view of Emilia. The article connects this play to *A Midsummer Night's Dream*, where Theseus also tried to impose a husband on an unwilling woman.

Mincoff, M. "The Authorship of *The Two Noble Kinsmen*." *English Studies* 33 (1952):97-115.
Argues from internal and external evidence that Shakespeare contributed to *The*

Two Noble Kinsmen. When the play was first published in 1634, it was attributed to John Fletcher and William Shakespeare; the two were not then recognized as a team, so the attribution probably is correct, not an attempt to cash in on Shakespeare's popularity. Also, Fletcher and Shakespeare worked together on *Henry VIII* and *Cardano*. Style points to Shakespeare, with the play's rich imagery in act I. The use of nouns as verbs and the mixture of ornate diction and colloquialisms again suggest Shakespeare's style. Mincoff's argument has gained wide acceptance.

Spencer, Theodore. *"The Two Noble Kinsmen." Modern Philology* 36 (1939):255-276.
Shakespeare's part of the play is less theatrical, more static, than Fletcher's. Shakespeare has passed through experience and desires only contemplation. His style is that of an old man not totally committed to the enterprise. Spencer speculates that Shakespeare's retirement may not have been totally voluntary, that his "slow pageantry" may have ceased to please audiences more excited by Fletcher's "easy, accomplished manipulation." Spencer fails to do justice to the play as a whole and especially to Shakespeare's contribution, but the connections he makes with Shakespeare's other plays are useful.

The Winter's Tale

Bartholomeusz, Dennis. *"The Winter's Tale" in Performance in England and America, 1611-1976*. Cambridge, England: Cambridge University Press, 1982.
Looks at sixty-two productions. Bartholomeusz sees the play as a successful fusion of diverse elements—pagan myth and Christianity, Arcadian romance and realism, time and eternity. He then judges performances on how well they realize this complexity. The work is well researched and well illustrated; Carol J. Carlisle called it "a fascinating record of the ways in which actors, directors, and theatrical artists have attempted to complete Shakespeare's creation through performance, always aware of contemporary tastes and interests." She maintained that the book is "easily one of the best . . . that have been published on Shakespeare in the theatre" (*Shakespeare Quarterly* 36 [1985]:365,366).

Battenhouse, Roy. "Theme and Structure in *The Winter's Tale*." *Shakespeare Survey* 33 (1980):123-138.
The play operates on many levels: emotional, moral, metaphysical, religious, and social. On each of these levels, the work ends triumphantly after a period of sorrow. The world of *The Winter's Tale* is governed by a beneficent deity. The play's theme emerges from its structure. Throughout the play, events echo each other to produce "a grandly architectonic network of integrated symbols." Battenhouse compares Robert Greene's *Pandosto*, Shakespeare's source, with the

play to show how *The Winter's Tale* expands on the idea of romance. Autolycus parodies the courtly views of Leontes and Polixenes, while Paulina serves as the true Good Samaritan.

Bethell, S. L. *"The Winter's Tale": A Study*. London: Staples Press, 1947.
A Christian reading of the play. Shakespeare presents "a changeless divine order whose redemptive function is providentially effective within the time process." Bethell praises the verse of the romances; in *The Winter's Tale*, "its varied and contorted rhythms, its stress and strain, suggest an energetic confronting of reality, even in the most Arcadian setting." Shakespeare chose to set his story in a world "remote from contemporary life" because of the popularity of Arcadia, but also because this fairy tale motif more readily allows for the providential. J. H. Walter questioned the doctrinaire interpretation but conceded that Bethell "has shown new aspects of power and nobility in the play that have made his study well worth while" (*Modern Language Review* 43 [1948]:415).

Bryant, Jerry H. *"The Winter's Tale* and the Pastoral Tradition." *Shakespeare Quarterly* 14 (1963):387-398.
The Winter's Tale draws on classical, Italian, and native English pastoral traditions, but Shakespeare transforms the conventions of the genre to comment on illusion and reality. Bryant examines the three influences to show how Shakespeare borrows from them, but the play subordinates the love of Perdita and Florizel to an examination of the nature of truth. Hermione and Leontes, not the young lovers, control the last scene. Florizel recognizes the truth about Perdita beneath her common appearance. Autolycus also knows the truth, though he plays with it.

Draper, R. P. *"The Winter's Tale": Text and Performance*. London: Macmillan, 1985.
In part 1, Draper examines the play as a three-part structure that moves from winter in the court of Sicily to spring and summer in the countryside of Bohemia and then back to Sicily for the autumnal conclusion in which the court is regenerated and Leontes' repentance bears fruit. Part 2 considers four productions: Trevor Nunn's 1969 Royal Shakespeare Company version, the 1976 Royal Shakespeare Company production directed by Nunn and John Barton, the 1980 BBC television version, and the 1981 Royal Shakespeare Company interpretation. The two earlier ones, highly unconventional, reveal the play's vitality and theatricality. Of the four, considers the BBC's the least successful.

Frey, Charles. *Shakespeare's Vast Romance: A Study of "The Winter's Tale."* Columbia: University of Missouri Press, 1980.
Opens with a survey of criticism of the play, followed by a discussion of sources and the place of the play in Shakespeare's literary development. The final section

of the book presents an analysis of the work. According to Frey, Leontes rejects love and so, in Shakespeare's economy, denies life itself. The play shows that Leontes erred. Here Shakespeare fuses art and nature, and, as in the other romances, "society and nature are freshly feminized, made nurturant in the promise of new birth."

Gurr, Andrew. "The Bear, the Statue, and Hysteria in *The Winter's Tale.*" *Shakespeare Quarterly* 34 (1983):420-425.
The appearance of the bear shatters the realistic tragedy of the first half of the play and introduces the comic, romantic part of the work. The shepherd's quotation from Evanthius' definition of comedy and tragedy—the latter dealing with death, the former with things new born—emphasizes the transition in III, iii. The bear also shows how nature dominates the artificial world of the court. In the second half, art rules nature and pastoral. Hermione's statue appears to live, but that life is only stage illusion, like the rest of the "tale" that is the play. The bear and statue both reveal the artificiality of the work.

McDonald, Russ. "Poetry and Plot in *The Winter's Tale.*" *Shakespeare Quarterly* 36 (1985):315-329.
The syntax in *The Winter's Tale* often relies on the periodic sentence, in which meaning becomes clear only at the end of the statement. So, too, events become clear only at the end of the play. "The late plays present a world that is not immediately comprehensible, but one that eventually rewards bewildered characters and spectators with understanding and happiness." In constructing his poetry and play as he does, Shakespeare imitates Providence, which demands patience and faith, a belief that difficulty will be overcome and that words and events will cohere.

Martz, Louis L. "Shakespeare's Humanist Enterprise: *The Winter's Tale.*" In *English Renaissance Studies: Presented to Dame Helen Gardner in Honour of Her Seventieth Birthday*, edited by John Carey. Oxford, England: Clarendon Press, 1980.
Argues that Shakespeare enhances the classical Greek elements of his source. The names in the play are more typically Greek, more of the action occurs in the Greek colony of Sicily (where Aeschylus died), and the first half of the play draws on aspects of Greek tragedy as Leontes commits crimes against guests, family, and the gods. If the opening resembles *Agamemnon*, the play proceeds through the *Oresteia* to scenes of forgiveness when Orestes, before the statue of Athena, is redeemed by the goddess herself. *The Winter's Tale* can be read as having three parts: tragedy, pastoral, and miracle. Similarly, it progresses from ancient Greek to pagan humanism to Christian humanism as "faith, nourished by art and grace, may witness a triumphant restoration of the world to goodness." The deaths of Mamillius and Antigonus, like the aging of Hermione, add elements of realism.

Nuttall, A. D. *William Shakespeare: "The Winter's Tale."* London: Edward Arnold, 1966.

An introduction by a partisan of the play; Nuttall calls it Shakespeare's "most beautiful" work. This study proceeds through *The Winter's Tale* and argues that it is realistic, giving life to an improbable but possible story. At the same time, it has the quality of myth. Offers sound comments about the characters, outlook, structure, and meaning of the play, discussing some earlier critics along the way. Includes a brief bibliography.

Overton, Bill. *"The Winter's Tale."* Atlantic Highlands, N.J.: Humanities Press, 1989.

In part 1, Overton surveys a variety of approaches to the play, including New Criticism, genre studies, Marxism, psychoanalysis, feminism, and performance-based analysis. Part 2 offers Overton's assessment of the play as he looks at questions of power and patriarchy, the play's theatricality, the significance of Autolycus, the role of women in the play (the women restore "the proper power of affection"), and the play's last scene, which mirrors the work as a whole in its mingling of the serious and the comic and which demonstrates the taming of patriarchy.

Pyle, Fitzroy. *"The Winter's Tale": A Commentary on the Structure.* London: Routledge & Kegan Paul, 1969.

A plodding scene-by-scene analysis, though along the way Pyle makes a number of challenging observations. For example, he offers an allegorical interpretation of the characters without denying their humanity: Perdita is "an ideal expression of maidenhood," Florizel is a "heightened representation of an honourable young man in love," and Leontes is "tyranny, then humility." Pyle gives an optimistic reading of the play, relating it to Shakespeare's other works and to Francis Beaumont and John Fletcher's *Philaster*. Appendices look at Shakespeare's chief source, *Pandosto*, and the influence of the indoor theaters on the play. Pyle finds that these private theaters are less influential than G. E. Bentley argued. Ernest Schanzer called this "an important addition to the literature on *The Winter's Tale*" (*Review of English Studies*, n.s. 21 [1970]:202).

Sanders, Wilbur. *"The Winter's Tale."* Boston: Twayne, 1987.

As usual with the Twayne volumes on the plays, Sanders first presents a brief overview of the work's stage history and critical reception. He then examines the play systematically, act by act. Sanders sees the play as ending happily despite the strained silences, and he argues for the work's unity. Denies that the piece lacks realism; the ending responds to the hope of the audience as well as of Leontes. "The supreme fiction has triumphed, not by defying but by expressing the realities of the human psyche that demands such a fiction." Brian Vickers maintained that this is an "outstanding critical study [by] a critic engaging freshly with a play as if it mattered to his, and our life" (*Times Literary Supplement*, August 26, 1988, p. 935).

Williams, John A. *The Natural Work of Art: The Experience of Romance in Shakespeare's "The Winter's Tale."* Cambridge, Mass.: Harvard University Press, 1967.

In the debate between Perdita and Polixenes in act IV, the former rejects art for nature and the latter sees art as perfecting nature. In the context of the romance, both are right. Art can operate only when nature provides the proper resources, but art is nature's ally, not its enemy. Each character in *The Winter's Tale* has a partial knowledge of truth, but none sees the providential rule that controls the action. Nature is beneficent, not destructive.

THE POEMS

General Studies

Baldwin, T. W. *On the Literary Genetics of Shakespeare's Poems and Sonnets.*
Urbana: University of Illinois Press, 1950.
Claims that Shakespeare is essentially an Ovidian poet. *Venus and Adonis* draws
from George Buchanan, Ovid, and Virgil. *The Rape of Lucrece* derives from
Ovid and Livy. Ovid's funeral oration for the parrot in his *Amores* influences *The
Phoenix and the Turtle*, and the sonnets also show Shakespeare's knowledge of
the Roman poet. Although Shakespeare employed the rhetorical techniques taught
in grammar schools, he shaped his material in his own way to create his enduring
verses. Baldwin tries to date the composition of the early plays and poems based
on their interrelationships, but he is not especially successful. Still, good as a
source study.

Knight, G. Wilson. *The Mutual Flame: On Shakespeare's Sonnets and "The Phoenix
and the Turtle."* London: Methuen, 1955.
Knight sees the sonnets as "a semi-dramatic expression of a clearly defined
process of integration, pointing towards the realization of a high state of being."
The youth (though real) represents the Apollonian, the Dark Lady (also real) the
Dionysian. Shakespeare tries to fuse these two elements and finds the resolution
within himself and in eternity. Hence, the sonnets such as 126 reveal a sense of
calm; Knight calls this integrated condition the "Christ-state." In *The Phoenix
and the Turtle*, the male turtle is the poet, the female phoenix all those things
that inspire him. From these emerges not a child but a new phoenix, "the bird
of loudest lay" of the first line; the bird represents the poet's creativity. In his
discussion, Knight examines a variety of images to explain their symbolic
significance within the poems and plays. He ignores the context of the words and
imposes meanings that sometimes seem strained.

The Phoenix and the Turtle

Buxton, John. "Two Dead Birds: A Note on *The Phoenix and Turtle*." In *English
Renaissance Studies: Presented to Dame Helen Gardner in Honour of Her
Seventieth Birthday*, edited by John Carey. Oxford, England: Clarendon Press,
1980.
After discussing the immediate event that prompted Shakespeare's poem—the
knighting of John Salusbury—and the poetic model for it—Robert Chester's
verses celebrating Salusbury's marriage in 1586—Buxton observes that *The
Phoenix and the Turtle* is for an occasion but not about it. While making some

useful comments about the birds summoned and the meter, Buxton's chief
concern is to refute those who seek to extend the poem's meaning to current
affairs (Elizabeth and Essex; Sir John and Lady Salusbury). The Phoenix leaves
no posterity because it denied its sexless nature in uniting with another. The
poem exploits a paradox to produce art, not political or social commentary.

Copland, Murray. "The Dead Phoenix." *Essays in Criticism* 15 (1965):279-287.
Sees no contradiction in a married phoenix and rejects overly mystical readings
of the poem. Shakespeare uses platonic ideas about human love and presents them
in a metaphysical fashion. The poem does not deal with immortality but mortality; the death of the phoenix is the culmination of the metaphysical surprises in
the poem. Links the poem particularly to Lord Edward Herbert of Cherbury's
"Ode upon a Question Moved, Whether Love Should Continue Forever" and
John Donne's "The Ecstasy."

Ellrodt, Robert. "An Anatomy of *The Phoenix and the Turtle*." *Shakespeare Survey*
15 (1962):99-110.
Dating the poem from 1600-1601, Ellrodt finds here the same mood that informs
Hamlet. Truth, beauty, love, and constancy are linked in the phoenix and turtle,
but they are dead. All that remain are "either true or fair" but not both. The
article surveys earlier critical interpretations of the poem and other poetic
treatments of the phoenix up to Shakespeare's time; Ellrodt notes Shakespeare's
originality in handling his material.

Empson, William. "*The Phoenix and the Turtle*." *Essays in Criticism* 16 (1966):147-
153.
Dates the poem from 1598 or early 1599 rather than the more traditional 1601,
when it was published. Empson believes that Robert Chester established the
theme as "married chastity," so both Ben Jonson and Shakespeare employed the
idea. Shakespeare's poem culminating in the death of the phoenix and turtle
without issue is not the last word but rather sets the stage for John Marston to
follow with his views rejecting the annihilation of the avian pair.

Garber, Marjorie. "Two Birds with One Stone: Lapidary Re-inscription in *The
Phoenix and Turtle*." *Upstart Crow* 5 (1984):5-19.
Claims that the poem fuses elegy and epithalamion, death and marriage, because
for the phoenix the two are one. The poem as self-conscious artifact keeps
renewing itself in its circular structure of invocation, anthem, threnos, and prayer
(which harkens back to invocation). Shakespeare introduces a second voice, that
of reason, but logic proves inadequate to comprehend the phoenix and turtle.
Shakespeare transforms the material he is given, presenting his vision in a
manner that draws on sources such as Ovid's *Amores* and Geoffrey Chaucer's
Parliament of Fowls but transcends them.

Matchett, William H. *"The Phoenix and the Turtle": Shakespeare's Poem and Chester's "Loves Martyr."* The Hague: Mouton, 1965.

Based on literary and historical evidence, Matchett argues that the phoenix is Elizabeth, the turtle Essex. The poems of *Loves Martyr* were begun in 1599 to urge the marriage of Essex and Elizabeth. After Essex's treason and execution in 1601, the volume was readdressed to Robert Chester's patron, Sir John Salusbury. Shakespeare refers to both birds as dead because he believed Elizabeth to be essentially dead without Essex. Thomas P. Harrison observed that "Matchett's analysis of the meaning and interrelations of the appended poems (to *Loves Martyr*) is interesting and valuable; his conclusions with regard to their authors and their supposed views of the Essex-Elizabeth tangle rest on slender evidence" (*Modern Philology* 64 [1966]:156.) Frank Marley similarly found Matchett's interpretation "extremely interesting" but not persuasive (*JEGP* 66 [196]:448).

Underwood, Richard A. *Shakespeare's "The Phoenix and Turtle": A Survey of Scholarship.* Salzburg, Austria: Institut fur englische Sprache und Literatur, Universitat Salzburg, 1974.

Includes virtually all studies of the poem between 1938 and 1970, as well as some published earlier. The thematic arrangement allows for useful comparisons of views on various issues but makes it hard to examine a specific item. The first chapter treats the text, authenticity, and date of composition. Chapter 2 looks at allegorical significance; Underwood rejects any particular personal references and regards the poem as treating love idealistically. Later he suggests another possibility, that "this is a poem about the making of a poem." Chapter 3 addresses "Classical and Source Studies"; chapter 4, "Critical and 'Dramatic' Interpretations," considers the literary milieu of the work. Underwood's "Critical Afterward" deals with the versification. One appendix traces the phoenix legend, and the other treats three studies omitted from the body of the text. Heinrich Straumann recommended the book as valuable "to all those bent on finding their own approach to one of the greatest shorter poems in the language" (*Modern Language Review* 71 [1976]:888).

The Sonnets

Bermann, Sandra L. *The Sonnet over Time: A Study in the Sonnets of Petrarch, Shakespeare, and Baudelaire.* Chapel Hill: University of North Carolina Press, 1988.

Argues that the sonnet has retained its popularity over six hundred years. Bermann examines the treatment of this lyric form by three major poets. Petrarch emphasizes "sound and meaning," draws on classical models, and focuses on the "I" of the poem. Shakespeare's "I" interacts with two other figures, the fair youth and Dark Lady, to depict a "distinctly human world." In *Les Fleurs du Mal*, Charles Baudelaire relies on irony and allegory to present the human condition without an "I" in the poem at all. Bermann offers close readings of a number of the sonnets as she develops her thesis.

Booth, Stephen. *An Essay on Shakespeare's Sonnets*. New Haven, Conn.: Yale University Press, 1969.
Booth attributes the sonnets' enduring popularity to their skillful manipulation of patterns. His book therefore looks at such matters as formal, logical, and syntactical patterns, phonetic patterns, and patterns of diction. As readers move through the sonnets, they receive pleasure from the interplay of these various devices, which also contribute to the meaning of the text. To demonstrate this principle, Booth offers good close readings of a number of sonnets. Booth concludes that Shakespeare's achievement in the sonnets lies in his multiplying complexity to create a greater sense of "likeness . . . to the experience of disorderly natural phenomena" but still in a controlled, patterned way.

Bray, Denys, Sir. *The Original Order of Shakespeare's Sonnets*. London: Methuen, 1925.
Various critics and editors from 1640 onward have sought to rearrange the sonnets as they appear in the 1609 quarto. Bray, shunning the subjective, devised a scheme based on "rhyme-link." Thus, sonnet 44 contains the words "gone" and "moan," sonnet 45 "gone" and "alone." These two must therefore be linked. Bray then joins other sonnets separated in the quarto: 24 and 46 become 28 and 29 in his scheme; 27, 43, and 61 in the original are in Bray's edition 38, 39, and 40. Bray claims to have tested this scheme by examining subject matter, repetition of words, the use of "thou" and "you" (the "you" sonnets were, according to Bray, composed after the "thou" sonnets). He notes that rhyme and word links are common in Elizabethan sonnet cycles. Bray's theory of the sonnet order has not won support. Apart from the lack of textual authority, the rearrangement divides sonnets that seem clearly linked, such as the two "Bath" sonnets (153 and 154) or 97 and 98, which sound so much alike.

Campbell, S. C. *Only Begotten Sonnets*. London: Bell & Hyman, 1978.
Campbell believes that the sonnets were addressed to the third Earl of Southampton and were written in the early 1590s. The rival poet is a composite of Christopher Marlowe and George Chapman. Shakespeare's break with Southampton resulted from the publication in 1594 of Henry Willoughby's *Willobie His Avisa*. Campbell would place the Dark Lady sonnets before those depicting the reconciliation with the fair youth. Campbell suggests that the Dark Lady may be only a lustful avatar of the friend, though the woman may also be a real person. Campbell believes that Shakespeare wrote two sonnets on each manuscript leaf of a notebook and that certain pairs of sonnets were misplaced in the 1609 edition,

perhaps intentionally, to mask their homosexuality, too closely glanced at by *Willobie His Avisa*.

Duncan-Jones, Katherine. "Was the 1609 *Shake-Speare's Sonnets* Really Unauthorized?" *Review of English Studies*, n.s. 34 (1983):151-171.
The general view is that the 1609 (first) edition of Shakespeare's sonnets appeared without the author's approval and may have been suppressed at his urging, since so few copies survive. Duncan-Jones disagrees, arguing that the publisher, Thomas Thorpe, produced only one unauthorized book, and that one was a joke. Also, the sonnets as they appear in the 1609 quarto have "thematic and structural coherence." The article pursues these two points in some detail and concludes that Shakespeare probably sold the copy of the sonnets to Thorpe but did not correct the work as it was being printed, hence the various textual anomalies.

Fineman, Joel. *Shakespeare's Perjured Eye: The Invention of Poetic Subjectivity in the Sonnets*. Berkeley: University of California Press, 1986.
A dense, Lacanian reading of the poems, which Fineman sees as relying on *chiasmus*, a crossing that at once repeats and inverts. This pattern appears in various sonnet couples (for example, 27 and 28, 97 and 98) and within individual poems. The dominant tone of the sonnets is mock praise. In the first 126 sonnets, visual imagery predominates, signifying union of subject and object. The sonnets addressed to the Dark Lady focus on language, which deceives. Yet these differences are more apparent than real; Fineman notes that both the young man and the Dark Lady betray the poet. He sees the sonnets as a "fundamental rewriting of the assumptions of the poetry of praise," drawing on but subverting the tradition from which they derive. The poems become a mirror for all Western literature. Sonnets 135 and 136, punning on the poet's name, mark a break from older perceptions of self by allowing the writer to observe the self observing. A book probably not for undergraduates, though it contains many fascinating observations even in the footnotes.

Giroux, Robert. *The Book Known as Q: A Consideration of Shakespeare's Sonnets*. New York: Atheneum, 1982.
The Q of the title refers to the 1609 quarto of the sonnets, which Giroux argues were written to honor Henry Wriothesley, third Earl of Southampton. Much of the case rests on the similarity between the dedication to Southampton of *The Rape of Lucrece* (1594) and sonnet 26. According to Giroux, the sonnets were written in the period from 1592 to 1595; the rival poet is Christopher Marlowe. Giroux assigns sonnet 107 to 1603 and sees the enduring of the lunar eclipse as referring to Southampton's release from prison. Includes a facsimile of the 1609 quarto.

Hammond, Gerald. *The Reader and Shakespeare's Young Man Sonnets*. Totowa,
N.J.: Barnes & Noble Books, 1981.
Accepts the order of the sonnets 1 to 126 in the 1609 edition and sees in them
a movement from dependence on the young man to the writer's self-sufficiency.
The turn comes at sonnets 32 through 35 and proceeds to "final and quite
damning criticism of the young man" in sonnet 99. Sonnet 121 depicts "a self-
regarding poet, impervious to the young man's needs or the world's opinions."
By sonnet 126, the writer can face the death of the young man without regret.
Paul Ramsey rejected Hammond's overall argument but concluded his review (in
Shakespeare Quarterly 34 [1983]:127-128) by praising "the specific interpretations [and] textual comments," as well as the book's survey of criticism of the
sonnets.

Hubler, Edward. *The Sense of Shakespeare's Sonnets*. Princeton, N.J.: Princeton
University Press, 1952.
Believes that the sonnets were composed from about 1592 to 1596 or 1597 and
accepts the conventional division: 1 to 126 addressed to the fair youth and 127
to 152 written to the Dark Lady, with the two concluding poems translated from
the Greek. The poems do not, however, tell a story. Rather, "they are a collection of lyrics on a variety of subjects expressing a variety of moods and psychological states." Traces an evolution in Shakespeare's thinking about mortality and
how to overcome it, on friendship and love, on writing, and on reputation. An
appendix addresses the question of Shakespeare's homosexuality, which Hubler
denies.

_____,et.al. *The Riddle of Shakespeare's Sonnets*. New York: Basic Books,
1962.
Presents the text of the sonnets, essays by Hubler, Northrop Frye, Leslie Fiedler,
Stephen Spender, and R. P. Blackmur, along with Oscar Wilde's *The Portrait
of Mr. W. H.* Hubler outlines the various critical responses to the sonnets and
notes various efforts to identify the Dark Lady, the rival poet, and other characters in the poems. Frye finds in the sonnets the full range of love's emotions,
from Petrarchan idealism to Proustian disillusion, but he rejects an autobiographical reading. Fiedler treats the corruption of the male by the female, Spender notes
Shakespeare's treatment of emotion in a way that applies to all but accepts a
factual basis, and Blackmur analyzes the conscious and unconscious voices in the
work.

Krieger, Murray. *A Window to Criticism: Shakespeare's "Sonnets" and Modern
Poetics*. Princeton, N.J.: Princeton University Press, 1964.
In "The Mirror as Window in Recent Literary Theory," Krieger rejects as
inadequate both the notion of art as imitation of reality (art as window) and the
view of art as self-referential (art as mirror). Instead he argues for contextualism,

which considers how art does and does not act as a window on the world. Part 2 turns to the sonnets, which Krieger sees as considering "the problem of unity and duality in love and in the metaphors of religion." Part 3 seeks to unite the other two, finding in the sonnets "a microcosm that illuminates the macrocosm of poetry" and "a key to the nature of metaphor, of poetry, and of poetics as well." Hugh N. MacLean wrote that "when Krieger gets down to detailed analysis of sonnet groups, he can be extraordinarily penetrating" (*Studies in English Literature* 5 [1965]:187).

Landry, Hilton. *Interpretations in Shakespeare's Sonnets*. Berkeley: University of California Press, 1963.
Landry is not interested in rearranging the order of the sonnets as they were first published, nor does he seek to solve the mysteries of date of composition or the identities of the young man, the Dark Lady, or the rival poet. He begins by looking at sonnet 94, interpreting it within the context of sonnets 87 through 96 and seeing it as a retelling of the parable of the talents. Landry concludes that the octave is ironic. Altogether, Landry discusses the relations among some twenty-five sonnets and presents careful readings of another nineteen. Hallett Smith called this "a useful commentary, not wide in scope but fine in texture" and found the contextual readings illuminating (*Shakespeare Studies* 1 [1965]:332).

_____, ed. *New Essays on Shakespeare's Sonnets*. New York: AMS Press, 1976.
A helpful collection of nine essays. Rodney Poisson begins the volume with a look at the theme of friendship in sonnets 18 through 126, showing how the poems trace the breakup of a relationship between two men of unequal rank. Martin Seymour-Smith offers a psychological reading of the first forty-two sonnets and argues that, while Shakespeare was physically attracted to the young man, they were not homosexual lovers. (Seymour-Smith thus recants his earlier belief that they were). This essay, too, sees a falling off of the relationship. W. G. Ingram looks at imagery and structure, as does Winifred Nowottny for sonnets 97 through 126. Anton Pirkhoffer links the poems and plays for their stress on self-knowledge but sees a tension in the sonnets between poet and dramatist. Hilton Landry defends the poems against the strictures of Yvor Winters and John Crowe Ransom. Marshall Lindsay evaluates the twenty-three French translations of the sonnets from 1821 to 1976, finding them generally unsatisfactory. Paul Ramsey looks at the meter of the sonnets, and Theodore Redpath concludes the volume with his study of punctuation in the 1609 quarto and his recommendations for modern editors.

Leishman, J. B. *Themes and Variations in Shakespeare's Sonnets*. London: Hutchinson University Library, 1961.

The chief purpose of this study is to examine Shakespeare's sonnets in the light of classical literature, Petrarch, Michelangelo, Geoffrey Chaucer, Torquato Tasso, Pierre de Ronsard, and other Elizabethan sonneteers. Focuses on three themes: poetry, time, and love. While offering a study of Shakespeare's indebtedness to other writers, Leishman also emphasizes the "notness" of the sonnets, the way in which they differ from other poems. For example, the theme of *carpe diem* is absent from the work. On the other hand, Shakespeare is Horatian in his attitude towards the power of poetry to confer immortality and outlast time. Though diffuse, the book stimulates thought and is often illuminating.

Martin, Philip. *Shakespeare's Sonnets: Self, Love, and Art*. Cambridge, England: Cambridge University Press, 1972.
Paul Ramsey concluded his review of this book by observing that "Martin is a balanced and perceptive critic. . . . He nicely explores relationships between self, self-love, and selves, between the moral and the artistic. He understands that poems build through rhythms; he is good on the uncertainties of Shakespeare's irony" (*Shakespeare Quarterly* 25 [1974]:366). Martin ignores questions of dating, the identification of the young man and the Dark Lady, and sequence. The first three chapters look at self-love, which in the poems is not necessarily a flaw. His study considers particularly sonnets 1, 33, 34, 35, 55, 57, 62, 65, 94, 116, 129, 130, and 138. Martin also treats the popularity of the sonnet in the Renaissance, compares Shakespeare and John Donne (Donne is more vivid and immediate, Shakespeare more mature and patient), and concludes that art, in arresting time's ravages, is a form of love.

Melchiori, Giorgio. *Shakespeare's Dramatic Meditations: An Experiment in Criticism*. Oxford, England: Clarendon Press, 1976.
A study of sonnets 94, 121, 129, and 146 to understand Shakespeare's views. Sonnet 94 deals with ethics of power, sonnet 121 with the ethics of social behavior, sonnet 129 with the ethics of sex, and sonnet 146 with the ethics of religion. Melchiori notes the prevalence of the second person pronoun that makes Shakespeare's sonnets into a dialogue, which, in turn, explores tensions without resolving them. As W. L. Godshalk commented, "This is a book which every devoted student of the Sonnets should read—and reread. It is delightful and instructive" (*JEGP* 77 [1978]:433). Sylvan Barnet called it "the keenest reading of the sonnets that I know of" (*Renaissance Quarterly* 30 [1977]:404).

Muir, Kenneth. *Shakespeare's Sonnets*. London: George Allen & Unwin, 1979.
Muir dates the sonnets' composition to the early 1590s and accepts the 1609 order as likely the one Shakespeare intended. The four central chapters present Muir's interpretation of the sequence and examine Shakespeare's debt to preceding sonneteers. Muir finds Ovid's *Metamorphoses* the greatest influence. The study also examines the structure, sound, and imagery of the poems and the

question of autobiography. Muir sees the poems as deriving "partly from Shakespeare's dramatic sense and partly from actual events." R. L. Smallwood praised Muir's study as "a guide characterized throughout by meticulous attention to the evidence, constant good sense, and genuinely helpful exposition of theories and solutions to problems. 'Judicious,' indeed, is the epithet one would wish to apply to his whole enterprise" (*Modern Language Review* 76 [1981]:667).

Padel, John. *New Poems by Shakespeare: Order and Meaning Restored to the Sonnets.* London: Herbert Press, 1981.
Supports the view that the sonnets were written for William Herbert, third Earl of Pembroke. Padel divides the first 126 sonnets into thirty-one "tetrads" and the Dark Lady sonnets into seven "triads," leaving seven sonnets that become four "proems." The "new poems" of the title are these tetrads, triads, and proems. Padel dates the poems from 1597 to 1606 and regards George Chapman as the rival poet. This account sees Lady Mary Pembroke as the most likely editor of the sonnets; she rearranged them to obscure certain events that the poems originally described, such as Pembroke's sexual initiation by the Dark Lady with the connivance of the poet and the Pembrokes. A charming piece of fiction.

Peguiney, Joseph. *Such Is My Love: A Study of Shakespeare's Sonnets.* Chicago: University of Chicago Press, 1985.
Drawing on possible double meanings in the sonnets, Peguiney makes the questionable assumption that the words have sexual connotations. He believes that the speaker in the sonnets is Shakespeare, not a persona, and that Shakespeare reveals his homosexuality in the poems. The sonnet sequence 1 through 126 shows the growth (1 to 19), maturity (20 to 99), and decline (100 to 126) of the relationship with the fair youth. Argues that only Sir Philip Sidney comes close to Shakespeare's artistry in handling the sonnet sequence; Shakespeare surpasses all others "in depth of perception, in range and complexity of feelings and the sense of experiential authenticity they convey, and in their exemplary arrangement. A secret of their power lies in their remarkable insights into the psychologies of love, lust, jealousy, and homoeroticism and into the bisexual self who is the subject of these and other emotional responses and mental states—insights articulated in the consummate language and art of the greatest poetic genius."

Ramsey, Paul. *The Fickle Glass: A Study of Shakespeare's Sonnets.* New York: AMS Press, 1979.
Begins with a consideration of some standard questions. Ramsey dates the sonnets between 1591 and 1594, and he accepts the 1609 order and the conventional division of the poems—the first and larger group addressed to the fair youth, the later ones to the Dark Lady. The rival poet is Christopher Marlowe. Having

addressed "Problems," Ramsey turns to "Techniques," where he considers such matters as "metrical rules" and the role of rhetoric in the poems. The final section, "Meanings," examines "The Logic of Hell" and "The Theology of Love" and concludes with a survey of criticism. Cyrus Hoy wrote that "analysis of the rhetorical and syllogistic strategies of the sonnets contributes in essential ways to our understanding of Shakespeare's technique in these poems, and Ramsey's book has a number of good things to offer in its commentary on specific sonnets" (*Modern Philology* 79 [1982]:317).

Rowse, A. L. *Shakespeare's Sonnets: The Problems Solved*. New York: Harper & Row, 1973.
According to Rowse, the Dark Lady of the sonnets is Emilia Bassano Lanier, sometime mistress to Henry Carey, Lord Hunsdon, who, as Lord Chamberlain, was the patron of Shakespeare's acting company. Rowse believes that the punning on "Will" in sonnets 135 and 136 refers to both Will Shakespeare and William Lanier, Emilia's husband (actually named Alfonso). In *Othello*, Emilia takes a tolerant view of adultery, as did Emilia Lanier, and Bassanio in *The Merchant of Venice* suggests her family name. Other problems solved are the dating of the sonnets (early 1590s) and the identities of the fair youth (the third Earl of Southampton), the rival poet (Christopher Marlowe), and the "W. H." of Thomas Thorpe's dedication (William Harvey, the third husband of Southampton's mother). Includes Rowse's prose rendition of the sonnets, together with the originals. George Steiner summarized the book's merits, which lie not in actually unriddling the sonnets but in revealing "an absolutely fascinating vignette of daily life in the demimonde of astrology, entertainment, sex, and finance that surrounded the Elizabethan court" (*The New Yorker*, March 18, 1974, p. 149).

Schaar, Claes. *Elizabethan Sonnet Themes and the Dating of Shakespeare's Sonnets*. Lund, Sweden: C. W. K. Gleerup, 1962.
Examines parallels between the sonnets and other writers' works (chapter 1) and between the sonnets and Shakespeare's other works (chapter 2) to determine when the sonnets were written. Based on these similarities, Schaar concludes that most of the sonnets were written in the early 1590s, though some may be later. Schaar does not insist on the sonnets' telling a story but notes that they can be read that way, and he sees the poems as containing imagery and language that Shakespeare later develops in his plays.

Smith, Hallett. *The Tension of the Lyre: Poetry in Shakespeare's Sonnets*. San Marino, Calif.: Huntington Library, 1981.
Begins by looking at the "voices" of the poet in the sonnets. Some of the poems are addressed to the poet himself and are meditations. Others are addressed to a possibly fictional audience. Smith maintains that to the fair youth Shakespeare addresses poems dealing with constancy, nature, time, and poetry, whereas the

theme of the Dark Lady sonnets is "the world." Chapter 3 looks at the courtly world of the sonnets, and chapter 4 links the sonnets to Shakespeare's other works. Smith next considers "Order and Punctuation," rejecting the view that the 1609 punctuation has authorial sanction. The book concludes with a survey of some of the sonnets' interpreters, including John Keats, John Suckling, and various critics.

Stirling, Brents. *The Shakespeare Sonnet Order: Poems and Groups*. Berkeley: University of California Press, 1968.
The 1609 sequence shows a high degree of patterning, but some sonnets do not fit in their present location. Sonnets 69 and 70, for example, fit best after sonnets 91 through 93, and sonnet 94 should follow sonnet 97. Having argued for such rearrangements, Stirling in chapter 2 offers his edition of five groups and six "poems," which consist of anywhere from one to nine sonnets ("Poem 5," for example, consists of sonnets 109 through 112 and 117 through 121); he offers his comments on these pieces as well. Chapter 3 offers further support for the rearrangement. One of the more bizarre attempts at reordering the sonnets.

Wait, R. J. C. *The Background of Shakespeare's Sonnets*. New York: Schocken Books, 1972.
The sonnets trace Shakespeare's relationship with the third Earl of Southampton over a twenty-year period. First is an idealization of the patron, followed by disillusion with Southampton for stealing Shakespeare's mistress and for participating in the 1601 Essex rebellion. Later the poet reprimands himself for failing to support Southampton in the following years. Around 1609, the two were reconciled, and this rapprochement led to the sonnets' publication and to Shakespeare's ability to write the final, happy plays of his career. A fascinating tissue of unsupported hypotheses that reads well but fails to persuade.

Weiser, David K. *Mind in Character: Shakespeare's Speaker in the Sonnets*. Columbia: University of Missouri Press, 1987.
In chapter 1, Weiser looks at the speaker as an *eiron* in comedy. Aware of mutability, time, chance, and death, the speaker first examines the ironies of nature, then of poets and lovers, and lastly in himself. The "Soliloquy Sonnets" (chapter 2), not addressed to "you" or "thou," involve introspection that leads to greater awareness. Chapter 3 ("Dialogue Sonnets") examines the poems addressed to the fair youth, and chapter 4 shows how in the Dark Lady sonnets the speaker loses that sense of integration achieved earlier. Taken together, the sonnets trace a pattern of "personal growth, conflict and decline."

Wilson, Katherine M. *Shakespeare's Sugared Sonnets*. London: George Allen & Unwin, 1974.
Argues that Shakespeare's sonnets parody the conventions of love poetry. Wilson

looks first at the origins of the sonnet and then at Shakespeare's treatment of ornate verse in his plays. *Romeo and Juliet* and *Love's Labour's Lost* mock the extravagant language and posturing of traditional love poetry and favor plain speaking. The sonnets to the Dark Lady mock the prevailing mode, exemplified for example in Thomas Watson's *Hekatompathia* (1582) and *Tears of Fancie* (1593). The first seventeen sonnets parody arguments for marriage, and addressing sonnets to a man rather than a woman was another parodic device. One merit of this study lies in the parallels it draws between Shakespeare's sonnets and contemporary verse. Here one finds the convention upon which Shakespeare built. "Postscripts" treats the dedication to the sonnets by Thomas Thorpe, a sonnet sequence by Sir John Davies that he called *Gulling Sonnets*, the date of composition of Shakespeare's sonnets (1591 to 1593), and the question of Shakespeare's homosexuality.

Winny, James. *The Master-Mistress: A Study of Shakespeare's Sonnets*. London: Chatto & Windus, 1968.
Argues that the sonnets are neither narrative nor autobiography. Rather, they explore issues of truth and falsehood, increase and creation, in the same imaginative mode that Shakespeare employs in the plays. Both sonnet sequences, 1 through 126 and 127 through 152, reveal a failed relationship and the speaker's dual nature; the same concern informs Shakespeare's two narrative poems of the same period. Winny finds in the sonnets a psychological revelation of Shakespeare's mind, a duality in which the writer is at once friend and speaker, seeking integration but failing to find it; yet from that failure springs great poetry.

Witt, Robert W. *Of Comfort and Despair: Shakespeare's Sonnet Sequence*. Salzburg, Austria: Institut fur Anglistic und Amerikanistik, Universitat Salzburg, 1979.
"The friend, the dark lady, and even the poet are . . . creations of Shakespeare, and they function not necessarily to record events in Shakespeare's private life but to present larger insights. They function, in other words, as symbols." The sonnets echo neoplatonic sentiments derived from a variety of sources but primarily Baldassare Castioglione's *The Courtier*. The fair youth sonnets demonstrate love, the Dark Lady sonnets lust. The story of the sonnets is ascent of the Platonic scale of love through reasonable affection (1 through 126) and descent because of passion (127 through 152); the last two sonnets summarize this dual movement. Witt uses this theory to rearrange the 1609 sonnet order, though he keeps the basic division between the fair youth and Dark Lady poems. Except for this reordering, Witt makes a good case for his interpretation.

Narrative Poems

Allen, D. C. "Some Observations on *The Rape of Lucrece.*" *Shakespeare Survey* 15 (1962):89-98.

Begins by outlining the long-standing debate over Lucrece. To Tertullian and Jerome, she was the ideal pagan woman who killed herself rather than live infamously. Saint Augustine, however, in *The City of God* wrote that "if suicide is extenuated, adultery is proved; if adultery is denied, the conviction is for suicide." Although Shakespeare sympathized with Lucrece, the poem accepts Saint Augustine's vision. Though Lucrece's suicide is heroic, it is also unforgivable. The reference to fallen Troy reinforces this reading because to Renaissance allegorizers that city (like the body) was corrupt and had to be destroyed.

Donaldson, Ian. *The Rapes of Lucretia: A Myth and Its Transformations.* Oxford, England: Clarendon Press, 1982.

Discusses the treatment of Lucretia in literature and art from Ovid and Livy to Jean Giraudoux, with an emphasis on English eighteenth century works such as Samuel Richardson's *Clarissa.* Donaldson's central concern is "Christian Europe's attempt to reconsider ancient heroic values in the light of Christian teaching and belief, and to transform the heroes of the past." Hence, he can include a section on Cato's suicide because, like Lucretia's, Cato's is a suicide of honor. Donaldson also discusses paintings such as Artemisia Gentileschi's *Tarquin and Lucretia* and Titian's rendering of the subject. The book shows a movement away from heroic action towards inner experience and finds Shakespeare's poem unsuccessful because the work allows "the story to drift down its traditional narrative course."

Keach, William. *Elizabethan Erotic Narrative: Irony and Pathos in the Ovidian Poetry of Shakespeare, Marlowe, and Their Contemporaries.* New Brunswick, N.J.: Rutgers University Press, 1977.

Looks at a number of Ovidian poems from the 1590s and finds in them an ambivalence, a recognition of life's duality in the fusion of comedy and tragedy, love and death. Keach first surveys Ovid's treatment of myth and eroticism, which generates "a constantly active and poised awareness that sexual love can be humorous, grotesque, and animal-like in its savagery as well as beautiful, emotionally compelling, and an essential part of what it means to be human." Keach then examines six epyllia, beginning with Thomas Lodge's *Glaucis and Scilla* (1589). He discusses Christopher Marlowe's *Hero and Leander* and Shakespeare's *Venus and Adonis* as well as three later works that use Ovidian narrative for satiric ends. Barry Weller noted some reservations about the book but also found "shrewd observations throughout" (*Modern Language Notes* 92 [1977]:1077).

Levin, Richard. "The Ironic Reading of *The Rape of Lucrece* and the Problem of External Evidence." *Shakespeare Survey* 34 (1981):85-92.
Responding to Don Cameron Allen and other critics who believe that Shakespeare condemns Lucrece, Levin looks at contemporary responses to the poem to determine how others in the 1590s and early 1600s saw the work and its title character. All twelve references treat Lucrece as admirable, and Shakespeare's other references to Lucrece are also favorable. Levin therefore rejects the ironic reading of the poem.

Putney, Rufus. "*Venus and Adonis*: Amour with Humor." *Philological Quarterly* 20 (1941):533-548.
Responds to critics who find the poem unsatisfying and argues that the poem is "a sparkling and sophisticated comedy." To make his case, Putney looks at other Ovidian imitations of the period and finds comic effects in them, including Christopher Marlowe's *Hero and Leander*. Even Venus' lament at the end of the poem is exaggerated and therefore amusing rather than tragic. The poem is the trifle that Shakespeare calls it, but it is a successful, funny trifle.

Simone, R. Thomas. *Shakespeare and "Lucrece": A Study of the Poem and Its Relation to the Plays*. Salzburg, Austria: Universitat Salzburg, 1974.
First looks at the treatment of the Lucrece story in Livy, Ovid, Saint Augustine, and Geoffrey Chaucer. The second part offers an interpretation of the poem, which Simone sees as Shakespeare's first exploration of the nature of tragedy because it deals with the issues that will resurface in the later plays. Part 3 looks at the poem in the context of Shakespeare's career. Coming after his first plays, *The Rape of Lucrece* deepened Shakespeare's understanding and helps explain the improvement of *Richard II* over *Richard III*. The great tragedies mark the full flowering of the ideas in *The Rape of Lucrece*, and all the late plays are indebted to this poem. The poem thus marks the "turning point in [Shakespeare's] development." An epilogue traces the critical fortunes of the poem from the seventeenth century to the twentieth.

Sylvester, Bickford. "Natural Mutability and Human Responsibility: Form in Shakespeare's *Lucrece*." *College English* 26 (1965):505-511.
A study of the imagery and structure of the poem. Language reflects the fallen world of the work, while the shifting use of colors reveals the mutability of fortune. Sylvester finds careful balance and parallels in the poem. For example, through suicide Lucrece regains the mastery over her body that she lost when Tarquin ravished her. By placing the rape at the center of the poem, Shakespeare shows that Tarquin's physical triumph triggers his defeat.

Vickers, Nancy J. "The Blazon of Sweet Beauty's Best: Shakespeare's Lucrece."
In *Shakespeare and the Question of Theory*, edited by Patricia Parker and Geoffrey H. Hartman. London: Methuen, 1985.

Coppélia Kahn's "The Rape in Shakespeare's *Lucrece*" (*Shakespeare Studies* 9 [1976]:45-72) argues that the poem deals with male rivalry. Vickers extends this idea to the descriptions of Lucrece, which she sees as part of this competition. Collatine praises Lucrece's beauty and chastity to defeat Tarquin in description, and at the end of the poem again "men rhetorically compete with each other over Lucrece's body." The poem dealing with descriptive contests is itself part of that contest; through his descriptions of Lucrece, Shakespeare hopes to defeat rival poets for the patronage of the dedicatee, the third Earl of Southampton.

Walley, Harold R. "*The Rape of Lucrece* and Shakespearean Tragedy." *PMLA* 76 (1961):480-487.
In *The Rape of Lucrece*, Shakespeare developed techniques and ideas that pervade the histories and tragedies. His presentation of a historical event in human terms characterizes the history plays, and his vision of evil and moral responsibility in the poem is that of the tragedies. Tarquin resembles Macbeth; Claudius (*Hamlet*), Edmund, Goneril, and Regan (*King Lear*); and Iago (*Othello*). The plight of Lucrece raises questions about a moral universe. As in the tragedies, evil destroys itself.

Williams, Gordon. "The Coming of Age of Shakespeare's Adonis." *Modern Language Review* 78 (1983):769-776.
Sees the boar's goring of Adonis as equivalent to sexual initiation; the boar usurps Venus as Adonis' lover. Venus becomes more sympathetic as the poem progresses, changing from a grotesque would-be ravisher to bereaved maternal figure, "a suffering woman absorbing a sense of universal calamity into her own personal pain."

INDEX

INDEX

INDEX